Book of Edward
Christian Mythology

Volume II

God Does Not Change

Why will some Christians actually go to Hell? If you are a Christian, this book may save your eternal soul and the eternal souls of your family. Who is Jesus talking about when he said: "I never knew you" in Matthew 7:21-23? Christians! So, which Christians have broken the covenant of Jesus' blood on the cross? Why are they headed to Hell instead of Heaven? The answers are inside.

The Apostle Edward

Introduction

Book of Edward
Christian Mythology

Copyright © 2005 by Edward G. Palmer
Published by JVED Publishing
Elk River, Minnesota 55330

    ISBN 0-9768833-1-7 (Volume II: God Does Not Change)
    ISBN 0-9768833-4-1 (4 Volume Set)

Palmer, Edward G.
    1. Faith—The Apostle Edward   2. Bible Prophecy—Christian Mythology
    3. Christianity—Christology

Printed in the United States of America.

All rights reserved. No portion of this book may be reproduced in any form without the written permission of the Author.

Notice. This book and its entire contents represents the sole opinion of Edward G. Palmer based upon his twenty-five plus years of in-depth Bible studies, his actual life experiences, his personal diaries and readily available public records. No part of this book is intended to offer professional counseling of any type especially that of legal advice. Persons involved in cultic churches, those in need of spiritual counseling, medical, legal or any other advice should seek competent professional help.

Capitalization Protocol. On all Bible citations, regardless of the translation used, and where the context clearly points to God Almighty or to Jesus Christ, this book makes the distinction between the two by using either small cap characters or lower case characters. For God Almighty, a small capitalized style protocol is followed and reflected in the format: CREATOR, FATHER, GIVER, HE, HIS, HIM, HIMSELF, YOU, YOUR, ME, MINE, MOST HIGH, MY, MYSELF, LORD and SAVIOR, ETC. For Jesus Christ, a lower case protocol is used except for Lord and Son. Hence, when these pronouns are used for Jesus, they show up as: he, his, him, himself, you, your, me, my, myself, savior, Lord, or Son. This has generally been followed throughout the book, but is not the case with every cited verse. It is used for those verses in which the context cannot be easily disputed or in the case of citing a quality or attribute, which belongs solely to God. For those interested in the original translation capitalization, the author refers them to the actual Bible version used for the cited text. A list of Bible translations is shown on the next page. In some other cases, capital letters used within the cited sentence structure were also changed on common words for ease of reading or modern grammar. In other cases, the capitalized letters were left as shown in the original translation. Hence the original Bible phrase "; Because" might appear as "; because." In all instances, Apostle Edward maintains complete integrity of translation and the writings herein can be traced back to the original Bibles to confirm the accuracy of presentation. While not perfect, the capitalization protocol is fairly consistent and enhances the reading and value of Apostle Edward's teachings.

Introduction

Translation Notice

The following Bible translations were researched for this book along with three Hebrew texts and one or more ancient manuscripts such as the Book of Enoch (ENO). Except where otherwise indicated and in regards to capitalization of words, all Scripture quotations are taken from the Holy Bible, New King James Version © 1979, 1980, 1982 by Thomas Nelson, Inc., Publishers. Verses that are followed by a two, three or four-letter capitalized identifier are from the following Bible translations or reference works.

Abbreviation	Bible Definition
KJV; NKJV	King James Bible[1]; New King James Bible[2]
AMP	Amplified Bible[3]
ASB; NASB	American Standard[4]; New American Standard Bible[5]
DB	Darby Bible[6]
ENO	Book of Enoch — Richard Laurence 1883 Edition[7]
GN; GNB	Good News[8]; Good News Apocrypha[9]-Today's English Bible
GW	God's Word Bible[10]
HEB	Hebrew Bible — English Translation JPS 1917 Edition[11]
JSB	Jewish Study Bible[12] - Jewish Publication Society 1985, 1999
LIV; NLT	Living Bible[13]; New Living Translation[14]
MB	MicroBible[15]
MLT	Morris Literal Translation[16]
MOF	James Moffatt Translation, Final Edition[17]
NIV	New International Bible[18]
NCV	New Century Bible[19]
NJB	New Jerusalem Bible[20]
REB	Revised English Bible[21]
RSV; NRSV	Revised Standard Bible[22]; New Revised Standard Bible[23]
SET	Simple English Translation[24]
TAN	Tanach - The Stone Edition 1996[25]
TB	Transliterated Bible[26]
WEB	Webster's Bible[27]
WEY	Weymouth's NT[28]
YLT	Young's Literal Translation[29]

Copyright 2005 Edward G. Palmer, All Rights Reserved.

Table of Contents

Page

Dedication vi

Foreword viii

Prophecies Fulfilled..x

Volume I
Matters Of The Heart

Chapter 1: It Starts With The Heart 1

Chapter 2: God Speaks To The Heart..11

Chapter 3: Repentance From The Heart 28

Chapter 4: God's Call Of The Heart 59

Chapter 5: Practice From The Heart...72

Chapter 6: The Heart Of An Apostle 93

Chapter 7: Choices From The Heart 131

Volume II
God Does Not Change

Chapter 8: Understanding God's Word 171

Chapter 9: Rationalization of Mankind 204

Chapter 10: The False Trinity Doctrine 242

Chapter 11: God's Eternal Character 312

Chapter 12: The False Salvation Doctrine..................................382

Chapter 13: A Light On My Path 416

Chapter 14: The Gift of Jesus 452

Introduction

Volume III
Itching Christian Ears

Chapter 15: Myth — God Heals Everyone 492

Chapter 16: Myth — God Owns Solid Rock 545

Chapter 17: Myth — Giving 10% Is A Tithe 615

Chapter 18: Myth — Abortion Doesn't Matter 678

Chapter 19: Myth — Sexuality Doesn't Matter................................. 749

Chapter 20: Myth — Politics Doesn't Matter 897

Chapter 21: Myth — Everybody Gets To Go 977

Epilogue.. 1039

Volume IV
Appendixes—Reference

Appendix A: A Real Salvation Prayer 1043

Appendix B: Baptism Doctrine 1046

Appendix C: Doctrinal Statement 1049

Appendix D: Jackie's Final Thoughts 1069

Appendix E: Ed's Goodbye Eulogy 1072

Appendix F: Cancer Killing Protocols 1083

Appendix G: Illustrations, Tables & Lists 1092

Appendix H: Notes & Bibliography... 1099

Appendix I: Bible Verse Cross Reference 1134

Appendix J: Index 1177

Introduction

Dedication

This book is dedicated to my beloved wife Jacqueline Lee (Bowers) Palmer whose love I was privileged to have on this earth for the thirty-nine years of our marriage and the four years of our teen love that preceded it from 1960-1964. On June 3, 2003, God gave Jackie her heavenly wings. This book was started during our thirty-seventh year of marriage and finished in what would have been our fortieth year.

In the forty-three years of earthly love that we shared, God used Jackie to teach me the simplicity of a genuine faith and the resulting earthly righteousness, which is manifested by that faith. Christian mythology has distorted the righteousness message of Jesus Christ. This book sets the record straight again about what it really means to accept God's Son.

———————

Introduction

God also used Dean H. Mattila, Jacqueline Mattila and Vernon Enstad to teach me. They are the three righteous people whom God chose for me, from within the church, to share the spiritual journey of this book with. These three alone had the courage to stand tall for the truth and stand by my side when we left a fellowship of Christians who long ago decided to turn their back on the truth and embrace mythology.

Then there is Michael and Maureen Gill, two righteous people whom God brought into my life uncommitted to Christ at the time and used by God to illustrate as HE did to Peter in Acts 10:34-35 NIV that, "How true it is that God does not show favoritism but accepts men from every nation who fear HIM and do what is right."

Jesus confirms the kingdom requirement of righteousness in Matthew 25:46 with his words: "Then they will go away to eternal punishment, but the righteous to eternal life." In Luke 5:32, Jesus further clarifies this by saying: "I have not come to call the righteous, but sinners to repentance."

This book is also dedicated to the memory of my first son Glen; to daughter Paula & husband James Kantorowicz; daughter Patty & husband Jon Morin; son Brian & wife Brandee Palmer; grandchildren Christopher, Paul, Kathryn, Bradley, Benjamin, Luke, Braiden, Bronson, those yet to arrive and to the memory of grandson Dylan.

This book is also dedicated to the memory of my parents and sister Barbara and all others whom have passed on, to my younger brother James Stanley, his wife Denise and sons Jimmy, John and Nick. This book is also dedicated to Karen and Amy whom God brought into my heart and who will always be like a daughter and granddaughter to me.

Finally, this book is dedicated to the Christian family that my wife and I were raised in. How wonderful to have lived life in a fellowship of people not afraid to talk about the Holy Bible, our God and what it means to have a genuine faith. To those in the family who have wondered why I chose to accept God's calling, the answers will be found in this book. I will always be grateful for all of these special people who shared in my life and I trust that our LORD will find them excellent members of HIS kingdom, even while on this earth and in this present existence. The Apostle Edward

Introduction

Foreword

It was a strange scene for me as I found myself watching television on a recent Sunday morning. As I prepared to leave to open the doors of my own church, I found myself instead surfing with the remote for a few moments. TV is not a high priority for me, but I was interested in seeing what was on the tube in the way of church services. Perhaps for my dear wife who would be taking care of grandkids at home that morning? Perhaps for my grandkids? Perhaps simply for some good content for my own church teachings? It didn't matter.

All of a sudden, I found myself watching the worship service of a church I had heard much about. It was an Assembly of God church in the Minneapolis metro area. The name is not important. What was important to me at the time was what I saw. I was watching a praise and worship service on television and it captivated my spirit. The church was reported by some to be "hot." You know, filled with the Holy Ghost and with signs and wonders. The service was "spirit-filled." I can tell you this by just watching as the people were giving their hearts to God in song, dance, praise and worship.

For years, it was wonderful for me to go up to the altar area, lift my head and arms as high as I could, and praise the LORD. I would sing and dance around the altar getting "drunk" in the Holy Spirit [see Acts 2:15-21]. The object of praise and worship for me was to press into God's Spirit and presence. We are taught in the Bible that through Christ Jesus, we are given the Spirit of truth. We are also taught that it is our ticket to step into the Holy of Holies to be with God.

For me, the worship service was very captivating to watch. I felt myself desiring to "sing, dance, praise and worship" God among those worshippers I saw. The "praise and worship" looked genuine and as my spirit was drawn in further, I sensed my heart crying out: "Make room for me!" There is simply something wonderful worshipping God. We are taught in the Bible that "In HIS presence" is fullness of joy. For me, that is exactly what "praise and worship" is all about—getting into company with HIM. I have never known the level of joy I feel with God in anything of this worldly existence. That isn't to say the world cannot provide you and I with joy. It can, but that kind of joy is short lived. With God, it is always there, it's eternal in nature: you just have to "press-in" to HIM.

Copyright 2005 Edward G. Palmer, All Rights Reserved.

Book of Edward—Foreword

Introduction

As much as I wanted to join the praise and worship service, I couldn't help but wonder: "Who in the crowd was worshipping God in vain?" Who in this particular crowd was going through the motions but inside were not "lovers of the truth?" Who in this particular crowd was still going to Hell yet thinking they were saved? The truth has been perverted from many pulpits and Paul's prophecy in 2 Timothy 4:3-4 was now fulfilled.

You see I recently left a church with this same type of "inviting" praise and worship service. However, Solid Rock Church turned out to be a den of thieves, filled with wicked and unrighteous people [Luke 19:46]. People who consider themselves Christian; yet, who routinely and without much thought ignore the truth. Turning their backs, God saw the fullness of their false witness.

God reminded me of HIS word in Matthew 15:8-9 "These people draw near to ME with their mouth, and honor ME with their lips, but their heart is far from ME, and in vain they worship ME, teaching as doctrines the commandments of men." And again it is written in Mark 7:7 that "They worship ME in vain."

Do you worship God in vain? Many, who call themselves Christians, and who think of them selves as being saved by the blood of Jesus, are simply deluding themselves on the way to their eternal home in Hell. Jesus tells us of this fact. Why? Does it have to be this way?

The message I received from God is to tell those who call themselves Christians that many of them will be going to Hell and that Jesus will serve up a very rude announcement to them as they plead for their eternal soul. However, by that time, it will be too late. So, who are these Christians?

Who is Jesus speaking to in Matthew 7:22-23? Jesus says: "Many will say to me in that day, 'Lord, Lord, have we not prophesied in your name, cast out demons in your name, and done many wonders in your name?' And then I will declare to them, I never knew you; depart from me, you who practice lawlessness." Jesus' message is clearly to those who call themselves Christian. To those who say: "I am saved by the blood of Lamb" or "I know Jesus." This book is a warning to Christians. Many of you are headed to Hell. Why?

The Apostle Edward

Copyright 2005 Edward G. Palmer, All Rights Reserved.

Book of Edward—Foreword

Introduction

Mythology Prophecy

"For the time will come when men will not put up with sound doctrine. Instead, to suit their own desires, they will gather around them a great number of teachers to say what their itching ears want to hear. They will turn their ears away from the truth and turn aside to myths."

2 Timothy 4:3-4 NIV

Truth Prophecy

"The coming of the lawless one will be in accordance with the work of Satan displayed in all kinds of counterfeit miracles, signs and wonders, and in every sort of evil that deceives those who are perishing. They perish because they refused to love the truth and so be saved. For this reason God sends them a powerful delusion so that they will believe the lie and so that all will be condemned who have not believed the truth but have delighted in wickedness."

2 Thessalonians 2:9-12 NIV

Prophecies Are Fulfilled

"The prophecies in 2 Timothy 4:3-4 and 2 Thessalonians 2:9-12 are fulfilled. Today, mythology is routinely taught from the pulpits of many Christian churches instead of God's Holy Word and many people attending Christian churches have turned away from the truth. These people are headed toward Hell unaware of their lost souls."

The Apostle Edward

Copyright 2005 Edward G. Palmer, All Rights Reserved.

God Does Not Change

Volume II

Chapter Eight
Understanding God's Word

"[God has] filled him [Bezaleel] with the Spirit of God, in wisdom, in understanding, in knowledge." Exodus 31:3

"[God] has filled him [Bezaleel] with the Spirit of God, in wisdom and understanding, in knowledge and ... HE [God] has put in his heart the ability to teach." Exodus 35:31-34

"Therefore be careful to observe [to actually do] them; for this is your wisdom and your understanding in the sight of the peoples who will hear all these statutes, and say, 'Surely this great nation is a wise and understanding people.'" Deut. 4:6

"Then God said to him: 'Because you have asked this thing, and have not asked long life for yourself, nor have asked riches for yourself, nor have asked the life of your enemies, but have asked for yourself understanding to discern justice, behold, I have done according to your words; see, I have given you a wise and understanding heart.'" 1 Kings 3:11

"[God] said, 'Behold, the fear of the LORD, that is wisdom, and to depart from evil is understanding.'" Job 28:28

"Through [God's] precepts I get understanding; therefore, I hate every false way." Psalm 119:104

"And we know that the Son of God [Jesus] has come [in the flesh] and has given us an understanding [to re-educate us], that we may [once again] know HIM [God] who is true."
1 John 5:20

Understanding God's Word

    I am just picking up my spiritual pen again to write for God. It has been four weeks since we learned of Jackie's inoperable and untreatable pancreatic cancer. That is the medical profession's judgment of her illness. However, her condition does seem to be responding to the power of prayer and to the metabolic [cell] nutrients that God has brought to our attention.

    As you seek a better understanding of God's Word, you should realize that God expects you to do your part. I.E. Would you pray about your lung cancer to God and then still keep on smoking cigarettes? Obviously not! Yet it might surprise you at just how many Christians have that mentality. I am also mindful of many Christians who will tell you to ignore symptoms that you may have. Yes, you heard me correctly. These people reason that if you actually admit that you have an illness [name your health problem here], then, you will have that illness [or health problem] for sure. Does that make sense or sound stupid? Yes, I have heard that reasoning from many charismatic Christians in the "name it and claim it" crowd [sect].

    Do you really want to understand God's Word? Then understand first of all that God has given you the "power of a strong mind." If something sounds stupid to you, then maybe it really is. If it just doesn't make sense, then maybe it's because it is nonsense. When it comes to understanding God's Word, realize that is exactly what God intended for you to do.

> **"For God has not given us a spirit of fear, but of power and of love and of a sound mind." 2 Tim. 1:7**

    When you understand God's Word, you can begin to reason as the Psalmist does. You understand in your heart that "your times are in HIS hand." In the case of a serious illness in your family, you also understand that they are in God's hand just as you are! Then, all of you do your part.

> **"But as for me, I trust in YOU, O LORD; I say, 'YOU are my God. My times are in YOUR hand.' " Psalm 31:14-15**

When You Trust God, You'll Understand!

Copyright 2005 Edward G. Palmer, All Rights Reserved.

Understanding God's Word

The Psalmist continues with the unquestioned reality of this earthly life when he writes:

"Our days on earth are like grass; like wildflowers, we bloom and die. The wind blows, and we are gone—as though we had never been here." Psalm 103:15-16 NLT

You need to fully understand that you will be dead a lot longer than you are alive on this planet. You need to understand that we are all just passing through an earthly existence bound for either Heaven or Hell. God has provided us with the free will to choose our eternal destination. Yet if you do not believe in those two eternal destinations, you cannot understand God; you lack a fundamental perspective needed for reading the Bible.

Ignorance of God's Word will not be a viable excuse in Heaven. If you think this, then you are mistaken. Consider the words of Jesus.

"Jesus answered and said to them, you are mistaken, not knowing the Scriptures nor the power of God." Matt 22:29

EXERCISE: Stop for a moment and count the remaining days of your life. I.E. If you plan to live to age 70, you would have a total of 365 x 70 or 25,550 days in your life. If you are now 40, you only have 30 years left or 10,950 days remaining. Eventually you will die no matter how long you live. Understand that good and evil exist together in this earthly existence. Understand also that God separates good and evil in the next life. Which eternal destination do you choose? If you fail to make a conscious decision, your actions and behavior will make the choice for you. When you acknowledge the reality of an eternal life, you begin to understand God.

PRAYER: "God Almighty, my Heavenly FATHER and the God of my brother Jesus Christ whom YOU alone sent in the flesh to re-educate YOUR people, hear my prayer. Enlighten the understanding of those who read these words that YOU have given me to write. Take the veil of deception off of all Christians. And above all, Glory and Honor be to YOU and blessed be YOUR ONENESS." The Apostle Edward

Understanding God's Word

Have you ever heard of Bezaleel, the son of Uri, the son of Hur, of the tribe of Judah? He seems almost as obscure as Jabez. Do you recall that Jabez' prayer was answered by God? In the case of Bezaleel, God did a little more than answer a prayer. God "injected" Bezaleel with the "Spirit of God" in wisdom, in understanding, in knowledge, and in all manner of workmanship. Further, God gave him the ability to teach others. You can read more about it in Exodus 31-35. So, why did God choose Bezaleel? My guess is that Bezaleel, like Jabez, had a sincere heart for God. There was a desire from deep within Bezaleel to serve and please God Almighty.

When You Give God Your Heart, You'll Understand!

Once your heart is in the proper place, God provides understanding and many other skills. I used the word "injected" above because God made it clear to Moses that it was HE who put these characteristics into Bezaleel.

> **"See [Moses], I have called by name Bezaleel ... and I have filled [injected] him with the Spirit of God, in wisdom, in understanding, in knowledge, and in all manner of workmanship, to design artistic works, to work in gold, in silver, in bronze, in cutting jewels for setting, in carving wood ... and all manner of workmanship." Exodus 31:2-5**

> **"And HE has put in [Bezaleel's] heart the ability to teach, in him and Aholiab ... HE has filled them with the skill to do all manner of work of the engraver and the designer and the tapestry maker, in blue and scarlet and fine linen, and of the weaver—those who do every work and those who design artistic works." Exodus 35:34-35**

Bezaleel didn't go to a seminary, trade school, college or graduate school to gain his wisdom, knowledge and understanding. No, instead, God "filled" him with the Spirit, wisdom, understanding, knowledge and the ability to teach others. Therein lies a big quandary for mankind. The world system lays down a gauntlet of educational requirements for specific trades and employment positions. However, God Almighty says: "When your heart gets right, I will give you everything [all the skills] you need."

Copyright 2005 Edward G. Palmer, All Rights Reserved.

Understanding God's Word

Wow, what a contrast. In one case, you study for years to gain what you and those of the world believe to be a true understanding [skills]. In the other, God Almighty gives you everything you need in an instant of time.

This, of course, brings us to another important issue when it comes to an understanding of God. Is God still active in the lives of men and women today? Or, is God a pacifist sitting on the sidelines of humanity? The short answer from me is that God is very active in the lives of men and women who have a sincere heart for HIM and HIS ways. HE also will intercede in human events to ensure that HIS will unfolds. If you want to understand God, you also have to understand that while HE has given us a free will, our will does not trump God's will or the will of other people.

Recall the discussion in chapter 6 [p 97] where you were taught that God respects our free will. Revelation 22:11 is cited as a Scripture proof. While it is true that HE respects our free will, it is the free will to choose our eternal destination. HIS love for us will constantly provide additional input in which we can re-evaluate our eternal choice. Therefore, at any moment or time in life, before our physical death, we can have a sincere change of heart and find ourselves in the arms of a loving God. The fact that we have free will does not alter God's will or the outcome that HE ordains. That means God will intercede in human events, as HE deems necessary or desirable to accomplish HIS goals. When and where God will intercede and whom HE will use to accomplish HIS goals are God's choices. We can only observe those who are with God and those who are against God. Remember, we will know them by their fruits [actions]. It is a simple matter of good and evil.

An activist God is either very frightening or it is very comforting to people. I suspect this is the case for a variety of reasons and may not be an accurate indication [in itself] of which side of the fence people are on. I know I have scared a few people by telling them that God is as real to me as they were. In fact, I could touch God just like I could touch them. Does this scare you? Why? To me, the fact that God will intercede on my behalf and give me direction to follow is not scary. It is both comforting and thrilling to me. Knowing I can walk with God brings great joy into my spirit. God is not some abstract idea floating around in my mind. God is real and I have seen HIM time and again manifest HIMSELF to me in the physical realm. I

Understanding God's Word

have had some prayers answered so fast that I haven't even had the chance to write them down in a prayer journal. Indeed, I have had prayers answered in mere moments or minutes. Some prayers have yet to be fully answered.

Back to the activist God and our free will. The point I am trying to illustrate can be shown clearly in Scripture at Daniel chapter 2. You may recall that King Nebuchadnezzar had received a dream and was demanding that a wise man provide an interpretation or that "he would destroy all the wise men of Babylon." Of course, Daniel knew that this included him and his friends so he asked God for an interpretation of the King's dream. Here is an example of a prayer request with a certain time specific deadline.

Daniel sought mercy "from the God of Heaven concerning this secret, so that Daniel and his companions might not perish with the rest of the wise men of Babylon. Then the secret was revealed to Daniel in a night vision. So Daniel blessed the God of Heaven." Daniel answered God and said:

> **"Blessed be the name of God forever and ever, for wisdom and might are His.**
>
> **And He changes the times and the seasons; He removes kings and raises up kings;**
>
> **He gives wisdom to the wise and knowledge to those who have understanding. He reveals deep and secret things;**
>
> **He knows what is in the darkness, and light dwells with Him.**
>
> **I thank You and praise You, O God of my fathers; You have given me wisdom and might, and have now made known to me what we asked of You, for You have made known to us the king's demand." Daniel 2:20-23**

> # When You Interact With God, You'll Understand!

Copyright 2005 Edward G. Palmer, All Rights Reserved.

Book of Edward—Chapter 8

Understanding God's Word

Note the prayer of thanksgiving that Daniel presented to God after he received the answer he was seeking. Note the characteristics of God that Daniel enumerates. Then, understand in your heart that God has not changed. If you will interact with God today, HE will interact with you.

Yes, God manifests HIMSELF today in undeniable ways. God is not some abstract [fire insurance] concept like a lot of Christians believe. To really believe in God means accepting the reality of the God that Daniel knew. Indeed, I assert to you in no qualifying terms, that I know the God that Daniel knew. I am free in my heart to ask of God just like Daniel asked. And as Daniel received answers, I too receive answers. Is this the God that you know? If not, you need to dig deeper within your heart to find God.

When You Understand God, You'll Get Answers!

If you cannot operate on this level of intimate prayer and dialogue with God, you do not understand God. In fact, it is very doubtful that you have even found God. His doctor told my dear friend, Dean, that he didn't have a physical heart ailment. Instead, what Dean really needed was to get on a quest to find God Almighty. I can tell you that Dean found God and that you too can find HIM if you just try hard enough. The bottom line is that God is not very hard to find. HE simply requires that your whole heart be involved with your search. So, stop holding back with God Almighty and you will *then* find that HE won't hold back with you.

It's Your Whole Heart!

"For I know the thoughts that I think toward you, says the LORD, thoughts of peace and not of evil, to give you a future and a hope. Then you will call upon ME and go and pray to ME, and I will listen to you. And you will seek ME and find ME, when you search for ME with all your heart."
                                                                    Jeremiah 29:11-13

If You Involve Your Whole Heart, You'll Understand!

Understanding God's Word

The Holy Bible, unlike any other book in recorded human history has been digested and analyzed almost to the point of absurdity. Out of this analytical study of the Holy Bible has come the terms hermeneutics, exegesis and exegete or exegetist. All of these terms refer to the mining of the biblical text for truth. This mining could be concerned with any particular translation of the Bible or it could be concerned with the original Hebrew and Greek manuscripts.

The Second College Edition of the American Heritage Dictionary[1] provides the following definitions:

Hermeneutics (hûr´ ma noo´ tiks) n. The science and methodology of interpretation, esp. of the Bible. The field of hermeneutics is derived from the base word hermeneutic which means either *interpreter* or *to interpret*.

Exegesis (ek´ sa-je sis) n. Critical explanation or analysis, esp. of a text.

Exegete (ek´ sa-jet) Or **exegetist** (ek´ sa-jet´ ist) is a person skilled in exegesis or the critical explanation or analysis of a written text.

Plainly put, someone who is skilled in critical analysis of any written text would be called an *exegete*. His or her critical explanation or analysis of the text would be referred to as an *exegesis*. Part of the methodology he or she used in the exegesis might be from the field of *hermeneutics*, which is the science and methodology of Bible interpretation.

You might surmise that various interpretations might be extreme and wildly opposing of one another. If so, you would be right. Depending upon how you read the Bible, your conclusions can be dramatically different. You can observe this as a fact when you listen to pastors from different denominations.

Copyright 2005 Edward G. Palmer, All Rights Reserved.

Book of Edward—Chapter 8

Understanding God's Word

If you want, you can even locate complete study guides on the field of hermeneutics to guide your thinking about the Bible. These guides can help you sort out the historical influence of the Bible writers. They can help you sort out poetry from history, etc. In many cases, they can enlighten you on how to read actual Scripture.

But beware; at least one author has written a complete encyclopedia of what the Bible really means. I would estimate it at between 30-40 books or more. Think about that. Instead of just trying to read your Bible, you could read 30-40 times the amount of material that is in the Bible just to understand God's Word [the Bible]. In fact, that is exactly what Satan would like you to believe. The message is clear from Satan's crowd that you cannot understand your Holy Bible without a comprehensive educational background in hermeneutics. Why, are you an expert Bible *exegete*?

If you believe this and take that educational path, make sure you also take the time to read the Bible instead of just reading what writers are telling you about the Bible. I've listened to enough Christians and pastors to know that the majority of them have never even read the Bible from front to back. I know pastors that tote around a denominational guidebook to answer questions instead of toting around the Holy Bible. Believe me when I tell you that you should always be instructed from the Bible and not from some denomination guidebook. I.E. A Lutheran, Catholic or other denomination's ministerial guide or instruction book [often unaccompanied by the Bible].

Some charismatic pastors are especially good at dragging Strong'S Concordance into their teachings to cite the different meanings of Hebrew or Greek text. The import to the congregation is "that you cannot understand the Bible without first being able to understand Hebrew or Greek." And, of course, there is that rather important matter of being trained in hermeneutics and exegesis. If you listen long enough to those types of teachings, you will give up on understanding the Bible for yourself. You will become a lap dog for whatever dogma that emerges from the pulpit of your church. Yet, is this really what God intended? For only a few select people to understand the Bible? Is the Bible really that tough to read and understand?

Understanding God's Word

Here is one list of "Principles of Biblical Interpretation" culled from an Internet guide on hermeneutics.[2]

Hermeneutic Principles Of Biblical Interpretation!

1. Meditate, pray, obey and be open.
2. Assume the clarity of Scripture.
3. Stress the priority of the original languages.
4. Look at the literary context.
5. Remember the basic unit of Scripture.
6. Let Scripture interpret Scripture.
7. Avoid confusion between truth and inspired record.
8. Never determine the doctrine from the illustration.
9. Check out the historical and cultural meaning.
10. Aim for one interpretation with many applications.
11. Always proceed from then to now.
12. Be careful about spiritualization.
13. Allow for the fuller meaning of Scripture.
14. Determine the teaching intention of the author.
15. Distinguish between the cultural and the transcultural.
16. Discern what is more critical and what is less critical.
17. Recognize the fact of progressive revelation.
18. Comprehend the biblical covenants.
19. Differentiate between Israel and the Church.
20. Separate between the rapture and the return.
21. Submit to the hierarchy of Scripture.
22. Know the different types of language.
23. Understand the use of language.
24. Highlight the theme of salvation.
25. Appreciate that all truth has not been revealed.
26. Acknowledge that the finite cannot completely fathom the infinite.
27. Beware of pride and prejudice.
28. Watch out for hobbyhorses and pet peeves.
29. Respect the insight of other Christians.
30. Consider the historical interpretations of the text.

Copyright 2005 Edward G. Palmer, All Rights Reserved.

Book of Edward—Chapter 8

Understanding God's Word

Many of the items on the above list are excellent ideas on how to read and understand your Bible. I will not comment on each one individually. I only include the list to provide a point of reference for you on hermeneutics. However, modern day Nicolaitans make a special effort at using item #21. They scream, "Submit to the hierarchy of scriptures!" However, this is often Satan's code language used to make a case that the Apostle Paul's writings supercede the thoughts and writings of the other apostles and of Christ, our head apostle. They claim Apostle Paul is higher in the hierarchy of biblical teachings; closer to God; newer information from God; etc. You get the picture? Yet God says, "I do not change."

I hope you understand from the last two chapters the need to fully heed the instructions of God Almighty and of His Son Jesus Christ [who came in the flesh as a messenger of God] as contained in the Holy Bible. Any teaching you hear that contradicts God's instructions and those you received from Christ are of Satan. It is really that basic and it's time to leave your church when your pastor contradicts God or Christ.

Apostle Paul Is Not Higher Than God Or Christ!

The biggest problem with the above hermeneutics list is that it was derived from and operates from the false doctrines of past generations. Like all Christian schools today, it emphasizes apostasy long ago accepted as fact. This includes a number of doctrinal issues not the least of which is the false doctrine of the trinity, a co-equal three-part godhead. Try to find the trinity doctrine in the plain and simple language of the Bible. It is not there. Instead, there is plain and simple language showing you the true relationship between God and Jesus Christ [His only human begotten Son].

A complete discussion of "The False Trinity Doctrine" will follow shortly in chapter 10. However, for a moment think about what I just told you. I told you that your Bible does not support the doctrine of the trinity. If I just left it there and did not show you chapter and verse to the contrary, you would probably drop this book right now. Yet who benefits from your lack of a clear understanding of God and His Word?

Understanding God's Word

Who benefits from a mixed up understanding that eventually leads you off the goal you have in mind for yourself and your family? You have the big goal of eternal life for yourself and family, don't you? I will tell you simply that it is Satan that benefits from your misunderstanding of who God is and what HE wants from you.

A speaker I heard gave an excellent sermon once on how a slight shift in direction can lead you astray and cause you to miss your target. Think of traveling from one spot to the next. It is a long distance of say 2,000 miles and is a straight line. There are no obstacles in your path and let's assume it is an air flight. Now, imagine the pilot's navigational gauge is mis-calibrated and it is negative 2% from where it is suppose to be. It is virtually 98% correct, yet off a negative 2%. From the navigational point of view, 360 degrees times 2% means your plane is off a negative 7.2 degrees from its true flight path. Do you think you will arrive at your destination [target]? Guess again. This is illustrated by the graphic below.

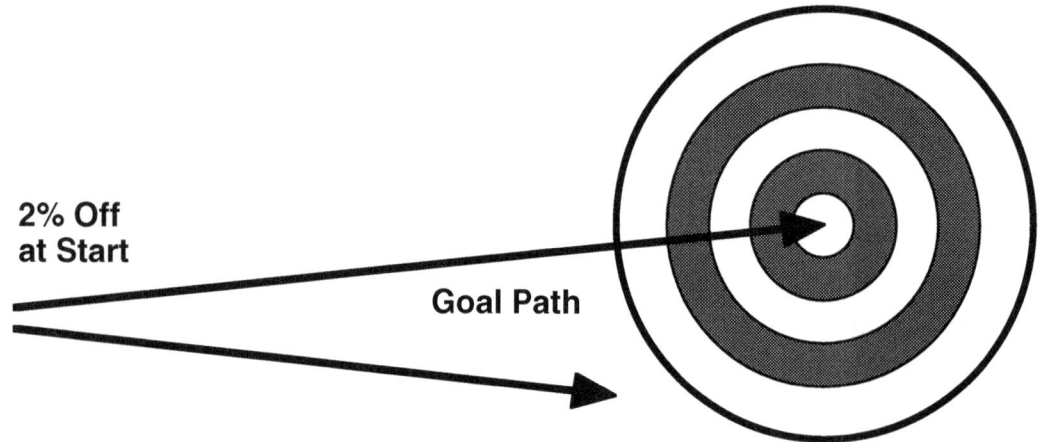

Satan's big picture goal is to take you off target in a way that leads you into eternal damnation. Satan doesn't do this in ways that you can easily recognize the deception. His tool is to shift you slightly off course. To twist Scripture, ever so slightly. To use plausible intellectual arguments like Apostle Paul has provided "a higher teaching" than that of Christ. It is newer information from God. We Christians are somehow "different" than the Jews in the eyes of God. The rationalization of Satan goes on and on.

Copyright 2005 Edward G. Palmer, All Rights Reserved.

Book of Edward—Chapter 8

Understanding God's Word

The goal of Satan is to be discrete and subtle. At the beginning of the deception, the con should be so slight that the majority, if not all, of God's people will not catch it. That is what happens when you've got a "good" con going down. People don't get it and are along for the ride so to speak. In the above graphic illustration, the start of the con is not so obvious that you can tell you are off target. Indeed, the beginning of the journey looks like you are going exactly where you are suppose to. The con's message to you looks like the graphic below. You still think you are on target, even though your gut might tell you something is amiss. Even if something is weird and odd in your gut, you reason that you have to give the pastor the benefit of the doubt. After all, he or she is the Bible *exegete*. You don't express it that way, but you do believe he or she is the expert—don't you?

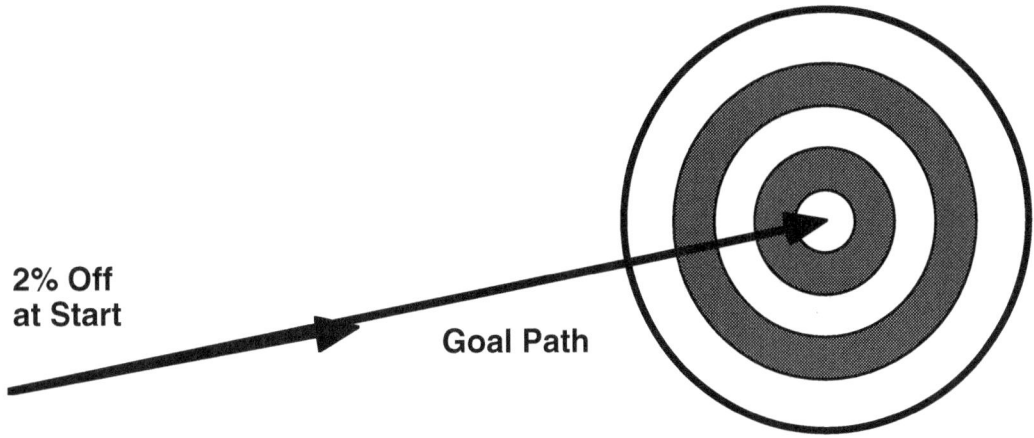

2% Off at Start

Goal Path

As time progresses along the journey towards your goal, the gap between where you are and where you want to be keeps growing wider and wider. However, very soon you are no longer concerned. You've decided that the pastor must know what he or she is doing and all will be well with your soul. You and some friends may have even talked about some oddity of the pastor's message or teaching. Yet since none of you know Hebrew or Greek and don't have the time to learn, you all let it go. That's why many in church lay back to enjoy the ride, never realizing that they are off course and headed for eternal damnation. That is the nature of a good con and it is Satan's strategy. Movies like Pinocchio illustrate this simple misdirection.

Copyright 2005 Edward G. Palmer, All Rights Reserved.

Book of Edward—Chapter 8

Understanding God's Word

The widening gap that grows with time looks like the graphic below. The original 2% error at is not where the con artist or lying pastor stops. Once you let your guard down, the con artist or false teacher then continues to introduce additional small 2% errors [apostasies]. These errors are again so small that you won't pick up on them either. If you do think something is odd, you are not likely to connect the current apostasy [lie] with a prior one. Thus, in almost all cases, you will never see and understand the cumulative effects of the apostasy con that is underway.

If you do want to see the cumulative effects, you will have to drop back some distance from the situation to gain perspective from a new and fresh larger setting. In the case of apostasy, you must rely upon your own common sense and the clear and plain language of the Holy Bible. It is the proverbial forest and tree scenario. You can be so absorbed by the trees [lies] that you do not understand you are in a forest [house of Satan].

You should also remember that the very idea of church swapping and moving into a new congregation is not an easy task. In fact, it is downright scary and filled with all sorts of emotions. Still, if you walk with God, you will chuck the human friendships when they are "committed" to apostasy.

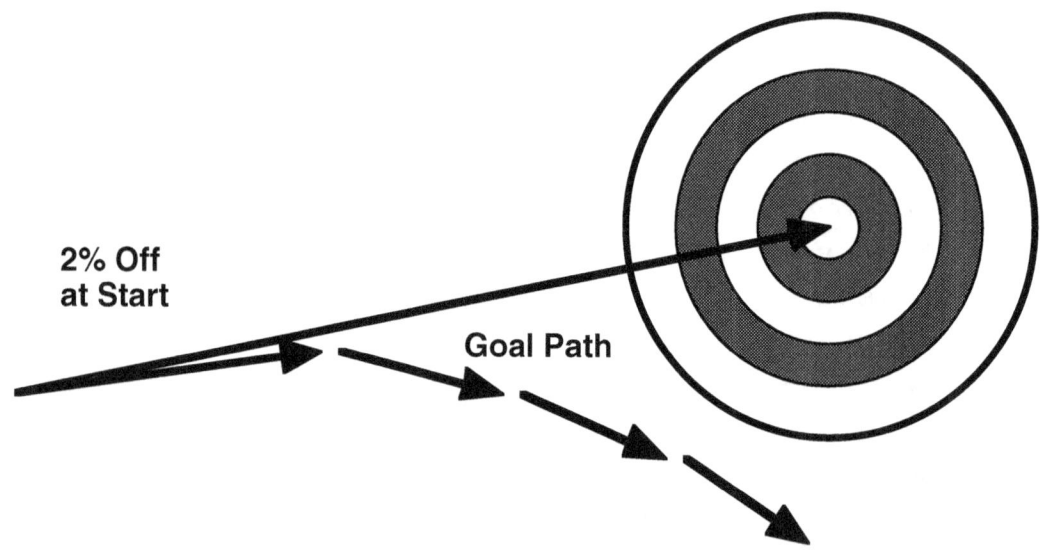

Errant Teachings Are Cumulative

Understanding God's Word

Notice that apostasy takes you in a downward direction. It is a path away from God and towards Satan. It is a path that moves you onto Satan's turf. As useful as these target illustrations are, they do not provide you with a complete understanding so I will use a couple of recent false teachings that I heard on national television. The first one came from the renowned Baptist preacher Charles Stanley. Several months ago, I accidentally tuned in for his televised message. Paraphrased below is what I heard Charles Stanley tell the people of his own Baptist congregation and the tens of thousands of national and international television viewers who were tuned in.

"You cannot obey the Ten Commandments. Nobody can. That is why you need Jesus. You need to understand that Jesus is God who came down in the flesh." Charles Stanley

I remember how dumbfounded I was when I heard Charles Stanley make that statement on television about God's Ten Commandments. The first thought that came to my mind was which one or ones couldn't Charles Stanley obey? What about his Baptist congregation? Which ones couldn't they obey? Was it?

1. You shall have no other gods before ME.
2. You shall not make for yourself a carved image …
3. You shall not take the name of the LORD your God in vain.
4. Observe the Sabbath.
5. Honor your mother and father.
6. You shall not murder.
7. You shall not commit adultery.
8. You shall not steal.
9. You shall not bear false witness against your neighbor.
10. You shall not covet your neighbor's wife …

Long before I knew God intimately, I had concluded in this earthly existence that I did not want to be a murderer, thief, adulterer, etc. Yes, I reckoned that the least I could do was to be a good citizen in America. Do you know that the majority of the Ten Commandments are incorporated into our Judeo Christian laws?

Understanding God's Word

Those who decide to just be a good citizen automatically wind up obeying a majority of the Ten Commandments with that simple decision. It is a simple choice for all of us to obey the laws of our country: to be a good citizen. Yet some people choose to be criminals.

The choice with God is just as simple. You don't need Christ to obey the Ten Commandments; you only need an obedient heart. Yet some choose to be lawless. It is one of the reasons that Christ said: "I never knew you; depart from me, you who practice lawlessness." Jesus could have told you that you never committed your heart 100% to God and that you chose to operate on both sides of the line of righteous. In a world that teaches you can have it all, you thought that also applied to the turfs of righteousness and unrighteousness. That you could operate on both sides. That you could have you cake and eat it also. You should understand that God Almighty does not like second place. Remember God's first commandment?

Indeed, which of God's Ten Commandments cannot be obeyed without Jesus Christ? Do you think that God Almighty gave those instructions to dumb people who could not obey them? No, created in the image of our God, we have all been given "the power of a strong mind." Obeying God's Commandments therefore really boils down to where our heart and spiritual choice is with God. This is NOT a matter of espousing Christ from our mouth. That is the stuff of Christian mythology.

What does it really mean to be born again? It doesn't mean accepting Christ so you can have a pass on your sins. That too is the stuff of Christian mythology. Being born again means giving your heart 100% to God Almighty and choosing to be HIS servant with or without the benefit of Jesus Christ. That means everyone throughout the world can choose God!

The false doctrine of Jesus being God will be dealt with later. For now, think about the statement: "You cannot obey the Ten Commandments. Nobody can. That is why you need Jesus." This seems simple enough to verify in scriptures. If what the Bible says contradicts Charles Stanley, would it matter to you? If it does, then consider the following scriptures.

Copyright 2005 Edward G. Palmer, All Rights Reserved.

Book of Edward—Chapter 8

Understanding God's Word

Job Was Blameless & Upright!

"There was a man in the land of Uz, whose name was Job; and that man was blameless and upright, and one who feared God and shunned evil." Job 1:1

Abraham Believed God!

"For what does the Scripture say? Abraham believed God, and it was accounted to him for righteousness." Romans 4:3

Zacharias & Elizabeth Were Both Righteous!

"There was ... a certain priest named Zacharias, of the division of Abijah. His wife was of the daughters of Aaron, and her name was Elizabeth. And they were both righteous before God, walking in all the commandments and ordinances of the LORD blameless." Luke 1:5-6

There comes a very basic and fundamental question that confronts every true believer who has a heart for God. Should you believe the learned pastor or should you believe the written word of God? While every pastor admonishes their congregation to read the written word of God, few people actually do read it. Believe me, the pastor knows this fact. Those who start to read and study the word of God in any serious way will have to confront this basic question of whom they will believe sooner or later.

What will it be? God's Word in the plain and simple language HE has given or the pastor's doctrine? Given the power of a strong mind that God has provided, it cannot be both ways. That is to say, the pastor cannot teach opposite of the word of God with impunity. Who makes the apostasy call? You do. It is done based on your knowledge of Scripture.

Understanding God's Word

The above-cited scriptures raise some very interesting questions since neither Job, Abraham, Zacharias nor Elizabeth had the benefit of "accepting Jesus in their hearts." In every instance, Jesus was not even born yet. So who was in their hearts? It was God Almighty that was in their hearts.

Who was it that they obeyed? It was God Almighty. What was it that they obeyed? It was the "commandments and ordinances" of God. The next time that some pastor teaches that you cannot be righteous, point out the fact that the Bible illustrates the opposite instructions. The Nicolaitans like to misquote Paul in this area. When Paul stated that "no one is righteous," he was lamenting like King David did about the seemingly unrighteousness of humanity as a whole. I too lament today over the seemingly unrighteousness of the Christian community as a whole. I also lament over the unadulterated and unchecked apostasy from the leaders of the Christian Church.

Is Charles Stanley right or is the word of God right? Don't try to tell me that you cannot discern the difference between Stanley's assertions that you cannot obey the Ten Commandments and the Bible references that directly contradict his false doctrine. If you cannot discern the difference, then you are one of the Christians that Jesus is talking about when he said, "I never knew you."

If you think you cannot make the choice because you would have to study the Hebrew or Greek behind the above cited verses, you are also one of those Jesus is talking about. This is an example of the plain and simple language of the Bible and how it is being perverted. If you cannot relate to the importance of this apostasy, you are simply not meant to. Go about your earthly business. If you can relate, then hold your pastor accountable for the teachings from his or her pulpit. Make sure those teachings conform to the Bible you base your salvation on. This is NOT a game; it is eternity!

I am amused by the notion that you can just pick and choose what you want to believe in the Bible. God's Holy Bible is a 100% take it or leave it proposition. If you can't understand the basics, reassess where you heart is.

Copyright 2005 Edward G. Palmer, All Rights Reserved.

Book of Edward—Chapter 8

Understanding God's Word

Not everything in the Bible is as easy to understand as the above illustration between the word of God and Charles Stanley's false doctrine. I estimate that ninety-eight percent of the Bible is exoteric in nature. This means that 98% of the Bible is meant to be understood by all who read it. The remaining two percent of the Bible is esoteric in nature. Only a few people will understand the spiritual implications in the esoteric parts of the Bible. This is by God's design and it is nothing for you to be concerned with. The 98% that God intends for you to understand can be illustrated as:

The Holy Bible is 98% Exoteric!

God meant for you to understand.

(2% Esoteric)

You will not get in trouble with God because you do not understand some cryptic esoteric passage of Scripture. Likewise, it doesn't matter if you cannot keep up with whom begets whom. Understanding genealogy will not impede your entrance into Heaven. You will get in trouble with God because you fail to observe the very basics of HIS commandments. It is items like the Ten Commandments and behavior that demonstrates true repentance. God has intended for you to understand the Bible, almost in its entirety (98% or more). Once again, your understanding "requires" a dedicated heart.

Understanding God's Word

Charles Stanley's false doctrines are derived from mankind's need to rationalize the trinity doctrine. This matter of rationalization is discussed in the next chapter. For now, think about the above implication when it comes to righteousness. If you can be righteous and obey the Ten Commandments on your own, why did Jesus come? What was Jesus' purpose? Does this individual righteousness mean that the Jewish people and the Muslim people can be saved without Christ Jesus? Which God do the Jews and Muslims worship? Is it the same God that Christians worship?

Christian apostasy doesn't know any boundaries because of the need of the Church to rationalize the trinity and "make" Jesus our God. Salvation is another issue that needs to be addressed. If you listened to Christian mythology, you would conclude that salvation arrived on the scene with Jesus. It didn't. Go get some Bible software and search on the word "salvation" and you will start to understand God a little better. Salvation did not arrive with Jesus. The "Gift of Jesus" is an upcoming chapter.

From the above example of Charles Stanley, you can observe that some pastors will teach a message that the Bible itself does not support. This is Bible apostasy. As bad as this apostasy is: What about the pastor that tells you to actually change the wording of your Bible?

It was only a few days ago when I tuned into the Trinity Broadcasting Network (TBN) on the satellite dish. I love God's Word and I am always interested in listening to it preached. It was now Rod Parsley, the pastor of the Worldwide Harvest Church on the television. This pastor was teaching out of the book of Joshua concerning the victory at Jericho. Observe the word of God at Joshua 6:18

> **"And you, by all means abstain from the accursed things, lest you become accursed when you take of the accursed things, and make the camp of Israel a curse, and trouble it."**
> **Joshua 6:18**

God sent the Israelites into the city to conquer and destroy it. Are you familiar with the story of Jericho?

Understanding God's Word

Before going into Jericho, God made His plan clear in verse 17.

"Now the city shall be doomed by the Lord to destruction, it and all who are in it. Only Rahab the harlot shall live, she and all who are with her in the house, because she hid the messengers that we sent." Joshua 6:17

Note that the city was doomed for destruction. "It and all who are inside of it except Rahab and all who are with her [in her house]." God Almighty had cursed the city of Jericho and its contents with the exception of Rahab and those in her home. This destruction applied to every other physical and living thing.

In verse 18, God instructed to the people of Israel to "abstain from the accursed things." In other words, don't take any personal souvenirs. Don't take any battle trophies. Destroy everything physical and all of the people [with the sole exception God noted]. If you read further into the story, you will find out that "Achan took of the accursed things; so the anger of the Lord burned against the children of Israel." Joshua 2:1

The story of Jericho is a story about the collective obedience of Israel. God expected everyone in Israel to do what He told all of them collectively to do. God also defined what was *"accursed."* He defined "the accursed things" as the entire city, all of its contents and its entire people with the sole exception of Rahab and those in her home.

The Second College Edition of The American Heritage Dictionary[3] defines the word accursed as follows:

Accursed 1. Under a curse; 2. Abominable; hateful

Both of these definitions fit God's description and His intention of the word "accursed." God cursed Jericho because it was an abomination and a hateful place in His eyes. However, Pastor Rod Parsley gave instructions to his congregation and television viewers to alter the Bible's clear language.

Understanding God's Word

Pastor Rod Parsley's instructions to his congregation and television viewers were to "cross out the word <u>accursed</u> and change it to the word <u>sanctified</u>." Here is what Rod Parsley says the Bible verse should look like.

"And you, by all means abstain from the ~~accursed~~ <u>sanctified</u> things, lest you become accursed when you take of the ~~accursed~~ <u>sanctified</u> things, and make the camp of Israel a curse, and trouble it." Joshua 6:18

The Second College Edition of The American Heritage Dictionary[4] defines the word sanctified as follows:

Sanctify   (**fied**) 1. To set apart for sacred use; consecrate. 2. To make holy; purify.

Take the time now to compare the definition of word <u>accursed</u> with the definition of word <u>sanctified</u>. Would you consider them of equal value? Absolutely not! It is bad enough that pastors would teach opposite of what the Bible clearly states. However, for a pastor to change something that was abominable to God into something that is sanctified to God is absolutely evil and I cannot put it in any less than that terminology. Those who seek to alter the written word of God with their teachings are engaging in evil works whether they are consciously aware of it or not. In the case of Rod Parsley, I believe he knew specifically what he was doing with this errant teaching.

Pastor Parsley's instructions continued on as he stated: "Jericho was a kind of first fruit. A kind of seed and you don't mess with God's seed." Of course this dialogue now involved money. That is always the meaning of a "first fruits" message from a charismatic pastor. The implication is to "bring in the money to the church and anyone who doesn't is in big trouble with God." This is a twisted tithe theology that perverts and contorts God's Word for personal gain. The tithe mythology will be discussed in a later chapter.

Parsley has twisted a collective punishment of Israel when one person "took of a cursed thing" into a message on giving money.

Understanding God's Word

You should be seriously concerned when your pastor misrepresents what the Bible says. Concerned enough to immediately confront him or her with their apostasy. You should contact the elders or others who may have oversight authority and take whatever action you can. Do not live with apostasy, as God will hold you personally accountable for doing so.

When your pastor wants you to change the wording of the Bible, get up and walk out and never return again. Whether you realize it or not, you are in a house of Satan if the pastor teaches and instructs you to alter God's Word. Both of the above pastors have congregations that number in the thousands of members, but I didn't see one of the members of either of these congregations rise to challenge the apostasy from their pastor. There is a herd mentality that is characteristic of any large group of people, which makes it difficult to speak out. The days of God holding the entire group accountable for the sins of an individual like he did with Jericho are over. It is a different covenant. Today, he holds individual sinners accountable!

Those who alter the word of God in any way will find themselves in serious trouble with a never changing God who says PLAINLY and CLEARLY: "DON'T MESS WITH MY WORD [INSTRUCTIONS]!"

These pastors and others haven't learned the fundamentals of teaching the word of God. Yes, they don't even understand the basics. God says you should not add anything to or remove anything from HIS Word. Let me repeat God's instructions [commandments] once again for those who would be bold enough to teach the Word in any way that alters its plain meaning.

> **"Whatever I command you, be careful to observe it; you shall not add to it nor take away from it." Deut. 12:32**

> **"If anyone adds to these things, God will add to him the plagues that are written in this book; and if anyone takes away from the words of the book of this prophecy, God shall take away his part from the Book of Life, from the holy city, and from the things which are written in this book." Rev. 22:18-19**

Understanding God's Word

When You Standup For The Word, You'll Understand!

It is Jesus who taught us that we could have eternal life if we only obeyed the Ten Commandments. Jesus even made it simpler to understand by teaching us that if you loved God and your neighbor that you would have eternal life. When you love God with all your heart, obedience and external love for your neighbor are no longer issues. <u>Consider these words of Christ</u>:

> **"Whoever therefore breaks one of the least of these commandments, and teaches men so, shall be called least in the kingdom of Heaven; but whoever does and teaches them, he shall be called great in the kingdom of Heaven."**
> **Matthew 5:19**

Ask yourself this question, are pastors that break the commandments of God telling you the truth or is Jesus Christ, whom you now claim as your savior? If you stand up for your pastor and deny the words of Jesus, don't be surprised if Jesus denies you in Heaven by saying "I never knew you." If you know Christ, you obey Christ. It is not enough to "know of" Christ as even demons know of him. It always comes back to obedience.

When You Obey Jesus, You'll Understand!

Well, so what about Jesus? Did he attend a seminary? Was he also degreed? Where did he get his knowledge and understanding? Think about this Scripture in Mark for a moment until it sinks into your heart and spirit.

> **"And when the Sabbath had come, he began to teach in the synagogue. And many hearing him were astonished, saying, where did this man get these things? And what wisdom is this, which is given to him, that such mighty works are performed by his hands!" Mark 6:2**

The message is clear that Jesus Christ spoke with understanding and wisdom. But isn't this Joseph the carpenter's son? What gives?

Understanding God's Word

Who did Jesus speak for? Whose deeds did he perform? The Bible is clear that God the FATHER imbued Jesus Christ with the power of HIS Holy Spirit. Jesus was God's messenger and represented God on this earth. He had a job to do for God and Jesus made this very clear to mankind.

> **"HE [the FATHER] who sent me is true." John 7:28**

> **"I can of myself do nothing." John 5:20**

> **"I [Jesus] fully obey God." John 8:55**

> **"I must work the works of HIM [God] who sent me." John 9:4**

> **"Nor is he who is sent [Jesus] greater than [God]." John 13:16**

The same kind of understanding that God Almighty placed earlier into Bezaleel for the building of HIS temple HE put into Jesus Christ so the kingdom of God could be properly preached and taught to others. Neither Bezaleel nor Jesus had to attend a seminary school. That is not how God Almighty works. The scriptures below illustrate some of the characteristics that they received from God. They can belong to you when you give God the unquestionable loyalty of your heart.

> **"For the Holy Spirit will teach you in that very hour what you ought to say." Luke 12:12**

> **"But the Helper, the Holy Spirit, whom the FATHER will send in my name, HE will teach you all things, and bring to your remembrance all things that I said to you." John 14:26**

> **"But the anointing which you have received from HIM abides in you, and you do not need that anyone teach you; but as the same anointing teaches you concerning all things, and is true, and is not a lie, and just as it has taught you, you will abide in HIM." 1 John 2:27**

Understanding God's Word

The controversy over whether Jesus is God seems ridiculous to me in light of the many scriptures that teach exactly the opposite, especially the recorded words of Jesus Christ. While this matter will be dealt with more fully later, consider these scriptures from the Apostle John if you want to understand our God.

> **"Whoever confesses that Jesus is the Son of God, God abides in him and he in God." 1 John 4:15**

> **"Who is he who overcomes the world, but he who believes that Jesus is the Son of God?" 1 John 5:5**

Apostle John makes it clear that Christ is *not* God Almighty as does the prior verses of Jesus that were cited. You will never understand God if you persist in trying to morph Jesus into God. Indeed, the word of God makes it plain to us that there is a different and special relationship. Then there are also clear statements from Christ that the FATHER is his God. Look at this plain and simple statement from Jesus Christ in Scripture.

> **"I am going back to my FATHER and your FATHER, to my God and your God." John 20:17 NCV**

When You Treat Jesus As The Son, You'll Understand!

Jesus and the other apostles of God have not come to give you a pass on your sins as much of modern Christian mythology teaches. Instead, they all call you back into obedience of God's simple commandments. When you obey the simple commandments of God, you wind up back into the loving arms of our heavenly FATHER [God]. God has not changed and Christ is not God; that doctrine is Christian mythology. God's call back to obedience through Christ and the other apostles should be natural to all of mankind as God has set HIMSELF into the hearts and minds of everyone. We inherently all know what is right and wrong. What is missing is the choice to obey and to stop rationalizing away our sins and spiritual responsibilities.

Copyright 2005 Edward G. Palmer, All Rights Reserved.

Understanding God's Word

It is simple to understand God when you acknowledge the internal set of instructions God already gave your brain and heart [computer metaphor].

> **"None of them shall teach his neighbor, and none his brother, saying, 'Know the LORD,' for all shall know ME, from the least of them to the greatest of them."**
> **Hebrews 8:11**

Understanding Is Second Nature To Committed Hearts!

SIDE NOTE: Did you realize that the matter of where your heart is with God was not on the hermeneutic list previously shown? Yet, make no mistake about it, salvation and understanding both start with your heart.

Now think about whether you really need that seminary school degree or whether you should simply give your heart to God and rely upon HIS ability to provide HIS teachings and whatever else you need such as wisdom and understanding?

When you get down to where the rubber meets the road, there exists a significant understanding paradox. That paradox is the fact that no matter how much schooling or education you achieve, you will never gain wisdom and understanding until you connect with God. You could have a Ph D degree and be as ignorant as a moron when it comes to wisdom and understanding without God. Indeed, there are those who continually seek higher levels of education for wisdom because they feel a lack of wisdom and understanding inside. They are incomplete without God and always will be. Conversely, you could be a sixth grade drop out and have wisdom beyond measure simply because you have given your heart to God.

> **"If any of you lacks wisdom, let him ask of God, who gives to all liberally and without reproach, and it will be given to him." James 1:5**

Note: See James 1:6-8 for some conditions that might apply.

Understanding God's Word

I first stumbled across an important observation on the relationship between spirituality and truth in the book titled <u>The Magic of Believing</u>[5] by Claude M. Bristol *Pocket Books, 1948.* In the book is a short quote that got my attention 2-3 decades ago. It came from an author known as Paracelsus.

"Men who are devoid of the power of spiritual perception are unable to recognize anything that cannot be seen externally."
Paracelsus

Over the years I have observed the reality of Paracelsus' observation. There is a physical reality that exists which is easily detectable by our physical senses of sight, touch, hearing, etc. However, there is a different reality that is only perceptible to people who have the power of spiritual perception. I can tell you that the full truth of any given situation is not understandable by people without spiritual perception. In essence, they only get part of the picture. The entire picture of any given situation is composed of the physical plus the spiritual. The spiritual in this sense is from God.

"For as the heavens are higher than the earth, so are MY ways higher than your ways, and MY thoughts than your thoughts." Isaiah 55:9

In times of great stress from my limited physical observations, I have to remind myself that God's reality is very different than what I can sense physically. That God's understanding is higher than mine and the only way to fully grasp the situation is to engage my spirit and connect it to HIS. I have become pretty adept at this and most of the time I can now see two sets of reality in front of me. One reality is what the world sees and is limited by all of our physical senses. The other reality contains spiritual insights and includes many options and alternative outcomes from God.

"Trust in the LORD with all your heart, and lean not on your own understanding." Proverbs 3:5

Without God's Help, You'll Never Fully Understand!

Understanding God's Word

These two realities can get interesting and humorous if you operate in areas of the sciences like I do. For me, I know that people who lack spiritual insights also lack understanding and wisdom. Where then is the SOURCE of wisdom and insight? It is God Almighty. Consider these words of Job.

"From where then does wisdom come?
And where is the place of understanding? [21]

It is hidden from the eyes of all living,
And concealed from the birds of the air. [22]

Destruction and Death say,
'We have heard a report about it with our ears.' [23]

God understands its way,
And HE knows its place. [24]

For HE looks to the ends of the earth,
And sees under the whole heavens, [25]

To establish a weight for the wind,
And apportion the waters by measure. [26]

When HE made a law for the rain,
And a path for the thunderbolt, [27]

Then HE saw wisdom and declared it;
HE prepared it, indeed, HE searched it out. [28]

And to man HE said,
'Behold, the fear of the LORD, that is wisdom,
And to depart from evil is understanding.' " Job 28:20-28

When You Depart From Evil, You'll Understand!

Understanding God's Word

Job asks the question of where does wisdom come from and where is the place of understanding in verse 20 and then gives the answer in verse 28. To gain perspective on understanding God, you must understand that you are not equal to God and that you are inherently a very limited human being without HIM. Of course, a little humility will go a long way in these regards. Humankind often operates on a high ego platform and men especially have a hard time admitting that they do not know it all.

The story of Job illustrates these limitations and God's answer to Job is very poignant in terms of the limits to our human understanding.

> **"But there is a spirit in man, and the breath of the Almighty gives him understanding." Job 32:8**

God's Breath Gives Us Understanding!

Get into a study of every use of the word "understanding" in the Bible in the Old and New Testaments if you want to explore this subject further. You will enjoy the effort and God will enhance your understanding of HIS Word in a great way. You will learn many things including:

1. Understanding of the times provides know how. 1 Chron 12:32
2. Understanding is in the visions of God. 2 Chron 26:5
3. Some men have understanding. Ezra 8:16
4. Some nations have no understanding. Deut. 32:28
5. Understanding grows with age. Job 12:12
6. God sometimes takes away understanding. Job 12:24
7. God sometimes hides understanding from hearts. Job 17:4
8. Gain understanding before you speak. Job 18:2
9. God's understanding controls weather. Job 26:12
10. If you have understanding, you listen. Job 34:10
11. Wisdom is placed in the mind. Job 38:36
12. Understanding is placed in the heart. Job 38:36

Copyright 2005 Edward G. Palmer, All Rights Reserved.

Understanding God's Word

After Job takes his turn questioning God, God Almighty responds with His own set of questions. "Tell Me, if you know all this" says God in Job 38:18. The questions that God asks Job illustrate the limits of our human understanding. Indeed, the greatest education that I ever got was the knowledge of just how little I really know when it comes to the universe of knowledge available and known by God. Yes, I completely realize that without God I am only a small part of what is possible for my life. But with God I can be all that He wants me to be. God asks Job "Who placed wisdom in the mind of man?" He then asks Job "Who placed understanding in the heart of man?" Who did these things Job?

**"Who has put wisdom in the mind?
Or who has given understanding to the heart?" Job 38:36**

Think about the organ of our heart for a moment. We know that there is life inside the blood. We also know that it is the heart organ that pumps this life throughout our body. When God places understanding in our heart, God knows this understanding will also be pumped throughout our entire being. We rely upon the blood being pumped by our heart to bring life to our physical being. Likewise, we can rely upon the understanding being pumped by our heart to bring life to our spiritual being (our spirit-soul).

God Gives Understanding To The Committed Heart!

When it comes to understanding God's Word, a complete science has emerged called hermeneutics. This science seeks to pick apart the word of God and sift through it for truth and meaning. However, early in this book I told you that you couldn't read the Bible with only your intellect. You need a heart for God to understand God's Word. With only your intellect, you are reading someone else's mail. You will have no intimacy with the subject and you will not see behind the scenes for God's meaning. Therefore you will lack perspective on what you read. In a way, it is like reading a recipe card that sounds simple enough to understand [cook, bake or make] with one big exception. The units of measure are totally unknown to mankind.

Understanding God's Word

In contrast to the field of hermeneutics, God simply offers to place understanding into your heart just like HE did with Bezaleel and Jesus. With that understanding, you will find simple and plain language in the Bible. Don't let anyone alter this simple language by trying to convince you there is more to it. You do not need a college education to understand the Bible. You can understand God's Word because it is 98% exoteric. God expects you to read and understand it all *after* you give HIM your heart. The Bible is written at a sixth grade level for ease of reading. If anyone you know cannot accept the simple and plain language that God has provided, it is because his or her heart does not fully belong to God.

> **"God will give your heart understanding when you give God a full 100% of your heart." The Apostle Edward**

> **"The fear of the LORD is the beginning of wisdom; a good understanding have all those who do HIS commandments. HIS praise endures forever." Psalm 111:10**

Your Obedience Demonstrates Your Understanding!

> **"And all who heard [Jesus] were astonished at his understanding and answers." Luke 2:47**

> **"And we know that the [begotten] Son of God [Jesus Christ] has come and has given us an understanding, that we may know HIM [God Almighty —Yahweh] who is true."**
> **1 John 5:20**

Jesus Gives Us An Understanding Of God [FATHER]!

Copyright 2005 Edward G. Palmer, All Rights Reserved.

Book of Edward—Chapter 8

Seven Keys To Really Understanding God's Word!

1. Give your heart 100% to God.
2. Start interacting with God on an intimate level.
3. Ask God for wisdom and understanding.
4. Accept the simple and plain language of the Bible.
5. Do not tolerate teachings that are opposite of the Word.
6. Do not tolerate teachers who alter God's Word.
7. Read your Bible daily for truth.

The above list is quite different than the prior hermeneutics list. It is a lot simpler and it doesn't involve the rationalization of mankind. God says to give HIM your heart and HE will supply everything else that you need in this earthly life. Mankind says to go get a Ph D in hermeneutics to explain the word of God. Yet no amount of education will get you an understanding of God's Word. That understanding only comes as a spiritual gift.

"And HE opened their understanding [HE gave the gift of], that they might comprehend the Scriptures." Luke 24:45

PRAYER: "Heavenly FATHER, God of my brother Jesus Christ, and all that I am on this earth and ever hope to be, hear this poor apostle's prayer. Enlighten those who read this book. Place the gift of understanding into every committed heart. Let no person leave this book without a greater sense of individual spiritual knowledge and power. LORD, heal my beloved wife Jackie of the cancer that threatens to take her life; she is my love in this earthly life whom YOU gave me as half of my flesh." The Apostle Edward

You Really Did Give God Your Heart!
Now, Your Obedience Demonstrates You Are ...
Understanding God's Word

Chapter Nine
Rationalization of Mankind

"If a son asks for bread from any father among you, will he give him a stone? Or if he asks for a fish, will he give him a serpent instead of a fish?" Luke 11:11

"Hatred stirs up strife, but love covers all sins." Proverbs 10:12

Jesus answered them, "Many good works I have shown you from my FATHER. For which of those works do you stone me?" John 10:32

"Then they took away the stone from the place where the dead man was lying. And Jesus lifted up his eyes and said, 'FATHER, I thank YOU that YOU have heard me.' " John 11:41

"But the rest of mankind, who were not killed by these plagues, did not repent of the works of their hands, that they should not worship demons, and idols of gold, silver, brass, stone, and wood, which can neither see nor hear nor walk." Rev. 9:20

"You are to live clean, innocent lives as children of God in a dark world full of crooked and perverse people. Let your lives shine brightly before them." Philip. 2:15 NLT

"There is no limit to the rationalization of mankind concerning God's Holy Word. This is especially true when it comes to the rationalization of the trinity doctrine." The Apostle Edward

Rationalization of Mankind

I asked God why doctrines that were exactly opposite of HIS written word existed in Christianity. For example, when Jesus raised Lazarus from the dead, Jesus lifted his eyes unto Heaven and said: "FATHER, I thank YOU that YOU have heard me." [John 11:41] Jesus spoke words of thanksgiving to God. Thank you God for hearing and answering my prayer! That is what Jesus prayed. Note: Jesus did not say: "Thank you Jesus for hearing Jesus' prayer." That sounds stupid, doesn't it? In other words, Jesus was NOT talking to himself. He was praying to his God. You know, the God that Jesus told us that he was returning to as cited in the last chapter. Remember, Jesus stated clearly and plainly that his FATHER and his God were also our FATHER and our God. This statement of Jesus is plain and clear and it does not leave anything to the imagination from a communications point of view.

Jesus preceded his prayer of thanksgiving to God with the statement to Martha in John 11:40. Jesus said: "Did I not say to you that if you believe you would see the glory of God?" Once again, Jesus was not talking about Martha seeing his glory: he was talking about Martha seeing God's glory.

Jesus prayed to his God. He did not pray to himself!

Jesus said it would be God's glory that Martha saw. Not his!

So I asked God. "Why would the doctrine of the trinity exist given this and other clear and plain words spoken by Jesus throughout the New Testament?" Obviously, they teach opposite such doctrine. Why God?

God gave me understanding and told me: "It is the rationalization of mankind." I have now studied this subject in depth and I can tell you I have to conclude that there is no limit to the rationalization of mankind. This is especially true when it comes to the Christian doctrine of the trinity.

If you actually believed in the trinity doctrine, you would have to check your brain in at the front door of the church. That is because your Bible studies would come up against the above words of Jesus and more.

Copyright 2005 Edward G. Palmer, All Rights Reserved.

Book of Edward—Chapter 9

Rationalization of Mankind

We know that God has given us "the power of a strong mind." We also know that God meant for us to understand the Bible. Yet if Jesus is really God in the flesh, then there are some stupid and nonsensical verses in the Bible. In other words, if the trinity doctrine were true, the Bible would not make intellectual sense and cannot be read in its simple, plain and easy to understand language. Verses like those above, where Jesus prays to God and demonstrates God's glory to Martha would then become unintelligible and cryptic messages.

If the trinity doctrine were true, a lot of Jesus' words would become stupid, nonsensical, unintelligible and cryptic. The above two verses are two examples of Jesus' plain and clear words. However, the acceptance of the trinity doctrine by the author Nikos Kazantzakis may be the reason that he wrote the book, The Last Temptation of Christ[1]. The book presents Jesus as a stupid and bungling idiot? The author could certainly have concluded that much if he believed in the trinity doctrine. Director Martin Scorsese took this author's book and translated it into a cinema apostasy in which Jesus was actually portrayed on the movie screen as a stupid and bungling idiot.

An Internet description of the movie states: "Despite controversy surrounding the production, Scorsese's film is an honestly felt and in many ways sympathetic contemplation of Christianity." The movie was so offensive in the first 10 minutes that I refused to watch it for several years. Having now watched the entire movie, I can tell you that it remained very offensive throughout its entirety.

Is Jesus a stupid and bungling idiot? Are the words Jesus spoke to us, given to him directly from God Almighty, meant to be understood in their plain and clear language? Or, given the trinity doctrine, are Jesus' words stupid, nonsensical, unintelligent and cryptic messages from God? It would appear that this is the basic choice you and I have got to make if we are going to study the Bible. Perhaps we should just give up on understanding? No, that is exactly what Satan wants you to do. Don't read your Bible is a message that the church at large is very comfortable with. Why?

Rationalization of Mankind

Do you remember the story of the transfiguration on the high mountain where Jesus took Peter, James and John his brother? Do you remember the thrilling moment when God Almighty looked down upon Jesus and said: "This is MY beloved Son, in whom I am well pleased?" Remember also that God told us to listen to Jesus? Hear him! In other words, take the words of Jesus to heart. This is a favorite passage of mine and it never ceases to thrill me when I imagine myself being with Jesus and hearing the words of God Almighty. Consider this verse.

"While he [Peter] was still speaking, behold, a bright cloud overshadowed them; and suddenly a voice came out of the cloud, saying, 'this is MY beloved Son, in whom I am well pleased. Hear him!' " Matthew 17:5

It doesn't take much Bible study to come to an important question concerning this verse. If Jesus is God in the flesh, then Jesus must have been talking to himself, right? I reasoned that this must be concluded as fact if the trinity doctrine were to hold true. You cannot have such clear and plain language of the Bible and simply ignore it. Therefore, if you accept the trinity doctrine, you must accept that Jesus was talking to himself. I speculated in my Bible studies that eventually someone would have to write about this and explain it to Christianity. Well …

Sixteen months ago I was in Houston, Texas on a business trip. I made a presentation at the Energy Venture Fair II where I sought investment capital for SolarAttic, Inc. This is a small energy technology company that I founded in 1986. God gave me an understanding of how to use the heat energy inside of attics. Today, several patents later, we know how to use the attic to heat homes, hot water and swimming pools. I.E. We can heat a swimming pool for $10 per month in electricity, which eliminates $500 per month in natural gas costs. Big energy savings are available for consumers. While I was in Houston, I stayed at the JW Marriott hotel. Directly across the street was a huge shopping mall covering several square blocks. It was called the Galleria.

Rationalization of Mankind

The physical location of the JW Marriott and Galleria center looked like the graphic shown below. The map shows the circuitous path of a very interesting trip to the B. Dalton bookstore that God took me on just before I left Houston.

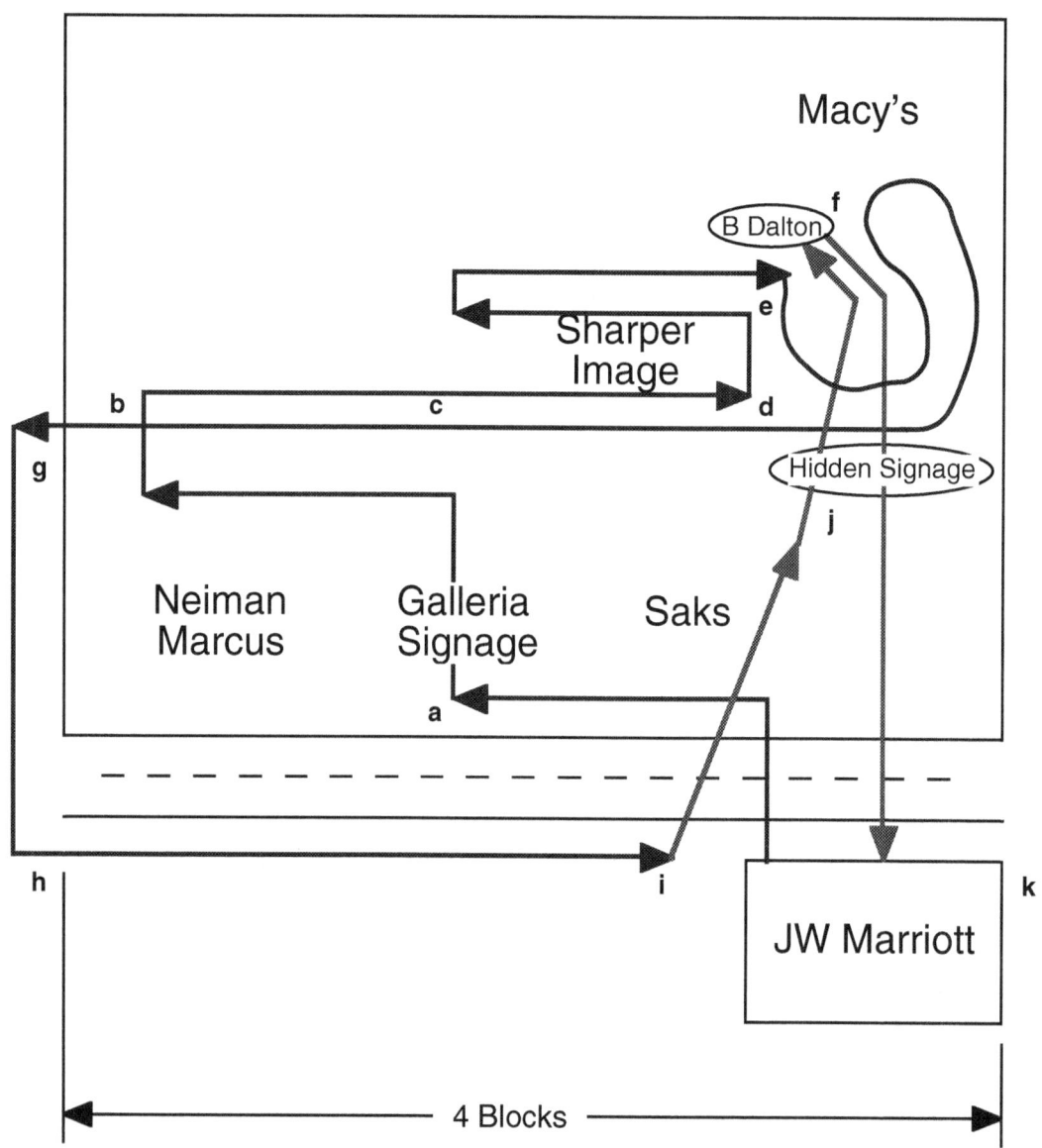

I checked out of the Marriott hotel at about 11 a.m. and I had two hours before the airport shuttle arrived. Now what?

Copyright 2005 Edward G. Palmer, All Rights Reserved.

Book of Edward—Chapter 9

Rationalization of Mankind

The Concierge at the Marriott recommended that I go check out the Sharper Image store in the Galleria across the street. A couple of days earlier I had ventured out into the neighborhood to check out the lay of the land. This is fun just to find out what the local shopping area looks like. I had wandered down the street four blocks and just past half way is where I had seen a huge Galleria sign [point "a"]. So that is where I thought the Galleria was located.

I wasn't particularly interested in the Sharper Image store albeit their catalogue is filled with very interesting products. I entered the Galleria at point "a" and proceeded down towards the Neiman Marcus store. The Galleria turned out to be a sprawling three level complex that occupies at least a four-block by two-block area. When I got down to point "b", I found a directory and noticed that a B. Dalton bookstore was located close to the Sharper Image store on the opposite end past Saks 5th Avenue. Bookstores are one of my favorite places to visit so the B. Dalton bookstore became my primary destination. In Minnesota, we have some large B. Dalton bookstores so I am familiar with them and their signage.

I never realized at the time that the direction I was heading was back towards the way that I came from. My wife is the navigator in the family. I am the adventurer. She likes to go boating but my desire to check out the weedy lily patches and remote areas of the lake stresses her out. Likewise when I want to go off the paved road onto the dirt road, she doesn't get very excited. And often I am on cruise control not really paying attention to the navigational details of the road. Just enjoying the cruise and the visual aspects of local spots of interest. When I started walking towards the bookstore, I had no conscious awareness of its physical relationship to the Marriott. I didn't even realize that the Saks 5th Avenue store was the same Saks' sign that was directly across from the Marriott. Duh! I was just trying to pass some time away before the airport shuttle arrived.

I meandered down the sprawling retail complex. Along the way toward B. Dalton, I stopped for a white-hot chocolate at the local cappuccino cafe and also to observe some ice-skating in a lower level ice rink.

Rationalization of Mankind

I encountered the Sharper Image store [point "d"] where I spent some time looking at all the gadgets that they had. Suffice to say that if you are rolling in money, you can get a lot of physical gadgets. A wise man once taught me to watch out for assets because someone has to take care of them. It is wise advice and I didn't buy anything. The B. Dalton bookstore was supposed to be in the same area but I could not find it. B. Dalton stores in Minnesota are rather large ones and I was looking for a big bookstore sign.

I couldn't find the big B. Dalton sign I was looking for so I walked up to the next level thinking it was upstairs. I still couldn't find it so I said "tough" and proceeded to leave the complex. I walked half way back on the second level to where I started from and studied another directory to locate a bathroom. I found that the nearest bathroom was back towards the Sharper Image store but in a hidden hallway next to Macy's second floor entrance. The map above doesn't convey store layouts and the hidden hallway well.

After a brief restroom visit [2nd floor point "e"], I realized that I must be directly over the B. Dalton store if it even existed. So I went back downstairs and just before Macy's and hidden with a very small sign, I found the bookstore [point "f"]. It was the smallest B. Dalton bookstore I've ever seen.

I remember commenting to myself how small the store was. As I walked in my eyes started to scan the limited shelves for books of interest. Immediately I spotted the book. It had a big cross on its cover for Christ. I approached the book with a strong and compelling spiritual sense that I had to see it. When I arrived, I found that the title read:

Christ ✝
A Crisis in the Life of God[2]

It was written by an ex-Jesuit Priest named Jack Miles and published by Alfred A. Knoft, 2001. Jack is now a journalist. Think objectivity here or the lack of it depending upon your perspective of journalists. He also wrote another book entitled "God: A Biography."

Rationalization of Mankind

I started pondering why God was supposed to have had a "crisis" in HIS life. I flipped to the very back of the book for a summary statement. That is when I almost got knocked off of my feet in sheer amazement. Less than two weeks earlier I had concluded that if you believed in the trinity doctrine, and were intellectually honest, you would have to conclude that God is talking to HIMSELF. That is the only way to justify Mark 1:11 in which God says: "You are MY beloved Son in whom I am well pleased."

Here inside of Jack Miles' book on page 244 [3] is written:

"At the start of HIS public ministry as a human being, God submitted to a rite of repentance in the waters of the Jordan and, speaking from Heaven, with HIS Holy Spirit hovering visibly over HIS human brow, HE declared HIMSELF well pleased with what HE had done and who HE had become. HE had become a lamb, and HE was pleased, as HE had not been since the last day of creation."

"Repentance in the Greek of the Gospels is *metanoia*, a changing of the mind. The changing of the mind of God is the great subject, the epic argument, of the Christian Bible."

Get the picture? Jack Miles writes that God is talking to HIMSELF and repenting while getting baptized via immersion by John the Baptist. If this author thinks God talks to HIMSELF during baptism, I must conclude that he also believes it happened during the transfiguration.

After some further explanation, Miles writes: "So HE [God] broke HIS promise." Miles reasons that God failed to save the entire nation of Israel at the time HE had promised. Therefore, the only thing God could do would be to repent on the cross for HIS [God's] sin.

What is right with this book is that is provides an honest intellectual rationalization of the trinity doctrine. What is wrong with this book is that it ignores and contorts the simple and plain language of the Bible from God to accomplish its objective.

Rationalization of Mankind

You already learned from Scripture that:

1. God does not change
2. God does not repent

Therefore, the author's arguments are without merit or foundation when it comes to God's Word in these two regards. Then, there are the crystal clear words of Jesus concerning his FATHER and God. Remember, Jesus telling us that his God is <u>also</u> our FATHER and God? Remember Jesus telling us that we are his brother or sister if we too will do God's will? Well then, what gives with this book?

What gives is the need within established Christianity to supply a plausible intellectual rationalization that fully supports the trinity doctrine since Scripture itself does not support such a doctrine.

The Trinity Doctrine Needs Rationalization!

If you really want to understand Christianity and its rationalization and arguments for the trinity and other doctrines, this is the book to read. Miles cites plenty of Scripture and does his best to present a reasonable rationalization of the trinity. However, Miles has God doing the following:

1. Changing
2. Repenting
3. Needing a way to fail [p222] [4]
4. Talking to HIMSELF
5. Committing Suicide
6. Breaking Promises
7. 100% Man and 100% God

"That the Son and the FATHER are *identical* gives Jesus' prayers a peculiarly contemporary cast inasmuch as HE is praying to HIMSELF ..." [p225] [5]

Rationalization of Mankind

Jesus Prays To God, Not Himself!

Again, the choices for any serious Bible student are the following:

1. Is Jesus a stupid and bungling idiot?
2. Are the words of Jesus, given by God, meant to be understood?
3. Are Jesus' words stupid, nonsensical, unintelligent and cryptic?

There are many works such as Martin Scorsese's movie and Jack Miles' book that seek to understand and rationalize the trinity [and other false doctrines]. You've seen in the Word that understanding is a gift from God. You've learned that the plain and clear language of the Bible can stand on its own. And you don't need a Ph D to understand that these two works are humanistic and filled with apostasy. Anytime someone writes or speaks in anyway that contradicts God's written word, it is apostasy. No exceptions. Not even in this book. To do so shows a lack of understanding.

I could cite a lot of Scripture that contradicts the trinity doctrine of mankind here, but I will save it for the next chapter. This chapter is mainly to point out the nature of rationalization and why it exists.

I'll never quit being amazed at the absolute rationalization and sheer fantasy of people who write books about God. How can they ignore what God has told us in plain and simple terms? Unless it is Satanic?

No, I am sorry to have to tell Martin, Jack along with the others who would perpetuate this nonsense that: "Jesus is not God and never was." He was the first of God's creation and he is only God's Son. Jesus is not even on the same "power level" since Jesus said: "God is greater than I am."

So—who is Jesus? Why not just pick up a red lettered New Testament and read the words of Jesus in red? Skip everything not in red letters and let Jesus tell you God's story! Then, obey the words of Jesus and God will open up your mind to an understanding of all of His Word.

Rationalization of Mankind

What I suggest is that you get the answers from Jesus by skipping everything not shown in red letters. Jesus explains quite nicely who he is and who God is and he speaks in plain and clear language. I heard God telling me for months: "Ed, everything is in the words of MY Son Jesus!" And why not, Christ told us that he only spoke what God told him to say and only did what God told him to do. He was God's spokesperson on earth. Read and understand the words of Jesus and you will find yourself understanding God and HIS intent for mankind. Then, maybe you will obey the simple commandments of God Almighty.

I didn't buy Jack's book at the time. I didn't want to lug it home and reasoned that I could buy it when I got back from the trip. I was still a little disoriented from a navigational standpoint so I walked all the way back and out of the Neiman Marcus store [point "g"] and down to point "h". As I got closer to the JW Marriott hotel, I glanced across the street at the building. That is when my eyes caught another Galleria sign hidden behind some trees. This smaller Galleria sign was not visible from a direct line of sight at the front of the Marriott. My mind started to put two and two together. Was that the place where I had finally found the bookstore? Was the B. Dalton bookstore actually just across from the Marriott behind that Saks' sign?

I decided to go up to the doors and check it out. I knew by now that God had me on another spiritual quest and I needed to know. Yes, both the Sharper Image store and the B. Dalton bookstore were accessible through the doors directly across from the Marriott. I had walked a circuitous route of almost a mile to find a book that God wanted me to find. I almost quit before I found the bookstore, but God guided me until I found it. That little voice inside gave me a nudge to keep going.

Then, as a way of ensuring that I would never forget, God showed me the crazy circuitous route that I traveled to get to that book. I knew before I got on the airport shuttle that I had just walked with God once again and HE gave me an answer to the trinity doctrine. God confirmed to me that the trinity doctrine is the rationalization of mankind. It was the need for man to morph Jesus into God. A god better suited for man's continued desire to sin.

Rationalization of Mankind

How did the trinity doctrine develop? Where did it come from? I can't say for sure and it is not the purpose of this book to delve into the history and development of Christian apostasy. Instead, this book is written for Christians to enlighten them on whom Jesus is referring to when he says: "I never knew you." By now you should be getting the bigger picture of what both God and Jesus' expectations are for our behavior. That salvation is a gift from God's grace cannot be denied. Yet the recipients of that gift demonstrate an understanding that they have received it and know how precious it really is. Our receipt of God's grace is acknowledged and demonstrated by our <u>new</u> behavior. Indeed, if we are "In Christ" — we have truly become a new person with new awareness of God and new behavior.

If you want to understand aberrant Christian doctrine [apostasy] that does not line up 100% with Scripture, consider the following graphic and its implications. For over two millennial now, mankind has been digging in a mining site called Christianity. Modern theological schools now teach the doctrines that have evolved out of this old dig [mining site for God's truth].

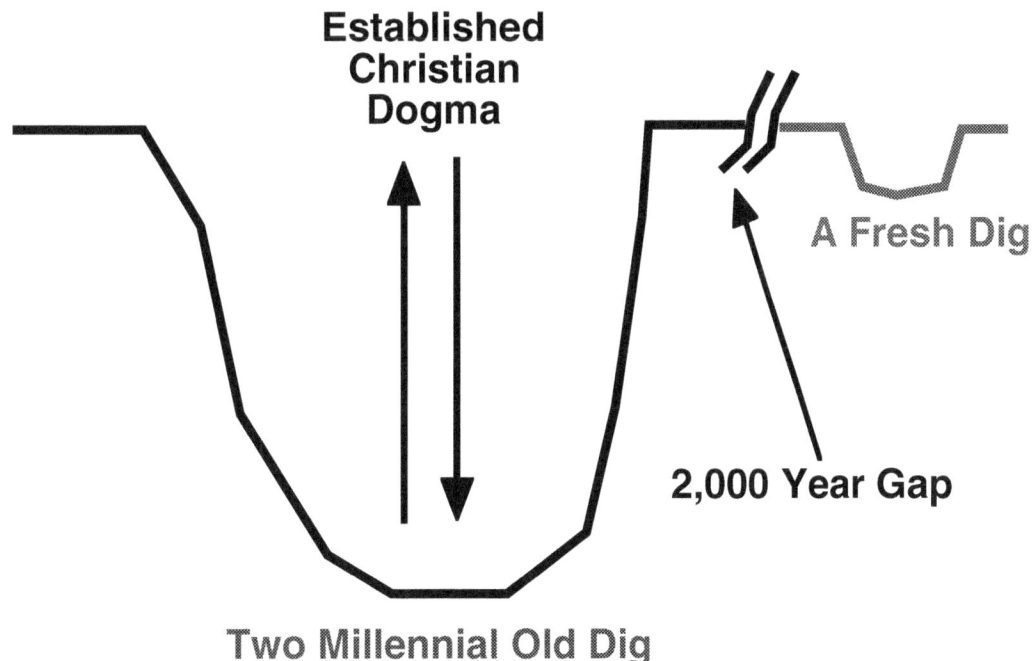

Copyright 2005 Edward G. Palmer, All Rights Reserved.

Book of Edward—Chapter 9

Rationalization of Mankind

Think back 2,000 years and consider what prospective theologians had to work with. In those days and under the best of circumstances, you would have been lucky to get your hands on a copy of some Hebrew or Greek text. Therefore, it was a rare individual that could search the word of God for spiritual truth. Next consider how that individual would have searched the word of God. Did he or she have a concordance? How about some computer software? What about some reference books like this one pointing to various Scriptures?

Two thousand years ago the Bible was searched by hand and read in a sequential way. Connecting the various Scriptures together in a cohesive manner like a <u>Chronological Bible</u>[6] or a <u>Parallel Bible</u>[7] does today would have been impossible. In fact, one would have to rely mainly upon his or her memory of where various teachings were located. That and any notes they might have written to guide their teachings. Finding printed reference works such as this to guide their studies would have been impossible.

That is the condition that existed as various doctrines emerged in the Christian Church. It is the condition that existed when the trinity doctrine emerged. A few select people postulated the trinity doctrine early in the first millennium after Christ taught for purposes I would only consider as Satanic in nature. While that may sound harsh, you will have to keep reading to fully understand the gravity of what the doctrine represents to mankind. Now fast-forward 2,000 years.

Today there is a fresh dig going on concerning Scripture. God has many small cells of people armed with incredible resources to search for His truth. As I look at my own resources on my desktop, I find I have at least twenty different Bible translations. Most of these are on computer software for ease of search and study. When I study a word like "understanding," I simply input the word into the Bible's search engine and search away. I can locate every single use of the word throughout the Bible. I can even isolate the study to one of the books in the Bible or even the three major sections of the Old Testament, Apocryphal or New Testament. I can readily compare what the Word says in any of the books or sections with the others.

Rationalization of Mankind

In addition to many Bible translations, I have <u>Today's Dictionary of The Bible</u>[8], a <u>Hebrew Dictionary</u>[9], a <u>Greek Dictionary</u>[10], software that converts Hebrew or Greek to English, Bible commentaries, two parallel Bibles, more than one concordance, Bible lists, etc. I could go on and on but you get the picture. In addition to a massive personal library, I have a high-speed DSL [digital subscriber line] to my personal computer network of four computers and four printers. From a communications perspective, I can be reached 24/7 with messages via email, facsimile or voice mail. I have multiple web sites and I use the Internet itself as a massive virtual library to find anything I want to. I haven't stumped the Internet yet. I.E. If I want to research one of the so-called lost books of the Bible such as the <u>Book of Thomas</u>[11], I can locate it with ease and obtain it immediately on a moments notice.

Now, who do you think can search the word of God for truth better? Someone who is armed with an individual Bible or someone armed with the resources listed above? It is simply no match.

Today, the average Christian totes a single Bible and only opens it to where the pastor tells him or her to read. They are like lambs led to a slaughter because the tiny glimpse of truth they do get is never followed up on with a more complete Bible study. This book cites a lot of Scripture. If you want to debate or argue with me about its contents, you had better get some resources. And I can tell you that you will find yourself arguing with the word of God very fast. That is because it is not my opinion I seek to enlighten you with. It is God's Holy Word that I seek to enlighten you with.

If you want to understand why the trinity doctrine and other apostasies are in trouble, you only need to look at the incredible resources now available to anyone who will simply acquire them. If you don't want to spend money, you can go to a library and use their Internet connection to find and search through many different Bibles free. Therefore, money should not be a concern to those who are serious about mining God's Word for truth. Just reading the ENTIRE BIBLE would surprise you. Try it!

Truth Is Opposite Of Rationalization!

Rationalization of Mankind

In the big picture, rationalization is just the opposite of truth. When someone engages in rationalization, they attempt to create their own truth. There is no limit to the degree of rationalization by mankind and you can even find rationalization in the sciences.

Science is a field that is supposed to be objective, rational and without emotion. Even so, science finds itself steeped in matters of humanism to get its own version of the truth across to the public. You need only consider the length that evolution scientists will go to support their ridiculous theories. If you believe in evolution, you believe in the scientific rationalization of many non-existent scientific facts. There is virtually no basis in science to support the theory of evolution. Not even any aspect of the theory. Scientific facts actually support the Bible in its statements of creation in Genesis. Excellent books have been written debunking the evolution myth so I will not add any more to it here. Go and study the subject. I mention it here only because it is another example of the rationalization of mankind in which mythology is now widely accepted as known fact. Repeat a myth long enough, and what?

Still, like Christian theologians that continue to support the trinity doctrine, evolution scientists continue to support a fully debunked theory. In the case of the trinity, the doctrine cannot stand up against the written word of God. In the case of evolution, the theory cannot stand up against well-established scientific facts, which include historical fossil records.

God's Word tells you how the truth can set you free. However, it is Christian mythology that "you can know the truth and the truth will set you free." This widely repeated statement in Christianity fails to acknowledge the conditional qualifications under which the truth will make you free. Consider the entire word of God on this subject and its <u>conditions</u>.

> **"Then Jesus said to those Jews who believed him, 'If you abide in my word, you are my disciples indeed. And you shall know the truth, and the truth shall make you free.'"**
> **John 8:31-32**

Rationalization of Mankind

Since Jesus spoke what God told him to say, the proper translation of this verse would be as follows. Once you believe, you start to abide in the Word. As you abide or "live in" the Word, you become Disciples of Jesus Christ. <u>At that time</u>, you will <u>know</u> the truth. Finally, then the truth shall make you free. This is a five-step process to getting set free with truth.

1. Believing in Christ [and his FATHER our God].
2. Abiding and living in Christ's word [the word of God].
3. Becoming a disciple of Christ [another servant of God].
4. Knowing the truth [not learning but "knowing" from God].
5. Getting set free by the truth.

It is important to realize that Jesus said this "to those Jews who believed HIM." Therefore, believing in God <u>and</u> HIS Son was the very first condition. A sincere heart is a companion to real belief. The above verse in John is just another way of saying Christ will open up your understanding to truth. The source of all truth lies within God's Word. To stand for the truth means that you are rational and are taking your emotions out of play.

"For if we are out of our minds, it is for God; if we are rational, it is for you." 2 Cor. 5:13 NAB

In the above verse, the Apostle Paul uses the word "rational" to make a contrast between "speaking in tongues" [without understanding to man] vs. speaking in plain language that all can understand. Speaking in tongues is a language of the spirit in which God's Holy Spirit interprets what we speak. This is the only use of the word "rational" in the entire Old and New Testaments. However, the Apocryphal book of 4 Maccabees in the NRSV[12] translation contains the following verses.

"The subject that I am about to discuss is most philosophical, that is, whether devout reason is sovereign over the emotions. So it is right for me to advise you to pay earnest attention to philosophy."

Rationalization of Mankind

"For the subject is essential to everyone who is seeking knowledge, and in addition it includes the praise of the highest virtue—I mean, of course, rational judgment. If, then, it is evident that *reason rules over* those emotions that hinder self-control, namely, *gluttony and lust*, it is also clear that it masters the emotions that hinder one from justice, such as malice, and those that stand in the way of courage, namely anger, fear, and pain. Some might perhaps ask, 'If reason rules the emotions, why is it not sovereign over forgetfulness and ignorance?' Their attempt at argument is ridiculous! For reason does not rule its own emotions, but those that are opposed to justice, courage, and self-control; and it is not for the purpose of destroying them, but so that one may not give way to them." 4 Maccabees 1:1-6 NRSV

Rational Judgment Rules Over Emotions!

"Now reason is the mind that with sound logic prefers the life of wisdom. Wisdom, next, is the knowledge of divine and human matters and the causes of these. This, in turn, is education in the law, by which we learn divine matters reverently and human affairs to our advantage. Now the kinds of wisdom are rational judgment, justice, courage, and self-control. Rational judgment is supreme over all of these, since by means of it reason rules over the emotions. The two most comprehensive types of the emotions are pleasure and pain; and each of these is by nature concerned with both body and soul." 4 Maccabees 1:15-20 NRSV

Rational Judgment Is A Part of Wisdom!

Copyright 2005 Edward G. Palmer, All Rights Reserved.

Rationalization of Mankind

> "Just as pleasure and pain are two plants growing from the body and the soul, so there are many offshoots of these plants, each of which the master cultivator, reason, weeds and prunes and ties up and waters and thoroughly irrigates, and so tames the jungle of habits and emotions. For reason is the guide of the virtues, but over the emotions it is sovereign.
>
> Observe now, first of all, that rational judgment is sovereign over the emotions by virtue of the restraining power of self-control. Self-control, then, is dominance over the desires. Some desires are mental, others are physical, and reason obviously rules over both. Otherwise, how is it that when we are attracted to forbidden foods we abstain from the pleasure to be had from them? Is it not because reason is able to rule over appetites? I for one think so. Therefore when we crave seafood and fowl and animals and all sorts of foods that are forbidden to us by the law, we abstain because of domination by reason. For the emotions of the appetites are restrained, checked by the temperate mind, and all the impulses of the body are bridled by reason."
>
> 4 Maccabees 1:28-35

Rational judgment is sovereign over the emotions of man by virtue of the restraining power of self-control. This is how our unlimited desires are checked. 4 Maccabees points out that wisdom, of which rational judgment is a part, is conditioned by the knowledge of both divine and human matters. See verse 1:16. Therefore, being rational involves keeping the emotions in check and simply examining the facts of the matter for truth. Those who seek to be rational about a matter seek truth. When it comes to the truth, however, one must be knowledgeable in the matters of the divine. One must have spiritual understanding, which is a gift from God Almighty.

You Cannot Be Rational Without Knowledge Of God!

Rationalization of Mankind

      Therefore, those who are truly rational and exhibit this aspect of wisdom are not just knowledgeable in human matters. They are also knowledgeable in spiritual matters and can demonstrate an understanding of God's written word. From where does wisdom come from? It comes from God. Becoming fully rational about any matter in life is a worthy goal. It is precisely why the philosopher Paracelsus made the statement: "Men who are devoid of spiritual perception are unable to recognize anything that cannot be seen externally." Truth and rationalization can be illustrated graphically as shown below. Note that they are inversely proportional to one another.

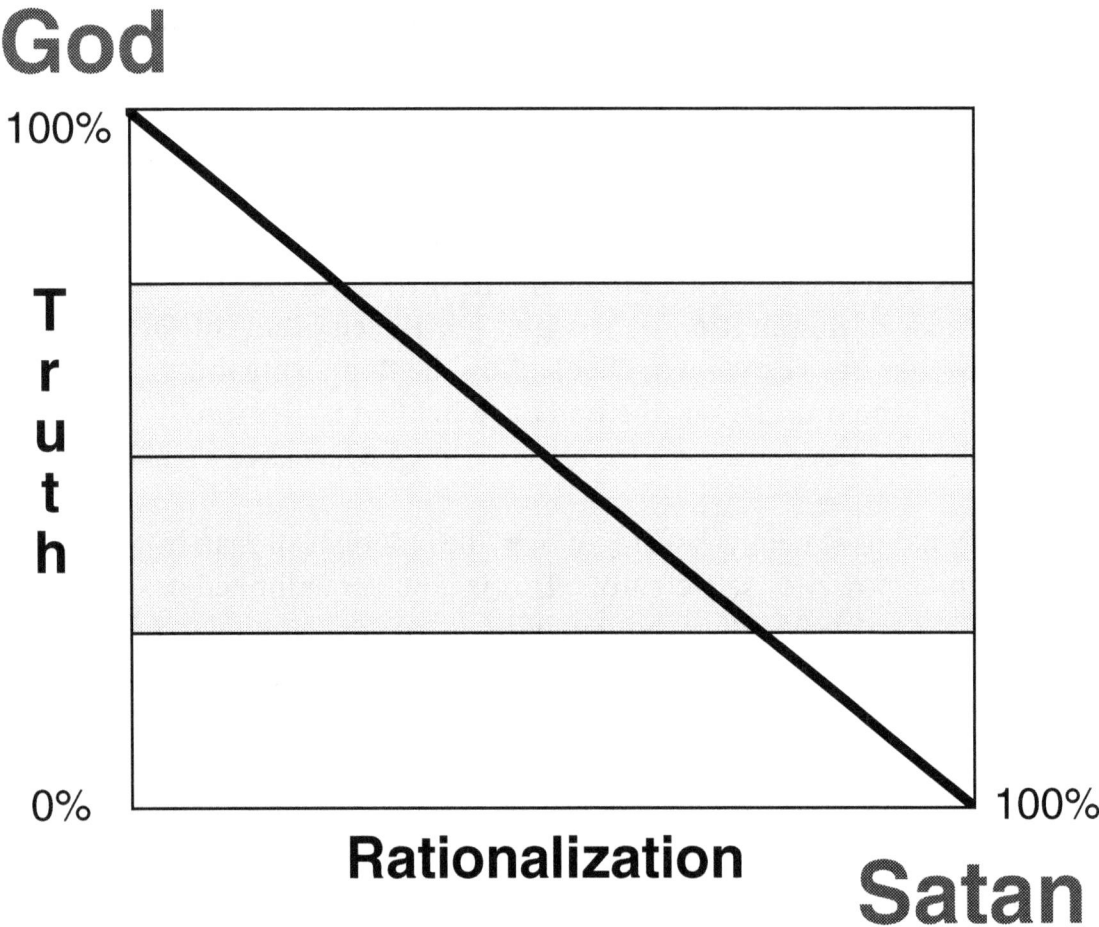

Copyright 2005 Edward G. Palmer, All Rights Reserved.

Book of Edward—Chapter 9

Rationalization of Mankind

At 100% of the truth, you are fully rational. Your reasoning then represents only reality and what is true or factual [in the eyes of God]. At 0% of the truth, you are at 100% of rationalization. Basically, you are lying 100% and trying to rationalize or morph something you believe or accept as being true into the truth. Virtually every human being alive rationalizes something into the truth at one time or another in his or her life. It is human inclination to want what we believe to be true to actually be true, especially when it comes to rationalizing our sins away. The simple act of repeating a lie over and over again has a tendency to create an air of acceptance as fact.

The following definitions are found in the Second College Edition of The American Heritage Dictionary[13].

Rational 1. Having or exercising the ability to reason. 2. Of sound mind; sane. 3. Consistent with or based on reason; logical.

Rationalize 1. To make rational. 2. To interpret from a rational standpoint. 3. To devise self-satisfying but incorrect reasons for (one's behavior).

Truth 1. Conformity to fact or actuality. 2. Fidelity to an original or standard. 3. Reality; actuality. 4. A statement proven to be or accepted as true. 5. Sincerity; integrity. 6. Truth. God.

It is a sad commentary that there are so many promoters of "gray" matter in the 21st Century when it comes to truth. Situational dynamics that render different sets of truth are simply man's rationalization to have it anyway that is satisfactory to cover the desires of sin.

Consider a common notion today that God supports the homosexual lifestyle and that practicing homosexuality is just another form of "love." This is man's rationalization using certain Scriptures to promote this sin while ignoring others that severely condemn it. It is most important in the rationalization of this and other sin that Jesus is morphed into God.

Rationalization of Mankind

By morphing Jesus into God, mankind shifts the character of God from one that is holy and requires repentance to one that no longer seems to care about much except "forgiveness." That is the essence of today's false Christian teachings. Christianity has created a more user friendly God by implying incorrectly that sin no longer matters to God "as long as you have Jesus." This is a cheap grace doctrine that literally won't hold any salvation.

The doctrine is a spiritual salvation sieve where what appears to be eternal salvation simply leaks away leaving the holder of the sieve empty handed when it comes to eternal life. Homosexuality is just another example of the preposterous rationalization of mankind that goes on today in modern Christianity. So many believe this "love doctrine" that practicing lesbians and homosexuals are now ordained as priests, bishops, etc.

Those who rationalize sin away will be among those whom Jesus says: "I never knew you." Those who teach others that sin no longer matters to God will have a special punishment awaiting them. Get to know your Bible and you will find this is a factual teaching from God's perspective. It is not rationalization on my part. I only inform you what you should know and expect from God's Word.

Besides rationalizing aberrant sexual behaviors like homosexuality and lesbianism, mankind seeks to rationalize many other sins in life. For example, it is amazing those who still rationalize that smoking won't harm their body. I know of nurses that smoke packs of cigarettes daily. That doesn't say much for their health education, does it? You should know that knowledge itself is totally useless. The old adage that knowledge is power is mythology. It is *applied knowledge* that is power. Applied knowledge is stuff that you have learned and then put into practice. That is why the Bible says, "Those who practice righteousness are righteous like Christ."

Alcohol and drugs won't hurt you? I could supply a lengthy list here of various and sundry rationalizations of mankind. Mostly all of these rationalizations involve some type of sin. It is stuff that mankind wants to be true, but isn't. At least it is not true from God's perspective.

Rationalization of Mankind

What about me? Haven't I rationalized a little in life? You'd better believe it. And in many ways. Remember I told you earlier that I recently suffered for four days in the grief of rationalization before God released me from it? I'll get to that event and explain it in a moment. For now you need to understand that when you walk with God, truth must reign supreme. As you get close to God, rationalization of any kind becomes anathema to you. It is literally something that can make you spiritually and physically sick. Why? Because you recognize it for what it is. Rationalization is SIN and it is a force opposite of TRUTH. Think again about the TRUTH PROPHECY.

> **"The coming of the lawless one will be in accordance with the work of Satan displayed in all kinds of counterfeit miracles, signs and wonders, and in every sort of evil that deceives those who are perishing. They perish because they refused to love the truth and so be saved. For this reason God sends them a powerful delusion so that they will believe the lie and so that all will be condemned who have not believed the truth but have delighted in wickedness."**
>
> **2 Thessalonians 2:9-12 NIV**

They Perish Because They Refused What?

Think about the words of Apostle Paul above. Paul told you that deception is coming. I tell you that deception has arrived. Paul teaches, "They perish because they refused to love the truth and so be saved." He goes on by saying, "That all will be condemned who have not believed the truth but have delighted in wickedness."

What or who is the truth? It is God Almighty and HIS Holy Word. That is truth! The sixth definition in the dictionary on truth recognizes God as truth. As a Christian, you should love the truth of God's Word. When you love the truth, you love God. Could Paul's words be clearer? Have you been given understanding? Do you now seek the truth at all costs? Those who love the truth will die for it. That is what Apostle Paul did.

Rationalization of Mankind

Now let's revisit the subject of homosexuality briefly and consider the words of Apostle Paul. The question before us at the moment is whether the doctrine of accepting homosexual behavior holds up to the truth? The truth is God's Word. Or, is the current acceptance of homosexual behavior "a refusal to love the truth and delighting in wickedness?" This subject will be dealt with more completely in a later chapter. However, for this discussion on rationalization, consider the following four Scriptures.

> **"[Homosexuals are] filled with all unrighteousness, sexual immorality, wickedness, covetousness, maliciousness; full of envy, murder, strife, deceit, evil-mindedness …"**
> **Romans 1:29**

> **"[Homosexuals have] exchanged the truth of God for the lie, and worshiped and served the creature [Satan] rather than the CREATOR." Romans 1:25**

> **"For this reason God gave [homosexuals] up to [their] vile passions." Romans 1:26**

> **"You shall not lie with a male as with a woman. It is an abomination." Leviticus 18:22**

The fact that God loves sinners cannot be denied. However, it is also fact that God holds sinners accountable for sins. To think or teach otherwise is simply rationalization. If you are able to reason, you have wisdom. The reason attribute of wisdom that you exhibit is because you not only know man's ways but you also know God's Word.

From this knowledge of God's Word, you reason correctly that you cannot condone homosexuality. This does not mean you cannot provide spiritual support to teach a homosexual the truth. To love the sinner and still hate the sin is fundamental to those who walk with God. Support in God's perspective means to teach the truth. You must not condone or fellowship with those who persist in a lifestyle of abomination unto God. Not if you love the truth.

Rationalization of Mankind

Today, the homosexual political lobby is very strong and their intent is simple. This is an "in your face" homosexual lobby that seeks nothing less than the full acceptance of their sinful lifestyle. They would have all of society believe that homosexuality is a valid alternative lifestyle on a par level with that of heterosexuality. They even seek marital benefits and special protections from governments and large corporations to elevate their status in society. All of their efforts are nothing but rationalization and cannot be reasoned from God's Word. While they will extract various benefits from governments and corporations, they will wind up short handed from Jesus who will tell all practicing homosexuals, "I never knew you."

Are you still with me? That's good. It means you seek the truth despite the hard teachings in the above homosexual illustration from God. It is not mankind's rationalization of homosexuality that is true. It is the word of God. To think otherwise, does not love the truth. Instead, it is engaging in and delighting in wickedness. What every Christian needs to understand fully is that God is the ONE who defines what truth is. It is not some college professor doing a scientific study on the makeup of the homosexual brain that defines truth. Now, let's reexamine the MYTHOLOGY PROPHECY.

> **"For the time will come when men will not put up with sound doctrine. Instead, to suit their own desires, they will gather around them a great number of teachers to say what their itching ears want to hear. [4] They will turn their ears away from the truth and turn aside to myths."**
> **2 Timothy 4:3-4 NIV**

Turning To Myths Is Turning Away From Truth!

Turning To Myths Is Practicing Rationalization!

Rationalization of Mankind

The Apostle Paul told you that a time is coming when people will turn away from the truth. I tell you that time has arrived. The truth of God's Word is being ignored by mainstream Christians and Charismatics alike. In virtually every church, mythology is often practiced and various doctrines are rationalized. In order to accept those rationalizations, members of the congregations have to turn their brains off. Indeed, they worship God in vain like Jesus said. True worship must involve truth, not rationalization.

Jesus said: "God is Spirit, and those who worship Him [God] must worship [God] in spirit and truth." John 4:24

Note: These are the words of Jesus Christ telling us to worship God and that we are to worship God [not Christ] in both our spirit and <u>truth</u>.

Those who are serious students of the Bible cannot find a place of real comfort in churches filled with apostasy. Therefore, if you stand firm for all of God's truth, you are most likely in some small fellowship. You are a remnant of God. Are you part of the remnant if you know the truth and yet elect to remain silent within the apostate church? We know from the book of Revelation that God has remnants within various churches. However, I wonder how silent those remnants can be about God's truth?

"Even so then, at this present time there is a remnant according to the <u>election</u> of grace." Romans 11:5

"You have a few names even in [the church of] Sardis who have not defiled their garments; and they shall walk with Me in white, for they are worthy." Rev. 3:4

I suspect that God has His people in virtually every church on earth. I cannot say exactly why they are there, why they remain. However, those who belong to God and remain in an apostate church will be witnesses before God Almighty of the apostasy and rationalization of mankind. They also have not "defiled their garments" — which I take to mean that they do not tolerate sin. Even in a sinful church, they do not partake in the sin and they do not condone it. They are agents of righteousness.

Rationalization of Mankind

As a small businessman, I have hired family and friends for various jobs in the past. If you want to find someone who rationalizes behavior away, go locate a small businessman who employs either family or friends. It took me a while to realize that when it came to family and friends, that I simply was not being fully rational. I could not reason with full wisdom because my emotions got in the way. Often my objectivity got thrown out of the window so to speak. Why?

It is because "love covers all sins." Proverbs 10:12

Your love for your family and friends can color your objectivity. This remains true until you fully harness God's wisdom and can reason over your emotions and speak the simple truth. I have a natural tendency to be rational and not involve emotions. If you listen to some people who know me, they might say I am insensitive. However, even this natural tendency does not help me to easily confront those who are close to my heart.

Then there is the matter of my son, Brian. I am much better with him today now that he is over 30. However, when he was a youth growing up and behaving badly—I could literally go brain dead. Many fathers will pull out all the stops so that their child will win. Win at all costs. Think about the ridiculous sports fiascos that take place, where fathers try to ensure "their" child will win. Why do we do this? It certainly has a little to do with our natural human inclinations.

"If a son asks for bread from any father among you, will he give him a stone?" Luke 11:11

Fatherly love does cover a lot of sin and objectivity is often lost when it comes to those who are closest to us. Mothers are certainly not immune from rationalization when it comes to children. They can be quite good at it.

What keeps our emotions in check and our reason in control is our knowledge of God's Word. Reason puts a check on our emotions. But only to the extent we possess knowledge of God's laws. With such knowledge we can reason properly and not rationalize bad behavior away.

Rationalization of Mankind

What I am really trying to say here is that we can be honest with God and honest with ourselves if we have HIS wisdom. Only then can we reason with integrity. That is what our aim should be in our spiritual lives. Our goal is to always be honest by using our reason correctly. And to not allow emotions to cloud our righteous judgment.

As they approached, Jesus said, "Here comes an honest man—a true son of Israel." John 1:47

Being honest with yourself and others means that you seek the truth of all matters and that you reject rationalization. Being honest means to seek to adhere to God's laws. It means that you do not gloss over, condone or hide sin. You don't make excuses for sin. In fact, you confront sin. If you walk with God, you seek to deal with sin in a way that true repentance is rendered. This is a real solution to bad or sinful behavior. If you hide sin, you are engaging in rationalization and Jesus may say to you, "I never knew you."

Let us go back to 4 Maccabees 2-3, for a moment to fully understand the nature of reason controlling our emotions. Starting at 4 Maccabees 2:1 in the NRSV we read.

[1] **"And why is it amazing that the desires of the mind for the enjoyment of beauty are rendered powerless?**

[2] It is for this reason, certainly, that the temperate Joseph is praised, because by mental effort he overcame sexual desire. [3] For when he was young and in his prime for intercourse, by his reason he nullified the frenzy of the passions.

[4] Not only is reason proved to rule over the frenzied urge of sexual desire, but also over every desire.

[5] Thus the law says, "You shall not covet your neighbor's wife or anything that is your neighbor's."

Book of Edward—Chapter 9

Rationalization of Mankind

[6] In fact, since the law has told us not to covet, I could prove to you all the more that reason is able to control desires.

Just so it is with the emotions that hinder one from justice. [7] Otherwise how could it be that someone who is habitually a solitary gormandizer, a glutton, or even a drunkard can learn a better way, unless reason is clearly lord of the emotions?

[8] Thus, as soon as one adopts a way of life in accordance with the law, even though a lover of money, one is forced to act contrary to natural ways and to lend without interest to the needy and to cancel the debt when the seventh year arrives. [9] If one is greedy, one is ruled by the law through reason so that one neither gleans the harvest nor gathers the last grapes from the vineyard.

> **In all other matters we can recognize that reason rules the emotions.**

[10] *For the law prevails* even over affection for *parents*, so that virtue is not abandoned for their sakes.

[11] *It is superior to love* for one's *wife*, so that one rebukes her when she breaks the law.

[12] *It takes precedence over* love for *children*, so that one punishes them for misdeeds.

[13] *It is sovereign over* the relationship of *friends*, so that one rebukes friends when they act wickedly.

[14] Do not consider it paradoxical when reason, through the law, can prevail even over enmity. The fruit trees of the enemy are not cut down, but one preserves the property of enemies from marauders and helps raise up what has fallen.

[15] It is evident that reason rules even the more violent emotions: lust for power, vainglory, boasting, arrogance, and malice.

Rationalization of Mankind

[16] For the temperate mind repels all these malicious emotions, just as it repels anger—for it is sovereign over even this.

[17] When Moses was angry with Dathan and Abiram, he did nothing against them in anger, but controlled his anger by reason. [18] For, as I have said, the temperate mind is able to get the better of the emotions, to correct some, and to render others powerless.

[19] Why else did Jacob, our most wise father, censure the households of Simeon and Levi for their irrational slaughter of the entire tribe of the Shechemites, saying, 'Cursed be their anger?' [20] For if reason could not control anger, he would not have spoken thus.

[21] Now when God fashioned human beings, he planted in them emotions and inclinations, [22] but at the same time he enthroned the mind among the senses as a sacred governor over them all. [23] To the mind he gave the law; and one who lives subject to this will rule a kingdom that is temperate, just, good, and courageous.

[24] How is it then, one might say, that if reason is master of the emotions, it does not control forgetfulness and ignorance? *4 Maccabees 3:1 now starts.* [1] But this argument is entirely ridiculous for it is evident that reason rules not over its own emotions, but over those of the body.

[2] No one of us can eradicate that kind of desire, but reason can provide a way for us not to be enslaved by desire. [3] No one of us can eradicate anger from the mind, but reason can help to deal with anger. [4] No one of us can eradicate malice, but reason can fight at our side so that we are not overcome by malice. [5] For reason does not uproot the emotions but is their antagonist.

[6] Now this can be explained more clearly by the story of King David's thirst. [7] David had been attacking the Philistines all day long, and together with the soldiers of his nation had killed many of them. [8] Then when evening fell, he came, sweating and quite exhausted, to the royal tent, around which the whole army of our ancestors had encamped.

Copyright 2005 Edward G. Palmer, All Rights Reserved.

Book of Edward—Chapter 9

Rationalization of Mankind

[9] Now all the rest were at supper, [10] but the king was extremely thirsty, and though springs were plentiful there, he could not satisfy his thirst from them. [11] But a certain irrational desire for the water in the enemy's territory tormented and inflamed him, undid and consumed him. [12] When his guards complained bitterly because of the king's craving, two staunch young soldiers, respecting the king's desire, armed themselves fully, and taking a pitcher climbed over the enemy's ramparts. [13] Eluding the sentinels at the gates, they went searching throughout the enemy camp [14] and found the spring, and from it boldly brought the king a drink. [15] But David, though he was burning with thirst, considered it an altogether fearful danger to his soul to drink what was regarded as equivalent to blood.

[16] Therefore, opposing reason to desire, he poured out the drink as an offering to God.

[17] For the temperate mind can conqer the drives of the emotions and qench the flames of frenzied desires; it can overthrow bodily agonies even when they are extreme, and by nobility of reason spurn all domination by the emotions." 4 Maccabees 2:1-3:18

The writer of 4 Maccabees gives many examples where the reason of the mind or "rational judgment" is sovereign over the emotions or the flesh. The illustration of Joseph rejecting the advances of Pharaoh's wife is particularly poignant. "In his prime for intercourse, Joseph overcame his sexual desires via mental efforts." Joseph reasoned in his mind that it was ill advised to "covet" the wife of Pharaoh no matter what her desires were. That is because God's Word says, "Thou shalt not covet." When you walk with God, you are obedient to HIS truth and you don't rationalize away your lust, you tame it. You confront your lust [or other sin] with reason, the kind of reason, truth and wisdom that comes from understanding God.

An ex-president of the United States, who totes his Bible into many churches, would do well to consider these simple teachings on reason and its relationship to wisdom. It can help control his sexual urges as God also says, "Thou shalt not commit adultery."

Rationalization of Mankind

The information on reason and wisdom from the Apocryphal Book of 4 Maccabees should be enough for you to obtain a Bible with these forgotten books. Most of the Apocryphal books are in the Catholic Bible. However, I only found 3 & 4 Maccabees in the NRSV Apocryphal. The other three translations in my Parallel Bible did not have these books. Protestant Bibles started to delete the Apocryphal books somewhere around 1300-1500 A.D.

You will find some wonderful writings in the Apocryphal books so I highly recommend them. Apocryphal is a word that refers to questionable authorship and the reason these books were excluded by Protestants is related to an inability to verify their authenticity or authorship. Having read them, I certainly feel they are of comparable writings to the rest of the Bible.

The United States Senate collectively rationalized and condoned adulterous sexual behavior at the very highest level of government in the United States. The Democratic Party in the Senate functioning in solidarity could not find the collective wisdom to admonish and remove a president that dishonored the office he was sworn to uphold. Instead, during the sexual fiasco of President William Jefferson Clinton, the leaders of the Democratic Party sought repeatedly to isolate his moral behavior from his ability to govern as president. Should we now elect immoral Presidents in the United States? Is that the kind of leadership we want? Yet isn't this the thinking in much of our society now? There has been a huge moral shift in just the last fifty years. I bear witness for God to increased immorality.

Just forty years ago, Democrats were concerned about whether John Kennedy, a Catholic, could be elected President. Now, at the beginning of a new millennium, Democrats seek to rationalize immoral and indecent behavior in the highest elected office of our land. Do you also rationalize President Clinton's behavior? Are boys just being boys like a lot of women think? You know, boys can't help themselves? What about the other immoral aspects of the Democratic Party and other political parties? Do you rationalize the killing of babies as a woman's right? What about euthanasia?

God Expects Reason Not Rationalization!

Rationalization of Mankind

For most of our U.S. history, the world could reason correctly that the United States was a moral nation. Now almost half of the U.S. voters will vote for immoral candidates and for laws that support licentiousness. Does politics matter to God? We do have moral people in this country. But make no mistake about it, we can no longer be reasoned as a moral nation by much of the world today. Much of the world has to now rationalize the idea of the United States being a moral nation. Why? It is because of the unchecked increase in immorality that exists across the U.S. We have a long way to go to get back to the point where it is universally reasoned by the rest of the world that the United States is still a moral nation.

Can The United States Remain A Moral Nation?

Before I knew God, I reasoned that abortion was okay. For me, it was the simple matter that no one should tell my wife what she could do with her own body. I wasn't into morality; I was into my family's legal rights. I just assumed she would never want to abort my children. But what if she had? How would I have felt about that? After all, it is her body isn't it? What she does with her body isn't anyone else's business, is it? I can certainly tell you that whatever you do is God's business. HE is looking and HE sees it all. Nothing is hidden from God and "the wages of sin is [eternal] death."

Was I reasoning or rationalizing about abortion? I was rationalizing because reason has to take into account God's Word on the subject. That is what wisdom is all about. Remember, you get half the picture or less if you operate only from a human perspective. You must also consider the DIVINE to get the total picture. What can be reasoned from God's Word? What does mankind rationalize?

Abortion Is Rationalization!

Excusing An Immoral President Is Rationalization!

Rationalization of Mankind

4 Maccabees is not the only good book in the Apocryphal collection. Consider the following verses from the Book of Sirach.

"If you fear the LORD, you will accept HIS correction."
Sirach 32:14

"Study HIS Law, and you will master it, unless you are insincere about it, in which case you will fail." Sirach 32:15

"If you fear the LORD, you will know what is right ..."
Sirach 32:16

"Sinners have no use for correction, and will interpret the Law to suit themselves." Sirach 32:17 GNB

Do you remember that President Clinton stated he studied the Bible and couldn't find any oral sex in it? And that is why he concluded that he wasn't really having "a sexual relationship" with the White House intern Monica Lewinsky? He was rationalizing his sexual sin, wasn't he? There is no limit to the rationalization of mankind. God knows that "sinners have no use for correction, and will interpret the Law to suit themselves." And God knows that lawyers like to parse words and twist the common meaning of the language. Clinton said in his testimony that whether or not he was lying depended on whether the word "Is" — is in the past or the present tense. Would Jesus think or talk that way? The answer is in the next chapter.

Is mankind dumb? We think we are being cute and that no one will find out about our sins because we sin in the privacy of our Oval office. But mankind has always engaged in the same sins and sexual immorality is well addressed in the Bible. Indeed, it is Jesus who said, "There are no excuses." Jesus means that there will be no rationalization [excuses] for your sin with God. Remember what God said in Isaiah 1:18 about reasoning?

"Come Let Us Reason Together," Says the LORD!

Copyright 2005 Edward G. Palmer, All Rights Reserved.

Book of Edward—Chapter 9

Rationalization of Mankind

If you are going to reason with God, you have to understand God's Word because that will be the basis of your ability to reason correctly. Ignorance cannot be pleaded as God has placed HIS Law on our hearts and in our minds. You can rationalize with man, but you cannot rationalize with God. HE knows the inner workings of your heart and your motives.

You Cannot Rationalize With God!

For four days and nights I was reasoning intensely with God about the subject of my own rationalization. At the same time I had been rationalizing in my own mind for several weeks about a subject that was gnawing at me. To put it bluntly, I found myself in a difficult position with God. On the one hand, I felt justified from a human perspective to rationalize about this subject. On the other hand, God ensured that I knew I was rationalizing.

I remember at one point I laid face down in a prostrate position on the floor and begged God to take the burden of rationalization off of my mind. I confessed to HIM that I recognized that such rationalization was not walking in the truth. You see I knew that rationalization is an opposing force to truth. You cannot be rationalizing and telling the truth at the same time. They are opposing forces and these two forces move in opposite directions.

To be rational is to simply tell the truth. With God Almighty, I was rational. In between conversations with God, I was rationalizing or as the dictionary says, "trying to make rational." I was trying "to devise self-satisfying but incorrect reasons for my behavior." Put another way, I was trying to morph my rationalized thoughts into some form of plausible truth.

Within a few hours after I prostrated myself in prayer to God, HE gave me release from the problem. HE also gave me the message to share the story with you as an illustration. That is why I had to spend four days in mental anguish over the issue. God wanted me to fully understand the logic and methods of mankind's rationalizations. HE reasoned that I could start by fully understanding my own areas of rationalization.

Rationalization of Mankind

I had already learned a lot about the issue of rationalization since I recognized that, when it comes to family and friends, I had to be especially diligent with reason. I had observed that in raising children and in the hiring of friends and family that I did not think as clearly and as objectively as I needed to think. Then there is the relationship to my wife. How objective do you think I can be with the woman I have loved for 43 years?

These *close relationships* skew our objectivity and heighten our emotions. Indeed, close relationships unduly influence our emotions because they are similar to a mother failing to discipline a child for fear of losing that child's love. Close relationships test your ability to keep your emotions in check and whether or not you can reason correctly. The lesson is: "When you exercise rational judgment, your reason will put into check your emotions. Then, your reason is sovereign over your emotions." With understanding and wisdom from God, you reason that God's Law:

1. Prevails even over the affection for parents, so that virtue is not abandoned for their sakes. 4 Mac 2:10
2. Is superior to love for one's wife, so that one rebukes her when she breaks the law. 4 Mac 2:11
3. Takes precedence over love for children, so that one punishes them for misdeeds. 4 Mac 2:12
4. Is sovereign over the relationship of friends, so that one rebukes friends when they act wickedly. 4 Mac 2:13

Reason Is Tested By Close Relationships!

This might be a good time to reexamine the priorities list on page 13. Reflect upon those priorities and on the above methods of dealing with those who are emotionally close to us. The Priorities list teaches you to put God first. The instructions in 4 Maccabees, teaches you how to keep God first.

Reason Keeps Your Priorities Straight!

Rationalization of Mankind

For years now we have been systematically taking God out of our lives. This includes taking God out of our schools, relationships and even our government. We rationalize incorrectly that God does not belong any place except in the privacy of our minds. That is why prayer has been excised from schools. That is why immorality invaded the White House office of the President. There is even a legal movement underway by an atheist to eliminate the phrase "under God" from our pledge of allegiance.

If we ever fully understood that God's law must be a part of our wisdom and that it contributes to our ability to properly reason in the exercise of our behavior, we would not have the levels of sin that exist today. When we reason properly, we fully observe the instructions shown above from 4 Maccabees and we are not afraid to exercise those instructions in any setting. That includes our job, church, family & social meetings or government offices. God has not told us to shut down our brain to make it easy on those who are around us engaging in sin or wickedness. It is man's rationalization that says, "Let's not talk politics or religion."

The issue I was trying to rationalize was that of an old advertising debt in my business. If there is any place to simply pour money down a drain, it is in advertising. All media sources promise increased business and in a sense that is the big lure of advertising. In all my life in business, I have yet to see a single advertising agent's promise fulfilled.

Advertising can be frustrating to a businessman and it is somewhat of a Catch 22. If you don't advertise, how will people know of your goods or services? The trick is to find your target audience with as little expenditure of funds as possible.

The basic facts

A) I had authorized five thousand dollars of additional radio advertising in the "hope" that business investments would come in from the ads to cover their costs. I had already prepaid ten thousand dollars of ads and the phones were ringing off the hook.

Rationalization of Mankind

B) The advertising failed to deliver the investments to offset the cost of the ads and we were caught short with the inability to pay.

C) 9/11 came along and sunk the business further into a deeper cash flow crisis forcing me to retreat even further.

D) The radio station aggressively pursued collection efforts and eventually started a lawsuit.

The simple truth of the matter is, that had I obeyed God's Law and refused to use credit, I would have never gotten into trouble with this debt. That is because I would have never had it. You see I too am still learning about our heavenly FATHER and the power of HIS Word. I have learned some painful lessons about debt. Nothing in my life has created such misery as the use of debt. And no use of debt has ever produced the promised results. A businessman can easily rationalize the use of debt. Just give us an Excel spreadsheet. Indeed, business schools teach leverage of assets through the use of debt. Suffice to say that God has different ways. A wise man once taught me, "What God decides, HE provides."

Therefore, if God wanted me to run those additional radio ads, HE would have supplied the resources to pay for them upfront. Likewise, if God wants you to go on that trip to Israel, HE will provide the resources to pay for the trip *before* you have to commit. The exercise of faith is not trusting in God to pay off your debt after you make the commitment and get back from Israel. The exercise of faith is remaining obedient to God's Word. Romans 13:8 says: "Owe no man anything except for love." — That should settle the question of whether we should borrow the money or use debt. The radio lawsuit was just another reminder of my own rationalization along with the rationale that I used at the time the ads were placed.

Going Into Debt Is Rationalization!

"And my God shall supply all your need according to HIS riches in glory by Christ Jesus." Philip. 4:19

Rationalization of Mankind

I filed a response to the lawsuit, which basically rationalized why I shouldn't have to pay. It is easy to create a laundry list of reasons when we do not want to recognize the true reality of any given situation. In part, the job of lawyers is to help both parties recognize the truth of the situation.

Part of my reasoning with God included beseeching HIM for the resources to simply settle this lawsuit. Settling would prevent further crisis for the small technology company that I am managing. God did provide a settlement to the issue. God also provided the financial resources to pay for the settlement. However, all of this took place after God showed me the depths of the rationalization that was possible from man. It was after I understood God's message that I got spiritual relief.

Why did I suffer so much anguish? I suffered because I desire to walk with God every day. In every waking hour of my life I am talking and dialoging with God. My heart desires to always be in God's presence and until you have entered into the Holy of Holies [God's presence], you cannot even imagine the joy that is located there. I knew that my rationalization was the opposite of the truth. I suffered because I knew that when I was busy with rationalizing that I could not be with God. God did not allow me to move on until I understood the issue so I could write this chapter. If you are engaged in rationalization, God confronts you with HIS commandment to "not bear false witness." Isn't that the gist of what rationalization is really all about? Yes, rationalization is about denials, lies, half-truths, colored statements and ultimately the resultant act of bearing false witness.

"When the rationalization of your mind yields to the truth of God's Holy Word, you will find yourself talking with God!" The Apostle Edward

"You Shall Not Bear False Witness!"
Is God's Confrontation To The ...
Rationalization of Mankind

Chapter Ten
The False Trinity Doctrine

"For I [Jesus] have given to them the words which You [God Almighty, my Father] have given me [to tell them]." John 17:8

"The words that I speak to you I do not speak on my [Jesus'] own authority." John 14:10

"It is the Spirit who gives life; the flesh profits nothing. The words that I speak to you are spirit, and they are life." John 6:63

"Therefore, it was necessary for Jesus to be in every respect like us, his brothers and sisters, so that he could be our merciful and faithful High Priest before God. He then could offer a sacrifice that would take away the sins of the people." Hebrews 2:17 NLT

"He [Jesus] with an oath by Him [God Almighty] who said to him [Jesus]: 'The Lord [God Almighty] has sworn and will not relent, you [Jesus] are a priest forever according to the order of Melchizedek.' " Hebrews 7:21

"He who overcomes, I will make him a pillar in the temple of my [Jesus, our High Priest] God." Rev. 3:12

"And to the angel of the church of the Laodiceans write, these things says [Jesus] the Amen, the Faithful and True Witness, the Beginning of the creation of God." Rev. 3:14

The False Trinity Doctrine

I imagine you might have just picked this book off of the bookshelf and turned directly to this chapter. After all, doesn't this chapter represent a really big issue for you and all of Christianity today, when it comes to God Almighty? Is Jesus really God in the flesh like so many teach today? If we worship Jesus, are we engaged in worshipping God Almighty or are we actually committing idolatry by worshipping a false god?

And God spoke all these words, saying:

[3] "You shall have no other gods before ME."

[4] "You shall not make for yourself a carved image, or any likeness of anything that is in Heaven above, or that is in the earth beneath, or that is in the water under the earth."

[5] "You shall not bow down to them nor serve them. For I, the LORD your God, am a jealous God, visiting the iniquity of the fathers on the children to the third and fourth generations of those who hate ME, but showing mercy to thousands, to those who love ME and keep MY commandments."

[7] "You shall not take the name of the LORD your God in vain, for the LORD will not hold him guiltless who takes HIS name in vain." Exodus 20:3-7

Maybe you listen to Charles Stanley [see p185] and other teachers today who state that you "cannot obey the Ten Commandments." Therefore, you no longer care about God's Ten Commandments. If so, stop right here as you are one of those whom Jesus is talking to when he said, "I never knew you." If you want to hold onto such a belief, nothing I can write here will change your mind.

You see the first aspects of the trinity conundrum you are confronted with are the words of God as shown above. There is only ONE GOD!

The False Trinity Doctrine

There is only ONE GOD and HE does not change, so what makes anyone think they can ignore HIS first commandment? The next question is did Jesus Christ teach us something different or did he repeat God's instructions to us? We need only look at Jesus' words to get the answer.

> **Jesus said to him, "You shall love the LORD your God with all your heart, with all your soul, and with all your mind. This is the first and great commandment. And the second is like it: You shall love your neighbor as yourself. On these two commandments hang all the Law and the Prophets."**
> **Matthew 22:37-40**

At this point, it almost seems paradoxical to me that I even have to have this discussion. Yet at least half of Christianity is now confused by a theology that alters who God Almighty is and seeks to negate God's first commandment and the confirmation of it by Jesus Christ. God wants to know, will HIS Word reign supreme in your heart or will tradition? Once again, Jesus provides some guidance for us on the subject.

> **[Jesus] answered and said to them, "Why do you also transgress the commandment of God because of your tradition?" Matthew 15:3**

Over two thousand years ago, Jewish teachers negated the word of God with their teachings. Not just any word. Their teachings negated the effect of at least one or more of God's Ten Commandments. Why? Today, Christian teachers also negate the effect of God's Ten Commandments. In fact, they have expanded on this by indicating to you, "they no longer apply to your life." Why? There is no other basis except Satan.

Do you recall that when Jesus said: "I never knew you" he also said, "Depart from me you who practice lawlessness?" [Matthew 7:23] The instructions from Jesus start at verse 21. Jesus states clearly that only those who do the will of God Almighty shall enter Heaven. Therefore, the heart of the question presented here is whether or not you will get into Heaven if you worship Jesus as God. Is worshipping Jesus the will of God?

The False Trinity Doctrine

The words of Jesus indicate that your obedience to the will of God Almighty will be the factor in whether you get into Heaven. Lawlessness is what we are before we are born again. The opposite of lawlessness is lawfulness. Being lawful and obedient to the law or Ten Commandments is the result of being born again in the spirit.

Obedience is the result of true repentance and it is the outcome of putting on the new man. It is the proof of those who are really "in Christ." The words of Jesus stand in direct contradiction to the teachings of pastors like Charles Stanley who rationalize that you can do whatever you want in life and still get into Heaven. This "eternal salvation" theology reckons once you proclaim Jesus as your savior that you can be as evil as you want to for the rest of your life. Once saved always. This type of apostasy has been discussed in prior chapters. God is not mocked. Whatever a man sows, that he shall reap. Whether or not one can mouth Jesus as Lord is immaterial to one's persistent evil behavior. Remember Hebrews 10:26? Righteousness?

Jesus says that if you practice lawlessness you do not get into Heaven. What is practicing lawlessness except willfully and continuously operating on Satan's turf? See the discussion on turfs in chapter 7. Doing evil instead of good gets you into Heaven, as long as you can proclaim Christ as savior? Such theology is preposterous given God's Holy Word. Only Bible ignorant Christians headed for Hell are able to accept such apostasy.

God Almighty said to worship only HIM as God and Jesus reaffirmed God's first commandment. The next aspect of the trinity conundrum is, exactly who did Jesus say he was? Can we seriously claim that Jesus is God Almighty when Jesus provided us with an abundance of opposite teachings?

"My FATHER ... is greater than all." John 10:29

"My FATHER is greater than I." John 14:28

Jesus said to her, "I am ascending to my FATHER and your FATHER, and to my God and your God." John 20:17

Copyright 2005 Edward G. Palmer, All Rights Reserved.

Book of Edward—Chapter 10

The False Trinity Doctrine

This chapter will present you with the simple truth that Jesus Christ is not God Almighty. Instead, Jesus is the Son of God who came to represent God to mankind and once again call for the repentance of sinners. Instead of just coming with the prior game plan of demanding repentance, Jesus came with a unique offer from God Almighty. Jesus came with the offer of the indwelling Spirit of God to those who would believe "Jesus was the SON of God." A full exploration of the gift of Jesus and what it means for mankind follows later. For now, the issue is whether Jesus is God. Is Jesus God?

If you did just flip to this chapter without reading the prior nine chapters, I must warn you. You may, like a lot of Christians, be embarking on a path that takes these writings out of the larger context that God has provided me with. I note that this is precisely the tenth chapter and that God has provided a lot of background material and Scripture prior to this point to bring you mentally and spiritually up to speed, to bring your understanding current. I will do my best to make this chapter stand on its own. However, my spirit is very aware of the many Christians who are intellectually lazy and who do not want to accept all of God's Word. That is why the Bible is taken out of context so often.

If you are looking for some fast and easy answers, there aren't any. You will need time, your Bible and your heart to get the most out of this book. You will also need to read it from the first page because that is the sequence of how God is giving it to me. Virtually every page that has been written has been without prior design. In fact, all of my prior designs for chapters have fallen away as I have consistently had to shed my thoughts in favor of HIS thoughts. In addition, God shows me only the next few pages of each succeeding chapter and I have even had to alter every chapter to fit HIS design. Therefore, it might be wise to go back and restart from the very beginning to get all of what God wants you to have.

There exists the larger contextual issue of the unchanging character of God. Often, it is God's character that is ignored in today's teachings. Within that overall character is HIS love for HIS creation. A love running so deep that God would provide additional help for the salvation of mankind.

The False Trinity Doctrine

Indeed, the Bible is not a book about Jesus Christ as many postulate. Instead, the Bible is a book about God Almighty HIMSELF. A God so loving that HE would give us a second chance with a more excellent opportunity for eternal life [success] through the shed blood of HIS only begotten Son Jesus.

Did Jesus alter the unchanging character of God? What about God's requirement of repentance as a condition of eternal life? Do you know that this requirement is in both the Old and New Testaments? Do you know that repentance before God is evidence of your spiritual rebirth? The proof of being born again? Did Jesus bring us help in the form of God's Spirit of truth to those who believe he was God's Son in the flesh? Is God's Spirit of truth or "Baptism of Fire" that Jesus gives us something different from prior salvations through repentance alone? Why?

Ask yourself this question. Did salvation exist in the Old Testament? What about deliverers? Did they exist in the Old Testament? How about people who came and spoke exactly what God told them to say. Did they exist in the Old Testament? If you believe that Jesus was the first savior sent by God to HIS people, you are wrong. If you believe that salvation did not exist prior to Jesus, you are wrong. If you believe that only Jesus spoke for God, you are wrong again. Think about these matters for a while. Study!

In Jesus' time, I believe that many people lost their faith in God Almighty and whether God actually existed. Their individual behavior demonstrated unbelief and exactly what was in their hearts, licentiousness. After all, if you *really* believe in God, you always want to be on your best behavior, don't you? Behavior is the precursor of our eternal destination and it betrays our deeply held beliefs, whether we like it or not. If it was difficult for people to believe that God existed, can you imagine the trouble they had believing that Jesus was God's Son? Do you think that God presented an easier proposition to mankind in terms of ease of belief? In the former situation, you were asked to believe in a God. Now, with Jesus, you are not only asked to believe that God exists, you are also being asked to believe that God's Word was manifested physically in the person of Jesus Christ. In a way, Jesus was "in your face" detailed instructions from God.

The False Trinity Doctrine

Yeah, sure you say, I might believe that God exists. I just don't think HE really matters that much on this earth if HE does exist. At the time that Jesus started his ministry, I believe that was the attitude of many towards our God. Not only did people lose their spiritual connection to God [spiritual power plug]—the teachers negated God's commandments in favor of their own manmade traditions. How much did those teachers believe in the reality of God if they willy-nilly would alter HIS commandments? In Jesus' time, Scripture availability was limited, so who could argue with the dictates of the spiritual leaders. Today? What's your excuse for Bible ignorance?

Enter Jesus Christ onto the scene as God's teacher, in the flesh, to reintroduce us to God. Think about this question again. If people choked at believing in a relevant God that holds them accountable for their sinful and evil behavior, how difficult would it be for them to believe that Jesus was now on site and delivering the word of God? That Jesus was the Word incarnate? That Jesus was God's truth, in the flesh and in your face?

Jesus was *not* God made incarnate [in the flesh]. He was only the Word of God in the flesh, because God gave HIS Word to Jesus so he could speak to us what God wanted him to say. Is this so difficult to understand? Did not God speak to many prophets and tell them exactly what to say? Those prophets then spoke for God, didn't they? It is the same thing here with Jesus, who also spoke for God. Jesus was God's spokesperson and messenger.

Jesus Gave Us <u>God's</u> Instructions! John 17:8

Do you sense the added difficulty in believing in the Son, that God now presented to the Jewish people? Yet Jesus taught that if we could believe in him as the Son, that we, in essence, would believe in God the FATHER. This makes common sense from the ability to believe, since belief in the more difficult [Son] renders a true belief in who sent him [God].

Belief In The Son Translates To Belief in God!

The False Trinity Doctrine

In other words, the fact that you believe in Jesus means that you must <u>also</u> believe in God. It does not mean that you believe that Jesus is God. It means that you <u>also</u> believe in "HIM who sent Jesus." It is a spiritual reality that belief in Jesus as God's Son translates into a belief in God the FATHER. If you believe in Jesus who was sent, you also believe in God who sent Jesus. It is nothing more than what you do when the pizza delivery guy arrives at your front door. Do you not also believe that the pizza shop owner exists? Do you not also believe that the pizza shop sent the delivery person? Why this is so complicated to many Christians I do not know.

Then Jesus cried out and said, "He who believes in me, believes not in me but in HIM who sent me." John 12:44

Belief In Jesus Acknowledges That God Exists!

Jesus is making it clear in the above verse that you exercise belief in God Almighty when you believe in God's Son. Have you ever heard the saying, "He looks like his father?" Have you ever read the line that we are created in God's image? Immediately after the above verse, Jesus adds:

"And he who sees me sees HIM who sent me." John 12:45

Indeed many sons look exactly like their fathers. Jesus' words in John 12:45 are not teaching people that he, Jesus, is God. Instead, Jesus is using a spiritual metaphor indicating that you needn't look any further than Jesus for what God has to say. Jesus is also providing us with the spiritual insight that those who see Jesus also see God. In other words, our spirits are connected to both Jesus and God Almighty. We are "plugged in" spiritually and we see the source of all truth. We also recognize that the Son is part of the family.

Yet many Christians think that this verse means that Jesus is God. It doesn't! If it did, then you would have to conclude that Jesus is not telling the truth in John 10:29; John 14:28; and John 20:17 as shown above. Hearing Jesus was both hearing & seeing God metaphorically speaking.

Copyright 2005 Edward G. Palmer, All Rights Reserved.

The False Trinity Doctrine

> "No one can come to me unless the FATHER who sent me draws him; and I will raise him up at the last day."
>
> "It is written in the prophets, 'and they shall all be taught by God.' Therefore everyone who has heard and learned from the FATHER comes to me." John 6:44-45

What might seem like some cryptic verses are simply telling you that if you know God already, you will recognize and know Jesus Christ as the human begotten Son of God. In many respects it is like bumping into a familiar person at any store. You don't recognize the person completely but you know he or she resembles someone you know. You walk up and ask the simple question, are you related to so and so? You look familiar.

Jesus made it clear that those who walked with God would recognize that he was there representing God and indeed was God's Son. Jesus also makes it clear that only those whom the FATHER draws spiritually can come to Jesus for salvation. Indeed, it is not Jesus who is in control; it is God Almighty the FATHER. Jesus makes it abundantly clear he exists to do the FATHER's will. The statement of the prophets that all of us shall be taught by God recognizes that God has placed his instructions on everyone's hearts and mind. This is the essence of the new covenant that Jeremiah spoke of.

It is those who are listening to God that seek Jesus out. When you listen to the instructions that God has provided, you understand spiritual matters. You also behave well knowing that God holds us accountable. God taught us through the prophet Jeremiah …

> "Behold, the days are coming, says the LORD, when I will make a new covenant with the house of Israel and with the house of Judah—not according to the covenant that I made with their fathers in the day that I took them by the hand to lead them out of the land of Egypt, MY covenant which they broke, though I was a husband to them, says the LORD."

The False Trinity Doctrine

> "But this is the covenant that I will make with the house of Israel after those days, says the LORD: I will put MY law in their minds, and write it on their hearts; and I will be their God, and they shall be MY people."
>
> "No more shall every man teach his neighbor, and every man his brother, saying, 'Know the LORD,' for they all shall know ME, from the least of them to the greatest of them, says the LORD. For I will forgive their iniquity, and their sin I will remember no more." Jeremiah 31:31-34

If you don't know God, you are not listening to HIS soft voice inside your heart and mind. You need to settle down into a quiet state. Many people simply drown out God's voice with a busy lifestyle that leaves no room for dialogue with God. Some people do this intentionally. They know that God's voice rises up inside of them. It is the wicked lifestyle they seek to enjoy that keeps them ignoring HIS instructions.

> "Be still, and know that I am God; I will be exalted among the nations, I will be exalted in the earth!" Psalm 46:10

Be Still, And Know God!

So, if you are not making progress with understanding Jesus, you should know that he is asking you to understand God first. Start listening to the still quiet voice inside of you. When you start acknowledging God, you will start recognizing Jesus. It all starts with some obedience and that is exactly what Jesus demonstrated while on this earth. He didn't call the shots. He was obedient to God the FATHER who called the shots. Think about this fact if you persist in treating Jesus as God. Jesus was obedient to God.

> "You say HE is our God, but you do not even know HIM. I know HIM. If I said otherwise, I would be as great a liar as you! But it is true—I know HIM and obey HIM."
> John 8:55 NLT

The False Trinity Doctrine

Jesus Christ Obeys God, Do You?

Apostle John quotes Jesus saying, "I know [God] and obey [God]." These words of Jesus are the next aspect of the trinity conundrum you have to deal with. Jesus indicates he is subservient to God Almighty. However, the trinity doctrine espouses a three-part co-equal godhead comprised of the Son, the FATHER and the Spirit. The essence of God Almighty being equal and identical in each part of the different parts of the godhead. Three parts all co-equals with each other in every respect.

If the trinity doctrine were true, then Jesus would be equal to the FATHER in all respects. It would also make Jesus a liar again when he tells us that he is obedient to the FATHER. And what about stuff that Jesus does not know? Remember that Jesus states in Matthew 24:36 that, "only my FATHER knows?" Three parts, co-equal, each knowing what the other knows does not describe the Jesus of the Holy Bible since Jesus did not know what the FATHER knew.

People use water to explain this three-part godhead. Is God analogous to water in a solid (ice), liquid (water), and vaporous (steam) state (3 in 1)? Graphics have also been used by Christians, over the last two millennial, to symbolize and explain the trinity. I.E. — The trinity symbol below is used on the letterhead of the Trinity Episcopal Church in West Virginia.[1]

Copyright 2005 Edward G. Palmer, All Rights Reserved.

The False Trinity Doctrine

The website article from the "Trinity Times Electronic Edition 01/18/99" [2] shows the above symbol with the following remarks. "The symbol is known as a triquetra and circle, and it has for many years represented the Christian doctrine of the holy trinity. This doctrine, argued powerfully by the early Christian theologian Tertulian, and others, says, in simple but formal language: The FATHER is not the Son or the Holy Spirit; the Son is not the FATHER or the Holy Spirit; the Holy Spirit is not the FATHER or the Son; the FATHER is God; the Son is God; the Holy Spirit is God. Three persons (or natures) of the one true God — God who has been from time and forever."

"Formed by three conjoined 'fish tracings' (Christianity's first symbol) or by interlocking three of the cabbalistic symbols for purity and innocence (a leaf-like pair of arches) or by arcs of a circle meeting the edge of an equilateral triangle, it represents the interwoven balance, strength, symmetry, and beauty of the holy trinity. When the triquetra is set within a circle there is added to the power of the symbol the circle's representation as something without beginning or end — infinity. Additionally, the three-part triquetra (which is Latin for 'three-sided') are contained as one — 'three in one' from the doctrine of the trinity. The tips protruding from the circle that we may experience or 'know' each part of the trinity distinctly."

Part of the dialogue in the above newsletter is a defense of this trinity symbol. Today, gangs of thugs and evildoers widely use this and other Christian symbols for their own evil logos, jewelry, etc. This appropriation causes some to think the trinity symbol represents the sign of Satan (666). Consider the trinity symbol used on the New King James Bible.

The False Trinity Doctrine

The authors of the New King James Bible state that this symbol is also a historical trinity symbol similar to the previous one. However, a Christian movement with at least 100,000 or more adherents declares the NKJV is the ultimate apostasy since it purports to be a simple update of the revered King James Bible. In fact, they state that the only English version not filled with error is the King James Version (KJV). This subject was discussed in detail earlier and shown to be without merit. For now, consider that the debate[3] also focuses on the NKJV trinity symbol as a sign of Satan.

Three interlocked fishes instead of three interlocked 6's? It does not take much imagination to see three interlocked fishes. However, you have to use a little more imagination to see the 6's. Who draws a six this way? This is how people visualize interlocking fishes and interlocking 6's.

Interlocking Fishes?

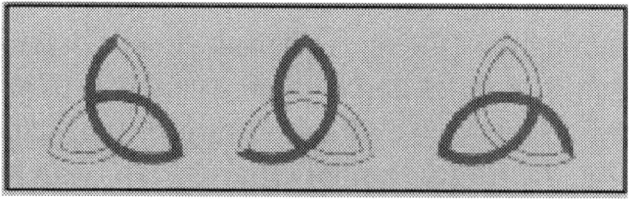

Interlocking 6's?

Are the above trinity symbols interlocked fishes representing a trinity doctrine that was adopted in the early years of the Christian church? Or, are they signs of Satan carried and used by those taken in by Satan's deception? I have no concern about the symbol used on the NKJV Bible. I believe that the symbol is just interlocking fishes and another manmade visualization of a doctrine adopted in the early years of the church. Does this mean that the trinity symbol is completely innocent? I'm not so sure.

Copyright 2005 Edward G. Palmer, All Rights Reserved.

The False Trinity Doctrine

Now let's examine the trinity writings of Pastor John Hagee in his *Prophecy Study Bible* [4], *NKJV Thomas Nelson Publishers, 1997.* This is the Holy Bible that I use regularly. I would highly recommend it as a base study Bible with the single caveat to beware of any teaching on Christian tradition such as the trinity doctrine. John Hagee [5] is a preacher of righteousness and he provides some great study aids and timelines in his *Prophecy Study Bible*.

The NKJV is the Bible that I compare all Scripture with in order to see the subtle variations on wording and whether doctrine agrees or disagrees. I have stated I believe all Bibles are basically in 99% agreement. However, Bibles often include commentary on Christian doctrines and the *Prophecy Study Bible* is no exception. Therefore, Hagee provides another explanation of the trinity and offers some "proof" scriptures for illustration. Here then is Hagee's orthodox trinity perspective and explanation from page 1429 of his *Prophecy Study Bible*. [6]

"No one should be surprised that when we try to describe God we run into problems with the inadequacy of both our concepts and our words. Take the idea of the trinity. 'Trinity' is not a word found in the Bible. Christians created it in response to the biblical information about the nature and relationships of the FATHER, Son, and Holy Spirit."

"The doctrine of the trinity asserts that there is one God who exists in three persons; one divine essence which expresses itself always in three coequal, coeternal subsistences: the FATHER, the Son, and the Holy Spirit. There you are—hard words and difficult concepts."

"Islam and Judaism have historically charged Christians with tritheism, the worship of three distinct gods. Some from within the Christian ranks have felt compelled to stress the unity of God to the point that only the FATHER is conceived of as fully divine. The Son is regarded as the highest creature, and the Holy Spirit usually as an impersonal force. Others have stressed the unity of God and explained the FATHER, Son, and Holy Spirit as ways the one God expresses HIMSELF at different times. All of these positions are heretical to orthodox trinitarian Christianity."

Copyright 2005 Edward G. Palmer, All Rights Reserved.

The False Trinity Doctrine

"Various metaphors have been used through the years as ways of imagining the idea of three-in-one. St. Patrick supposedly used the shamrock to explain the trinity to the first Irish Christians. Ice, water, and steam are three states of the same compound. The three sides of a triangle comprise one geometric figure. A person consists of body, soul and spirit. Yet, any one of these or the many other illustrations does nothing more than hint at the idea."

"The biblical evidence that compels Christians to adopt the trinitarian position consists of passages that treat each person of the trinity as equally divine and passages that persistently group the FATHER, Son, and Spirit together. It's easy to agree that the FATHER is God (Rom. 1:7; Gal. 1:3). The evidence for the full deity of Jesus also permeates the New Testament (John 1:1, 18; Heb 1:3, 8; Rev. 22:13). The New Testament says less about the Holy Spirit than about the FATHER and Son. However, in the Ananias and Sapphira incident, lying to the Holy Spirit (Acts 5:3) is called lying to God (v. 4).

In the following passages, the members of the trinity are grouped together by various New Testament writers as a special expression of God's character or work: Matthew 3:16, 17; 28:19; John 14:15-23; 15:26; 16:13-15; Acts 2:32, 33; 1 Corinthians 12:4-6; 2 Corinthians 13:14; Galatians 4:4-6; Ephesians 1:2-14; 2:18; 4:4-6; Philippians 3:3; Hebrews 10:10-15; 1 Peter 1:2; 1 John 5:1-12." Hagee references twenty-five *trinity*-supporting verses.

I believe John Hagee presents the best thoughts on the trinity doctrine from an orthodox trinitarian Christian perspective. He seeks to back up the doctrine with twenty-five cited scriptures. *So, let's examine every single Scripture citation to see if support for the trinity doctrine really exists.* Get your Bible out now and turn to Romans 1:7, which is Hagee's first citation.

> **"To all who are in Rome, beloved of God, called to be saints: Grace to you and peace from God our FATHER and the Lord Jesus Christ." Romans 1:7**

Copyright 2005 Edward G. Palmer, All Rights Reserved.

The False Trinity Doctrine

John Hagee's comments confirm, "Christians created it [the trinity doctrine] in response to the biblical information about the nature and relationships of the FATHER, Son, and Holy Spirit."

Christians Created The Trinity Doctrine!

It is true; you won't find the word "trinity" in Scripture. Mankind in response to what man believed the Bible said created the word trinity and its doctrine. I should point out that the early church, without the resources that exist in the 21st Century, created it. What you need to ascertain here is whether such a doctrine formulated on limited resources and perpetuated as truth into the 21st Century, is still valid. Is the trinity doctrine still valid today based on the resources we have available to compare, search and understand the word of God? Or, is the trinity a myth now accepted as fact?

Does Scripture Support The Trinity?

It is clear that John Hagee thinks that Scripture points to the trinity. Yet, if you were going to edit any Christian Bible and posit any commentary within it, would you dare <u>not</u> support the trinity doctrine? Hagee's prior comments indicate that anything other than supporting the trinity doctrine is <u>heretical</u> within the orthodox Christian community. In other words, it would be almost impossible for someone to be established in orthodox trinitarian Christianity and then posit any teaching except orthodox Christian dogma. In a way, it is like medical doctors who risk being discredited and losing their livelihood if they stray from well established and commonly accepted medical practices fully supported by the American Medical Association.

Enter The Apostle!

Now enters the apostle who doesn't care about the establishment and the tradition of the church. Instead, the apostle cares about God's truth and about HIS Holy Word …

The False Trinity Doctrine

    Can you understand why God would send someone from the outside to remind those on the inside [the Church] of what they are expected to believe? Isn't this who Jesus was? An outsider sent by God Almighty to remind mankind of the truth and of God's commandments, because they freely transgressed them? And what about today? Is there obedience?

    I respect John Hagee and his ministry and I firmly believe that you won't find any better explanation and better supporting scriptures than what John offers. Knowing, as John Hagee knows, that his Bible commentary would come under very heavy scrutiny by orthodox Christianity, I believe some incredible energy went into his trinity commentary. I believe the Scripture John provides represents the best support that is available for the doctrine. Got your Bible opened up to Romans 1:7 yet? Now is the time to examine the Scripture citations of John Hagee.

    It is clear in Romans 1:7 that the FATHER is God and that Jesus is a separate entity. "Peace from <u>God our FATHER</u> and the <u>Lord Jesus Christ</u>." Note that if Jesus was really God Almighty that Paul could have written a more simple form of the sentence. He could have written, "Peace from God our FATHER who is also our Lord Jesus Christ." He could have rephrased the sentence, but didn't. As we track the Scripture citations of John Hagee, we will give them a simple check mark for either clearly and directly supporting a trinity doctrine or clearly and directly not supporting a trinity doctrine.

Rating Hagee's 25 Trinity Citations

#	Verse	Comment	Speaks Directly to Trinity Doctrine?	
			Yes	No
1	Romans 1:7	FATHER is God		✔

Most Of Scripture <u>Will</u> Speak For Itself!

Copyright 2005 Edward G. Palmer, All Rights Reserved.

Book of Edward—Chapter 10

The False Trinity Doctrine

If the Word is not plain, clear and speaking directly to any doctrine, the Word does not support that doctrine. Instead, the doctrine then requires a leap of faith. Does Scripture connect the dots for you or do you need either orthodox Christian dogma or man's opinion to accept the teaching? Review chapter 6, pages 117-118, for a detailed discussion of this Scripture issue.

Again, most of Scripture simply speaks for itself. Where I have given you a spiritual interpretation, that interpretation does not change or alter the basic meaning of Scripture. In other words, you don't have to take my word for the scriptures that I seek to clarify for you. You only need to think about whether the explanation I provide you with holds some common sense.

Many of the scriptures that Christians use to justify the trinity doctrine not only require a leap of faith to accept, they also blatantly ignore other Scripture on the subject that is clear and not controversial. Besides ignoring other Scripture, simple common sense explanations of how we operate in our human environment are also ignored.

I do not say to you to ignore all other interpretations and only accept mine. You should ignore all interpretations that do not coincide with the simple and clear language of the Bible and your own common sense. The only thing you need to use is the clear and plain language of the Bible and your common sense human understanding of the subject. These two items and a heart for God get you all the understanding you need of Scripture.

Hagee's next Scripture citation is Galatians 1:3. Hagee acknowledges this and the prior one as supporting the FATHER as God. However, he doesn't comment on the distinct separation of the FATHER and the Son within this simple verse. Are there not two distinct entities identified by Paul?

"Grace to you and peace from God the FATHER and our Lord Jesus Christ." Galatians 1:3

Hagee ref #2.   *Is it direct support for trinity doctrine? No!*

The False Trinity Doctrine

Now let's move through the rest of the Scripture citations that could support the trinity doctrine. Compare your own Bible to the verses shown below and see if you agree with my assessment of whether the verse provides any clear and direct support for the trinity doctrine. Where there are simple and clear verses opposing the one cited by Hagee, I will provide them along with commentary, if needed, directly below Hagee's citation.

"In the beginning was the Word, and the Word was with God, and the Word was God." John 1:1

Hagee ref #3.   Is it direct support for trinity doctrine? No!

Commentary: John 1:1 is an oft referred to verse in support of a trinity. However, there is no direct support for the trinity doctrine in this verse. There is only implied support, but you need man's opinion to accept such a doctrine. You cannot read the Word and clearly see such a doctrine. We know that the Word of God incarnate was Jesus Christ. However, there is nothing here that indicates Jesus did not just get a "download" from God of HIS Word. Whose word is it anyway? It is God Almighty's Word. That HE gave the Word to Christ to speak cannot be denied.

Running directly opposite to this verse are the words of Jesus Christ in Revelations 3:14 stating clearly "[I Jesus am] the Beginning of the creation of God!" The NCV translation reads, "[I Jesus am] the Beginning of all that God has made." These very words of Jesus are clear and in opposition to the implied trinity of John 1:1. Which do you accept as truth? Jesus words? In one case, you will need a leap of faith because the Scripture itself does not support the doctrine. In the second case, you need only accept what Jesus has said. Note that Jesus did not state he was present at the beginning of creation. Jesus said, "He _was_ the beginning of creation." Note also that Jesus said it was God's creation, not his own.

Note: At the end of Hagee's trinity citations I will provide a summary table of all the verses cited and their direct support or lack of direct support for the trinity doctrine. Hagee's next Scripture citation is …

Copyright 2005 Edward G. Palmer, All Rights Reserved.

Book of Edward—Chapter 10

The False Trinity Doctrine

> "No one has seen God at any time. The only begotten Son, who is in the bosom of the FATHER, he has declared HIM."
>
> **John 1:18**

Hagee ref #4.   Is it direct support for trinity doctrine? No!

> [3] "Who being the brightness of HIS glory and the express image of HIS person, and upholding all things by the word of HIS power, when he had by himself purged our sins, sat down at the right hand of the Majesty on high, [4] having become so much better than the angels, as he has by inheritance obtained a more excellent name than they. [5] For to which of the angels did HE ever say: 'You are MY Son, today I have begotten you?' And again: 'I will be to him a FATHER, and he shall be to ME a Son?' [6] But when HE again brings the firstborn into the world, HE says: 'Let all the angels of God worship him.' [7] And of the angels HE says: 'Who makes HIS angels spirits and HIS ministers a flame of fire.' [8] But ~~to~~ [of] the Son, he [Jesus] says: 'YOUR throne, O God, is forever and ever; a scepter of righteousness is the scepter of YOUR kingdom.' " **Heb. 1:3-8**

Hagee ref #5   Is it direct support for trinity doctrine? No!

<u>Commentary</u>: Hebrews 1:3-8 is set up by verses 1-2. In verse 1, it teaches that God "at various times and in different ways spoke in <u>time past</u> to the fathers by the prophets." In verse 2, [God] "has <u>in these last days</u> spoken to us by HIS Son [Jesus], whom HE [God] appointed heir of all things, <u>through whom</u> also HE [God] made the worlds." Translation: God first created Jesus and then used Jesus to help create the worlds. Note the words "But when HE again brings the firstborn [Jesus] into the world, HE says: 'Let all the angels of God worship him [Jesus].' " In verse 4 we see how Jesus, "having become so much better than the angels," was elevated in status by God. We also see that, "[Jesus] has by inheritance obtained a more excellent name than they [the angels]." The comparison to his prior brethren [angels] cannot just be ignored for the sake of a trinity doctrine.

The False Trinity Doctrine

Far from supporting a trinity doctrine, Hebrews 1:1-8 actually reinforces the statement of Jesus in Revelation 3:14 about being the "first of God's creation." Jesus as the "firstborn angel" was *again* brought into the world as the "firstborn of mankind's spiritual rebirth." The first time Jesus came to this world was as an angel to help God finish HIS creation for we know that all things "were created *through* Jesus." The second time Jesus came to this world was as the Son, in the flesh, to help God reconcile mankind's sinful nature. What will you believe the next time Jesus comes?

Jesus was originally an archangel of God and the *very first* of God's creation. When he became a man in the flesh, Jesus literally became God's only begotten human Son [in the flesh and 100% just like you and I are]. Do you bleed? Jesus bled. Can you die physically? Jesus died physically. Can you become one with God? Yes. So did Jesus.

"There were giants on the earth in those days, and also afterward, when the sons of God came in to the daughters of men and they bore children to them. Those were the mighty men who were of old, men of renown." [Genesis 6:4] This time with Jesus, it was God Almighty doing a work "with a daughter of man" to resolve the sin of mankind. God's Spirit came to Mary and impregnated her egg with the DNA of Jesus. Is this a difficult task for the God of the universe, to impregnate a virgin without the benefit of sexual intercourse? Does the creator of our cellular structures have any trouble modifying cells? No! Yes, it was a virgin that gave birth.

Note also that in Hebrews 1:3, it is clear that Jesus sits at the right hand of the throne of God. Jesus does <u>not</u> sit on the throne because he is not God. Clearly Jesus is the Son and God Almighty is the FATHER. In Hebrews 1:8, the word "to" should be "of" according to the NRSV, REB, and NAB translations. Therefore, Jesus Christ is telling God Almighty "YOUR throne, O God, is forever and ever ..."

Some may think that Hebrews 1:8 is God telling Jesus that he [Jesus] is now God, but that requires that you drop your brain off at the front door. You must interpret Scripture in a way that is consistent with the context of the immediate verses both before and after the verse in question.

The False Trinity Doctrine

You must also interpret Scripture in the context of other Scripture and within the greater context of God Almighty and HIS relationship to Jesus as HIS Son. Since it is clear that Jesus is speaking for God [v2] and sits at the right hand of God [v3], it must also be correct that the word "to" should really be "of" in verse 8 of the NKJV and other translations. The verse is then correctly read "But of the Son, he [Jesus] says [to God Almighty], 'YOUR throne, O God, is forever and ever; A scepter of righteousness is the scepter of YOUR kingdom?" Note that "righteousness" is the scepter of the kingdom of God. What about your own righteousness, do you have some?

The author of Hebrews is unknown and chapter 1 verse 9 complicates the discussion because it is esoteric in nature. Verse 9 [not shown] is out of context with the prior 8 verses and appears to be a repeat of Psalms 45:7. Back to verse 8. If this was interpreted to read, "But to the Son, HE [God] says: 'YOUR throne, O God, is forever and ever' "— then, you are "making" Jesus God. You also have a direct contradiction with Revelation statements and the *seating* arrangements at the throne. Consider Rev. 5:4-9 ...

"So I wept much, because no one was found worthy to open and read the scroll, or to look at it. [5] But one of the elders said to me, 'Do not weep. Behold, the Lion of the tribe of Judah, the Root of David, has prevailed to open the scroll and to loose its seven seals.' [6] And I looked, and behold, in the midst of the throne and of the four living creatures, and in the midst of the elders, stood a Lamb as though it had been slain, having seven horns and seven eyes, which are the *seven* Spirits of God sent out into all the earth. [7] Then he [Jesus] came and took the scroll out of the right hand of HIM [God] who sat on the throne. [8] Now when he [Jesus] had taken the scroll [from God], the four living creatures and the twenty-four elders fell down before the Lamb [Jesus], each having a harp, and golden bowls full of incense, which are the prayers of the saints. [9] And they sang a new song, saying:

> You are worthy to take the scroll,
> And to open its seals;
> For you were slain,
> And have redeemed us to God by your blood
> Out of every tribe and tongue and people and nation."

Copyright 2005 Edward G. Palmer, All Rights Reserved.

The False Trinity Doctrine

Therefore, there is a distinct line of separation between God and H<small>IS</small> Son Jesus. God sits on the throne. Literally speaking, Jesus sits at God's right hand in another chair, at your left as you face the throne of God. Jesus sits in a place of honor with God and "in the midst" of the throne. Being at this location means Jesus is a central part of the area surrounding the throne of God. Jesus [the Lamb] is the only one who is able to take the scroll from God, open it up, read it and loose the seals [v5]. It is Jesus walking up to God Almighty to take the scroll from God's right hand [v7]. Hebrews 1:8-9, are reason enough to have more than one Bible translation for your studies.

When any verse in your Bible sounds weird, go get one or more additional translations and seek clarity. Better yet, get a parallel Bible so you can see four translations simultaneously side by side with each other.

You <u>will</u> run across some odd Bible verses. However, when your heart is with God, H<small>E</small> will give you understanding. As I studied this section of Hebrews, the understanding that I got was to go with the word "of" in verse 8 and to simply ignore verse 9. If it sounds odd that I would do that, think about these apparent lost books of the Bible for a moment.

Lost Book Referenced in Bible	Scripture Reference
Book of Jasher	Joshua 10:13
Book of Nathan	1 Chronicles 29:29
Book of Gad	1 Chronicles 29:29
Book of Shemaiah	1 Chronicles 12:15
Book of Jehu	2 Chronicles 20:34

1 Kings 12:22 reads, "But the word of God came to Shemaiah the man of God" and 1 Chronicles 12:15 refers to the Book of Shemaiah. Where are these missing books? Wouldn't you like to know what is inside of them? After all, God gave Shemaiah H<small>IS</small> word and he was "the man of God!" Etc.

Don't get confused. I am trying to point out to you that you cannot take God's Word out of its immediate contextual setting, the context of other Scripture, the context of the character of God Almighty and the context of the relationship between God Almighty and H<small>IS</small> Son Jesus.

Copyright 2005 Edward G. Palmer, All Rights Reserved.

Book of Edward—Chapter 10

The False Trinity Doctrine

You need to dig deeper if something doesn't make sense to you. You do this by gathering more resources to study the Word. I am also trying to point out to you that Bible study can get very sophisticated and you should not try to make the Bible into a 100% literal and 100% error free book. To do so will only mess up your mind. That is because, on occasion, you will run across Scripture oddities like Hebrews 1:8-9 and those "missing books." When you've given God your heart, HE will give you understanding.

The immediate context of any Scripture text is the preceding 10 verses and the following 10 verses. Those verses provide the immediate contextual setting. You would be amazed at the apostasy you will uncover in teachings if you simply read back and forward ten more verses from that being taught. Then compare what you have read to the nature of what is being taught. Context also involves other Scripture. For example, the tithe doctrine is always taken out of context in regards to Deut. 14:22-29. Check out those verses at your next tithe sermon. Understanding the character of God and the relationship of God and HIS Son Jesus provides the largest context, which is very much abused in sermons today.

More than one Bible translation provides greater study resources. In more than 25 years of study, additional translations have not failed to clear up and eliminate misunderstandings. Remember also, that an estimated 98% of the Bible is exoteric in nature and not controversial or esoteric like the above two verses in Hebrews 1:8-9.

Before I leave this commentary, I want to point out Revelation 5:6. Take a closer look at the words "which are the *seven* Spirits of God sent out into all the earth." As you think about the rationalization of Jesus and the Holy Spirit as God, you may want to start considering that there are actually *seven* Spirits of God. The trinity doctrine only counts one of them. Isn't this odd? Why were the other six Spirits ignored in the trinity doctrine? Most likely, they were ignored because of a lack of study resources to fully understand the word of God. A further discussion follows. For now, let's move on to the next Hagee citation.

The False Trinity Doctrine

> **"I am the Alpha and the Omega, the Beginning and the End, the First and the Last." Rev. 22:13**

Hagee ref #6.   Is it direct support for trinity doctrine? No!

Commentary: The "Alpha and the Omega" will also be covered further and in depth later on in this chapter. However, for now, this verse does not provide any direct support for the trinity doctrine. In fact, the verse speaks only of a single entity or person, not three.

> **But Peter said, "Ananias, why has Satan filled your heart to lie to the Holy Spirit and keep back part of the price of the land for yourself? While it remained, was it not your own? And after it was sold, was it not in your own control? Why have you conceived this thing in your heart? You have not lied to men but to God." Acts 5:3-4**

Hagee ref #7.   Is it direct support for trinity doctrine? No!

Commentary: Lying to the Holy Spirit is lying to God because it is God's Holy Spirit that we are talking about. Jesus said in John 15:26, "But when the Helper comes, whom I shall send to you from the FATHER, the Spirit of truth who proceeds from the FATHER, he will testify of me." Therefore, the Spirit of truth [Holy Spirit] proceeds forth "from the FATHER." Indeed, the Spirit of truth is one of *seven* Spirits that *belong* to God Almighty.

> **"When he had been baptized, Jesus came up immediately from the water; and behold, the heavens were opened to him, and he saw the Spirit of God descending like a dove and alighting upon him." Matthew 3:16**

Hagee ref #8.   Is it direct support for trinity doctrine? No!

Commentary: It was the "Spirit of God" that descended upon Jesus. In other words, the Spirit belonged to God. This is one of several verses that

The False Trinity Doctrine

use the words Jesus, Spirit and God within the same sentence. That seems to be the only basis of the trinity doctrine. However, the fact that Jesus, God and God's Spirit is mentioned within the same verse does not prove that God is composed of three equal and separate entities. Once again the verse does not directly support the trinity doctrine. In fact, it doesn't even imply a trinity in and of itself.

> **"And suddenly a voice came from Heaven, saying, "This is MY beloved Son, in whom I am well pleased." Matthew 3:17**

> *Hagee ref #9.   Is it direct support for trinity doctrine? No!*

Commentary: Many verses used to support the trinity do not even have three elements to them. They are like this verse that point to the duality of the FATHER and the Son.

> **"Go therefore and make disciples of all the nations, baptizing them in the name of the FATHER and of the Son and of the Holy Spirit." Matthew 28:19**

> *Hagee ref #10.   Is it direct support for trinity doctrine? No!*

Commentary: The baptismal formula in Matthew contains the FATHER, Son and Holy Spirit. However, as previously noted from the words of Jesus, *it is* God's Holy Spirit. The verse should be read and understood to mean we should baptize to honor God, HIS begotten Son Jesus, and HIS Holy Spirit, which is the Spirit of truth.

> **"If you love me, keep my commandments. [16] And I will pray the FATHER, and HE will give you another Helper, that HE may abide with you forever—the Spirit of truth, whom the world cannot receive, because it neither sees HIM nor knows HIM; but you know HIM, for HE dwells with you and will be in you. I will not leave you orphans; I will come to you. A little while longer and the world will see me no more, but you will see me. Because I live, you will live also.**

The False Trinity Doctrine

> **[20] At that day you will know that I am in my FATHER, and you in me, and I in you. He who has my commandments and keeps them, it is he who loves me. And he who loves me will be loved by my FATHER, and I will love him and manifest myself to him. Judas (not Iscariot) said to him, 'Lord, how is it that you will manifest yourself to us, and not to the world?' [23] Jesus answered and said to him, 'If anyone loves me, he will keep my word; and my FATHER will love him, and WE will come to him and make OUR home with him [or her]." John 14:15-23**

Hagee ref #11.   Is it direct support for trinity doctrine? No!

Commentary: Again, in verse 16 Jesus makes it clear that God will provide HIS Spirit of truth to us. "I [Jesus] will pray [to] the FATHER, and HE [God] will give you another Helper [Spirit of truth]." Note also verse 20. Jesus is in the FATHER and we are in Jesus and Jesus is in us. And in verse 23, both God and Jesus will come to live within us. Does the fact that we are one with God and Jesus also make us God Almighty? No. It is a spiritual metaphor meaning we are one in the Spirit. Same thing with Jesus when he said: "I and my FATHER are one." It didn't make him God and it doesn't make us God. However, it does make us like gods.

Jesus answered them, "Many good works I have shown you from my FATHER. For which of those works do you stone me?" [33] The Jews answered him, saying, "For a good work we do not stone you, but for blasphemy, and because you, being a man, make yourself God." [34] Jesus answered them, "Is it not written in your law, 'I said, you are gods?'"

[35] If HE called them gods, to whom the word of God came (and the Scripture cannot be broken), [36] do you say of him whom the FATHER sanctified and sent into the world, 'you are blaspheming,' because I said, 'I am the Son of God?' [37] If I do not do the works of my FATHER, do not believe me; [38] but if I do, though you do not believe me, believe the works, that you may know and believe that the FATHER is in me, and I in HIM." John 10:32-38

The False Trinity Doctrine

> **I say, "You are gods**
> **and children of the MOST HIGH.**
> **But in death you are mere men.**
> **You will fall as any prince,**
> **For all must die." Psalm 82:6-7 NLT**

What the Jews failed to understand is that Jesus was not saying he was God Almighty. That was a human hang up over the issue of what is divine. Or who is God? The issue still exists today. Instead, Jesus was saying that the FATHER was in him and he was in the FATHER. This spiritual oneness exists for all who will choose to serve God. The Jews objected to Jesus using words they equated with being divine.

However, as the Psalmist indicates, those who are children of the MOST HIGH are all called gods by God Almighty. In the human sense of the word, it also means that they are all divine [a god]. However, this does not make them God Almighty. It just makes them of a nature like God.

> **"But when the Helper comes, whom I shall send to you from the FATHER, the Spirit of truth who proceeds from the FATHER, HE will testify of me." John 15:26**

Hagee ref #12.   Is it direct support for trinity doctrine? No!

Commentary: Again, the Spirit of truth proceeds from the FATHER. This is simply another Bible verse in which the words FATHER, Spirit and Jesus are associated. From the FATHER are the operative words in the above verse. There is no support for the trinity doctrine of orthodox Christianity.

> **"However, when he, the Spirit of truth, has come, he will guide you into all truth; for he will not speak on his own authority, but whatever he hears he will speak; and he will tell you things to come. He will glorify me, for he will take of what is mine and declare it to you. All things that the FATHER has are mine. Therefore I said that he will take of mine and declare it to you." John 16:13-15**

The False Trinity Doctrine

Hagee ref #13.   Is it direct support for trinity doctrine? No!

<u>Commentary</u>: Since Jesus did not speak on his own authority, it is reasonable to assume that the Holy Spirit, which proceeds from the FATHER, does not speak except that which the FATHER provides. Just as the FATHER has provided Jesus with words to speak, HE [God] also provides the Spirit with the words to speak to our spirits.

"If anyone wants to do HIS [God's] will, he shall know concerning the doctrine, whether it is from God or whether I [Jesus] speak on my own authority." [John 7:17] Don't confuse who Jesus speaks for just because God has given him all authority in Heaven and earth.

"And Jesus came and spoke to them, saying, 'All authority has been given to me in Heaven and on earth.' " [Matthew 28:18] Both Jesus and the Spirit speak for God Almighty and operate on HIS behalf. This is what spiritual oneness means. When you are one with God, you do HIS will. You yield to HIS plan for your life.

"This Jesus God has raised up, of which we are all witnesses." Acts 2:32

Hagee ref #14.   Is it direct support for trinity doctrine? No!

"Therefore being exalted to the right hand of God, and having received from the FATHER the promise of the Holy Spirit, he [Jesus] poured out this which you now see and hear." Acts 2:33

Hagee ref #15.   Is it direct support for trinity doctrine? No!

The False Trinity Doctrine

> "There are diversities of gifts, but the same Spirit. [5] There are differences of ministries, but the same Lord. [6] And there are diversities of activities, but it is the same God who works all in all." 1 Cor. 12:4-6

Hagee ref #16.   Is it direct support for trinity doctrine? No!

Commentary: The same Spirit is from God. The same Lord is Christ Jesus the Son of God. The same God is Yahweh or God Almighty. Nothing in this citation can be construed to create a trinity doctrine. The words speak for themselves.

> "The grace of the Lord Jesus Christ, and the love of God, and the communion of the Holy Spirit be with you all. Amen." 2 Cor. 13:14

Hagee ref #17.   Is it direct support for trinity doctrine? No!

Commentary: The apostle's benediction in 2 Corinthians 13:14 again provides an association of Jesus [as the grace of God manifested to mankind] by the love of God Almighty [Yahweh] who also provides a fellowship or communion with HIS Holy Spirit [God's Spirit of truth] to all of us who are "in Christ." Once again, other than an association of the three entities inside of a single verse, there is nothing in the verse supporting the trinity doctrine of orthodox Christianity.

> "But when the fullness of the time had come, God sent forth HIS Son, born of a woman, born under the law, to redeem those who were under the law, that we might receive the adoption as sons. And because you are sons, God has sent forth the spirit of HIS Son into your hearts, crying out, 'Abba, FATHER!'" Galatians 4:4-6

Hagee ref #18.   Is it direct support for trinity doctrine? No!

Commentary: Does your heart cry out Abba, FATHER? If not, why?

The False Trinity Doctrine

> "Grace to you and peace from God our FATHER and the Lord Jesus Christ. Blessed be the God and FATHER of our Lord Jesus Christ, who has blessed us with every spiritual blessing in the heavenly places in Christ, just as HE chose us in HIM before the foundation of the world, that we should be holy and without blame before HIM in love, having predestined us to adoption as sons by Jesus Christ to HIMSELF, according to the good pleasure of HIS will, to the praise of the glory of HIS grace, by which HE has made us accepted in the Beloved. In him we have redemption through his blood, the forgiveness of sins, according to the riches of HIS grace which HE made to abound toward us in all wisdom and prudence, having made known to us the mystery of HIS will, according to HIS good pleasure which HE purposed in HIMSELF, that in the dispensation of the fullness of the times HE might gather together in one all things in Christ, both which are in Heaven and which are on earth--in him. In him also we have obtained an inheritance, being predestined according to the purpose of HIM who works all things according to the counsel of HIS will, that we who first trusted in Christ should be to the praise of HIS glory. In HIM you also trusted, after you heard the word of truth, the gospel of your salvation; in whom also, having believed, you were sealed with the Holy Spirit of promise, who is the guarantee of our inheritance until the redemption of the purchased possession, to the praise of HIS glory." Ephesians 1:2-14

Hagee ref #19.   Is it direct support for trinity doctrine? No!

<u>Commentary</u>: Think carefully about this verse. "Blessed be the God and FATHER of our Lord Jesus Christ." There are some wonderful words in the above Scripture. However, you will not find any direct support for the orthodox trinity doctrine. Clearly there is a distinct relationship between "God the FATHER" and the "Lord Jesus Christ."

The False Trinity Doctrine

> "For through him [Jesus] we both have access by one Spirit to the FATHER." Ephesians 2:18

Hagee ref #20.   Is it direct support for trinity doctrine? No!

Commentary: This is another verse simply referencing three entities. Note that there is no direct or implied support for the orthodox trinity doctrine. Instead, one of the main benefits of being "in Christ" is cited. It is access to "the FATHER [God]." Accepting Christ results in God's indwelling Spirit and also the spirit of Christ within us. We are indeed one with God and Son and therefore have access to the FATHER [God] through HIS Spirit.

> "There is one body and one Spirit, just as you were called in one hope of your calling; [5] one Lord, one faith, one baptism; [6] ONE God and FATHER of all, who is above all, and through all, and in you all." Ephesians 4:4-6

Hagee ref #21.   Is it direct support for trinity doctrine? No!

Commentary: The verse makes it clear that there is "one God and FATHER of all." And there is also "one Spirit" and "one Lord [Jesus Christ]." This verse is the same as others that simply references all three entities. But look at the words and their plain meaning. Only a confused person who does not understand God can contrive a trinity doctrine using this verse.

> "For we are the circumcision, who worship God in the Spirit, rejoice in Christ Jesus, and have no confidence in the flesh." Philip. 3:3

Hagee ref #22.   Is it direct support for trinity doctrine? No!

Commentary: Again the three entities in a single verse are not enough to contrive a trinity doctrine. Note clearly that we are to "worship God in the Spirit." Note the contrast that instead of worshipping Jesus, we are to "rejoice in Christ Jesus." We are not to worship Jesus; we are supposed to worship God. Jesus confirms this worship instruction in John 4:24.

The False Trinity Doctrine

> "By that will we have been sanctified through the offering of the body of Jesus Christ once for all. And every priest stands ministering daily and offering repeatedly the same sacrifices, which can never take away sins. But this Man, after he had offered one sacrifice for sins forever, sat down at the right hand of God, from that time waiting till his enemies are made his footstool. For by one offering HE has perfected forever those who are being sanctified. But the Holy Spirit also witnesses to us; for after he had said before." Hebrews 10:10-15

Hagee ref #23.   Is it direct support for trinity doctrine? No!

Commentary: We know that the priest's sacrifices did atone for the sin of man. However, those sacrifices did not alter mankind's behavior. Man continued to sin and the priests continued to offer more sacrifices for the atonement of the new sins. There was a continued cycle of atonement, sin, atonement, sin, atonement, sin, etc. However, Jesus' sacrifice alters this cycle by altering our behavior. Those "in Christ" cannot continue to willfully sin because the Spirit of God and Christ dwell within us. That does not mean we are perfect on our own. It means we practice righteousness and do not willfully sin. See prior chapters. "For by one offering HE [God] has perfected forever those who are being sanctified." Are you sanctified? Set apart for God now, free from sin's control over you now and holy now?

> "Elect according to the foreknowledge of God the FATHER, in *sanctification* of the Spirit, *for obedience* and sprinkling of the blood of Jesus Christ: Grace to you and peace be multiplied." 1 Peter 1:2

Hagee ref #24.   Is it direct support for trinity doctrine? No!

Commentary: Has the Spirit sanctified you into obedience through the sprinkling of Christ's blood? Or, are you one of those whom Jesus will say, "I never knew you?" Obedience is the opposite of lawlessness!

The False Trinity Doctrine

> "Whoever believes that Jesus is the Christ is born of God, and everyone who loves HIM who begot also loves him who is begotten of HIM. By this we know that we love the children of God, when we love God and keep HIS commandments." 1 John 5:1-2

Hagee ref #25.   Is it direct support for trinity doctrine? No!

Commentary: It is ironic that the last Scripture cited as supporting the trinity doctrine brings us back to the beginning. Have no other Gods. Those who are children of God — keep God's commandments. Everyone who loves God [HIM who begot] also loves Jesus [him who is begotten of God]. Far from supporting a trinity doctrine, Hagee's citations clearly point out the separation of the entities from each other. There is the FATHER who is God. There is the obedient Son, who is Jesus. Then, the Spirit who belongs to God and emanates from God is one of *seven* Spirits of God.

Accepting the trinity doctrine is like checking your brain at the front door of the church. Scripture simply does not support a trinity doctrine and in fact makes it clear that distinct persons [entities] and distinct relationships do exist and that there is only ONE GOD. Back in chapter 6, I presented the graphic below to illustrate a teaching fundamental. You should not have to take a leap of faith to understand Scripture. Scripture speaks for itself.

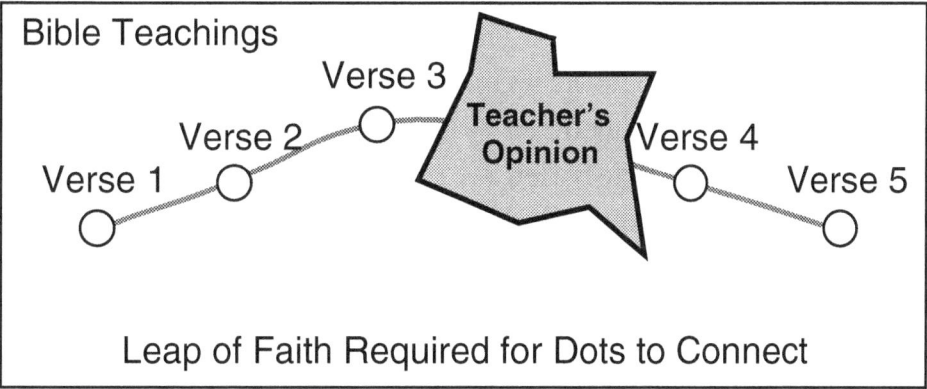

Book of Edward—Chapter 10

The False Trinity Doctrine

	Hagee Trinity Citation Summary		Scripture Speaks Directly to the Trinity Doctrine?		
#	Verse	Specific Teaching	Note	No	Yes
1	Romans 1:7	FATHER is God	3	✔	
2	Galatians 1:3	FATHER is God	3	✔	
3	John 1:1	Word was God in Beginning	3	✔	
4	John 1:18	Jesus has declared God	3	✔	
5	Hebrews 1:3-8	Jesus at right hand of God	1	✔	
6	Rev. 22:13	Refers to single entity	4	✔	
7	Acts 5:3-4	Lie to Spirit = Lie to God	3	✔	
8	Matthew 3:16	Spirit belongs to God	3	✔	
9	Matthew 3:17	Jesus is God's Son	3	✔	
10	Matthew 28:19	Baptismal association	2	✔	
11	John 14:15-23	God gives us the Spirit	2	✔	
12	John 15:26	Spirit proceeds from FATHER	2	✔	
13	John 16:13-15	Spirit speaks for God	2	✔	
14	Acts 2:32	God raised Jesus	3	✔	
15	Acts 2:33	Jesus at right hand of God	2	✔	
16	1 Cor. 12:4-6	One God	2	✔	
17	2 Cor. 13:14	Benediction association	2	✔	
18	Galatians 4:4-6	God sent forth Jesus	2	✔	
19	Ephesians 1:2-14	FATHER is God	2	✔	
20	Ephesians 2:18	Jesus gives us access to God	2	✔	
21	Ephesians 4:4-6	One God and FATHER of all	2	✔	
22	Philippians 3:3	Worship God	2	✔	
23	Hebrews 10:10-15	Sanctified by body of Christ	2	✔	
24	1 Peter 1:2	Sanctified for obedience	2	✔	
25	1 John 5: 1-2	Keep God's commandments	3	✔	

Table Notes
1. If misinterpreted and taken out of context, this verse implies a trinity doctrine.
2. Scripture text expressing three entities and not supporting a trinity doctrine.
3. Scripture text expressing two entities and not supporting a trinity doctrine.
4. Scripture text expressing one entity and not supporting a trinity doctrine.

Copyright 2005 Edward G. Palmer, All Rights Reserved.

The False Trinity Doctrine

Mankind Created The Trinity Doctrine!

Indeed, as Pastor John Hagee points out in his analysis on page 1429 of his <u>Prophecy Study Bible</u>[7], the trinity doctrine was "created" because the FATHER, Son and Spirit are all associated within several verses. Yet, can we ignore the clear teachings of those verses in favor of a fantasy doctrine that holds no merit whatsoever? Look at some of the principal teachings of these trinity support verses as shown in the table above.

In fact, most of these reference verses speak directly against the trinity doctrine; they do not support the doctrine. The closest support you can muster for the trinity doctrine from these verses is Hebrews 1:8. However, in order to support the trinity doctrine with this verse, you have to take the verse out of its context and ignore other Scripture. The notes I have provided in the above table can be summarized as follows.

Reality of Trinity Citations	Quantity
Single Entity in Verse	1
Two Entities in Verse	14
Three Entities in Verse	9
Implied Trinity Support	1

If you analyze the verses based on the amount of entities discussed in the verses, there are only 36% that even have all <u>three</u> entities. Most of the verses simply speak of the duality of God and HIS Son. If it was Tertulian of the third or fourth century that postulated this doctrine, clearly he did not possess the biblical text and resources that now exist.[8] One commentary indicates Tertulian may only have only possessed a few books of the Bible.

When a myth is perpetuated long enough, it takes on a life of its own. Today, many Christians accept the trinity doctrine as truth. However, it is clear that Scripture does not support the doctrine. The trinity myth is only supported by man's tradition. Mankind has transgressed the commandments of God by its tradition again. This time it is not the Jews; it is the Christians.

The False Trinity Doctrine

Scripture Does Not Support The Trinity Doctrine!

Christian Tradition Supports The Trinity Doctrine!

This ends the analysis of Pastor John Hagee's scriptures supporting the trinity doctrine. <u>Always check</u> lists of scriptures supporting doctrines.

Years ago while traveling I would catch Herbert W. Armstrong[9] on the radio. As he taught Bible lessons, he would also cite Scripture references that he claimed supported his radio teachings. I would write down the citations and later check them. I rarely found any to support the doctrines that I heard. I just thought I had mistaken the citation. Some time later, I started to read Hal Lindsey and his prophesy books. Hal would make a statement and then cite Scripture to support it. I would read the Scripture and sure enough, it supported exactly what Hal Lindsey taught. Therefore, Hal Lindsey's writings became my gold standard for teaching Scripture. If a doctrine is taught and backed by a Scripture, you must be able to read it directly from Scripture. It is easy for people to claim that Scripture supports a doctrine. The true student of the Bible will always check the Scripture citations for themselves. Again, most teachers know people do not check scriptures so they usually get away with false teachings because of this fact.

Just for fun, check out the following verses cited in the St. Joseph Medium Size Edition of <u>The New American Bible</u>[10], *copyright 1970, The Confraternity of Christian Doctrine, Washington, D.C.* This is a Catholic Bible. On page 347, it provides the following definition of purgatory.

Purgatory	A middle state of souls, suffering for a time on account of their sins, <u>is shown by those many texts</u> of Scripture which affirm that God will render to every man according to his works, so that such as die in lesser sins shall not escape without punishment.

Copyright 2005 Edward G. Palmer, All Rights Reserved.

Book of Edward—Chapter 10

The False Trinity Doctrine

Just below the definition, a list of nine scriptures that were said to support the purgatory doctrine is shown. Here are the Scripture citations.

>2 Maccabees 12:43-46   1 Cor 3:15
>Matthew 5:25   1 Peter 3:18-20
>Matthew 12:32   1 John 5:16
>Luke 12:58   Revelation 5:3
>   Revelation 5:13

Take some time and see for yourself whether those scriptures directly support the purgatory doctrine. If you are a Catholic, the scriptures might surprise you. Check them out yet? If you did, you were left scratching your head wondering where the purgatory doctrine came from. In stark contrast to the purgatory doctrine, the word of God says the following.

"And as it is appointed for men to die once, but after this the judgment." Hebrews 9:27

I am sorry, there are no holding zones where others petition for your eternal transfer to a better "cell" so to speak. You'd better get it right before you die. That doesn't mean you can't pray for relatives and friends right up unto the *Judgment Day*, you can. *See* Apocryphal book of 2 Esdras 7:105.

What's the point here? God wants you to know that both of the above lists were derived from printed Christian Bibles. God also wants you to know that HIS Word takes precedence over Bible lists. Remember, the lists and commentaries that you find in Christian Bibles espouse established orthodox Christian dogma.

Think about this. Jesus is the Word of God incarnate. Therefore, if you know Jesus, you know God's Word. Right? If you know God's Word, you will obey Jesus and God the FATHER. It just might be that some of those whom Jesus said "I never knew you" — never knew the Word at all.

If You Know Jesus, You Know God's "Word!"

The False Trinity Doctrine

The wealth of information available to us today on Christianity is staggering. That also includes the Internet as a virtual library on Christian apologetics. However, when it comes to Christian teachings, orthodoxy pervades the dialogue and the rationalization of the trinity is at the top of the list. Consider the following statements and lists (I – III) that rationalize Jesus as God. The lists shown below are part of a dialogue entitled "The True Jesus." The information was obtained online at a Christian web site.[11] My comments are shown below each list. Look up the scriptures.

   I. The Jesus of the Bible is prayed to
      1. Acts 7:55-60*
      2. Psalm 116:4**
      3. Zech. 13:9**
      4. 1 Cor. 1:1-2*

   *Calls on the name of Jesus vs. "prays to"
   **Prayer is to Yahweh and not Jesus [LORD v. Lord]

The Internet writer misrepresents the above-cited scriptures by his opening line of "The Jesus of the Bible is prayed to." Even if there were many verses indicating that Jesus was prayed to, does this alter whom Jesus taught us to pray to? Many people, wowed by Jesus' miracles, must have thought that he was God. No doubt they prayed to him just like modern day groupies worship at the feet of rock idols and other stars. That is human nature when it operates in a worldly mode. Who did Jesus say to pray to? Jesus taught us to pray to God the FATHER. It doesn't matter what the crowd does, it only matters if we do what we are taught [that we obey]. Consider Jesus' words.

> "But you, when you pray, go into your room, and when you have shut your door, pray to your FATHER who is in the secret place; and your FATHER who sees in secret will reward you openly." Matthew 6:6

Jesus Taught — Pray To The FATHER [Our God]!

The False Trinity Doctrine

    II. The Jesus of the Bible is worshipped
        1. Matthew 2:2
        2. Matthew 2:11
        3. Matthew 14:33
        4. Matthew 28:9
        5. John 9:35-38
        6. Hebrews 1:6

That Jesus is worshipped cannot be denied. In part, it is explained in the previous paragraph. Hebrews 1:6 —commands that angels shall worship Jesus *upon his return*! Who did Jesus tell us to worship? If we claim Jesus as our savior, shouldn't we actually obey Jesus? Consider his words.

"God is Spirit, and those who worship HIM must worship in spirit and truth." John 4:24

The Bible expounds further on whom to worship with these verses.

"For we are the circumcision, who worship God in the Spirit, rejoice in Christ Jesus, and have no confidence in the flesh." Philip. 3:3

"And I fell at his feet to worship him. But he said to me, 'See that you do not do that! I am your fellow servant, and of your brethren who have the testimony of Jesus. Worship God! For the testimony of Jesus is the spirit of prophecy.'"
                                                                      Rev. 19:10

The testimony of Jesus is that his God is real and that we will face either eternal salvation or eternal damnation. Jesus did not come here pretending to be God. Neither did he teach us to worship him. Worshipping Jesus is the epitome of Christian mythology. It is also idolatry.

Jesus Taught — Worship God In Spirit And <u>Truth</u>!

The False Trinity Doctrine

    III. The Jesus of the Bible is called God
        1. John 10:28
        2. Hebrews 1:8

The author does not understand the first Scripture and misrepresents John 10:28. We've already discussed Hebrews 1:8 at length.

Jesus Taught — I Return <u>To</u> My God <u>And</u> Your God!

What is the point here? Once again, God wants you to know that it is easy for Christians to get zealous and lift Scripture out of context. For almost two millennium Christians have gotten the message from God mixed up. Many Christians are very eager to demonstrate their own rationalization of the trinity doctrine in writing. Yet, it is not what those authors or I say that matters. It is what Scripture and Jesus says. You will not be able to use an author's opinion with God. But you can use Jesus' opinion with God.

It is not just millions of exuberant individuals wanting to rationalize the trinity doctrine to prove they understand it. There are at least two major Christian denominations that seek to rearrange Scripture to fit their salvation doctrine. Consider for the moment the Jehovah Witnesses and the Church of God denominations. Both believe that when you die, you go into the ground instead of either to Heaven or Hell. Of course, your memory flows back into God Almighty to wait for the moment of resurrection. Heard of this stuff?

The doctrine rationalizes that "no one has gone to Heaven" yet. This can get quite complicated and I will not go into all the details. However, you might discern that such a doctrine would have some holes in it from a scriptural perspective. If so, you are right. One of those little holes is the dialogue that Jesus had with the thief on the cross next to him. Consider.

"And Jesus said to him, 'Assuredly, I say to you, today you will be with me in Paradise.' " Luke 23:43

Copyright 2005 Edward G. Palmer, All Rights Reserved.

Book of Edward—Chapter 10

The False Trinity Doctrine

If "Jesus is talking to himself on the cross" seems offensive to you, think about this question. What if Jesus talked and sounded like William Jefferson Clinton? Would Jesus parse the simple words like this infamous lawyer did? In other words, would Jesus use simple words in such a manner and speak in such a clever way to actually deceive the people into believing something that were not true? Well, to rationalize the salvation doctrine of the above denominations, a comma has to be shifted in Luke 23:43.

Think about this. Jesus says "Assuredly, I say to you, TODAY you will be with me in Paradise." The words are clear enough. Jesus is telling the thief that he would be with Jesus in Paradise *that very day*! Whoops. Nobody goes to Heaven yet according to the present doctrine. Sounds like the statement of Jesus interferes with the doctrine of these churches? Of course, the only thing to do is to rationalize around Luke's statement. In this case, it is the comma that is the real problem. Yes, that comma was simply placed in the wrong spot by the translators. I might add it was placed in the wrong spot multiple times by multiple translation teams and that they all got it wrong. Since nobody gets into Heaven until after Jesus comes back, the verse is really suppose to read as follows.[12]

"And Jesus said to him, 'Assuredly, I say to you today, you will be with me in Paradise.' " Luke 23:43 [Comma moved.]

Note that the comma is moved to the opposite side of the word "today" in the above view. Thus the new meaning is "I'm telling you that sometime in the future eons of time that you will be with me in Paradise." Get the drift? The people who postulate this comma shift now expect you to believe that Jesus would mislead people like William Jefferson Clinton did! Is this the Jesus you know? It is not the Jesus I know. Jesus wouldn't offer needless hope to the thief in such a manner. He had no reason to. If he wanted, Jesus could have simply said: "Don't worry, someday you will be with me in Paradise. For the moment though, you will have to rest in the ground for a while. I don't know when I will return for you, but not to worry, I <u>will</u> come back <u>sometime</u>." Wow. This rationalization of Scripture leads to incredible apostasy and back to Scorsese's stupid Jesus.

The False Trinity Doctrine

There are countless denominations and sects in Christianity. It seems like each one has to have its own special belief or truth to attract members. This doctrine is no different. However, once again there is Scripture and the multiple translations that can be referenced for truth. So let's go get some translations and see how they compare Luke 23:43. Where is the comma supposed to be?

Bible	Comma before or after the word today?
KVJ	Verily I say unto thee, Today shalt thou be with me in paradise.
NKJV	Assuredly, I say to you, today you will be with me in Paradise.
LIV	Today you will be with me in Paradise. This is a solemn promise.
NLT	I assure you, today you will be with me in paradise.
NJB	In truth I tell you, today you will be with me in paradise.
NIV	I tell you the truth, today you will be with me in paradise.
RSV	Truly, I say to you, today you will be with me in Paradise.
NRSV	Truly I tell you, today you will be with me in Paradise.
NAB	Amen, I say to you, today you will be with me in Paradise.
NASB	Truly I say to you, today you shall be with me in Paradise.
GW	I can guarantee this truth: Today you will be with me in paradise.
NCV	I tell you the truth, today you will be with me in paradise.
GNB	I promise you that today you will be in Paradise with me.
REB	Truly I tell you: today you will be with me in Paradise.
DB	Verily I say to thee, To-day shalt thou be with me in paradise.
YLT	Verily I say to thee, To-day with me shalt thou be in the paradise.
AMP	Truly I tell you, today you shall be with me in Paradise.
WEY	[T]his very day you shall be with me in Paradise
WEB	Verily I say to thee, This day shalt thou be with me in paradise.
SET	I am telling you the truth: Today you will be with me in paradise.

There are twenty (20) different Bibles listed in the above table and not one suggests that the comma be shifted to the other side of the word "today" to alter the meaning of the verse. The lesson is simple enough. You are to let Scripture speak for itself. Do not modify the expressed meaning of any Scripture to suit your doctrine. If in doubt about a doctrine, go fetch a bunch of Bibles to compare against each other.

The False Trinity Doctrine

Those who support the doctrine of going into the ground and not Heaven probably won't care about the above reference table. But you should think about the ramifications of the table above. There had to be literally hundreds of translators involved in the above Bible works. I suspect that every single one of them was more intelligent than I am. For any Christian to just categorically ignore these translations is foolish and demonstrates a lack of wisdom. Want understanding? Give God your heart and get some Bible resources. For years I have attended Bible studies with at least 7-10 translations opened to the Word. Try that out and find out how fun it can be. You won't be bored and I guarantee that the Spirit will flush out the truth.

You don't surf Bible translations to pick and choose the verses out of them that you like. You surf Bible translations for the truth of God's Word. If you do not like the truth, God will not give you understanding. Now consider that Jesus is preparing a place for you and plans to come back for you.

> **"My FATHER's house has many rooms. If that were not true, would I have told you that I'm going to prepare a place for you?" John 14:2 GW**

> **"If I go to prepare a place for you, I will come again. Then I will bring you into my presence so that you will be where I am. You know the way to the place where I am going."**
> **John 14:3-4 GW**

Every Christian has the opportunity to enter into God's Holies of Holies right here while on planet earth. Jesus Christ gives this to us as a result of believing that he is the Son of God. That is when the Spirit of God and the spirit of Christ come to dwell inside of us. I live there and since I can freely fellowship with God right now, I cannot imagine going into the ground and having less than I have now. No, God has made it clear to this poor servant that there is only Heaven to look forward to once I die. THAT is when judgment for sinners occurs or transfer takes place for believers [me].

The False Trinity Doctrine

Are you still in the ground with your thoughts? Then, consider the following verses and remember that if a single Bible verse speaks directly against this doctrine, then the doctrine cannot stand the test of God's Word. God is not the author of confusion.

> **"So all the days of Enoch were three hundred and sixty-five years. And Enoch walked with God; and he was not, for God took him." Genesis 5:23-24**

> **"By faith Enoch was taken away so that he did not see death, 'and was not found, because God had taken him'; for before he was taken he had this testimony, that he pleased God." Hebrews 11:5**

> **Jesus said: "But concerning the dead, that they rise, have you not read in the book of Moses, in the burning bush passage, how God spoke to him, saying, 'I am the God of Abraham, the God of Isaac, and the God of Jacob?' HE is not the God of the dead, but the God of the living. You are therefore greatly mistaken." Mark 12:26-27**

To use a Monopoly game metaphor, it looks like Enoch passed *Go* without getting jailed and collected $200. The Word teaches us "he pleased God." Do you?

This "in the ground" salvation doctrine claims that the dead hadn't had the chance to choose Jesus yet. Since they also teach you cannot get into Heaven without Jesus, they reason that the dead are not in Heaven. Both teachings are false doctrines. However, you will have to wait until chapter 12 for a discussion on the issue of salvation with and without Christ. For now, the word of God is clear—there are people in Heaven without the benefit of Jesus Christ. Think about the ramifications for your salvation.

> **Enoch walked with God; and he was not, for God took him!**

Copyright 2005 Edward G. Palmer, All Rights Reserved.

Book of Edward—Chapter 10

The False Trinity Doctrine

Alpha & Omega Scripture Analysis

"I am the Alpha and the Omega, the Beginning and the End, says the LORD, who is and who was and who is to come, the Almighty." Rev. 1:8

In a red letter Bible, the above verse is in red indicating it is Jesus speaking. Is Jesus the Alpha and Omega? A brother in Christ Jesus, Bryn Hendrickson[13], provided an analysis of the Alpha & Omega scriptures. I knew it came from God through Bryn because of its precise timing and the Spirit's confirmation of truth to me. Would someone alter the red lettering of the Bible? Or, is Jesus speaking for God and not for himself? Let's examine John's Revelation closer. Here are Bryn's basic conclusions.

To enhance the context of Rev. 1:8, let's back up to Rev. 1:4.

"John, to the seven churches which are in Asia: Grace to you and peace from HIM who is and who was and who is to come, and from the *seven* Spirits who are before HIS throne, and from Jesus Christ, the faithful witness, the firstborn from the dead, and the ruler over the kings of the earth.

To him [Jesus] who loved us and washed us from our sins in his own blood, and has made us kings and priests to his God and FATHER, to him be glory and dominion forever and ever. Amen. Behold, he [Jesus] is coming with clouds, and every eye will see him, even they who pierced him. And all the tribes of the earth will mourn because of him. Even so, Amen." Rev. 1:4-7

Notice who John says the greeting comes from. It comes from,

1. HIM who is and who was and who is to come; <u>and from</u>,
2. The *seven* Spirits who are before HIS throne; <u>and from</u>,
3. Jesus Christ, the faithful witness, the firstborn …

The False Trinity Doctrine

A) Notice that Jesus Christ *[#3]* is a different person than the first person who is described as "HIM who is and who was and who is to come" *[#1]*. Note that *seven* Spirits *[#2]* reside before HIS *[#1]* throne. John is talking about God Almighty in the form of the person identified as,

HIM who is and who was and who is to come *[#1]*

B) Now examine Rev. 1:8 again and observe that the one called the Alpha and Omega is also called,

HIM who is and who was and who is to come *[#1]*

C) If Jesus *[#3]* stands before the entity *[#1]* on the throne, which is identified as "HIM who is and who was and who is to come" (Rev. 1:4-5) — for the purpose of taking the seventh seal from HIS hand (Rev. 5:7), this clearly means that he, Jesus *[#3]*, is not the same person as *[#1]*.

D) If the Alpha and Omega is "HIM who is and who was and who is to come" as is stated clearly in Rev. 1:8, and Jesus *[#3]* is not, this would mean that Jesus is also *not* the Alpha and Omega.

Jesus Is Not The Alpha & Omega!

This analysis could go on for at least four more pages but I will stop here. Study the above phrases and who sits on the throne in Revelation. Note also that Revelation 1:10-11 in the KJV and NKJV contains the words "Alpha and Omega" which do not appear in many early Greek manuscripts and is considered a later addition. It is corrected in newer Bible translations. Other relevant scriptures to study are Rev. 1:13-16; Rev. 4:8; Rev. 11:16-18; Rev. 21:5-7; and Rev. 22:6-7, 12-13.

God The FATHER Is The Alpha & Omega!

The False Trinity Doctrine

Now let's return to the ex-Jesuit Priest Jack Miles and my discussion in the last chapter. Miles wrote the book <u>Christ: A Crisis in the Life of God</u>, *Copyright 2001, Alfred A. Knopf, NY.*[14] Do you recall seven conclusions Jack reached about God's character as he rationalized the trinity doctrine?

Miles in his trinity rationalization has God doing the following seven things. He believes they are attributes of the character of God. However, does Scripture really support these characteristics of God or does Scripture teach us something different altogether? Jack concludes that God is …

1. Changing
2. Repenting
3. Needing a way to fail
4. Talking to HIMSELF
5. Committing Suicide
6. Breaking Promises
7. 100% Man and 100% God

"That the Son and the FATHER are identical gives Jesus' prayers a peculiarly contemporary cast inasmuch as he is praying to himself." [15] Jack Miles believes that God prays to HIMSELF. Do you?

Remember, that if you want to accept the trinity doctrine, you have to conclude the same things that Jack Miles has concluded; at least if you are intellectually honest with yourself. If God allowed HIMSELF to die on the cross, God did commit suicide. If you did just start to read this book with this chapter, go back and read the last chapter as I cannot repeat it all again. You will miss foundational teachings if you do not. Indeed, Jack Miles reached some honest conclusions in his book with these characteristics.

If you want to understand Christianity, as it exists today, Jack Mile's book is a good place to start. I believe it is the best explanation of the trinity doctrine that you will find. However, it is a rationalization of man, which lacks <u>full</u> Scripture support. Remember this, if I show you a single Scripture that speaks directly against any Bible doctrine, then that doctrine is false according to Scripture.

The False Trinity Doctrine

You cannot simply postulate a biblical doctrine that contains loopholes and exceptions. If you do, you are not talking about what God does; you are talking about what man does. Let's compare the character attributes of God that Miles identifies against Holy Scripture.

Item 1. God changing? Answer: No!

"For I am the LORD, I do not change." Malachi 3:6

Item 2. God repenting? Answer: No!

**"God is not a man, that HE should lie,
Nor a son of man, that HE should repent." Numbers 23:19**

Item 3. God needs a way to fail? Answer: No!

"Has HE said, and will HE not do? Or has HE spoken, and will HE not make it good?" Numbers 23:19

Item 4. God talking to HIMSELF? Answer: No!

"For I [Jesus] have given to them the words which YOU [God] have given me [Jesus]; and they have received them, and have known surely that I [Jesus] came forth from YOU [God]; and they have believed that YOU [God] sent me."
                                                                John 17:8

Item 5. God committing suicide? Answer: No!

"And about the ninth hour Jesus cried out with a loud voice, saying, 'Eli, Eli, lama sabachthani?' that is, 'My God, my God, why have YOU [God] forsaken me [Jesus]?' "
                                                                Matthew 27:46

The False Trinity Doctrine

Item 6. God breaking promises? Answer: No!

"For all the promises of God in him [Christ] are yes, and in him [Christ] Amen, to the glory of God through us." 2 Cor. 1:20

Item 7. [Jesus is] 100% Man and 100% God? Answer: No!

"Therefore, in all things he [Jesus] had to be made like his brethren [the rest of mankind in a body of flesh and blood], that he [Jesus] might be a merciful and faithful High Priest [in the temple of our God] in things pertaining to God, to make propitiation for the sins of the people [the rest of us]." Heb. 2:17

My eyes welled up at the Scripture citation on Item 5 and my heart is broken at just the thought of Jesus' words on the cross. I can even feel Jesus on the cross speaking those words because his spirit resides inside of me. My spirit therefore cries out to God just like Jesus' did saying, "Abba FATHER." And aside from the tears and the ache inside my heart, it is an outright abomination to think that Jesus was talking to himself when he uttered those words of spiritual pain on the cross.

Jesus Had To Be Made Just Like Us! Hebrews 2:17

Honest men and women must conclude what Jack Miles does if they support the trinity doctrine. They must reach the above seven conclusions even though Scripture itself does not support those conclusions. They either rationalize the trinity doctrine like Miles, are simply ignorant of Scripture, or they have checked their brains in at the front door of the church. In the end, the trinity doctrine actually makes a mockery of the gift of Jesus. It counts the blood of Jesus as a "common thing" and eventually those who perpetuate the trinity doctrine will have to answer to God Almighty for the apostasy.

The False Trinity Doctrine

Wouldn't it be a simple thing for God to commit suicide? Yes it would. However, for God Almighty to behave in that way is nothing more than God duping mankind. It would be virtually nothing for God to commit suicide if that is what he wanted. If he did, does that really inspire you? Why? Is it some big thing for the God of creation to do suicide and then go back upstairs after HE repairs HIMSELF? The whole idea is both laughable and sad at the same time. Yet that is the state of Christian belief today.

Now think about this for a moment. God's only begotten Son Jesus falls down on his face in tears and asks of God [the ONE God] — "O my FATHER, if it is possible, let this cup pass from me; nevertheless, not as I will, but as YOU will." Matthew 26:39

Jesus never wanted to go to that cross. Yet, his heart was with God and in obedience he went and took the cross so that mankind would have a better shot at eternal life. When you believe in Jesus, the cross takes on real meaning as Jesus did die for the sins of the world. God resurrected Jesus. He did not resurrect himself.

In one illustration, God commits suicide. Ho hum. No big thing for God Almighty, is it? In the second illustration an obedient Son, who GOD ALMIGHTY MADE JUST LIKE THE REST OF US, gives up his own life for us in a HUMAN SACRIFICE on the cross. If God sacrificed HIMSELF, how does that teach us that we too as a human male or female can also be obedient to HIS commands, even unto death? However, Jesus as a human sacrifice carries special meaning. Indeed the body and blood of Jesus are to be remembered.

God's <u>Human</u> Son Jesus Was Sacrificed!

"For God so loved the world that HE gave HIS only begotten Son, that whoever believes in him [Jesus] should not perish but have everlasting life." John 3:16

It is only when you realize that the trinity doctrine is false that you can appreciate the full depth of God's love for us.

The False Trinity Doctrine

Indeed, God gave us the sacrifice of HIS only human Son [begotten and made just like us] Jesus on the cross. You should understand that God actually went through with the sacrifice that HE tested Abraham with. This time, it was the love of the Son for the FATHER that allowed the sacrifice on the cross to take place. If you understand this, then you will understand that it is to obedience that we are sanctified to, through the blood of Jesus Christ. Are you obedient to God's commands or do you rationalize your sin away?

Jesus taught us that the flesh [our human bodies] profits us nothing and that is one of many reasons he remained obedient to God. Giving up his flesh [life] on the cross, even though painful, was not only what God wanted for Jesus' life, it was also a point of transition back to God for Jesus. He knew this and chose the FATHER's plan. Indeed, all of us will be dead a lot longer than we will be alive. This earthly life is just a speck of dust in all of eternity. Can you shift your focus towards eternal life like Jesus?

> **"It is the Spirit who gives life; the flesh profits nothing. The words that I speak to you are spirit, and they are life."**
> **John 6:63**

Jesus Sanctifies Us Into Obedience!

I and my FATHER are one!
Analysis

Perhaps no other verse is as confusing to Christians today than John 10:30. I also suspect that no other verse is used as much to rationalize the trinity doctrine. This verse needs to be dealt with in more depth and here is my analysis. Want to continue misusing this verse or want understanding?

"I and my FATHER are one." John 10:30

Book of Edward—Chapter 10

The False Trinity Doctrine

The word "one" is not capitalized in the above verse, which I find curious. So, let's compile a table of Bible translations. I'll include Mark 10:18 since it and John 10:30 represent the words of Jesus Christ and have opposing meanings for the trinity doctrine. Those who insist on citing John 10:30 in the belief that Jesus is God, will have to reconcile their thinking with the words of Jesus Christ in Mark 10:18. Now take a few moments to think about these two verses in the twenty translations shown.

Bible	John 10:30 [Jesus' words]	Mark 10:18 [Jesus' words]
KVJ	I and my FATHER are one.	[N]one good but one, that is, God.
NKJV	I and my FATHER are one.	No one is good but One, that is, God.
LIV	I and the FATHER are one.	Only God is truly good.
NLT	The FATHER and I are one.	Only God is truly good.
NJB	The FATHER and I are one.	No one is good but God alone.
NIV	I and the FATHER are one.	No one is good--except God alone.
RSV	I and the FATHER are one.	No one is good but God alone.
NRSV	The FATHER and I are one.	No one is good but God alone.
NAB	The FATHER and I are one.	No one is good but God alone.
NASB	I and the FATHER are one.	No one is good except God alone.
GW	The FATHER and I are one.	No one is good except God alone.
NCV	The FATHER and I are one.	Only God is good.
GNB	The FATHER and I are one.	No one is good except God alone.
REB	The FATHER and I are one.	No one is good except God alone.
DB	I and the FATHER are one.	No one is good but one, that is God.
YLT	I and the FATHER are one.	No one [is] good except One—God.
AMP	I and the FATHER are One.*	[N]o one good except God Alone
WEY	I and the FATHER are one.	[None] good except One, that is God.
WEB	I and [my] FATHER are one.	[N]one good, but one [that is] God
SET	FATHER and I are united.	Only God is good.

With the exception of the Amplified Bible*, all other translations do not capitalize the word "one" in John 10:30. Is this important? I think it is to a point. The words "Him, him, Me, me, My, my, Your, your, One, and one" are very intriguing in some verses. At least, from a study perspective, these words can present challenges to the casual Bible student.

The False Trinity Doctrine

The use of the word "one" in John 10:30 is identified in StrongS' Concordance[16] as Greek word #1520. It is the Greek word *heis* [hice]; a prim numeral; *one:*—a (-n, -ny, certain), + abundantly, man, one (another), only, other, some. The usage of the word in John 10:30 is the same as the usage of the word in Mark 10:18.

> **Jesus said to him, "Why do you call me good? No <u>one</u> is good except God alone." Mark 10:18 GW**

Is there anyone that will look me in the eye and tell me that Jesus is God based upon what Jesus has said in Mark 10:18? Jesus has made it clear that there is only "ONE" that is good. He stated that this person is God. Jesus identified his God as the "FATHER" and many times. The two verses seem like polar opposites, don't they? Using John 10:30, Christians claim that the word "one" means Jesus is God. However, in Mark 10:18 it is obvious that Jesus is not God. Such is the nature of many verses in the Bible when man tries to rationalize a doctrine that is not supported by Scripture. The contradiction in meaning is not confusion on God's part, it is man trying to rationalize and morph the Bible into supporting a false doctrine.

Mark 10:18 is easy to understand when the trinity doctrine is simply recognized as false, but what about John 10:30? How is that explained? Again, we have to look at the words of Jesus closer. Not in isolation and lifted out of the larger contexts. We need to consider <u>all</u> of Jesus' teachings. Do yourself a favor. If you cannot explain a doctrine and back it solidly with Scripture, don't try. God is not the author of confusion.

> **"For God is not the author of confusion but of peace, as in all the churches of the saints." 1 Cor. 14:33**

> **"For where envy and self-seeking exist, confusion and every evil thing are there." James 3:16**

God Is Not The Author Of Confusion!

The False Trinity Doctrine

To understand John 10:30, let's turn to Matthew 19:4-6.

> **"And he answered and said to them, have you not read that HE who made them at the beginning 'made them male and female,' and said, 'for this reason a man shall leave his father and mother and be joined to his wife, and the two shall become one flesh?' So then, they are no longer two but one flesh. Therefore what God has joined together, let not man separate." Matthew 19:4-6**

Jesus states: "Man shall leave his father and mother and be joined to his wife, and the two shall become one flesh."

Jesus Says: "The Two <u>Shall</u> Become <u>One</u> Flesh!"

My wife and I will be married 39 years in less than two months. Our friends Dean and Jackie have been married 43 years. Our friends Vern and Inga have been married even longer. Recently I posed this question to all three couples. Did you and your spouse become one flesh like Jesus taught? Everyone answered yes, but how can that be? If you can understand this teaching of Jesus on "oneness of flesh," you can understand what he means when he says "I and the FATHER are one." Think about it for a moment.

In each marriage there are two people physically walking around, yet one flesh according to Jesus. All three marriages testify to the veracity of Jesus. Got any answers yet? Well, simply put, what Jesus is talking about is a "spiritual oneness of the flesh" that exists in true marriages. If you have never experienced this, you might think it odd. However, it is true. Jesus is teaching us about a spiritual fact that transcends our human ability to reason physical matters. Yet, this one flesh is something that everyone "knows" when he or she has it, even if they cannot explain it.

In the simplest explanation, Jesus is using a spiritual metaphor to explain the holy relationship between husband and wife. No doubt it is more complicated and profound, most likely beyond full human understanding.

The False Trinity Doctrine

Husbands and wives know when they have it [one flesh] as weird things occur such as either spouse completing the other's sentences. Or both starting to ask the same question of the other at the same exact moment in time. Or one spouse completing the other spouse's thoughts without the benefit of actually being able to find out what was on their mind. I.E. Stopping to pick up something seemingly on an impulse only to later find out that the exact moment you had the thought, that your spouse was thinking it would be nice if you did [name the action]. Indeed, one flesh exists between two people. I have experienced it. I have also experience a "oneness" with God.

That you can be one with God is yet another fact. Consider John 14:20, 23; and John 17:23.

> **"When I am raised to life again, you will know that I am in my FATHER, and you are in me, and I am in you."**
> **John 14:20 NLT**

> **Jesus replied, "All those who love me will do what I say. My FATHER will love them, and WE will come to them and live with them." John 14:23 NLT**

> **Jesus answered him, "Those who love me will do what I say. My FATHER will love them, and WE will go to them and make our home with them." John 14:23 GW**

> **"I in them and YOU in me, all being perfected into one. Then the world will know that YOU sent me and will understand that YOU love them as much as YOU love me."**
> **John 17:23 NLT**

Jesus said that he and the FATHER would come to us and make their home inside of us. Note that there is a condition that applies. Jesus states in John 14:23 that "those who love him will do what he [Jesus] says."

The False Trinity Doctrine

Jesus teaches — "He is in everyone who believes, God is in him, and as a result, we are all [God, Jesus, and the believer] perfected in one." Jesus taught that those who love him obey him and that is *when* God will *dwell* inside of them. Jesus in us, God in Jesus, and all of us in perfect oneness. In other words we are "one" with God and Jesus according to John 14:23. Are Jesus and God inside of you? If not, you need to check your obedience because <u>that</u> is the condition. They <u>are</u> inside of me!

True Believers <u>Are</u> "One" With God And Son!

Okay, here comes the really big question. Does the fact that you too can be "one" with God [and Son] make you God? If you answered no, you got the answer correct. Now comes the next really big question. If we are not God, what makes you think that Jesus Christ is God given the same language and metaphor? Indeed, Jesus is not God no more than you and I are. This is another profound "spiritual oneness of the flesh" that transcends our limited human ability to reason physical matters. Yet, those who walk with Jesus and God "<u>know</u>" when they are "<u>one</u>" with them.

Yesterday I spent almost twelve hours on this chapter. I was very nervous starting the day about the business matters I am ignoring just so I can accomplish this writing. I cannot even tell you what is in the huge pile of papers on my desk, because God has me focused on trying to complete this chapter. I had the same nervousness all of last week.

However, all last week I got blessed and blessed and blessed by several events. I told my wife, who was diagnosed with pancreatic cancer and sent home to die, that we had been enormously blessed in these certain matters all of last week. She concurred and is herself a living blessing since she is now able to eat and even has hunger pains once again. She is walking around and starting to gain energy. I pray that God has healed her.

I knew this would be a tough chapter to write; yet I couldn't help but marvel how God seemed to control my schedule and give me peace.

Copyright 2005 Edward G. Palmer, All Rights Reserved.

Book of Edward—Chapter 10

The False Trinity Doctrine

Even though nervous yesterday, I continued to press forward with this chapter. Once again we received a specific blessing yesterday afternoon. Now, <u>this</u> morning, I had the same nervousness again. The business pile is getting larger. I reasoned that God had control of the situation and since I had some input from HIM early this morning, I decided to proceed with writing this chapter. When you are "one" with God, you start to complete HIS thoughts in your head even before HE can. It is just a "fun" oneness thing somewhat similar to that of a husband and wife. Ever wonder why Jesus used the metaphor of the Bride [those "in Christ" vs. the church at large] and Bridegroom [Jesus] to explain our special relationship to him?

I decided to push ahead and while writing in the spirit, I had the musing thought to ask God to bring the same blessing to me *this day* as he had yesterday *as a sign* if this is what HIS will was for me today. I thought about Gideon's fleece test and I reasoned that such an event *this day* would give me peace that it was okay to continue writing. As fast as the thoughts came, they passed away. However, it didn't seem like 15 minutes had went by before God provided the specific thing that I requested. It was another Gideon moment for me and it wasn't the first time. I knew in my spirit that God was telling me, "Keep writing Edward!"

It <u>was</u> just like Gideon's fleece test. God <u>will</u> manifest HIMSELF to you physically if you will give HIM your heart. If you choose the Son in a manner that involves obedience to the Word, you will find God and Jesus making their home with you. Then get ready for a real adventure of "one."

> **"Then Gideon said to God, 'Do not be angry with me, but let me speak just once more: Let me test, I pray, just once more with the fleece; let it now be dry only on the fleece, but on all the ground let there be dew.' And God did so that night. It was dry on the fleece only, but there was dew on all the ground." Judges 6:39-40**

Study this section of Judges and learn more about how the God of the universe will interact in your life if you will trust and interact with HIM.

Copyright 2005 Edward G. Palmer, All Rights Reserved.

The False Trinity Doctrine

When you understand that Jesus spoke of a "spiritual oneness" when he said "I and the FATHER are one" — you can understand what he meant when he said the following.

> **"But he answered and said to them, 'my mother and my brothers are these who hear the word of God and do it.'"**
> **Luke 8:21**

Jesus said he would be your brother *if* you "hear the word of God and do it." Can you grasp the reality of the spiritual oneness that is being offered to you by God through Jesus? All it takes is obedience to the word of God.

Jesus Is *Your* Brother Only If *You* Obey God!

I don't want to leave you hanging on the issue of those words. The reason that the words "Him, him, Me, me, My, my, Your, your, One, and one" can be confusing in Scripture is that the capitalized version implies it is God. Quite frankly, it isn't always that way in Scripture and the use of caps adds confusion into the reading of some Scripture. Luke 8:21, is a good example where the sentence can be cleaned up and the understanding enhanced by reading it as follows. Note fathers are absent in this teaching.

> **"But Jesus answered and said to them, 'my mother, my brothers and my sisters are these who hear the word of God and do it.'" Luke 8:21** [Apostle Edward's understanding]

Jesus Is One With God, He's Just <u>Not</u> God!

This ends a very detailed discussion of the many ways in which man rationalizes the trinity doctrine. It is not meant to be complete as there is no limit to the rationalization of mankind when it comes to the trinity doctrine. However, no trinity rationalization can stand up against God's Holy Word.

The False Trinity Doctrine

It would be wrong to just leave this discussion without also pointing out some scriptures that speak directly against a trinity doctrine. There are scriptures that directly support the separate and distinct relationship of the FATHER and Son. There are also scriptures that speak direct to God's Spirits. This final section will start with a discussion of the *seven* Spirits of God. Can there be a trinity if God has *seven* Spirits? What are those Spirits? Did Jesus have them all? One more aspect of the trinity conundrum is that GOD has *seven* Spirits and the doctrine ignores six of them or 85.7%.

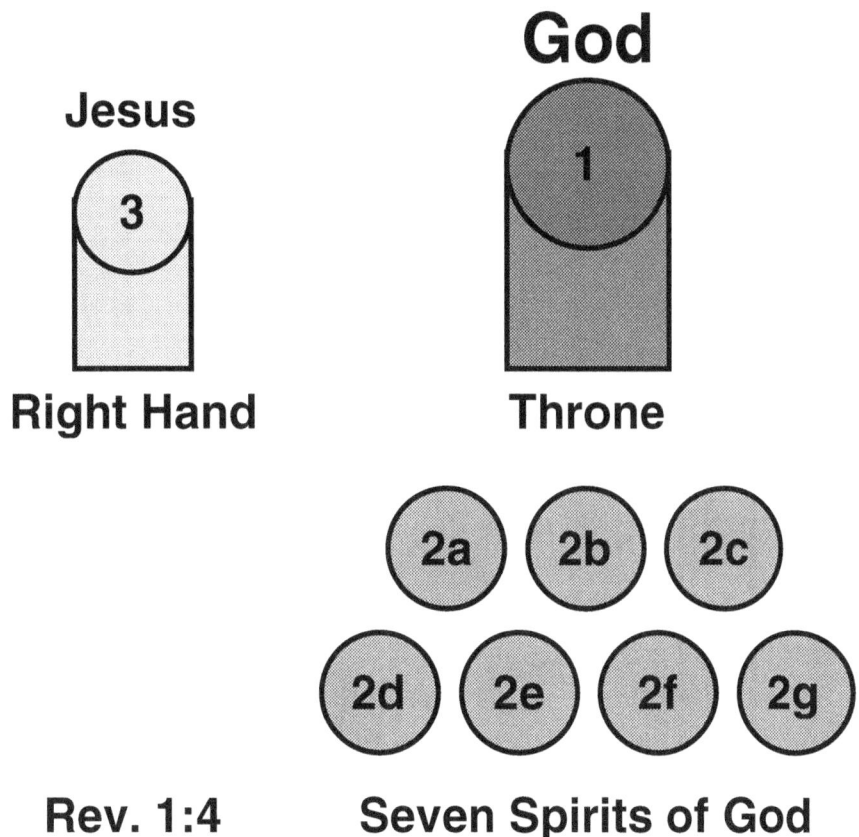

God Has Seven Spirits, <u>Not</u> One!

The False Trinity Doctrine

You might surmise that if you ignored 85.7% of any given subject, that you are for the most part completely ignoring the subject. For example, would a final grade of 14.3% on any college exam satisfy you? Is it any different with the *seven* Spirits of God? Can we claim to know God if we do not acknowledge all of His Spirits? Let's go back to Rev. 1 on page 287 for a moment and make the following observations about whom we are talking about. From Revelation 1:4-8 we learn the following truths.

Attribute of Jesus	Attribute of God
Faithful Witness	HIM who is and who was and is to come
Firstborn of the dead	Sits on throne
Ruler over kings of earth	Seven Spirits before HIS throne
Washed us with his blood	Jesus sits by HIS right hand
Makes us kings & priests to God	God Almighty
His God is the FATHER on throne	Alpha and Omega

I have used the same numbers identified in Revelations 1:4-5 in the above graphic. #1 is God Almighty. #2a-2g are the *seven* Spirits before God. #3 is Jesus Christ. If you are viewing the graphic in color [web site], you will observe that Jesus is a different color than the *seven* Spirits before the throne. As a result of becoming God's only begotten Son, Jesus is elevated above the angels and has been given God's *seven* Spirits.

If you believe in the trinity doctrine, the math does not add up now when it comes to the Spirits. Jesus *plus* FATHER *plus seven* Spirits adds up to the number nine, not three. Jesus *plus* FATHER *plus* Holy Spirit equals three. However, the Spirit of truth is only one of the *seven* Spirits of God stated clearly in God's Word. Consider the following scriptures now.

> **"John, to the seven churches which are in Asia: Grace to you and peace from HIM who is and who was and who is to come, and from the *seven* Spirits who are before HIS throne." Rev. 1:4**

Greetings From Seven Spirits Before God's Throne!

Copyright 2005 Edward G. Palmer, All Rights Reserved.

The False Trinity Doctrine

And to the angel of the church in Sardis write, "These things says he [Jesus] who has the *seven* Spirits of God and the seven stars: 'I know your works, that you have a name that you are alive, but you are dead.' " Rev. 3:1

Jesus Has The Seven Spirits Of God!

"And from the throne proceeded lightnings, thunderings, and voices. Seven lamps of fire were burning before the throne, which are the *seven* Spirits of God." Rev. 4:5

"And I looked, and behold, in the midst of the throne and of the four living creatures, and in the midst of the elders, stood a Lamb as though it had been slain, having seven horns and seven eyes, which are the *seven* Spirits of God sent out into all the earth." Rev. 5:6

Seven Spirits Of God Are Sent Out Into All The Earth!

Now that you know that there are *seven* Spirits of God and that Jesus has them all at his disposal, exactly who are these Spirits? You will find God's *seven* Spirits in the Old and New Testament as follows.

"The Spirit of the LORD shall rest upon him,
The Spirit of wisdom and understanding,
The Spirit of counsel and might,
The Spirit of knowledge and of the fear of the LORD."
Isaiah 11:2

"And I will pour on the house of David and on the inhabitants of Jerusalem the Spirit of grace and supplication; then they will look on me whom they pierced. Yes, they will mourn for him as one mourns for his only son, and grieve for him as one grieves for a firstborn." Zechariah 12:10

The False Trinity Doctrine

"The Spirit of truth, whom the world cannot receive, because it neither sees HIM nor knows HIM; but you know HIM, for HE dwells with you and will be in you." John 14:17

Spirit Of Truth Is One Of Seven Spirits!

"And declared to be the Son of God with power according to the Spirit of holiness, by the resurrection from the dead." Romans 1:4

"If you are reproached for the name of Christ, blessed are you, for the Spirit of glory and of God rests upon you. On their part he is blasphemed, but on your part he is glorified." 1 Peter 4:14

Summary of God's Seven Spirits

Specific Identity of God's Spirit	Bible Reference
Spirit of Wisdom and Understanding	Isaiah 11:2
Spirit of Counsel and Might	Isaiah 11:2
Spirit of Knowledge and Fear of the LORD	Isaiah 11:2
Spirit of Grace and Supplication	Zechariah 12:10
Spirit of Truth	John 14:17
Spirit of Holiness	Romans 1:4
Spirit of Glory	1 Peter 4:14

There is a lot more to God's Spirits that could be studied. Note that the Scripture references point directly to Jesus Christ. These are the *seven* Spirits that God gave Christ. Isn't it curious that the Spirit of truth is sent back to those who begin a new life "in Christ Jesus?" It is because God's manifested power in your life begins with HIS truth.

Copyright 2005 Edward G. Palmer, All Rights Reserved.

The False Trinity Doctrine

Finally in this chapter comes the essence of Scripture teachings, which deny by their very existence the possibility of a trinity doctrine. For those who are walking in the truth with God, meditate on these Scripture lessons.

Scripture Teaches Christians

Scripture Lesson	Bible Reference
Jesus gives you an understanding of God	1 John 5:20
You know God because you know Jesus	John 7:17; 1 John 5:20
You are to serve and worship only God	Matthew 4:10
You are to worship God in spirit and truth	John 4:23
Love God with your heart, soul, mind & strength	Mark 12:30
Love God and obey God's commandments	1 John 5:3; John 14:15
You are to pray to the FATHER [God] in Heaven	Luke 11:2
You no longer ask of Jesus, you ask of the FATHER	John 16:23
You are to ask of the FATHER in Jesus' name	John 16:23
You are to go directly to God with your prayers	John 16:23 LIV
There is only One God (not three in one)	Mark 12:32; 1 Cor 8:6
Jesus is the Son of God in the flesh	1 John 5:1
You are to resist sin	1 John 5:18
You are to practice righteousness	1 John 2:29
You are supposed to be slaves to righteousness	Romans 6:16-18
You are to purify yourself because Christ was pure	1 John 3:3
Jesus is your advocate before God	1 John 2:1
There are unintentional sins	Leviticus 4:2
There are unknown sins	Leviticus 5:17
There is willful sin	Hebrews 10:26
You are to stop all willful sin	Hebrews 10:26
You are to emulate Jesus	1 John 2:6
You are to walk a narrow walk	Matthew 7:13-14
You are to walk in the spirit, not the flesh	Romans 8:1
You are to be doers of the word, not hearers only	James 1:22
You are to know the kingdom of God is inside you	Luke 17:20-21
You manifest God's kingdom by your behavior	Luke 17:20-21

The False Trinity Doctrine

Scripture Teachings Continued

You are to be filled with the Spirit of truth	John 16:13
You are to pray to the FATHER [God] in private	Matthew 6:6
You are to purge evil from among you	Deut 13:5, 17:7, etc.
You are to seek justice through God's authorities	Romans 13
You are not to testify falsely in any dispute	Exodus 23:2
You are a new creation if you are "in Christ"	Galatians 6:15
You are witnesses for Christ	Acts 1:8
You get your praise from God, not from men	Romans 2:29
You understand Hell is a real place like Heaven	Matthew 10:28
You understand that sin in this life leads to death	Romans 2:12
You know that God's commands are not a burden	1 John 5:3
Your heart fears God and keeps HIS commands	Deut. 5:29
Your perfect love for God offsets your fear of God	1 John 4:18
You have a good understanding because you obey	Psalm 111:10
You do not fear the death of the body	Matthew 10:28
You fear the death of the soul into Hell	Matthew 10:28
You know eternal life comes from obedience	Matthew 19:16-19
You know obeying two commands is eternal life	Matthew 22:40
You know that some people are righteous people	Luke 1:6
You practice righteousness to be like Jesus Christ	1 John 3:7
You know that the Gospel of Jesus is repentance	Matthew 4:17
You know that Jesus preached the kingdom of God	Luke 4:43
You know that Jesus said God was greater than he	John 13:16; 14:28
You know that Jesus said God knew more than he	Mark 12:32
You know that Jesus spoke for God	John 8:27
You know that Jesus did what God told him to do	John 9:4
You know that Jesus always obeyed God	John 8:55
You know that Jesus did nothing of himself	John 8:28
You know that God created Jesus at the beginning	Revelation 3:14
You know that there is only One God the FATHER	1 Cor. 8:6
You know the FATHER is Jesus' God and also ours	John 20:17
You overcome when—Jesus is the Son of God	1 John 5:5

Copyright 2005 Edward G. Palmer, All Rights Reserved.

Book of Edward—Chapter 10

The False Trinity Doctrine

You might want to stop for a moment and place a check mark at every Scripture lesson in the above two tables in which you fully agree with. Then, you should examine those scriptures that you deny carefully. You should have the full understanding, from this apostle, that if you deny any of the Word, you may also be denying Jesus Christ. The power of God's sacrifice is manifested within those who accept all of His Word. If Jesus says to you in Heaven "I never knew you," maybe it's because you never did take the time to get to know the word of God.

> **"Who is he who overcomes the world, but he who believes that Jesus is the Son of God?" 1 John 5:5**

God's Word is clear enough on the subject of who Jesus actually is. The Apostle John also makes it clear that "those who overcome the world believe that Jesus is the Son of God, who has come in the <u>flesh</u>." John teaches us how to know the Spirit of God and the spirit of the Antichrist.

> **"By this you know the Spirit of God: every spirit that confesses that Jesus Christ has come in the flesh is from God, and every spirit that does not confess Jesus [in the flesh as a human] is not from God. And this is the spirit of the Antichrist, of which you have heard that it is coming; and now it is already in the world." 1 John 4:2-3 NRSV**

The phrase "come in the flesh" can only mean "human, exactly like you and I — made with blood and body flesh." Those who claim that Jesus was 100% man <u>and</u> 100% God will be disappointed when Jesus says that he never knew them. The Apostle John also teaches us that a claim of lack of humanity is from the spirit of the Antichrist. If Jesus was a human sacrifice on the cross, it means that we too should be obedient unto death. However, is it really a big sacrifice if God Almighty pulled a fast one and duped us on His cross with His powers? Christians who deny the "human begotten Son" Jesus Christ and his *total humanity* deny Christ and are of the Antichrist.

It Is The Spirit Of The Antichrist That Denies — The 100% <u>Total</u> <u>Humanity</u> Of Jesus!

Copyright 2005 Edward G. Palmer, All Rights Reserved.

The False Trinity Doctrine

If you are wondering why such doctrine is promulgated, the answer is simple. Today, in the 21st Century, Satan is playing a great shell game. The object of the game is to convince Christians that they are powerless. Indeed, they cannot even be righteous people. After all, it took "God" on the cross to cleanse us – "so we can continue our sin unabated" and with impunity. You know, "you just can't help yourselves." The object of the shell game is to alter the character of God into a user-friendlier God. It is a new God focused on forgiveness, which understands your shortcomings and simply forgives all of your continued willful sins and evil deeds. That Satan has convinced Christianity at large of such doctrine cannot be denied. Yet the word of God stands in opposition to such apostasy.

"Then the seventh angel sounded: And there were loud voices in Heaven, saying, 'The kingdoms of this world have become the kingdoms of our LORD [God] and of HIS Christ, and he shall reign forever and ever!'" Rev. 11:15

Kingdoms Of Our LORD And Of HIS Christ!

In many churches it is no longer God Almighty that is worshipped. The church has substituted its new user-friendly god of forgiveness and now calls him Jesus Christ. Doctrines have been developed to seemingly back up this apostasy. The trinity doctrine is the biggest but it does not stand by itself. There are many supporting doctrines of the trinity doctrine like the one about going into the ground temporarily until Jesus comes back. Mankind has to come up with supporting doctrines to rationalize the trinity doctrine. What is missing in Christianity is the simple adherence to the truth of God's Holy Word. Yet this is by Satan's design, not God's.

We live in the world of Christian mythology today and the trinity doctrine heads the list of mythologies and apostasies. The worship of Jesus has evolved into a full-fledged idolatry and God the FATHER is no longer even talked about in many churches. Talk about Jesus leads us to the forgiveness of sins that we cannot avoid. However, talk of God leads to the need for repentance, holiness, righteousness and a sin free life, a discussion to avoid.

Copyright 2005 Edward G. Palmer, All Rights Reserved.

Book of Edward—Chapter 10

The False Trinity Doctrine

Worship Of Jesus Has Evolved Into Idolatry!

God's first commandment is very clear. You should have no other gods before HIM. Not all Christians are confused. Some are starting to make the conscious choice to worship the FATHER as Jesus instructed us to. They have studied Scripture enough with an honest heart for God and have come to realize that worshipping Jesus is actually committing idolatry with God. Consider a recent Internet discussion.

Question: "If we must choose and one path leads to death while the other leads to life, shouldn't we make very sure we choose correctly?"

Carolyn's Answer: "Oh ABSOLUTELY. I choose YHWH and HIM alone."

Question: "If we esteem someone in YHWH's place, how is that not idolatry?"

Carolyn's Answer: "Since investigating Judaism and talking with so many wonderful Jewish people, my eyes have been opened to how Christianity has replaced the worship of YHWH with the worship of Jesus. So … I have changed how I worship. I love to sing songs of praise and worship to the LORD when I'm alone. I change all the references in the songs from Jesus to "FATHER" and sing to HIM exclusively. I also pray directly to YHWH. When on this earth, Jesus worshipped YHWH and prayed to HIM … his disciples did also. So, where and why did Christianity replace YHWH with Jesus? I've encountered a LOT of negativity from Christians when I discuss this with them. They insist Jesus is God and God is Jesus … but I no longer agree. I don't call myself a Christian anymore either … I don't know WHAT I am anymore. It's a scary place to be in, but I'm learning and growing daily … and I LOVE GOD. I believe that's what is important."

Carolyn, the answer of what to call you is clear. You are a <u>real</u> Christian because Jesus has given you an understanding of the FATHER. That is what a Christian was always supposed to be, someone with a relationship with God the FATHER as a result of having known HIS only begotten Son.

Copyright 2005 Edward G. Palmer, All Rights Reserved.

Book of Edward—Chapter 10

The False Trinity Doctrine

Carolyn doesn't have to worry about where she is heading. Unlike those who call themselves Christian and yet practice idolatry, she is headed for Heaven and God's open arms.

So, if a Christian stands firm on the word of God, why should they have to worry about others who are ignorant of God's Word? If those others with "negativity" really had a heart for God, they would be open to the reason of Scripture [James 3:17]. Yes, Christians are making the choice to worship YHWH [God Almighty], as they should. Why is this a problem?

Note: YHWH is the Tetragrammaton or Jewish word used in Hebrew text to describe God Almighty. Later on, Bible scholars started to use the words Jehovah, Yahweh or LORD whenever they encountered the word YHWH in Hebrew text. Jewish people, scared of using God's name in vain, substituted the word Adonai in its place to speak out loud about God.

Many Christians find themselves in the same awkward position that Carolyn did. They started to worship God Almighty [YHWH] and now find themselves at odds with family, friends and their own Christian church. Still others are silent and have given up on trying to really understand Scripture. Even learned and renowned scholars and preachers are confused or do not understand. Men of God, who understand Scripture, admit honestly that they do not comprehend the Christian trinity doctrine.

Consider these honest words of Billy Graham as spoken on KTIS Radio on December 8, 2002 after more than 50 years of Christian ministry. Billy said, "I never really understood how Jesus, the Holy Spirit and the FATHER are equal in all respects." Billy Graham went on to indicate that he had just read a new book on the trinity doctrine but still did not "get it." I've since watched Billy on satellite TV from about 25 years ago preaching. He acknowledged, at that time, that he didn't understand the trinity doctrine.

Let me ask you this question. If Billy Graham, a man of God and after HIS own heart, is honest enough to tell you that after fifty years he still does not understand the trinity doctrine, what makes you think you can?

The False Trinity Doctrine

Think about the number of times that Billy has read his Bible during the last fifty years. Think about the number of Bibles he has been exposed to. Think about the people he has brought to salvation with the honest and simple message that: a) You need Jesus Christ as the Lord of your life; and, b) You need to obey the teachings of Jesus Christ. Do those two things and you will not only get saved, you will also worship the FATHER, not Jesus.

So, what chance do you have of understanding a doctrine that can only be rationalized, a doctrine unsupported by Scripture? A doctrine Billy Graham cannot square with Scripture even after 50 years of study? Scripture speaks directly against the trinity doctrine! Indeed, it is an apostasy and honest men of God, like Billy Graham, will readily admit that they cannot comprehend the trinity doctrine. They also won't distort Scripture.

This is a doctrine of Christian mythology foisted on Christians to take us away from God. It is the backbone of other doctrines that allow sinful lives to flourish instead of ceasing. It is the reason practicing homosexuals and lesbians are ordained into ministry. It is the reason that great injustices are done by pastors and priests. After all, "Jesus will forgive me, won't he? I've got an excuse, don't I? Jesus will forgive my willful sin, won't he?"

> **Jesus said: "If I had not come and spoken to them, they would have no sin, but now they have no excuse for their sin." John 15:22**

"When you understand who sits <u>on</u> the throne, who's in <u>front</u> of it and who sits <u>next</u> to it, you won't try to rationalize the false trinity doctrine!"

The Apostle Edward

God Says: "Jesus Is MY <u>Son</u>!"
It Is Willful Sinners That Rationalize …

The False Trinity Doctrine

Chapter Eleven
God's Eternal Character

— Jesus' Instructions & Model Prayer —

"And when you pray, you shall not be like the hypocrites. For they love to pray standing in the synagogues and on the corners of the streets, that they may be seen by men. Assuredly, I say to you, they have their reward. But you, when you pray, go into your room, and when you have shut your door, pray to your FATHER who is in the secret place; and your FATHER who sees in secret will reward you openly. And when you pray, do not use vain repetitions as the heathen do. For they think that they will be heard for their many words." Matthew 6:5-7

"Therefore I say to you, whatever things you ask when you pray, believe that you receive them, and you will have them."
Mark 11:24

So he [Jesus] said to them, "When you pray, say:

Our FATHER in Heaven,
Hallowed be YOUR name.
YOUR kingdom come.
YOUR will be done
On earth as it is in Heaven.
Give us day by day our daily bread.
And forgive us our sins,
For we also forgive everyone who is indebted to us.
And do not lead us into temptation,
But deliver us from the evil one." Luke 11:2-4

God's Eternal Character

Your new life walking with God started at the very moment you gave God your heart. It was a huge CHOICE that you made directly from your heart. This should have been a point of total surrender to God's authority that you eventually came to in life. You may have reached that decision of your heart either through a great struggle or tragedy in your life or through simply a gift of understanding that God gave you. For me, personally, it was through the gift of understanding that God gave me on one particular day after 32 years of wandering around spiritually in life. Admittedly, it was a low point in my life and my heart was fully open to God's Spirit. It was an epiphany that I will never forget. I will tell you how I personally found God and became HIS apostle in an upcoming chapter. For now ...

It was Friday, May 2 when I finished Chapter 10 and posted it on the Internet for review. God had given me the first page and most of the above paragraph for this chapter before I stopped writing. I remember vividly how awestruck I was at God's providential hand in the life of Jackie and I. That night as I sat with Jackie watching some television, she started to sleep while resting on the couch. As I watched her intently, I couldn't help notice her continued labored breathing. I felt God was telling me once again that it was her time and that it would be soon. I found myself again praying to God for divine healing of Jackie's body. Healing did not come and Jackie died on June 3, a little over four weeks after that particular night.

It is now 5 pm on Friday, August 22 — a full 16 weeks or almost four months after God gave me the opening information for this chapter. I do not know if I am ready to resume. However, God told me this afternoon that it is HIS time. It certainly does not seem like I am emotionally ready yet and certainly things are not perfect. In fact, I have quite the mess on my hands in many regards. Yet today God brought back into my remembrance one of my favorite Bible verses. It is a comment from Solomon on the subject of "waiting for perfect conditions" and it is found in his book of Ecclesiastes.

> **"If you wait for perfect conditions, you will never get anything done." Ecclesiastes 11:14 LIV**

God's Eternal Character

Part of me wants to now rearrange the chapters of this book and just start talking about how awesome God was during the last ninety days of Jackie's life or about healing from HIS perspective. And especially about how HIS Holy presence consumed the atmosphere in our bedroom during Jackie's last days. Even now, tears come to my eyes and my throat swells up just thinking of how much I miss her. God has told me that all of this will be discussed in this book at some point, even some of it now. However, God has ordained this chapter to be focused on HIS eternal character.

Perfect conditions have never existed in my life and God has again reminded me to get on with life. The verse in Ecclesiastes is a literal view of the farmer and the issues with weather that he is up against when it comes to planting and harvesting his crops. Quite literally, "He that observes the wind won't plant [sow] his seeds for fear they will be scattered and he that regards the clouds won't harvest [reap] for fear that rain will damage the crop before he completes the harvest."

Sooner or later you need to get on with living. If you are waiting for events in the family to calm down before you quit smoking, drinking, take counseling or whatever else you have on hold—God's message is that you will never have those perfect conditions. You need to get on with living while you still can. In the thirty-nine years that Jackie and I were married, we had many times of relative calm. They always occurred in between life's stormy periods. We certainly never experienced any "perfect conditions." Today, God called me back to this book in a way that "I knew" it was HE who was talking. Take Solomon's advice and get on with your own life, in line with God's biblical instructions and not your own selfish human ways.

Before I get deeper into God's eternal character, you should know I am not just talking about the God of the Christians. I am talking about the God of the Jews, Christians and Muslims. Yes, these three major world religions claim to worship the same God who I describe in this chapter. How could this be since there has and continues to be so much theological conflict between these religions? The quick answer is that few people in any of these world religions *really* know God's eternal character. At least from a numerical perspective of those who claim they know God.

God's Eternal Character

I am not going to provide a complete list of God's characteristics here because that might encompass a book twice as big. Instead, I will give you the perspective on God that HE guides my spirit to write. If you want to know more about God, read and study your Bible daily for the rest of your life. As each day goes by, God will give you a greater appreciation of whom HE is. Yet, I doubt if we in this human flesh can ever fully comprehend HIS eternal character and nature, until we shed this earthly vessel and assume a heavenly one like Jackie has. In that regard, I am a little envious of her. Still, God has given us more than enough information to really "know" HIM.

Besides God's awesome love, you have already learned the following basic attributes and characteristics of God:

1. God does not change.
2. God does not repent.
3. God does not need a way to fail.
4. God does not pray to himself.
5. God does not worship himself.
6. God did not talk to himself on the cross.
7. God did not commit suicide on the cross.
8. God does not break promises.
9. God did not take the human form of Jesus.

Indeed, you learned that the perfect sacrifice of Jesus was that he was a human in all respects just like you and I. That with a willing heart for God Jesus chose to go to the cross. It was God's love for us that created this final and perfect sacrifice on the cross. It was Jesus' love for God and us that allowed him to be a willing participant in God's plan. Jesus knew the bigger picture and that the earthly trials we suffer must be placed into God's larger context. That is the essence of John 3:16. If you do not fully understand this yet, you should reread the last ten chapters.

The God I am talking about is the God that Jesus worshipped. And understanding the "oneness" that Jesus had with God is as simple as understanding the one flesh that God gives to married couples. How does HE do this? The following verse in the book of Malachi explains "oneness."

God's Eternal Character

> "But did HE not make them one,
> Having a remnant of the Spirit?
> And why one?
> HE seeks godly offspring.
> Therefore take heed to your spirit,
> And let none deal treacherously with the wife of his youth."
>
> **Malachi 2:15**

This section in Malachi teaches us to honor the wife of our youth as God has made us "one" with her. Did HE not make them one [of one flesh]? The prophet Malachi is talking about a covenant marriage made in God's eyes. It is the kind that Jackie and I shared for 39 years. It carries with it the oath of "till death do us part." Yes, HE did make them one [Jackie and I too] and God did it by placing in them and us a remnant of HIS Spirit. All who walk with God will become one with HIM just as Jesus Christ did for exactly the same reason. We choose God with our hearts and HE *then* places HIS Spirit inside of us because we *first* choose to be "one" with HIM. It is the greatest exercise of your free will that you can ever make. And, I might add the most exciting one you can make.

With God and the world, everything is reversed. The world tells you that God will cramp your lifestyle. However, life with God is more exciting than life in this world without HIM. You just don't have the privilege of knowing this until you make an irreversible choice of your heart. To quote some friends, "You can't experience the river of God until you jump into it and get neck deep." It is a real irony that what people think is dull is actually the epitome of excitement on this planet, walking with God. If you claim to be a Christian and you do not have this kind of excitement in this earthly here and now — it is a clear sign that you need a heart check up.

The God that Jesus knew is the same God that Jesus told us in his model prayer instructions to do the following:

1. To pray to God without vain repetitions like hypocrites do.
2. To pray in private and in secret so God will reward us openly.
3. To pray to our FATHER God in Heaven [not to Jesus].

Copyright 2005 Edward G. Palmer, All Rights Reserved.

Book of Edward—Chapter 11

God's Eternal Character

4. To praise God's name [hallowed be YOUR name].
5. To ask for God's kingdom to come, not Jesus'.
6. To ask forgiveness from God for our sins.
7. To forgive others like God forgives us.
8. To ask God to deliver us from sin, temptation and the evil one.

Perhaps you still hold onto the mistaken believe that Jesus is God in spite of the numerous Scriptures that I have already provided you with. If so, you have to believe that Jesus has the character and attributes of God in all respects. In other words, all of God's attributes and characteristics belong to Jesus. Given prior Scripture references, this would probably mean you are not serious about God's Holy Word and is also an indication of the need for a heart check up. Is it possible that Christian dogma or the word of your pastor or bishop is more important than the word of God to you? If Jesus was God, then the God that Moses talked to had to be Jesus. Right? Then consider this biblical teaching on God's character.

Moses went up to the mountain as God commanded to receive a second set of stone tablets of the Ten Commandments. The story is in Exodus 33. At one point, Moses asked God to show him HIS [God's] Glory. God responds to Moses with the following eternal characteristic of HIS.

But HE [God] said, "You cannot see MY face; for no man [flesh] shall see ME, and live." Exodus 33:20

An important characteristic of God is that no human flesh [man] shall see God and live to tell about it. Now ask yourself how many humans saw and dealt with Jesus Christ during his ministry on earth. If this is a true attribute of God as God HIMSELF states, then how can Jesus have been 100% God like so many preachers assert today? It can't be.

The story doesn't stop there. God explains exactly how HE will protect Moses from mortal death by even accidentally seeing God's face. God says HE will cover Moses with HIS hand as HE passes in front of him so "MY face shall not be seen" and you shall live! Who is right? God's Word or the preacher?

God's Eternal Character

> **And the L**ORD **said, "Here is a place by M**E**, and you shall stand on the rock. So it shall be, while M**Y **glory passes by, that I will put you in the cleft of the rock, and will cover you with M**Y **hand while I pass by. Then I will take away M**Y **hand, and you shall see M**Y **back; but M**Y **face shall not be seen." Exodus 33:21-23**

The Israelites in Deuteronomy carry on a discussion about speaking with God [and their fear of it] with the following words to Moses:

> **And you [Moses] said: "Surely the L**ORD **our God has shown us H**IS **glory and H**IS **greatness, and we have heard H**IS **voice from the midst of the fire. We have seen this day that God speaks with man; yet he still lives. Now therefore, why should we die? For this great fire will consume us; if we hear the voice of the L**ORD **our God anymore, then we shall die. For who is there of all flesh who has heard the voice of the living God speaking from the midst of the fire, as we have, and lived? You go near and hear all that the L**ORD **our God may say, and tell us all that the L**ORD **our God says to you, and we will hear and do it." Deut. 5:24-27**

Yes, fear of mortal death consumed the Israelites. Not from being able to actually "see" God as Moses had asked, but simply from being able to hear God's voice. "Moses, you go hear what God has to say and come tell us. For our part, we will hear it from your voice Moses and then do it." Get this picture of God as described in the Holy Bible? This is not Jesus!

After hearing the Israelites, God responds with the following dialogue to Moses.

> **"Then the L**ORD **heard the voice of your words when you spoke to me, and the L**ORD **said to me: 'I have heard the voice of the words of this people which they have spoken to you. They are right in all that they have spoken.' "**

God's Eternal Character

> **"Oh, that they had such a heart in them that they would fear ME and always keep all MY commandments, that it might be well with them and with their children forever!"**
>
> **Deut. 5:28-29**

What a remarkable dialogue in the Holy Bible to illustrate several characteristics of God Almighty. First, that HE is not Jesus is obvious as we were able to see and touch Jesus Christ — who was human like you and I in every respect. It had to be that way! Second, God acknowledges the Israelites fears of death and laments "Oh, that they had such a heart in them that they would fear ME and always keep MY commandments." Why? "That it might be well with them and their children forever!" You could interpret the word forever as "eternally" and it would also be correct.

What a contrast we have in today's society. Not only do preachers teach the apostasy that the commandments of God no longer matter, they also teach that it is okay to sin because Jesus has you covered. Isn't that the essence of the message of Christianity today, you just can't help but sin?

My spirit senses another part of God's lament that is not so apparent. I believe that God also feels sad that these Israelites are acknowledging that they do not have the faith inside of them to deal with God directly. Isn't it apparent that many of their hearts are not truly with God? If you want to fellowship with God directly like Moses, Jesus and even I, it starts with your heart. Part of that heart function is an actual fear in knowing that an eternal destination does await each of us, either Heaven or Hell. From that fear, we make conscious decisions not to sin. We reason correctly that sin will bring eternal damnation. Jesus Christ has not altered the characteristic of God in which punishment is certain. That is why Jesus said: "There are now no excuses for man's sin." Do you think that the Episcopalian bishops [1] who recently ordained an openly homosexual bishop in Minneapolis have any fear of God? Not only don't they fear HIM, it is evident that they do not have a foggy idea of who God is. Either that or they have simply chosen the wrong side of the fence. Surely as bishops they cannot be that ignorant of God's Holy Word on the subject of the "sin" of homosexuality. How could that be? All those years of studying, what were they reading?

Copyright 2005 Edward G. Palmer, All Rights Reserved.

God's Eternal Character

They certainly demonstrated a lack of 20/20 vision [understanding]! Hear God's Word, which summarizes the issue of fear of God and sin.

"That HIS fear may be before you, so that you may not sin."
Exodus 20:20

Moses fear <u>and</u> love for God from his upright heart allowed Moses to both dialogue with God and fall down on his face in worship and respect for whom God was. Moses is an example of what the New Testament means when it says "Perfect love casts out fear." Love for God from an upright heart is a counterbalance to the fear of God and both of these attributes allow us to keep God's commandments. Indeed, "Oh that all of us had such a heart for God." Moses certainly did. So did Jesus. Likewise, you too can have such a heart. You just need to get your biblical facts straight and only worship God and not worship a messenger of God [Jesus].

God is a God of love, but make no mistake about HIS promise of sure punishment for sin. If you think you can use Jesus as a kind of justification for willful sin in your life, you need to carefully consider that God is also a punisher of those who "sin." Study carefully the verses below and explain to me exactly which ones you think Jesus has changed for you.

God says: "I will judge you [each of us] for the way you have lived and will make you pay for everything you have done that I hate." Ezekiel 7:8 NCV

God says: "I will show no pity, and I will not hold back punishment. I will pay you back for the way you have lived and the things you have done that I hate. Then you will know that I am the LORD who punishes." Ezekiel 7:9 NCV

Now reconsider Hebrews 10:26 in the context of the above two verses. Any Christian [regardless of status] that teaches your sin no longer matters to God if you claim Jesus is a liar. The Spirit of God told me that they are "toast" and nothing but false prophets lying to God's people.

Book of Edward—Chapter 11

God's Eternal Character

God speaks out against lying prophets [teachers] in Ezekiel 13.

God says: "Say to those who make up their own prophecies: 'Listen to the word of the LORD.' " Ezekiel 13:2 NCV

God says: "Your prophets see false visions and prophesy lies. They say, 'This is the message of the LORD, when the LORD has not sent them. But they still hope their words will come true.' " Ezekiel 13:6 NCV

God says: "By lying to MY people, who listen to lies, you have killed people who should not die, and you have kept alive those who should not live." Ezekiel 13:19 NCV

God says: "By your lies you have caused those who did right to be sad, when I did not make them sad. And you have encouraged the wicked not to stop being wicked, which would have saved their [eternal] lives." Ezekiel 13:22 NCV

I've lost track of the false teachings foisted onto Christians ignorant of the Bible. How will you know the truth and if you are a real brother or sister in Christ? You will only know the truth by getting informed on God's Word. God says: "Listen to the word of the LORD." Isn't that a simple instruction?

In God's eyes, it is an absolute insult to claim that sin no longer matters with the blood of Jesus. God's eternal character says otherwise!

God says: "Is it unimportant that the people ... are doing the hateful things they have done here? They have filled the land with violence and made ME continually angry. Look, they are insulting ME every way they can."
                                                   Ezekiel 8:17 NCV

God says: "You did not live by MY rules or obey MY laws. Instead, you did the same things as the nations [people] around you [did]." Ezekiel 11:12 NCV

God's Eternal Character

Today it is estimated that 80% or more of the people in Israel are now secular in nature and have no respect for God. The news recently reported a Gay Pride[2] parade in Israel to celebrate the sin of homosexuality. In the United States, we are now busy kicking the Ten Commandments out of every institution in our land. In fact, a legal debate[3] now rages over even using the word God and whether our eyes should be exposed to the dangers of a public monument of the Ten Commandments in Montgomery, Alabama.

Secular social forces in the USA fight to prevent your eyes from even seeing the Ten Commandments in any public place. At the same time, these forces fight for open homosexuality and the right to teach your children the homosexual lifestyle. Even to broadcast unseemly sexual content into your home television during primetime evening hours. There is little doubt that a race is on to secularize the United States. It is a race to extricate God from every aspect of our lives. While 80% of the people in the USA might claim to believe in God, few of them do anything to support God and show HIM that they really do believe. I wonder if the United States isn't just as secular as Israel from a practical standpoint? Where is the voice of the masses of concerned believers in this country? Indeed, the masses are absent in the arena in pubic debate. The Montgomery Ten Commandments monument is a tell tale sign that few people nationally really do care about God's word. In the sixty's, thousands of protestors marched the streets for Negro rights. How many march the streets for the right to acknowledge God? Where are the masses in Christianity to defend even the idea of saying the word "God?"

Yet the new covenant of God no longer holds the nation collectively accountable. The new covenant of God holds each one of us individually accountable. That doesn't mean we won't suffer by living in a nation, state or city that is disrespectful or insulting towards God. We will. It rains on good and evil people simultaneously. What effects society at large will affect each individual in some way. None of us leads an isolated life.

Mankind has taken the blood of God's only begotten Son Jesus Christ and turned it into a huge insult and slam against God Almighty. It has done this with Christian teachings that promote "getting along" over God's Holy Word. God doesn't want us to behave like the heathens that surround us.

God's Eternal Character

That much is clear in Ezekiel. With or without Jesus in our hearts it makes no difference to God. Our behavior betrays who we are in God's eyes. Jesus is God's enforcer; he is not God's excuse maker. Jesus is also not an excuse you can use with God. The Apostle Paul asks: "Shall we continue in sin?" He then provides a direct answer with an emphatic "certainly not!" Hebrews 10:26 is the warning that eternal damnation awaits those who would treat the blood of Jesus as a common thing by continued willful sin. Anyone who supports a willful sin — commits a willful sin!

God also takes it as a huge insult when His Word is perverted to support any form of sin. To state in any way that God's Word or any part of it supports sin is a form of blasphemy against God's Spirit. It is a sin with severe consequences. Don't lie about what God's Word says and remember that sin is what God says we should not do. God is the ONE who defines what is sinful behavior. It is not your lesbian or homosexual bishop that defines sin! No, their job is to rationalize their sin just like the Apostle Paul states they did in his day [Romans chapters 1-2]. Sin is an old game.

God's Logic For Punishing Sinners!

Listen carefully to what I am about to say to you. God has a simple reason why HE punishes the person who sins. HIS logic for punishment of sinners and eternal life for those who do good is contained in Ezekiel. HIS ability to forgive is certainly one of HIS eternal characteristics. However, HIS ability to punish is something now totally forgotten in Christianity.

> **God says: "If I tell good people, 'You will surely live,' they might think they have done enough good and then do evil. Then none of the good things they did will be remembered. They will die because of the evil." Ezekiel 33:13 NCV**

> **God says: "When I tell the good man, 'You shall live,' and when he relies upon his goodness and commits iniquity [sin], none of his good deeds shall be remembered, he shall die for the iniquity [sin] he has committed." Ezekiel 33:13 MOF**

God's Eternal Character

> **God says: "When I shall say to the [uncompromisingly] righteous that he shall surely live, and he trusts to his own righteousness [to save him] and commits iniquity (heinous sin), all his righteous deeds shall not be [seriously] remembered; but for his perversity *and* iniquity that he has committed he shall die." Ezekiel 33:13 AMP**

Pastor Bill, if you are reading this, "Listen to the word of the LORD!"

If you call yourself a Christian, perk up your ears to the word of God. This is a very serious discussion and I am giving you God Almighty's logic to punish sinners. I have provided three translations. I like the New Century Version, but the Moffatt and Amplified translations make the point clear. I could have listed many other translations, but they are all basically the same.

Here is the main point. God does *not* reward you for doing one or more righteous deeds. HE rewards you for being a righteous [good] person all the time. HE knows you will make mistakes. That is not an issue with God. However, you cannot rely upon anything good you have done in the past as justification or offsetting for doing any thing evil today. Let me rephrase that a little. No amount of good you have done in the past will justify any amount of evil [iniquity, sin] you might want to do in the future.

You might think of your walk with God as being on a one-way street. You cannot turn back from righteousness and go the opposite way [towards sin] without incurring eternal damnation. You can also *not* play on both sides of the fence meaning doing good one day and then sinning the next. No one has salvation with God who is willfully both good and evil. That means if you think your Sunday church prayers will make up for the week of sins, you are mistaken. God doesn't expect one, two or even many [good] righteous deeds. HE expects righteousness for the rest of your life.

Copyright 2005 Edward G. Palmer, All Rights Reserved.

Book of Edward—Chapter 11

God's Eternal Character

I suspect that about now someone is thinking but "I have Christ Jesus." If you believe preachers like Charles Stanley, you might be right. But let me ask you this question. Is Charles Stanley's eternal salvation story a higher level of moral authority than God Almighty? Remember, the verses cited above are ones in which God HIMSELF is speaking. Charles or God?

Therefore, an important characteristic of God is that HE will punish sinners with or without Christ. I suspect God will punish sinners who claim Christ is their salvation much more severely for insulting the Spirit of grace. Do you remember that I showed you earlier where Christ said that there is a minimum righteousness standard? Christ is not your ticket to eternal life. Your new one-way walk of righteousness through Christ Jesus is! In fact, that new behavior actually demonstrates that Christ is in your heart and that you received God's message delivered by Christ. Remember Apostle John's teaching that "those who practice righteousness are righteous like Christ?"

Nothing that God has said in Ezekiel has changed with Jesus. The above punishment characteristic of God is eternal in nature as is HIS logic for punishing sinners. You might be now thinking that this characteristic, logic and word of the LORD runs counter to the salvation doctrine you've been taught in your Christian church. Guess what? You've been taught apostasy. You've been misled. I will tell you God's truth of salvation in the next chapter. For now, reflect on what God is trying to teach you. Also, reflect on how these words from God will affect those Episcopalians who openly support the willful sin of homosexuality. A righteous, practicing homosexual or lesbian? Not if you <u>listen</u> to the word of the LORD!

God is a God of forgiveness and always has been despite Christian doctrine that claims salvation is only through "accepting Jesus Christ in your heart." That too is a myth and a misrepresentation of God's Holy Word. HIS forgiveness is eternal and also shown in Ezekiel. Listen to the Word.

> **God says: "Or, if I say to the wicked people, 'You will surely die,' they may stop sinning and do what is right and honest. For example, they may return what somebody gave them as a promise to repay a loan, or pay [give] back what they stole."**

God's Eternal Character

> **"If they live by the rules that give life and do not sin, then they will surely live, and they will not die. They will not be punished for any of their sins. They now do what is right and fair, so they will surely live." Ezekiel 33:14-16 NCV**

Live By The Rules That <u>Give</u> Life!

Bill, if you are reading this, "Listen to the word of the LORD!" There is still hope for you and the other people involved in your thefts if you return the church and all other property that you stole from God, men and women. Nothing on this earth is worth losing eternal life over, especially material things. Not even your pride and the pride of your wife and family is worth losing the salvation of yourself and those whom you love. Think about it. This is God's Holy Word. Nothing you can do will alter HIS eternal nature and character. Your only hope is to comply with God's rules that give life!

God Is A Forgiver <u>And</u> A Punisher!

No doubt Bill and his fellow thieves might be thinking that God is unfair by establishing such standards for HIS people. It sounds like God now expects Bill and crew to give back all that they stole. Yes, that is exactly what God expects from them. It is a good trade too. They give back the material stuff they stole and turn their hearts away from wickedness and to righteousness and THEN they get eternal life. Sounds good. You can read the same "unfair" thoughts from the Israelites in Ezekiel as shown below.

> **God says: "Your people say: 'The way of the LORD is not fair.' But it is their own ways that are not fair. When the good people stop doing good and do evil, they will die for their evil. But when the wicked stop doing evil and do what is right and fair, they will live. You still say: 'The way of the LORD is not fair.' Israel [Christianity], I will judge all of you by your own ways." Ezekiel 33:17-20 NCV**

Copyright 2005 Edward G. Palmer, All Rights Reserved.

Book of Edward—Chapter 11

God's Eternal Character

Now, take a moment to reflect on your understanding of Christian teaching today. Do not Charles Stanley[4] and others preach that all you need to do is accept Jesus Christ as your Lord? That once this takes place nothing can keep you from your heavenly journey? Yes, if you thought that this teaching sounds a little like the expectations of the Israelites, you were right. They thought they had it in the eternal bag with God for a variety of reasons. Christianity has just consolidated all the reasons of the Israelites into the personage of Jesus Christ so that Christians can have only one good reason.

A lot of Christians like the concept of majority rule. You know that 51% of corporate shareholders control most corporations. A simple 51% majority also elects our congressmen and senators. 51% outweighs 49% in our way of thinking, doesn't it? That is the democratic way, isn't it? No doubt that many preachers in the past and present view sinning with God exactly that way. On balance, they say, I am good; because my life's 51% righteousness certainly outweighs my life's 49% evil. To this extent, you can view life as a simple stack of deeds. How about 100 for illustration?

Life As A Stack Of 100 Deeds

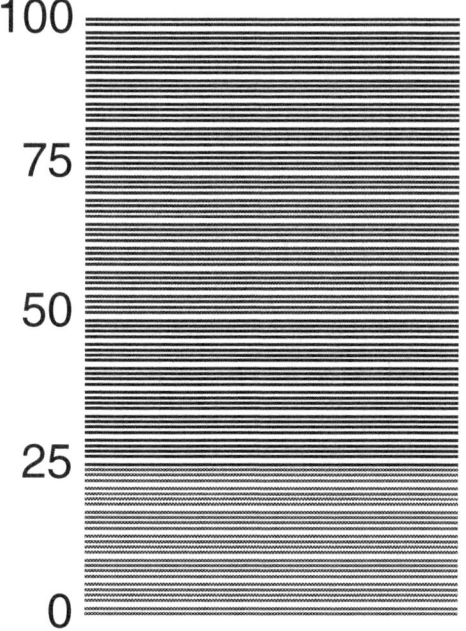

Copyright 2005 Edward G. Palmer, All Rights Reserved.

Book of Edward—Chapter 11

God's Eternal Character

Each deed in life can be either good or evil. You are the one that gets to decide. If your actions in life choose to support evil like the Episcopal bishops that voted to support the sin of homosexuality in the church of God, then that counts as an evil deed [sin] even if you are not the homosexual sinner himself. If you want to know why, you only have to consider what the Apostle James wrote about sin. It clarifies the matter of sin and is broader than any list of sins. The Apostle James writes …

"Therefore, to him who knows to do good and does not do it, to him it is sin." James 4:17 NKJV

"So any person who knows what is right to do but does not do it, to him it is sin." James 4:17 AMP

This is one of those times to perk up your ears to the word of God. This definition of sin will be applied to you in addition to the sins that God itemized such as homosexuality, etc. By the way, don't think for a moment that I am a homophobe. It is not my definition of sin! Therefore, if anyone wants to label me that way, they should know that it is God who is at the receiving end, not I. A classic tactic in the realm of justifying this and other sin is to call those who oppose the sin names. How childish in God's eyes.

I like this definition, especially the clarity of the Amplified Bible. It is tailor fitted to virtually every individual. That is because the standard shifts. Think about it. The average Episcopal Church member might be ignorant of God's Word on the sin of homosexuality, but those Episcopal bishops know better. Therefore, for those ignorant, God might view their supporting this sin as unintentional [assuming their heart is otherwise right with God]. However, it is certainly considered a willful sin by someone as knowledgeable as a bishop. Nice touch God. It really covers the sin bases.

In another illustration, I bore witness to the theft of Solid Rock Church. I have studied corporate law for my own business adventures for over 25 years. When the pastor manipulated the Articles of Incorporation and By-Laws, it went right over the heads of the average member of the church, but I understood. Do you think God holds me to a higher standard?

God's Eternal Character

Do you think that what the average member needed to do was a little different than what I needed to do? Exactly. What is determined to be right is in the eyes of each individual based upon the knowledge and information they have in hand. Not understanding that something evil had taken place left the average member of Solid Rock Church with virtually nothing to do. Understanding the depth of the pastor's evil left me with a lot to do.

I know a fellow named Gaylen who is very knowledgeable of the Bible. Gaylen once told me that he refused to be a teacher to others because God would hold teachers to a higher standard. This is true. However, what Gaylen fails to realize is that the knowledge he has acquired automatically puts him at a higher standard in the eyes of God. In other words, those who are more informed know better than those who are less informed. And it is not just what is in the Bible that matters. God has written HIS laws on our hearts and in our minds. Therefore, in the area of willfully supporting the sin of homosexuality in the church, I doubt if anyone who supports it has any excuse with God. To do so is sin, plain and simple.

Going back to the life as a stack of 100 deeds analogy. You can easily understand the visual patterns of a generally good and evil person.

Copyright 2005 Edward G. Palmer, All Rights Reserved.

Book of Edward—Chapter 11

God's Eternal Character

A Generally Evil Person

Besides the two graphics above, there is the "on-balance" graphic below. This graphic reflects the attitude of many Christians today. In the back of their minds, their deeds are weighed on a balance scale. With 51/49 in their favor, they feel that the scales of eternal life are tipped in their favor. They are, unfortunately, very wrong in their understanding of God's eternal nature and His view of what our life should be if we are really with Him.

On Balance, I am a Good Person

Copyright 2005 Edward G. Palmer, All Rights Reserved.

Book of Edward—Chapter 11

God's Eternal Character

God's idea is that when we are with HIM that we are on a one-way street and are now "slaves to righteousness." Therefore, there should be zero willful sin and only some unintentional or unknown sin as discussed earlier in the book. This is especially true for all who call themselves a Christian as one of the principal attributes of "putting on the new man" in Christ Jesus, is the rejection of anything evil in the eyes of God Almighty.

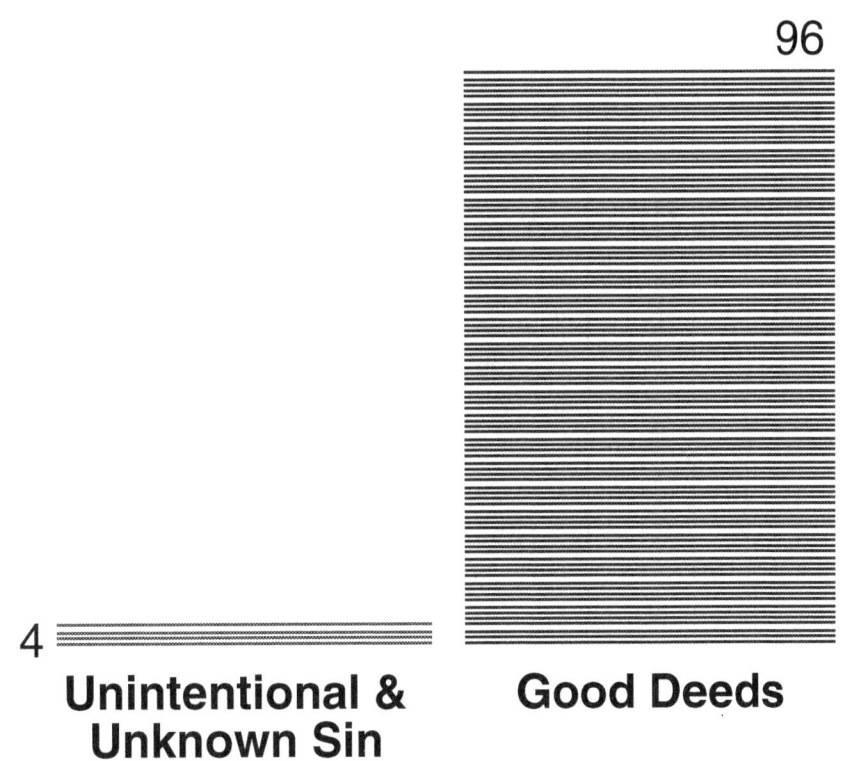

God gave me this graphic analogy to help explain why HE established the rules HE outlined in Ezekiel. You need to fully expect that God will forgive your sins, even without Jesus Christ, if you turn from your evil and wicked ways. You need to also understand that no matter how much you claim Jesus Christ as your savior, it will not keep you from eternal damnation if you lead a life of willful sin. When you appreciate these truths, you will understand whom Jesus means when he said: "I never knew you."

God's Eternal Character

It might have been easier for you to grasp had Jesus simply said: "Get away from me you who willfully sin." God said: "Listen to the word of the LORD!" Jesus Christ only told you what God told him to say. For the sake of your salvation and all whom you know, think about what Jesus Christ has taught us. The operative phrase is "you who practice lawlessness [sin]."

> **"Not everyone who says to me, 'Lord, Lord,' shall enter the kingdom of Heaven, but he who does the will of my FATHER in Heaven. Many will say to me in that day, 'Lord, Lord, have we not prophesied in your name, cast out demons in your name, and done many wonders in your name?' And then I will declare to them, 'I never knew you; depart from me, you who practice lawlessness!'" Matthew 7:21-23**

Depart You Christians Who Practice Lawlessness!

You simply cannot operate on both sides of good and evil with God. It goes against HIS eternal holy character, which does not change. Ezekiel came with the word of God and so did Jesus. Nothing has changed. Now examine carefully again the entire reference above and you will find out that Jesus is talking directing to Christians. Who doesn't make it? Christians who think they can do both good and evil, and that as long as their good stacks higher than their evil, they have eternal life. Guess again. If you put on the "new man" through Jesus Christ, it is a one-way street with God that does not permit willful sin in your life. You are now supposed to be a slave unto righteousness, not a willful sinner or an accomplice to sin.

Why didn't God through Jesus speak in clearer language so we could all understand that HE was talking about willful sin? God told me while proof reading this page that HE is looking for those who will make a free "choice of the heart" for HIM. Remember, HIS laws are in our minds and hearts. It is really a matter of people choosing not to listen. Indeed, some parts of the Word are confusing to people, but not to those whose hearts belong to God. HIS Spirit will enlighten them as needed in their life.

Copyright 2005 Edward G. Palmer, All Rights Reserved.

Book of Edward—Chapter 11

God's Eternal Character

Before leaving this discussion, let me summarize exactly what Jesus Christ does for the Christian with the graphic illustration below. When we put on the "new man" and shed the "old man", we are literally shifting from a life without God to a life with God. That shift is accompanied by a big change in our heart. Apostle Paul describes the second aspect of our salvation with the words "belief in our heart unto righteousness." Get the picture. If we are with God, sin is anathema to us in every form that it takes. For us, there is no more willful sin in our lives, only unintentional or unknown sins. God covers those sins with the blood of Jesus Christ.

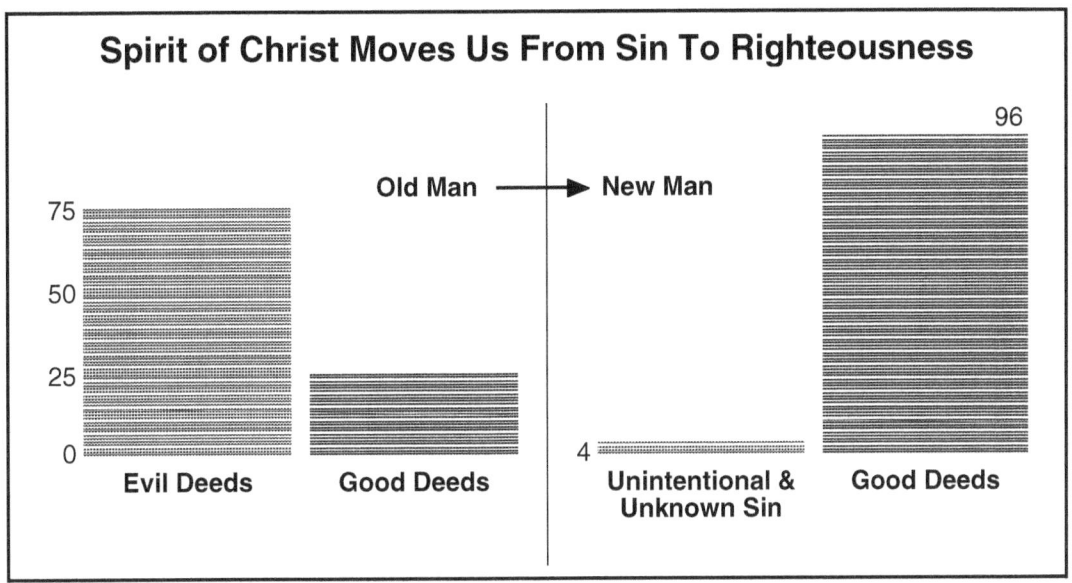

"What shall we say then? Shall we continue in sin that grace may abound? Certainly not! How shall we who died to sin live any longer in it?" Romans 6:1-2

"Knowing this, that our old man was crucified with him, that the body of sin might be done away with, that we should no longer be slaves of sin. For he who has died has been freed from sin." Romans 6:6-7

Those "In Christ" Have Died To Willful Sin!

God's Eternal Character

Now consider that the Episcopal bishops who voted to support the sin of homosexuality in the church have now directly sent people to their eternal death because they have failed to teach God's Word. That is the message of Ezekiel 13:22 from God HIMSELF. Therefore, God will reserve a special punishment for those who enable and support the sin of others. Here is HIS message. Do not do anything that will cause another person to sin. You will be held accountable to God. If you do not speak up when you know better, it is willful sin. If you turn your back and fail to take action, it is willful sin. If you know what is right to do, but do not do it, it is willful sin.

> **"But whoever causes one of these little ones who believe in me to sin, it would be better for him if a millstone were hung around his neck, and he were drowned in the depth of the sea." Matthew 18:6**

Note: When the Bible says you should not be relying upon your own righteousness, there are at least a couple of aspects to it. First, do not ever think that what you have done in life is ever good enough. That is clearly relying upon your own stack of good deeds to offset some evil in your life. You can see clearly that this is bad reasoning in the context of God's eternal character. Second, relying upon God or Christ's righteousness means that you rely upon "their definition" of what righteousness is. It does not mean you rely upon God or Christ's own righteousness. Jesus Christ's sacrifice is not a security blanket that covers continued willful sin; it is a spiritual end of sin in those who truly believe. Indeed, the spirit of Christ transforms our deeds, beliefs, attitudes, etc. into conformance with God's requirements.

We Conform To God's Requirements In Christ!

> **"I know that whatever God does,
>   It shall be forever.
>   Nothing can be added to it,
>   And nothing taken from it.
>   God does it, that men should fear before HIM." Eccles. 3:14**

God's Eternal Character

It is the nature of God that HIS character is eternal and unchanging. Now, consider Solomon's next verse, which reflects upon man's life.

> **"That which is has already been,**
> **And what is to be has already been;**
> **And God requires an account of what is past." Eccles. 3:15**

Long before modern man wrongfully accepted too much change back from the mistaken store clerk, he was doing it back in Solomon's time. Just yesterday, the store clerk at a local home building supply-company, failed to ring up $80.00 in paneling that I was purchasing. I mentally calculated my bill at about $260.00 right at the cash register. She rang up $180.00 because instead of nine ten-dollar panels, she only counted one. I could have simply walked out of the store with the ill-gotten gain of $80.00 but I did not do it. She told me that I probably slept better than a lot of people. She is right.

First, I reasoned that I know better. It is one thing when I am not with it mentally and the clerk makes an error I don't catch. While Jackie was dying, I walked out of the same store with an extra $110.00 worth of lawn furniture. I was totally unaware of the clerk's failure to ring it up. Quite frankly, I was also a little fried mentally. However, within a few hours, I was studying the store receipt and observed the clerk's failure to charge me. I went back to the store and made it right. The store gave me a discount on the chase lounge because I was honest. However, that was not my goal.

I always want to do what is right because that is precisely what God requires of me. Further, I want to help others like the store clerk do what is right because that is also what God requires of me. No willful sin and no enabling others to sin. All of God's rules of life are this easy to understand.

This is just one illustration of the opportunity to sin in the life of man. There are endless opportunities to sin or to do what is right. Nothing is new. Everything man does has already been done in regards to righteousness and sin. What we do today has already been done. What we will do in the future has already been done. And God requires an accounting of our past!

God's Eternal Character

God Requires An Accounting Of Our Past!

Mankind's nature runs endlessly on a sin treadmill never making any spiritual progress without intervention. That is because our inherent desire to sin does not change without us first getting a change of heart. Man's sin might seem comical to God if it weren't so sad. He probably says: "There they go again." What does alter our self-serving evil nature? It is the Spirit of God that sets us on the new path of rejecting sin at every turn in life. That Spirit is also one of the gifts of Jesus Christ. To activate it spiritually with Jesus requires a new and changed heart from us. We must acknowledge the truth of God and our sinful ways. This involves repentance [stop doing evil deeds]. Righteousness is then evidence of our "rebirth" and new motives. Indeed, that is how we get "reborn" in the spiritual sense as Christ taught.

> **"All the ways of a man are pure in his own eyes, but the Lord weighs the spirits." Proverbs 16:2**
>
> **"People may be pure in their own eyes, but the Lord examines their motives." Proverbs 16:2 NLT**
>
> **"I, the Lord, search the heart,**
> **I test the mind,**
> **Even to give every man according to his ways,**
> **According to the fruit of his doings." Jeremiah 17:10**
>
> **"For we speak as messengers who have been approved by God to be entrusted with the Good News. Our purpose is to please God, not people. He is the one who examines the motives of our hearts." 1 Thess. 2:4 NLT**

To Change Motives Requires A Changed Heart!

"If you claim Christ's salvation, you better have a new heart as shown by righteous behavior or it doesn't count with God!" The Apostle Edward

---

Copyright 2005 Edward G. Palmer, All Rights Reserved.

God's Eternal Character

Why would I say that? Is it anything different than what the Apostle James taught? What do we know that you don't? It gets back to knowledge of God's character and the words HE spoke to Ezekiel. Listen to the Word.

> **"I will put MY Spirit inside you and help you live by MY rules and carefully obey MY laws." Ezekiel 36:27 NCV**

Got Jesus? Really? If so, you've got God's Holy Spirit inside of you. Now ask these questions. If God's Spirit is really inside of you, do you think HE wants to hang out at the Gay and lesbian bar with you? How about watch porn movies with you? What about going down to the state office with you and filing false Articles of Incorporation so you can steal your congregational church away from its membership? How about going into a courtroom and bearing false witness with you? Do you think God wants to be there with you in any "sinful" situation? Got Jesus? Really? If so, you've got God's Holy Spirit inside of you. If your actions don't demonstrate it, you don't have it. Yes, your walk must match your talk with God or your mouth that espouses Jesus Christ, as savior, is nonsense to God.

> **"HE saved us, not because of the good things we did, but because of HIS mercy. HE washed away our sins and gave us a new life through the Holy Spirit. HE generously poured out the Spirit upon us because of what Jesus Christ our savior did." Titus 3:5-6 NLT**

In Christ, God's Spirit Is Poured Out Abundantly!

Indeed, to those in Christ Jesus, God pours out HIS Holy Spirit in abundance. This Holy Spirit is also called the Spirit of truth. Those who espouse salvation in Christ and then say that sinful lifestyles are okay with Christ and his salvation commit blaspheme against the Spirit of God. They crucify Christ again and again on the cross with each new sin they claim is sanctioned by Christ. You Episcopal bishops who voted to support the sin of homosexuality know better; Christ's salvation is only <u>unto</u> righteousness!

God's Eternal Character

> **"I do not enjoy seeing you die," the LORD God says. "Turn, turn and live!" Ezekiel 18:32 LIV**

In modern day parlance, the message is simply: "Get a new life!" It has always been God's character to continually offer you a chance to repent and start anew with HIM. God sees your repentance as sincere when HE witnesses the righteous behavior that stems and flows out of a changed and new heart. A heart within us that allows us to obey HIS "rules that give life."

God Judges According To Our Ways!

God will judge all of us according to what we have done in our lives. This is our motives, thoughts, actions, deeds, etc. Christians who willfully sin betray themselves as evil people destined for punishment. Then there is the matter of Christian confusion over the issue of judging. I talked to my friend Mike in Wisconsin last week. He met an Episcopalian and inquired of him exactly what the Episcopal Church and his beliefs were.

To Mike's astonishment, this Episcopalian stated that his church did not believe in judging anyone for any thing. If so, I guess that explains how their bishops sanctioned and even blessed the sin of homosexuality in their church. I also read a recent comment from another Episcopalian who said: "I don't really understand all the Bible has to say about homosexuality."

Judge not lest ye be judged. How often have you heard those words espoused from the pulpit? Today, in Christianity, it is not popular to judge anyone in the Church. It is not just Episcopalians that have the mistaken idea that judging is not an acceptable Christian behavior. After all, Christ said he did not come to judge the world, so why should we judge others? Once again we have a clear demonstration of the ignorance of God's Word and also the ignorance of God's eternal character in the Church.

Let me state that this type of message is often deliberately taught by preachers to cover their own sin and the sins of their congregation. But does the Bible really teach us not to judge others, to hide sin in the Church?

Copyright 2005 Edward G. Palmer, All Rights Reserved.

God's Eternal Character

On this side of the issue of judging, the message to Christians is that you do not judge anyone for anything if you are really saved. Let God take care of the issue is one instruction I've personally heard from Christian authorities. Really? Is that biblical?

On the other side of the issue of judging are people like Paul J. Hill [5], the 49-year old former Presbyterian minister who gunned down a Florida abortion doctor. His state execution is scheduled for tonight. Paul Hill said that he felt no remorse and suggested that the state will be making him a martyr. This is the first execution in the United States for anti-abortion violence according to the news on MSNBC.

For Paul Hill, this isn't "anti-abortion violence" like MSNBC [6] and other media sources euphemistically report. For him it is a fully rationale act easy to comprehend. If you just kill one abortion doctor, you can save hundreds perhaps thousands of babies from being killed. Paul Hill was executed in a humane way with a lethal injection. But in Paul Hill's mind, the abortion doctors are literally butchering new babies by tearing their limbs apart one at a time to excise them from their mother's uterus. No painkillers and it's not a pretty picture. There is a growing body of scientific evidence that supports his thinking. How about the fact that babies are now observed with ultrasound "running away" from the doctor's killing tools? That is to say they are trying to get the farthest away from the doctor in the mother's womb to avoid being killed.

How about the fact that fertilized eggs in the embryonic stage can be adopted out to an infertile woman and grown within her own uterus? The embryo then grows into a full-fledged baby. Some of these embryo implants are reported to be entering teen years or adulthood. Think about this. It is a fact that if we kill a fertilized egg in the embryonic stage, we kill human life in that stage of development. Placed in a willing mother's womb, the embryo has all he or she needs to grow into a full human baby. I suspect God is bringing science into the arena to help educate us on the miracle of childbirth. Quite frankly, Paul Hill has more than enough scientific facts to rationalize his position on killing what he would term legalized baby killers. Yet, did Paul Hill actually do God's will with his act of murder?

Copyright 2005 Edward G. Palmer, All Rights Reserved.

Book of Edward—Chapter 11

God's Eternal Character

Note: To give you a time reference, it is Sept 3 this day and Jackie has been gone for three full months. I am feeling the emotional pain of her loss today to accompany some very heavy physical pain I feel in my body. It is now twelve days since I restarted writing this chapter. God is with me.

The Reverend Michael Bray writes in an Internet article[7] on Sept 2 after quoting some Scripture and speaking of Paul Hill, "we jail or murder our own prophets." He goes on to conclude: "But let us not fail to honor him [Paul Hill] as one [prophet of God]." Really? Was Paul Hill a prophet of God as Mr. Bray and others believe? Did the State of Florida kill God's prophet when they executed Paul Hill? How do we determine if this is true?

We know that God will judge man according to his ways. So what about us? Are we really supposed to not judge others according to their ways? Aren't we created in the image of God? As we emulate Jesus, don't we emulate God's character as Jesus did? Wouldn't this include judging?

Will Paul Hill receive a "great reward" in Heaven like he believed? Will he be a martyr in God's eyes or is he just another sinner? Wasn't he supposed to know God's Word better than the average believer given his ministerial education? Here we have two examples of opposite positions in terms of Christians judging others. Let's resolve the issue of Paul Hill first and consider only the written word of the LORD to get our answers.

The issue of being of prophet must be dealt with to satisfy those in the Christian community like the Reverend Bray. The first thought that came to my mind was whether or not prophets premeditatedly murdered people. I don't think so. However, I will do a quick search of the biblical text. Nope. I cannot find any instance in the Bible where a prophet premeditatedly murdered someone. Elijah did execute four hundred-fifty false prophets for God in 1 Kings 18. However, the penalty for false prophets is death and Elijah was only seeing to it that the word of God was carried out.

God used prophets to deliver HIS news of impending doom or disaster. God also used prophets to either deliver HIS Word to the people at large or to a specific individual. Prophets were messengers of God, not murderers.

God's Eternal Character

If you believe in the awesome power of God Almighty like I do, I can assure you that HE doesn't need Paul Hill or anyone else to execute abortion doctors. How much more effective for the population would it be if God struck the doctor dead HIMSELF. Read the story of Elijah in 1 Kings 18 to see the impact that God had on the people by raining down fire from the sky.

God could have supernaturally consumed this abortion doctor in the public square at midday in a lasting fire from the sky that the television cameras could record. Imagine a toasted abortion doctor carried on world television with the clear message that it was God Almighty who did it. Now that would get the people's attention. Paul Hill's death didn't even register as a concern on the average person's mental radar screen. A recent poll of prolife supporters indicate that 66% believe Paul Hill actually hurt the cause of trying to put an end to abortion murder. Why? He violated God's law!

Example: Prophet Elijah asks God to rain down fire.

"Hear me, O LORD, hear me, that this people may know that YOU are the LORD God, and that YOU have turned their hearts back to YOU again. Then the fire of the LORD fell and consumed the burnt sacrifice, and the wood and the stones and the dust, and it licked up the water that was in the trench." 1 Kings 18:37-38

God's Character Is Also Metaphysical!

Metaphysical means originating not in the physical world but somewhere outside it. A rain of fire from the sky on the request of a prophet is metaphysical. God has intervened metaphysically in my life a number of times. That is to say God has altered the reality I faced in many instances by altering something physical. God's character takes on a metaphysical nature whenever HE decides. Therefore, I can tell you that it is no big deal for HIM to end a Florida abortion doctor's life whenever HE chooses to. God doesn't need Paul Hill or anyone else to premeditatedly murder any abortion doctor.

God's Eternal Character

Example: Prophet delivering some bad news of impending death.

"In those days Hezekiah was sick and near death. And Isaiah the prophet, the son of Amoz, went to him and said to him, thus says the LORD: 'Set your house in order, for you shall die, and not live.' " 2 Kings 20:1

God rendered HIS Word through prophets and we know that HIS Word does not change. Would God send prophets to "murder" someone when HE commands all men [including Paul J. Hill] that "You shall not murder?" To do so makes God a liar, doesn't it? Therefore, from the word of God alone it must be concluded that Paul J. Hill could not have been a prophet, as he did not represent the truth of God's Word to the people of the United States.

This is not to say that abortion is not evil and that this doctor did not deserve to die. That is an entirely different subject matter. I have no sympathy for any doctor who makes his or her living killing babies. Nor do I have any sympathy for those mothers who participate in such evil by allowing their own baby to be murdered [terminated]. God has said: "You shall not murder." That should be enough for all. Make no mistake about it; abortion is murder, even if it is legal in the nation's laws. God will hold everyone accountable, especially the Supreme Court Justices of the United States of America who sanction the murder of innocent babies in the womb.

A prophet of God is given words from God to speak to the people or to some individual. In this regard, Paul J. Hill left us with his thoughts on the subject of murdering abortion doctors. His thoughts can be found on the Internet in a fifteen-page essay he wrote in 1994 titled "Should We Defend Born And Unborn Children With Force?"[8] I have read and studied it. First, in his entire essay, Paul J. Hill fails to do what prophets do. The prophet would say: "Thus says the LORD God Almighty." Whatever God told the prophet to say would then follow this or any opening statement like it.

For example, God told me to tell Christians that many are going to Hell instead of Heaven as they think in their mind. Then God said to explain who those Christians are in this book. God gave me a message and orders.

God's Eternal Character

However, nowhere within Hill's essay are there any instructions from God. Therefore, Paul Hill himself does not complete the primary act of a prophet. He does not relate any words he received directly from God to the people or to any individual in particular. He does quote some Scripture, but his essay is simply a rationalization of the premeditated murder of abortion doctors. It mainly cites other men's opinions, not God's Word. You might want to read it yourself and then review the chapter on rationalization again.

Hill uses two Old Testament stories as the basis of his rationalization. He feels that if murder is accompanied by "righteous zeal," it is justified behavior in God's eyes. We will now examine these stories to see if they support premeditated murder. I suspect another lesson on God's character will emerge, because the Spirit is taking me in this direction. [Note: For your information, God does not forbid killing per se. HE often commanded the Israelites to do exactly this. The distinction of murder vs. killing per se is in the area of being preplanned and premeditated on our own. In other words, the killing itself is not from a command of God or out of passion nor is it unintentional. One has to plan to murder. Often killing is out of the passion of the moment and is an unintended consequence of conflict. Some killings are actually accidents [see Number 35:11]. Hill's first story is that of Moses killing the Egyptian in Exodus 2.

> **"Now it came to pass in those days, when Moses was grown, that he went out to his brethren and looked at their burdens. And he saw an Egyptian beating a Hebrew, one of his brethren. So he looked this way and that way, and when he saw no one, he killed the Egyptian and hid him in the sand. And when he went out the second day, behold, two Hebrew men were fighting, and he said to the one who did the wrong, 'Why are you striking your companion?' Then he said, 'Who made you a prince and a judge over us? Do you intend to kill me as you killed the Egyptian?' So Moses feared and said, 'Surely this thing is known!'"**
>
> **Exodus 2:11-14**

God's Eternal Character

> "When Pharaoh heard of this matter, he sought to kill Moses. But Moses fled from the face of Pharaoh and dwelt in the land of Midian." Exodus 2:15

Clearly Moses had some emotions in play during this event of his life. He looked out at the burdens of his brethren and then saw a [severe] beating. No doubt it was a severe beating as the life of a slave was not highly valued.

> "He looked all around, and when he didn't see anyone, he beat the Egyptian to death and hid the body in the sand."
> Exodus 2:12 GW

"God's Word" [GW] translation indicates that Moses "beat" the Egyptian to death. This was probably by using his bare hands. We have to consider that passion was certainly involved and that this was not a premeditated murder in the sense Paul Hill wants us to take it. Moses did not go out with the specific "intent" of killing this Egyptian taskmaster that day. Intent does make a difference, doesn't it?

The second story takes place in Numbers 25 where Phinehas kills Zimri and Cozbi his Midianite woman. Here again, Hill would have you believe this is the same type of "righteous" murder that he advocates against abortion doctors. Because the Israelites have committed harlotry, God has place upon them a plague. God is angry against those Israelites who have commingled with heathen women. God issues the command to kill all of the offenders. We pick the story up in Numbers 25:4 with God's command.

> "Then the LORD said to Moses, 'Take all the leaders of the people and hang the offenders before the LORD, out in the sun, that the fierce anger of the LORD may turn away from Israel.' So Moses said to the judges of Israel, 'Every one of you kill his men who were joined to Baal of Peor.'"
> Numbers 25:4-5

God <u>Issues</u> Command To Kill All Offenders!

Copyright 2005 Edward G. Palmer, All Rights Reserved.

Book of Edward—Chapter 11

God's Eternal Character

This is now the part Paul J. Hill uses to rationalize his murder.

"And indeed, one of the children of Israel came and presented to his brethren a Midianite woman in the sight of Moses and in the sight of all the congregation of the children of Israel, who were weeping at the door of the tabernacle of meeting [because of God's plague on the people]. Now when Phinehas the son of Eleazar, the son of Aaron the priest, saw it, he rose from among the congregation and took a javelin in his hand; and he went after the man of Israel into the tent and thrust both of them through, the man of Israel, and the woman through her body. So the plague was stopped among the children of Israel. And those who died in the plague were twenty-four thousand." Numbers 25:6-9

"Then the LORD spoke to Moses, saying: 'Phinehas the son of Eleazar, the son of Aaron the priest, has turned back MY wrath from the children of Israel, because he was zealous with MY zeal among them, so that I did not consume the children of Israel in MY zeal.' " Numbers 25:10-11

Here again, Paul Hill gets his Bible facts wrong. First of all, God had already commanded Moses that the offenders be killed. Moses had issued the command to kill the offenders to the judges of Israel. Both of these occurred before Phinehas ever picked up his javelin. Second, the plague had killed 24,000 people. This was serious business and no doubt passions were high. That is why the people were "weeping." Then there is the issue of Phinehas himself who was the grandson of Aaron the high priest. He was no doubt a priest himself or at least was in line to be one. Also, as grandson of Aaron, he was trained in God's laws and HIS ways.

Phinehas took his righteous action because God already commanded it. He did not act without that godly authority. He certainly did not preplan the murder of someone solely because they were wicked. It was "MY zeal."

God's Eternal Character

Paul Hill supposes that he will get a "great reward" because like Phinehas God will be pleased with his righteous zeal. However, Phinehas' zeal was inline with God's command to kill those specific offenders. God had already given the order. Phinehas was obeying that order. Yet, Paul Hill does not inform us that he received such a command from God against abortion doctors. That is because of God didn't say it. Hill could have also used the story of Jesus, the sword and the ear. But then that would not have served his purpose of rationalizing murder.

> **"And one of them struck the servant of the high priest and cut off his right ear. But Jesus answered and said, 'Permit even this.' And he touched his ear and healed him."**
> **Luke 22:50-51**

The lessons are many. Several just came to me by the Spirit. First, it is God's character to permit the death of certain people. Second, it is God's character to discipline His people. Third, it is God's character to protect His people. Fourth, it is only righteous zeal when it is righteous in God's eyes! Preplanned, premeditated murder is not righteous even if it is face to face and in the open as Paul Hill's murder was. In the age of a covenant in which each individual will be held personally accountable to God, Paul Hill did not teach people to be personally accountable to God. If he had, he would have focused his energies into the hearts of the mothers who willfully end the life of their own babies. For in the end analysis, abortion doctors would have no business if mothers did not want to kill their own babies.

Hill's logic is also flawed because if "violence against the unborn" is justification for murdering the abortion doctor, it is also justification for murdering the mothers who seek to do violence against their own babies.

You're Only Righteous If You Obey God's Commands!

Paul Hill's biblical rationale is also flawed. He ignores many of God's commandments that directly contradict his murder rationale.

God's Eternal Character

Abortion is not an option for any person who claims to walk with God. This applies to the mother, father, doctor, nurse, counselor, etc. When you walk with God, you obey HIM. See chapter 18 for more discussion.

> **"But the prophet who presumes to speak a word in MY name, which I have not commanded him to speak, or who speaks in the name of other gods, that prophet shall die."**
> **Deut. 18:20**

> **"Then the prophet Jeremiah said to Hananiah the prophet, 'Hear now, Hananiah, the LORD has not sent you, but you make this people trust in a lie.' " Jeremiah 28:15**

Perhaps the saddest thing is that some Christians will still believe that Paul J. Hill was a prophet doing God's will. This in spite of what God's Word says. There are many in Christianity with their own agenda and own version of God's Word. We are not the ones who can call God to change HIS ways. It is God who calls us to change our ways.

Paul Hill is like many who not only feel free to judge —they also feel free to take action. That is what makes his case an excellent illustration for God's Word. Remember we learned when a doctrine is established that goes against the word of God that it is a false doctrine; that it is manmade? I am also concerned about the senseless baby killings. It is clear that Hitler's murder of six million Jews does not even come close to the estimated forty-one million American babies that have now been murdered via the rulings of the U.S. Supreme Court. To state that both of these groups of murdered people represent genocide, evil and the immorality of man's ways is a gross understatement. Think about the mass of evil that abortion is in God's eyes.

Yet God has explicitly reserved vengeance for HIMSELF. Therefore, consideration of God's character must be at the forefront of any biblical analysis. Can we rationalize behavior that is against the character of God and then claim that we walk in HIS will? No, we cannot!

Consider these other instructions of God to us in this matter.

God's Eternal Character

"You shall surely rebuke your neighbor [the abortion doctor, the mother, the father, etc.], and not bear sin because of him [them]." Leviticus 19:17

"You shall not take vengeance." Leviticus 19:18

"You shall keep MY statutes." Leviticus 19:19

"You shall not murder." Exodus 20:13

"You shall not murder." Deut. 5:17

You Shall Not Sin Because Of Another's Sin!

You Shall Not Murder!

All of the above verses Paul Hill should have known. But he should also have known this verse on vengeance. It is a classic pulpit teaching.

"I will take vengeance; I will repay those who deserve it.
In due time their feet will slip.
Their day of disaster will arrive,
and their destiny will overtake them." Deut. 32:35 NLT

"Vengeance is MINE, and recompense." Deut. 32:35 NKJV

Vengeance Belongs To God, Not Man!

Paul Hill ignored a lot of God's Word when he passed judgment on the abortion doctor. He rationalized that the murder was justified in the eyes of God. It wasn't. No amount of good we do can rationalize any sin. That includes murder and all sin is evil. Paul Hill is an example of a preacher abusing God's Word. His teachings are part of today's Christian mythology.

Copyright 2005 Edward G. Palmer, All Rights Reserved.

God's Eternal Character

> ### God Seeks Vengeance On His Schedule, Not Yours!

Hill also used Numbers 35:33 to justify spilling the abortion doctor's blood. In his eyes, killing the abortion doctor would be atonement to God of the prior blood that was shed by the doctor's actions.

> **"So you shall not pollute the land where you are; for blood defiles the land, and no atonement can be made for the land, for the blood that is shed on it, except by the blood of him who shed it." Numbers 35:33**

However, Hill ignored the verse that immediately follows:

> **"Therefore do not defile the land which you inhabit, in the midst of which I dwell; for I the LORD dwell among the children of Israel.'" Numbers 35:34**

Verse 34 is the "because" verse that qualifies verse 33. The why of verse 33 is because God dwells "in the midst of the land." Paul Hill doesn't just lift verse 33 out of its immediate context, which is the place where God dwells; he lifts it out of the context of the entire chapter of Numbers 35. This is where God teaches the Israelites how to make the distinction between manslaughter [accidental killing] and murder [premeditated killing]. Verses 22-24 are God's criteria for sorting out the difference. In these verses, God explains how to discern "intent."

> **"However, if he pushes him suddenly without enmity, or throws anything at him without lying in wait, or uses a stone, by which a man could die, throwing it at him without seeing him, so that he dies, while he was not his enemy or seeking his harm, then the congregation shall judge between the manslayer and the avenger of blood according to these judgments." Numbers 35:22-24**

God Examines Your Intentions!

God's Eternal Character

Numbers 35 is the instruction from God to establish safe cities for those who accidentally kill someone [manslaughter]. Paul Hill also ignores the instructions in this chapter for those who intend to murder someone on purpose [like Paul J. Hill did]. Their punishment is summarized in the three preceding verses, which Hill ignores in his essay.

> **"Whoever kills a person, the murderer shall be put to death on the testimony of witnesses; but one witness is not sufficient testimony against a person for the death penalty. Moreover you shall take no ransom for the life of a murderer who is guilty of death, but he shall surely be put to death. And you shall take no ransom for him who has fled to his city of refuge, that he may return to dwell in the land before the death of the priest." Numbers 35:30-32**

The Rev. Michael Bray teaches that Paul J. Hill was a prophet. He is ignorant of God's righteousness. The Rev. Paul J. Hill teaches people that premeditated murder is justified in God's eyes as long as it is done with righteous zeal. He too is ignorant of God's righteousness.

Paul Hill is not a martyr because he was disobedient to God's written word and commandments. Paul Hill could have taken other non-violent approaches to try and stop this abortion doctor. He did not have to ignore God's Word. Like other sinners, his act of violence seemed justifiable in his own eyes [Proverbs 16:2]. Paul Hill thought that this zealous murder was a righteous deed for God. It wasn't.

Righteousness is what is right in God's eyes. It is not what we can rationalize to ourselves. Righteousness would have involved obedience to God's laws. So should we do evil for some type of good?

> **"If you follow that kind of thinking, however, you might as well say that the more we sin the better it is! Those who say such things deserve to be condemned, yet some slander me by saying this is what I preach!" Romans 3:8 NLT**

God's Eternal Character

> "And why not say (as some people slander us by saying that we say), 'Let us do evil so that good may come?' Their condemnation is deserved!" Romans 3:8 NRSV

Should we do evil so that some good might come? I don't think so. That is not God's requirements of us. It is not His character. Listen.

> "Repay no one evil for evil. Have regard for good things in the sight of all men." Romans 12:17

> "Beloved, do not avenge yourselves, but rather give place to wrath; for it is written, 'Vengeance is MINE, I will repay,' says the LORD." Romans 12:19

> "Since it is a righteous thing with God to repay with tribulation those who trouble you." 2 Thess. 1:6

Any person or group that purports to be with the God must submit to the righteousness of God Almighty as defined by His Word. Christianity at large operates on its own righteousness, not God's. That is why Episcopal bishops can ordain an openly Gay bishop to head up the New Hampshire Diocese. That is why Paul J. Hill a former Presbyterian minister can murder an abortion doctor. In both instances, there is a clear ignorance of God's righteousness and a situation where man seeks to establish his own righteousness. This is nothing new as the Apostle Paul wrote about it.

> "For I bear them witness that they have a zeal for God, but not according to knowledge. For they being ignorant of God's righteousness, and seeking to establish their own righteousness, have not submitted to the righteousness of God." Romans 10:2-3

What about just the idea of judging? Was Paul Hill out of touch with the idea that he personally had to come to a judgment about this abortion doctor? Was it okay to judge the doctor with a righteous judgment? The quick answer is yes, but there is more to consider when we start to judge.

God's Eternal Character

So let's discuss the opposite side of this issue and whether or not we should judge others. If you think it is un-Christian to judge others, you only demonstrate a lack of understanding of both God's character and HIS written word. There are nuances involved in judging and we are not supposed to judge some people. Who are they? Why shouldn't they be judged if we are supposed to judge others? The first question concerning judging the sinner is whether they are in the Church. Do they profess to be a believer? Are they claiming to walk with God? That is the starting point of our judging.

If the abortion doctor was a confessing believer in Jesus Christ, then you are required to judge this person with a righteous judgment. Of course, this simply means that you judge this person according to God's perspective and not your own. Remember that a righteous judgment is from only God's righteousness and not what you think is right. Doing that, you would come to the fast conclusion that the abortion doctor was not in God's will since he is willingly committing murder [sinning] on countless unborn babies in the womb. Therefore, God requires specific action in accordance with HIS Word. It means starting by rebuking the doctor and then collectively shunning him [socially isolating him].

Since we are not to live with evil in the Church, it means kicking the doctor out of the church or excommunicating this person; God would have expected that. Yet this punishment is seldom used today. The Church lives with wicked people inside its midst. Was this abortion doctor a member of some congregation that claims to be with God Almighty? If so, that congregation, its minister and teachings totally failed God in terms of repentance. It never taught this abortion doctor what was good or evil in the eyes of God, who expects us to cease doing evil. The ability to discern good and evil is seriously diminished in the Church today, because the Laws of God are no longer taught; this is the time of Christian mythology.

Make no mistake about it. If this abortion doctor had tried to commit baby murder in as little as 35 years ago, U.S. justice would have killed him. Or at the very least, when convicted, he would have spent the rest of his life in prison. Even in the United States, just 35 years ago, our society had the ability to recognize the "shedding of innocent blood" as being sheer evil.

God's Eternal Character

An eye for an eye and life for a life was the general rule given by God and we read the punishment for harming any baby still inside the mother's womb in Exodus. If you thought that the Bible did not speak directly against abortion, you were wrong.

> **"If men fight, and hurt a woman with child, so that she gives birth prematurely, yet no harm follows, he shall surely be punished accordingly as the woman's husband imposes on him; and he shall pay as the judges determine. But if any harm follows, then you shall give life for life, eye for eye, tooth for tooth, hand for hand, foot for foot, burn for burn, wound for wound, stripe for stripe." Exodus 21:22-25**

God's message is simple. Do not mess around with the baby inside of a mother's womb. Why? It's because, like it or not, God placed that baby into that womb. Mother's take heed. When you murder your baby by abortion, you murder the handiwork of God. Think about HIS Word.

> **"Did not HE who made me in the womb make them?**
> **Did not the same ONE [God] fashion us in the womb?"**
> **Job 31:15**

> **"For YOU [LORD] formed my inward parts;**
> **YOU covered me in my mother's womb." Psalm 139:13**

> **"As you do not know what is the way of the wind,**
> **Or how the bones grow in the womb of her who is with child, so you do not know the works of God who makes everything." Ecclesiastes 11:5**

> **"Thus says the LORD, your Redeemer,**
> **And HE who formed you from the womb:**
> **'I am the LORD, who makes all things,**
> **Who stretches out the heavens all alone,**
> **Who spreads abroad the earth by MYSELF.' " Isaiah 44:24**

God's Eternal Character

Listen. Perk up your ears again as we are going somewhere with God in this discussion. I am now explaining the issue of "submitting to the righteousness of God" that Apostle Paul wrote about in Romans 10:2-3. If you cannot get this straight in your mind, you will never understand the character of God. You must realize that all we do as humans, that we think is right in our own minds, is worthless unless it is right in the eyes of God. It is God's righteousness that matters in the realm of eternal life, not ours.

Man's Idea Of Righteousness Does Not Matter!

>>>> It Is God's Righteousness That Matters! <<<<

God's Righteousness Is Eternal & Does Not Change!

The issue of man's righteousness is fully illustrated in the Supreme Court's *Roe v. Wade* [9] decision that legalized the killing of babies inside the womb by abortion doctors. The United States and its Supreme Court "being ignorant of God's righteousness, established its own righteousness" in this matter of sin. And even as to whether or not we can call it human life or sin. The Church, through decades of apostasy has led the United States down this immoral path by failure to teach God's Laws. Along with women seeking the right to murder their baby, they have sought the right for easy divorce and the right for sexual freedom outside of marriage. I bear witness for God in these social matters and its evil. I bear witness to the mythology of the Church at large; who ignored these issues, some even advocating them.

The issue of God's righteousness is fully illustrated by the above verses concerning the subject of babies in the womb. When we submit to God's righteousness, we obey HIS Word and do not ignore it, modify it or abuse it. This is the only truth that matters to those who walk with God.

**Submitting To God's Righteousness,
Means Obeying HIS Word!**

Copyright 2005 Edward G. Palmer, All Rights Reserved.

God's Eternal Character

The United States as a nation for two hundred years submitted itself to God's righteousness. We built our nation's laws and justice based upon God's righteousness. HIS Word was the standard that we historically used. On the face of the U.S. Supreme Court building is a sculpture of Moses holding the Ten Commandments. For two hundred years we were blessed. Now, our society disclaims its godly heritage by creating vile laws that seek to redefine righteousness. The Church is aiding and abetting these vile new laws in its own attempt to redefine God's righteousness. The Church seeks acceptance of its own sin in the eyes of God. Yet as we move away from God, HE moves away from us. We are no longer a land in which God is the basis of moral authority. God help us because we are in trouble and ...

God's Righteousness Is The Only Righteousness!

So with judging, first ask yourself whether or not the sinner claims to be a part of God's people. If the sinner is part of God's people, then you must apply God's righteous judgment to the sinner. It involves knowing God's Word or else you would be judgmental [applying what you think is right] instead of judging [applying God's righteousness]. You are only judging if you apply God's righteousness. It is God HIMSELF who has made the judgment. Your job is to make the observation of sin and decide if God's judgment applies. The second step in judging is therefore to simply use God's Word [HIS standards] as the "sole" basis of your judging.

First Two Steps of Judging Summarized

Step One: Determine if the sinner is a part of God's people?

Step Two: If step one is false, ignore the sinner's ways unless it is unlawful. If it is unlawful, then report it to the proper civil authorities. [This is also a good time for the Good News.]

If step one is true, then apply God's righteousness to the sinner's ways. Determine what the church needs to do and whether the civil authorities need to be contacted. Do not hide sin. Sin is evil and those who hide it are doing evil.

God's Eternal Character

Suppose the doctor was just a secular atheist who could care less about what God wants? Then what? Should we still judge him? The answer is different and to understand all the nuances of judging, we have to consider some Bible verses on the subject. First consider the words of Jesus Christ in Matthew 7, which are usually taken out of context.

"Judge not, that you be not judged." Matthew 7:1

Now consider the entire context of Jesus' words and you will observe that Jesus really teaches, "Do not be judgmental."

"Judge not, that you be not judged. For with what judgment you judge, you will be judged; and with the measure you use, it will be measured back to you. And why do you look at the speck in your brother's eye, but do not consider the plank in your own eye? Or how can you say to your brother, 'Let me remove the speck from your eye'; and look, a plank is in your own eye? Hypocrite! First remove the plank from your own eye, and then you will see clearly to remove the speck from your brother's eye."
                                                                Matthew 7:1-5

Judgmental means that you "tend to judge or criticize the conduct of other people." Hypocrite means "somebody who gives a false appearance of having admirable principles, beliefs, or feelings." Jesus is teaching that we better be looking at our own sin and not just others. What about that plank in your eye? Isn't that greater than the speck in your brother's eye? Some think that we should keep our mouth shut regarding sin. I guess that is the basis of the "do not judge" theology. However God's Word teaches us something different regarding sin. It teaches us humility towards each other.

"Therefore confess your sins to each other and pray for each other so that you may be healed. The prayer of a righteous man is powerful and effective." James 5:16 NIV

Confess Your Sins To Each Other!

God's Eternal Character

It also teaches us humility towards God. You should keep a short list of your sins before God. Confess your sins daily to God and you will see results in your life. When you do that, your inner most being will become molded to God's righteousness. You will begin to take on HIS eternal character in all your deeds and actions; you will move to zero willful sin.

"If we confess our sins, HE is faithful and just and will forgive us our sins and purify us from all unrighteousness."
1 John 1:9

Stay with me now because I do not want you to get confused. Jesus is not teaching that we should not judge others, because he also taught …

"Do not judge according to appearance, but judge with righteous judgment." John 7:24

Judge With Righteous Judgment!

And what is that righteous judgment except that of God's laws and of what HE defines as righteous? Jesus taught that he did not judge anyone, but went on to say that if he did judge it would be by God's standards. In other words, Jesus would and will be applying God's righteous standards to our sin and not his own view of what is right or wrong in our human life.

"You judge by human standards; I judge no one, but if I judge, my judgment will be true, because I am not alone: the ONE who sent me is with me." John 8:15-16 NJB

"By myself I can do nothing; I can judge only as I am told to judge, and my judging is just, because I seek to do not my own will but the will of HIM who sent me." John 5:30 NJB

Judge With God's Righteousness!

God's Eternal Character

You can observe the standard that Jesus Christ applied. It was that of God's righteousness. As a Christian, you are to emulate Christ. Therefore, you must also apply God's righteousness as the standard of your life. This means you must know the Word and live by it. Understanding the purpose of Jesus Christ is as simple as understanding these words from Peter.

> **"He himself bore our sins in his body on the tree, so that we might die to sins and live for righteousness."**
> **1 Peter 2:24 NIV**

Die To Sins, Live For Righteousness!

It is God's eternal character that all of HIS people should die to sins and live for HIS righteousness. That is to say you obey HIS commandments. Yet in the world there are two groups of people, God's people and Satan's people. God's people are not to behave like the heathens or Satan's people that surround them. God's people follow God's "rules of life." Did God worry about heathen behavior and what they were doing, wickedness like murdering one another? I don't think so. In many respects, God held the wickedness up as an example to us of what we are not suppose to do.

So we have always had a mixed group collectively if you look at the geography. Good exists next to evil. Same thing exists with abortion. Those who cherish life [good] find themselves alongside those who support abortion [evil]. For those in God's camp, we are to judge them. However, the Apostle Paul provides a different answer for those not with God. Why? God has already condemned the world and those in it. If you were to worry about everyone evil around you, you would go nuts. Isn't that fact evidence that God's people are only a minority in the United States? Sheer numbers?

> **"In my letter, I wrote to you that you should have nothing to do with people living immoral lives. I was not including everybody in this present world who is sexually immoral, or everybody who is greedy, or dishonest or worships false gods [or supports abortion]—that would mean you would have to cut yourselves off completely from the world."**

Copyright 2005 Edward G. Palmer, All Rights Reserved.

Book of Edward—Chapter 11

God's Eternal Character

> "In fact what I meant was that you were not to have anything to do with anyone going by the name of brother [or sister] who is sexually immoral, or is greedy, or worships false gods, or is a slanderer or a drunkard or dishonest [or supports abortion]; never even have a meal with anybody of that kind."
>
> "It is no concern of mine to judge outsiders. It is for you to judge those who are inside, is it not? But outsiders are for God to judge. You must banish this evil-doer from among you." 1 Cor. 5:9-13 NJB

You Are To Judge Those In The Church!

You Are To Ban Evil Doers From The Church!

God Judges Those Who Are Outside The Church!

Note: I have added the "or supports abortion" comment because God has made it clear to this apostle that supporting abortion is also evil and would be applied to the verse today. I myself used to support abortion. Are you shocked? Yes, it is true. I will talk about how I came about changing my position later. Stay tuned.

There comes a time in which the world might demand that you do something that is directly against God's will, something evil and wrong. If so, you must stand your ground and say no. For example, if Paul Hill was a medical doctor, he might have had to face a situation where his supervisor demanded that he perform an elective abortion on some baby. Of course he would have said no, because God's Word makes that decision clear. If we walk with God, HE expects us to hold HIS righteousness higher than any law or demand of the world in our life. This is part of HIS eternal character.

God's Eternal Character

"Whether or not it is right to you authorities that we obey God, you decide. As for us, we cannot help but obey our God." That was the attitude of the apostles. What is your attitude about obeying men instead of God?

> **"But Peter and John retorted, 'You must judge whether in God's eyes it is right to listen to you and not to God.' "**
> **Acts 4:19 NJB**

You Must Obey God, Not Man!

When faced with the choice between obeying God's Word and even my own death if I don't, I will choose death. It is no big thing for me to do so, because I know that God's picture is larger than the one I see. Those who walk with God will also do the same thing. Not because they want to die, but because they know that to turn their backs on God is something that is eternal in nature. Doing so denies His character, His nature, and even our eternal life. Do you know like I do that God has a larger picture? Do you understand that we are only small players in His larger picture of life? This means that there are two realities. One reality we see and discern with our senses in the physical realm; and, the second larger reality is that of God's. His reality is also metaphysical in nature among other characteristics that are beyond our ability to fully comprehend. His ways are greater than ours.

> **"For now we see in a mirror, dimly, but then face to face. Now I know in part, but then I shall know just as I also am known." 1 Cor. 13:12**

The Apostle Paul teaches us that we can only know a small portion of what is really going on. However, when we get to Heaven, we will see God's whole picture. For me, I know like Paul does, that I am only a part of God's larger picture. Like Apostle Paul, I know I only see a part of it. In that respect, I envy my dear Jackie in Heaven who now not only has no more suffering, but she sees it all. She even sees all of who I am and how I will be known in Heaven. For now, I must be satisfied in knowing it is all in the hands of God Almighty. It is He who is sovereign over life, yours and mine.

Copyright 2005 Edward G. Palmer, All Rights Reserved.

Book of Edward—Chapter 11

God's Eternal Character

God's Picture Is Larger Than What You See!

And who can't understand this fact when God also says …

**"For MY thoughts are not your thoughts,
Nor are your ways MY ways," says the LORD.
"For as the heavens are higher than the earth,
So are MY ways higher than your ways,
And MY thoughts than your thoughts." Isaiah 55:8-9**

The Apostle Paul knew you shouldn't waste any time judging those on the outside because God has judged them. HE has identified who will be excluded from eternal life [unless they repent & change their ways]. I.E.

"Do you not realize that people who do evil will never inherit the kingdom of God? Make no mistake-the sexually immoral [fornicators, homosexuals, lesbians], idolaters, adulterers, the self-indulgent, sodomites, thieves, misers, drunkards, slanderers and swindlers [pastors who steal churches], none of these will inherit the kingdom of God. Some of you *used* to be of that kind: but you have been washed clean, you have been sanctified, and you have been justified in the name of the Lord Jesus Christ and through the Spirit of our God." 1 Cor. 6:9-11 NJB

Don't be tempted to say that after Christ washes you through the Spirit "everything is permissible". Paul writes that verbiage next in verse 12 [not shown] to teach us that, with the Spirit, God will guide our walk. It will not be the rules of men. If you take such a stand, it indicates that you are one of those people Jesus will say: "I never knew you." Those seeking to rationalize their sin, unfortunately, often abuse the teachings of Apostle Paul in this type of manner. The operative words in Paul's teachings are verse 11, which states, "Some of you used to be of that kind." To use 1 Cor. 6:12 as a justification to return to sin is a prime example of the modern teachings of Christian mythology. Get a new life, a life with God!

God's Eternal Character

It is God's eternal character to judge between the righteous [good] and sinners [evil]. Jesus reinforced this eternal character of God and told us that he would be using God's righteousness as his basis to judge. As Christians are to emulate Christ, we are also to judge. However, we are to apply God's judgment to those who claim to be part of the Church. Those who exhibit evil behavior are to be expelled from the Church. We are not to live with sinners inside the Church. We are not to judge sinners outside the Church.

Christian mythology includes the false teaching that there is no reward for a good man who does not know Jesus Christ. God's salvation will be discussed in greater detail in the next chapter. However, God's eternal character does include rewarding those who do good during this earthly life. Indeed, the righteous [good] people belong to God and HE will reward them even without Jesus Christ. This is not just semantics. That is why Peter said he was convinced that righteous people in all nations belonged to God!

> "The steps of a good man are ordered by the LORD,
> And HE [God] delights in his way." Psalm 37:23

> "A good man obtains favor from the LORD,
> But a man of wicked intentions HE will condemn."
> Proverbs 12:2

> "A good man out of the good treasure of his heart brings forth good things, and an evil man out of the evil treasure brings forth evil things." Matthew 12:35

> "But love your enemies, do good, and lend, hoping for nothing in return; and your reward will be great, and you will be sons of the MOST HIGH. For HE is kind to the unthankful and evil." Luke 6:35

> "For he was a good man, full of the Holy Spirit and of faith. And a great many people were added to the Lord." Acts 11:24

God Punishes Evil People & Rewards Good People!

God's Eternal Character

God is a jealous God! Everyone should know that attribute of HIS. From that characteristic, you may feel it is justified to take HIM seriously when HE says not to worship idols or otherwise engage in forms of idolatry. Would you worship Moses? Why do you worship Jesus? Did Jesus say to worship him? Of course not, Jesus taught us to only worship God who was his FATHER in Heaven. Worshipping Jesus is the epitome of idolatry and not what God sent HIS Son down here to accomplish. It is Christian mythology.

Worship Only The FATHER; God Is A Jealous God!

God is also sovereign. Many Christians want to take Mark 11:24 and apply it to every prayer that comes out of their mouth. "Ask and you shall receive, if only you really believe." That is the way the name it and claim it crowd views this and other verses. God in their mind is nothing more than a slot machine and HE cannot help but comply according to HIS Word. Place a demand on the anointing and God is compelled to take care of your desires? However, God looks at the intention of your heart and HIS bigger picture of your life. The Apostle James writes:

"You ask and do not receive, because you ask amiss." James 4:3

It isn't just a matter of asking in accordance with God's will; there is also the matter of actually respecting God. The Israelites felt that God owed them because HE made a promise to Abraham. Christians feel that God owes them because of Jesus Christ's salvation. God owes nothing to the man or woman that does not respect God. We demonstrate respect through our obedience to HIS Word. We demonstrate our disrespect for God through continued willful sin with or without the claim of Jesus Christ as our savior. The disrespect is graver when sin is claimed to be sanctioned by Jesus as it "counts the blood of God's only begotten Son as a common thing" thereby insulting God's Spirit of grace. Both desire and demand for respect are part of God's eternal character.

God's Eternal Character Demands Respect!

Copyright 2005 Edward G. Palmer, All Rights Reserved.

God's Eternal Character

Willful Sin Disrespects God's Eternal Character!

God will leave sinners to their own demise; this much is certain. Yet God is so awesome that when you just start to move near to HIM, HE will move closer to you. In fact, I believe God will match you step for step!

"Give yourselves humbly to God … and when you draw close to God, HE will draw close to you." James 4:7-8 LIV

Suppose that you are nine steps away from God. If you take one step closer to HIM, HE will also take a step towards you. God will meet you half way, if you have a heart for HIM. Listen carefully: "Your iniquities have separated you from your God; and your sins have hidden HIS face from you, So that HE will not hear [you]" - Isaiah 59:2. So, which way do you move?

```
You •   •   •   •   •   •   •   •   • God
  You •   •   •   •   •   •   • God
    You •   •   •   •   • God
      You •   •   • God
        You • God
      You •   •   • God
    You •   •   •   •   • God
  You •   •   •   •   •   •   • God
You •   •   •   •   •   •   •   •   • God
```

Draw Close To God & HE Draws Close To You!

God's Eternal Character

As you approach God, you will find yourself moving into His holy presence. This is the place that I want to be 24/7 with my life. It is not always possible, but you'd be surprised at how much you can live in His presence each and every day of your life. Indeed, draw near to God and He will draw near to you. This part of God's eternal character is very exciting.

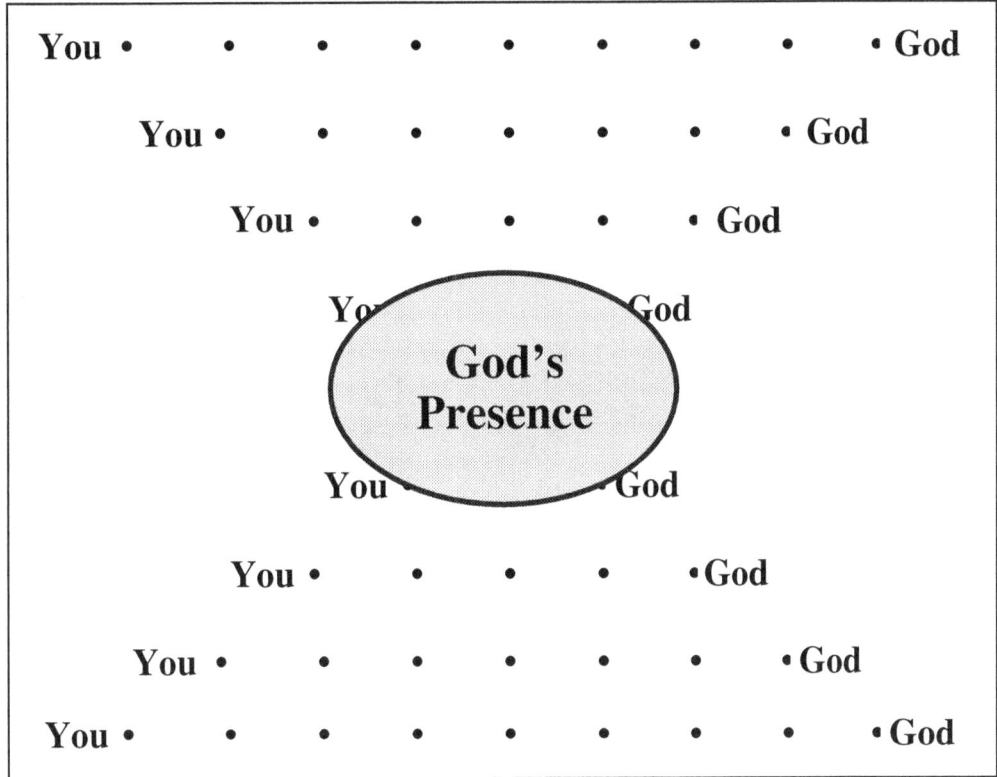

Once you have found yourself in God's presence that is where you will want to stay. That is because there is incredible love, peace and joy in His presence. You cannot find anything like it in this earthly life. It is why Jesus in Revelation 3:12 says to members of the church of Philadelphia the following:

"I will make you a pillar in the temple of my God, and you will not [have to leave His presence]." Rev. 3:12 *Paraphrased*

Until you have stepped into His holy presence with a whole heart for God, you cannot imagine or understand the joy that this graphic represents.

God's Eternal Character

Let's return briefly to the subject of who's God I am talking about. It is important to realize that three major world religions claim to worship the God of Abraham. In a highly simplified view, these three world religions can be view like the graphic below for comparative purposes.

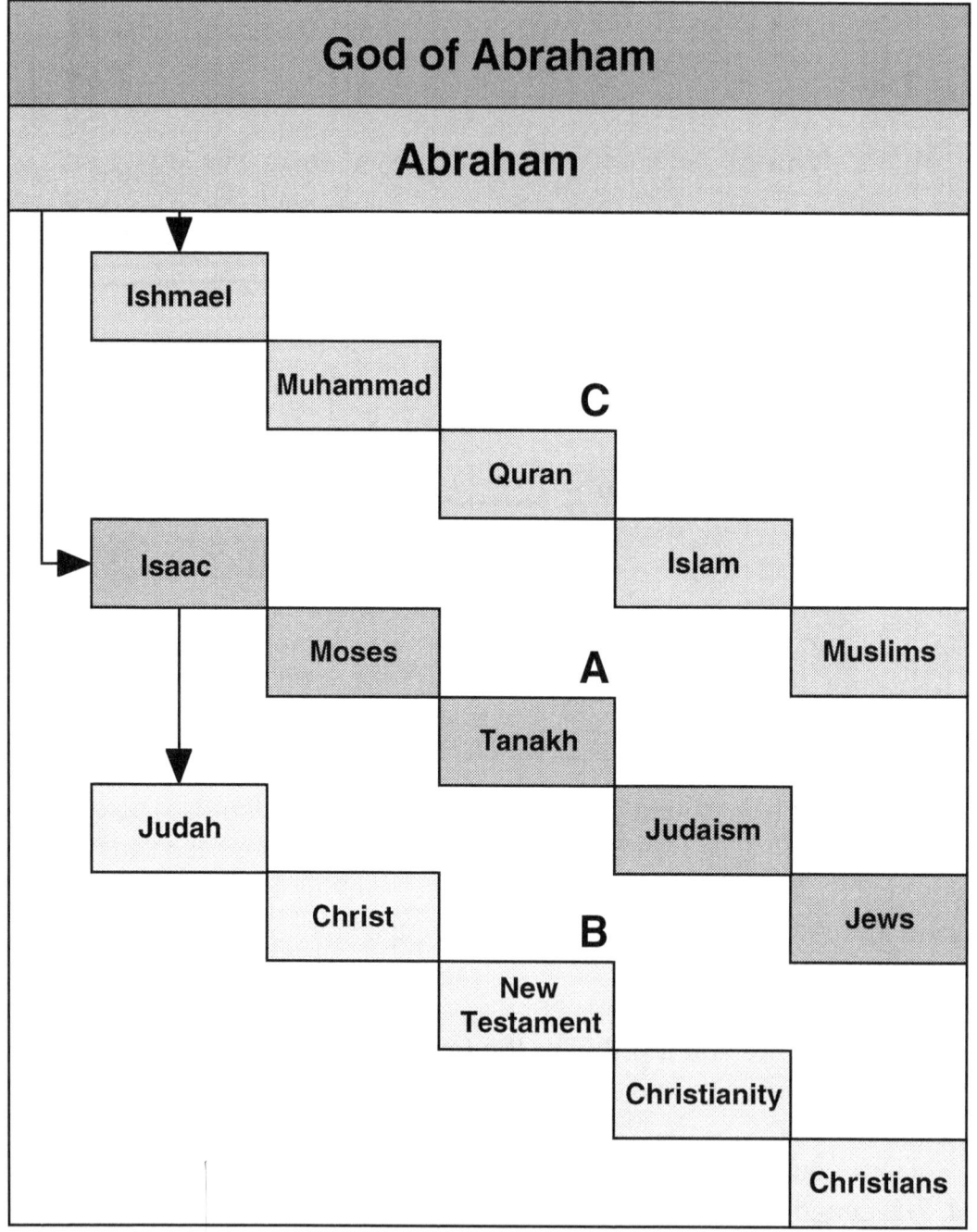

God's Eternal Character

Abraham gave birth to Ishmael and then Isaac. Through Isaac the Hebrew nation developed as a distinct Jewry culture. Jesus Christ was a Hebrew and his genealogy is traced back to Abraham through his son Isaac. Through Jesus Christianity developed as a second distinct religious culture. Through Ishmael the Arab nations developed as a third distinct culture.

Three distinct written works of God emerged and are related to one another according to Christian and Islam scriptures. The Hebrew Torah was the first to emerge. It is the first five books in Hebrew Scripture and is also called the Pentateuch, written by Moses in about 1400 B.C. The Torah combined with other Hebrew Scripture, totals 39 books and forms the "Holy Scriptures According to the Masoretic Text," [10] issued in 1916 by Jewish scholars. This is a standard in American Judaism. The complete list of Jewish Scripture written in Hebrew is also referred to as the Tanakh. In addition to actual Scripture, there is the Jewish Talmud, which consists of ancient Rabbinic writings in the Mishnah and the Gemara. The Talmud forms the basis of religious authority for traditional Judaism.

Christian Bibles[11] uses the same 39 books of the Jewish Bible in its Old Testament; but it alters the order of those books. It may also use either an original Greek or Hebrew manuscript in its many translations. This new order and one or more different Greek or Hebrew manuscripts form the Old Testament of the Holy Bible. Judaism is based specifically on the Torah and other Hebrew Scripture as well as the Talmud. Following the Old Testament writings, Christ's disciples wrote the New Testament. Whenever the word *Scripture* is used in the New Testament, it is a direct reference to the Jewish Holy Scriptures. For example, when Paul wrote that the Bereans *searched Scriptures* to see if he was telling the truth, it was the Jewish Holy Scriptures that were being searched for the "truth of God's Word." Therefore, Apostle Paul specifically acknowledged that his teachings on God were consistent with the teachings in Jewish Holy Scripture, which is the Old Testament.

Christianity is based on both the Old and New Testaments. Therefore, Christians claim to respect and acknowledge the basis of Judaism as written in the Old Testament Hebrew and Greek books. Christians therefore have acknowledged that the God of the Hebrews in the Old Testament is the same

God's Eternal Character

God that they worship. In addition to the many Bible translations, countless interpretations of the Scriptures have been authored and countless sects of Christianity now exist based upon those varied writings. Some are very cult oriented. I.E. The leader of the Branch Dividian in Waco, Texas had his own special twist on Scripture, which he indoctrinated his followers with. Thus, like Jewry, different sects or branches in Christianity have their own basis for religious authority. Often, that basis of authority exists outside of written Scripture in the form of countless volumes of written opinions. It could be the founder's opinion of any Christian branch or sect. Or, a so-called new truth [divine revelation] as revealed by the "Holy Spirit" invoked by an individual or group to get their way regarding church policy. Who would dare argue against the Holy Spirit? I'll tell you. It is anyone who is knowledgeable of the Holy Bible and knows something different is written.

Recently the Episcopalians, seeking rationalization to alter the word of God to ordain an openly Gay [homosexual] bishop did exactly that. They invoked the name of the Holy Spirit and said it was a new direction the Spirit of God was leading them into. Hello, anyone upstairs in those brains? Once again let me remind you that if any church doctrine goes against the written word of God, it is a man made doctrine and *not* God's.

Do you think that this book is just another one of those countless interpretations and or opinions of Holy Scripture? If so, you would be wrong since this apostle only seeks to inform you and other Christians of what the Scriptures say. That is the job God has ordained me to do because that is where Christians have gotten off track. They are so focused on man's opinion; they are ignoring God's Word. Consider what Solomon has told us regarding all of these countless books expressing countless opinions.

"But, my child, be warned: There is no end of opinions ready to be expressed. Studying them can go on forever and become very exhausting!" Ecclesiastes 12:12 NLT

Make a mental note. Opinions are the cheapest commodity in the world and everyone has them. Besides that, they are usually free. I've told you this before; you should be more concerned about God's Word than what anyone says about God's Word. That includes me.

Copyright 2005 Edward G. Palmer, All Rights Reserved.

Book of Edward—Chapter 11

God's Eternal Character

God is very disappointed with mankind's reinterpretations of HIS Word as given to all three major world religions. Our job is not to obey what any man, including me, has to say about God. Our job is to obey what the written Scripture given by God says. Now consider that our whole job in life as far as God is concerned can be reduced down to simple obedience. That is what Solomon writes in the last verse of Ecclesiastes.

"Here is my final conclusion: Fear God and obey HIS commands, for this is the [whole] duty of every person. God will judge us for everything we do, including every secret thing, whether good or bad." Ecclesiastes 12:13-14 NLT

Anyone who truly fears God will obey HIS commands. Consider HIS word as given by Moses in the book of Exodus. Once again, if you want 20/20 vision with God's instructions, it is as simple as Exodus 20:20.

And Moses said to the people, "Do not fear; for God has come to test you, and that HIS fear may be before you, so that you may not sin." Exodus 20:20

Indeed, it is the real fear of God that keeps you from continued and willful sin. That is the same message in the Old and New Testaments and Christ has *not* altered it one iota. Bishops at the Episcopalian convention in Minneapolis last month [August], however, would have you believe that Jesus Christ has altered God's message on sin. They did this when they openly ordained a practicing homosexual to head up the New Hampshire Diocese. This is an example of what I am talking about; mankind altering and reinterpreting what God has said. It is unequivocal blaspheme against God's Spirit. It is a form of the unforgivable sin that Jesus talks about in the New Testament. The 62 of 107 Episcopal bishops who voted to support ordaining practicing homosexuals should now be wondering about their own eternal damnation, as I firmly believe that they have crossed a line with God in which there is no return to eternal salvation.

Note: It is now September 9 at 8:30 p.m.

God's Eternal Character

Gay Bishop V. Gene Robinson said on NBC's Today Show, "I believe that the spirit that was here at the convention … will continue in the church, and that spirit pulls us together." There is no doubt "that" particular spirit will remain in the Episcopal Church. However, this is not God's Spirit because God does not speak against HIMSELF. Nor does HE change HIS mind. We learned that much in the last two chapters. Seventy-seven million Anglicans worldwide now have a choice to make concerning their own eternal salvation. They will choose between God's Word and man's doctrine. I can tell you that every individual will be held accountable to God's Word and you will not be able to plead confusion because your "bishop" taught you a "doctrine of man" opposite that of God's Word.

There should now be a mass exodus from the U.S. Episcopal Church and barring that, it will only indicate exactly how much Satan is in control of this denomination. These Episcopal bishops didn't just stop there; they approved the blessing of same sex marriages and are working towards openly Gay and lesbian marriages within the confines of God's church. Is this God's Word? Is this the Spirit of God? Get a life you Episcopal bishops and at least read the Bible that you claim supports your faith in the "ONE" God. Moving on, there is yet another or third book of God.

The third book written and claimed to be inspired of God is the Quran[12], which the Prophet Muhammad claims God gave to him around 600 AD. The Quran acknowledges both Judaism and Christianity and claims to respect the word of God contained in those two books as well as those two faiths. In Islam, this recognition would be understood to be within the context that Hebrew and Christian Scripture do not disagree with the information written in the Quran. Muhammad went on to write other information and once again we have countless writings on the interpretation of the Quran and the policies of its founder. The Quran and these other writings constitute Islam. It has also been written that the Quran cannot be interpreted properly without studying it in the Aramaic language in which it was given. Therefore, some sects of Islam would most likely disavow the English translation that sits on my bookshelf. In sequence then, Judaism's book was written first, Christianity's book second and the Islam's book third. You might think it is a gross simplification, but it's the basics.

God's Eternal Character

Do you get the picture? All three of the major world religions claim to worship the very same God based on these texts and the interpretations of those texts. All claim to be direct descendants of the same father Abraham. All three should now go back and reexamine their theologies to see if they still line up with the eternal character of the God of Abraham. That includes adhering to the righteousness of God. In the simplest terms, the following definitions[13] should apply to the practitioners of these three religions.

Hebrew — *Someone who established a personal relationship with God because of the teachings of Moses, the Torah and the Tanakh.*

Christian — *Someone who established a personal relationship with God because of the teachings of Jesus Christ and the Holy Bible.*

Muslim — *Someone who established a personal relationship with God because of the teachings of Mohammed and the Quran [Koran].*

Moses, the judges and prophets did not come to teach us we should worship them, their coffins, gravesites or their other personal artifacts. They all taught us to worship only the ONE God Almighty. Jesus Christ did not come to teach us to worship him. Jesus taught us to worship the ONE God Almighty. Mohammed taught the same thing. So, exactly who and what do you worship if you too claim to belong to the God of Abraham?

Do you remember that it all starts with your heart? Therefore, another eternal characteristic of God is this: HE searches the earth for those people who have a loyal heart to HIM. The Living Bible says God is "looking for people whose hearts are perfect towards HIM." Exactly where is your heart in relationship to the God of Abraham? That is the God, which I describe.

"For the eyes of the LORD run to and fro throughout the whole earth, to show HIMSELF strong on behalf of those whose heart is loyal to HIM." 2 Chronicles 16:9

God's Eternal Character

In God's larger picture, you and I are just a tiny part. All of God's eternal characteristics are unchanging and they belong only to HIM. This includes all salvation that is given through the acceptance of Jesus Christ. Why? It is because God gave salvation to Christ to offer us another chance, but Christ will only implement it the way that God Almighty already does. Thus, Christ offers you and I only the salvation that is already available directly from God HIMSELF and not something new, as Christian mythology would have you believe. Did not Jesus Christ say, "Repent and be saved?"

If you obey Christ, then you are obeying God. Not because Christ is God, but because that is what Jesus Christ commands us to do. Likewise, if you obey God, you automatically obey Jesus Christ. The Son of Man offers us a better understanding of God's eternal character; he provides a final and perfect sacrifice from God without further excuse for willful sin; and, the Holy Spirit is now given to us in abundance. Those who already know God will know Jesus Christ, because the Spirit testifies to them of Jesus' truth. The Good News isn't that Jesus Christ saves us; it is that God offers another chance to repent and obtain eternal life through HIS only begotten Son Jesus Christ. God is giving you and I another wake up call with HIS Son Jesus!

> **"Salvation belongs to our God who sits on the throne, and [God has also given it] to the Lamb [Jesus, who sits next to God's throne at HIS right side]!" Rev. 7:10**

> **"Then Jesus answered and said to them, 'Most assuredly, I say to you, the Son can do nothing of himself, but what he sees the FATHER do; for whatever HE does, the Son also does in like manner.' " John 5:19** - *Jesus executes only God's will!*

> **"For as our God has salvation in HIMSELF, so God has also granted Jesus the ability to offer salvation. God also gave Jesus the authority to execute HIS judgment, because Jesus is the Son of Man." John 5:26-27 [paraphrased]**

Salvation Emanates From God Almighty!

Copyright 2005 Edward G. Palmer, All Rights Reserved.

Book of Edward—Chapter 11

God's Eternal Character

Those who claim to walk with God will readily acknowledge Jesus Christ because the Spirit of God will testify to the truth of Jesus. Here again, it is Jesus Christ who explains this fact.

"It is written in the prophets, 'and they shall all be taught by God.' Therefore everyone who has heard and learned from the FATHER comes to me." John 6:45

I bear witness for God of the teaching of Jesus. For God has taught me and I readily come to HIS only begotten Son Jesus. God has a bigger picture and in that picture Jesus plays the role of HIS perfect sacrifice, which puts an end to willful sin in those who believe. There will not be another sacrifice in the temple next week or month so you can get forgiveness for your evil ways "again." The blood of Jesus, combined with the Holy Spirit puts an end to willful sin. This is why Jesus informed us that there are no more excuses for sin. Jesus brings us back to God through repentance.

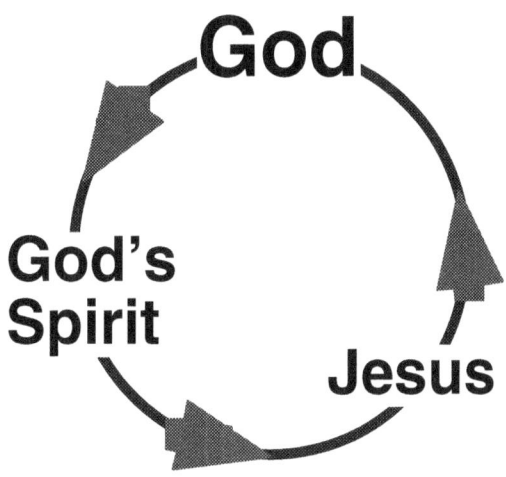

If you truly have Jesus, you have come back to God through him. It started when God sent Jesus Christ to call us back to repentance and eternal life. When Jesus rose, he asked God to send us a helper. God sent HIS Holy Spirit, which is the Spirit of truth [not lies]. The Spirit testifies to us that what Jesus taught is true. Jesus taught us to return to the FATHER, his God.

God's Eternal Character

Solomon tells us of some things that God Almighty hates. Indeed, he provides a list of seven (7) things that are an abomination to God in Proverbs 6:16. This is part of God's eternal character. HE hates these things. Listen.

Seven Abominations To God Almighty!

1. A proud look
2. A lying tongue
3. Hands that shed innocent blood
4. A heart that devises wicked plans
5. Feet that are swift in running to evil
6. A false witness who speaks lies
7. One who sows discord among brethren

Therefore, all abortion doctors will eventually find out that God will deal with their murder [shedding of innocent blood] on HIS own timing.

> **"Now the end has come for you, and I will send MY anger against you. I will judge you for the way you have lived, and I will make you pay for all your actions that I hate. I will have no pity on you; I will not hold back punishment from you. Instead, I will make you pay for the way you have lived and for your actions that I hate. Then you will know that I am the LORD." Ezekiel 7:3-4 NCV**

Somewhere along the path, Christian mythology started teaching that everyone can be saved and have eternal life. It is for all people. This is not true and Jesus teaches us the following in John to explain this fact.

> **"No one can come to me unless the FATHER who sent me draws him; and I will raise him up at the last day."**
> **John 6:44**

The fact is, some people are meant and predestined for evil and, no amount of proselytizing can alter their behavior. For example, Judas Iscariot. How about a pastor that steals the church from God? How about people who teach Bible lies and claim it is from God's Word, blasphemy?

God's Eternal Character

Blasphemy against the Spirit of God is the unforgivable sin that Jesus talks about. The Spirit that Jesus identifies is the Holy Spirit, which is also called the "Spirit of truth." This is one of *seven* Spirits of God that emanate from the throne of God. To attribute evil to God or His Son is blasphemy. That is because the Spirit of truth testifies to us concerning the truth of Jesus and God's Word. To take Jesus or God's truth and then turn it into a lie is blasphemy. Many in Christianity now speak lies concerning the word of God and His Son. But to take those lies to the next level and say that the Holy Spirit is telling you them, is blasphemy against the Spirit. It is the one unforgivable sin! Isn't this what the Episcopal bishops did when they said the Holy Spirit was now leading them in a new direction to sanction sin?

"Therefore I say to you, every sin and blasphemy will be forgiven men, but the blasphemy against the Spirit will not be forgiven men." Matthew 12:31

"But now you yourselves are to put off all these: anger, wrath, malice, blasphemy, filthy language out of your mouth. Do not lie to one another, since you have put off the old man with his deeds, and have put on the new man who is renewed in knowledge according to the image of HIM who created him." Col. 3:8-10

In the simplest of terms, blasphemy is disrespect for God. Therefore, whenever a preacher misuses God's Word for personal gain such as twisting the tithe Scriptures or to justify filing false state documents, that preacher is committing blasphemy against God. Yet, it is forgivable at that stage if amends are made. However, when the preacher takes his or her blasphemy another step forward and claims that it comes from God's Holy Spirit, he or she then crosses the line of what is unforgivable sin in God's eyes. Why? At this point they are attributing those lies directly to God Almighty and using HIM for whatever it is they seek to personally accomplish or justify.

Take care, anyone who says: "Thus sayeth the LORD" or "Thus sayeth the Holy Spirit" had better be right. That includes this poor apostle. You can discern truth when you are knowledgeable of God's eternal character.

God's Eternal Character

Christianity today is just like ancient Israel in its desire to sin. Indeed nothing has changed from Jeremiah's days. I bear witness of that for God.

> **"I listened and heard,**
> **But they do not speak aright.**
> **No man repented of his wickedness,**
> **Saying, 'What have I done?'**
> **Everyone turned to his own course,**
> **As the horse rushes into the battle." Jeremiah 8:6**

Self-righteousness rules today. The Episcopal bishop's actions and Paul J. Hill's murder are both tantamount to King David saying that God told him to send Uriah to the war front so he could get killed. Or that God said it was okay for him to commit adultery with Bathsheba, Uriah's wife. When confronted with his sin, King David repented unto God. It didn't just end there. God struck and killed David's first baby because of his adultery with Bathsheba. David's reaction to the illness and death of his first child with Bathsheba confused his servants so much that they asked him:

> **" 'What is this that you have done? You fasted and wept**
> **for the child while he was alive, but when the child died, you**
> **arose and ate food.' And he said, 'While the child was alive,**
> **I fasted and wept; for I said, who can tell whether the LORD**
> **will be gracious to me, that the child may live? But now he**
> **is dead; why should I fast? Can I bring him back again? I**
> **shall go to him, but he shall not return to me.' "**
> **2 Samuel 12:21-23**

King David Saw God's Bigger Picture!

God is sovereign over all aspects of HIS eternal character. This includes control over everyone's life, including yours. The Psalmist writes:

> **"But I trust in YOU, O LORD; I say, 'YOU are my God.'**
> **My times [life] are [is] in YOUR hands." Psalm 31:14-15**

Copyright 2005 Edward G. Palmer, All Rights Reserved.

God's Eternal Character

God preordained Jackie's time on this earth. HE specified the day and hour she would die. Before she died, Jackie told me: "God has told me that my time on this earth is finished." Before she died, God confirmed the same thing to my spirit. Not just that much either. God showed me the color of her casket ahead of time; HE showed me her laying inside the casket when I identified it; HE gave me her eulogy message; HE gave me the details of her funeral service, including the music that would be played; and, HE told me one week ahead of time the day she would die, the day of the wake, the day of the funeral service, and the day of her internment [all different days] at Fort Snelling National Cemetery in Minneapolis. If you think I wanted to hear this, you are wrong. I just wanted her to stay with me. Yet, God has showed me that this is all part of HIS bigger picture. I accept this from God and yet HE has left me free to still weep, as my spirit needs. Not so with the Prophet Ezekiel. God told <u>him</u> not to weep.

> **"Then the LORD spoke his word to me, saying: 'Human, I am going to take your wife away from you, the woman you look at with love. She will die suddenly, but you must not be sad or cry loudly for her or shed any tears. Groan silently; do not cry loudly for the dead. Tie on your turban, and put your sandals on your feet. Do not cover your face, and do not eat the food people eat when they are sad about a death.' " Ezekiel 24:15-17 NCV**

God has told me to move on beyond Jackie's death, but HE didn't say that I could not mourn. Ezekiel the prophet, however, was given a task to show the people of Israel that God was real. Doing so meant that he could not show any outward grief when his wife died. He obeyed God because he saw God's bigger picture and, we can all learn from Ezekiel's obedience.

Prophet Ezekiel Saw God's Bigger Picture!

Apostle Paul also saw God's bigger picture and writes that his followers should not lose heart because he had to suffer on their account.

God's Eternal Character

> "Therefore I ask that you do not lose heart at my tribulations for you, which is [for] your glory." Ephes. 3:13

Apostle Paul Saw God's Bigger Picture!

Then there is Joseph, who was sold into slavery to the Ishmaelites by his brothers. God blessed him and he became the Pharaoh's right hand man in charge of all affairs in Egypt. Joseph's brothers had planned evil to get rid of him because they were jealous. This story not only illustrates that Joseph saw the bigger picture of God, but also that God can turn around evil to work good for people.

> "The evil you planned to do me has by God's design been turned to good, to bring about the present result: the survival of a numerous people." Genesis 50:20

Joseph Saw God's Bigger Picture!

Sometimes God Turns Evil Into Good!

Then there is the issue of the Ishmaelites. Ishmael's descendants are Arab-Muslim people. The United States is now conducting a war against terrorism in the Middle East. The perpetrators of terror appear to be radical Islamists that think they are doing God's will by murdering innocent people. They do not know God's righteousness so they practice the "shedding of innocent blood" which is an abomination to God. We read about Ishmael in the Bible and Genesis 17:20 records: "He [Ishmael] shall beget twelve princes and I [God] will make him a great nation." However, God also records the character of Ishmael and tells us of future conflict.

> "He shall be a wild man; his hand shall be against every man, and every man's hand against him. And he shall dwell in the presence of all his brethren." Genesis 16:12

God's Eternal Character

Could it be that God set up the Middle East conflict we are now engaged in several millennial ago? John records this warning from Jesus.

> **"The time is coming that whoever kills you will think that he offers God service." John 16:2**

God Sees A Bigger Picture Than You Do!

In God's bigger picture, HE intends to test the hearts of those who claim to be with HIM. This is the group of people who have accepted HIS righteousness and given up on their own definitions. God's test will come to you in very subtle ways that will give you an easy pass to do evil. It might be a simple clerk's oversight that allows you to walk away with $80-110 totally unnoticed. It might be what you do in public that God will test you on. It might be things in private. It will be unrighteous things that you can get away with. That is how God will test your heart. Be ready and be right!

> **"The LORD tests the righteous, but the wicked and the one who loves violence HIS soul hates." Psalm 11:5**

In the typical Christian's eyes, there is no picture beyond what his or her senses can detect. This is another way of saying that Christians do not typically engage their spiritual intelligence. That is because they usually do not have any, preferring instead to simply lap up whatever their preacher delivers from the pulpit. Will you rely upon the preacher for your eternal salvation and that of your family? If you do, you may be very sorry in the end when you have to face God. Remember, even bishops will lie to you about what God's Word and what the Holy Spirit says. You can develop deep spiritual intelligence by understanding God's eternal character and also knowing HIS written word. The knowledge in this book can be a beginning.

Knowing God's Eternal Character & Written Word Gives You A Spiritual Intelligent Quotient!

Copyright 2005 Edward G. Palmer, All Rights Reserved.

God's Eternal Character

Judgmentalism is a close cousin to rationalization. When you are judgmental, you rely on your own sense of what is right and wrong. You fail to submit to God's righteousness as the Apostle Paul teaches us to do. In a literal sense, you use a set of lenses that color everything in life the way you want it to look. However, doing this totally misses the opportunity to have any perspective on God's eternal character and His bigger picture of what is actually going on around us. You must stop using your own set of criteria for what is right and wrong if you want eternal life. Only God's idea of right and wrong will matter at the time of your judgment with God.

God's big picture has many elements in it and we only get to see enough to understand that there is more to life. The big question mark represents all of the many things of God we do not even have a clue about.

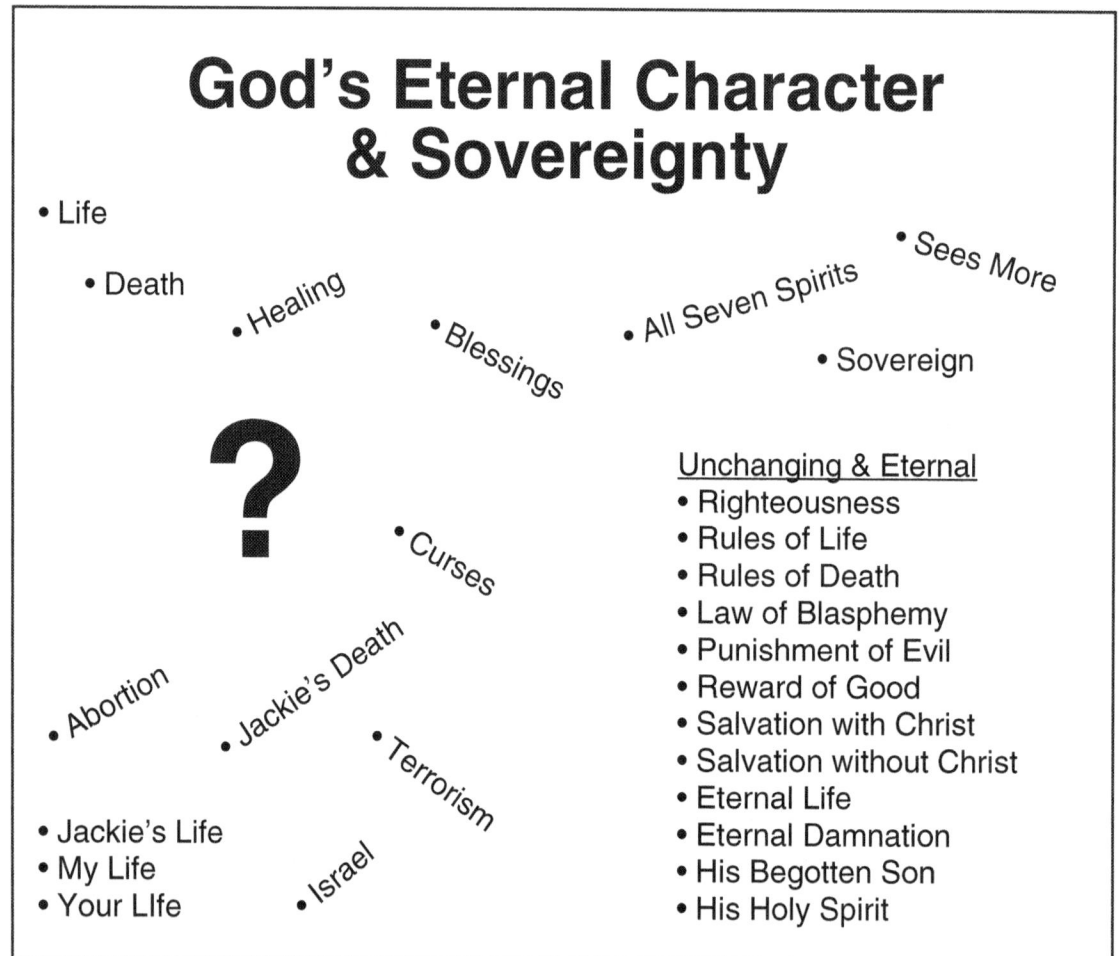

Copyright 2005 Edward G. Palmer, All Rights Reserved.

God's Eternal Character

Finally, when it comes to the issue of God's eternal character, there is the issue of HIS absolute sovereignty over every aspect of life. That means God will do as HE pleases in our life. HE is the only ONE who sees the total picture; we only see a small part of what is going on. It is the reason King David said: "Who can tell whether the LORD will be gracious to me, that the child may live?" It is one reason that some people are healed and others are not. It is one reason why some people live short lives and others live long lives. Listen to God's Word and understand that when you submit your life to HIM, you must acknowledge HIS Sovereignty over you, or life will not be easily understood during times of difficulty and trial.

> **"I will be gracious to whom I will be gracious, and I will have compassion on whom I will have compassion."**
> **Exodus 33:19**

> **"I will have mercy on whom I will have mercy." Rom. 9:15**

> **"But indeed, O man, who are you to reply against God? Will the thing formed say to HIM who formed it, 'Why have you made me like this?' Does not the potter have power over the clay, from the same lump to make one vessel for honor and another for dishonor?" Romans 9:20-21**

> **"HE has made everything beautiful in its time. Also HE has put eternity in their hearts, except that no one can find out the work that God does from beginning to end." Eccl. 3:11**

"When you know the God of Abraham, you'll know that HE doesn't change. Not for Hebrews, not for Christians and not for Muslims. You'll know that God's character is unchanging and eternal!" The Apostle Edward

When You Give God A Loyal Heart, You'll Start To Understand …

God's Eternal Character

Copyright 2005 Edward G. Palmer, All Rights Reserved.

Chapter Twelve
The False Salvation Doctrine

"Sing to the LORD, all the earth; proclaim the good news of HIS [Yahweh's] salvation from day to day." 1 Chron. 16:23

"Salvation belongs to the LORD [Yahweh]. YOUR blessing is upon YOUR people." Psalm 3:8

"The LORD [Yahweh] is my rock and my fortress and my deliverer; my God, my strength, in whom I will trust; my shield and the horn of my salvation, my stronghold." Psalm 18:2

"The LORD [Yahweh] lives! Blessed be my Rock! Let the God [Yahweh] of my salvation be exalted." Psalm 18:46

"The LORD [Yahweh] is my light and my salvation; whom shall I fear? The LORD [Yahweh] is the strength of my life; of whom shall I be afraid?" Psalm 27:1

"But the salvation of the righteous is from the LORD [Yahweh]; HE [God] is their strength in the time of trouble." Psalm 37:39

"Whoever offers praise glorifies ME [Yahweh, God]; and to him who orders his conduct aright I will show the salvation of God." Psalm 50:23

"Salvation belongs to our God [Yahweh] who sits on the throne, and to the Lamb [Jesus via God's delegation]!" Rev. 7:10

"For as the FATHER has life in HIMSELF, so HE has granted the Son to have life in himself." *Jesus' words in* — John 5:26

The False Salvation Doctrine

MEMO. It is October 7. I finished the last chapter on September 16 and posted it to the web. The preceding Sunday (14th) I almost split my gut laughing as I listened to a local televangelist named Mac[1] proclaim that he was starting <u>his</u> new series titled "Matters of the Heart." The fact that I had posted that section to the web two years earlier and had advertised the site for weeks in a paper that reached his membership had me musing whether or not some plagiarism was underway. It is often said that copying is a form of flattery. Is it a concern? No, and I pray that sooner rather than later every preacher will instruct their flock on the "Matters of the Heart."

However, the televangelist did teach something false that you need to properly understand. He said that at the time you came to Christ, your heart was not perfect. The message indicated to me that he thinks that your heart would grow towards God. Let me correct this teaching by stating that your heart, will either be with God or it won't. If it is with God, you will at all times be concerned about the things of God. Your heart will not grow to be with God. Being with God is a choice you make with the heart. It is true that the heart becomes more enduring towards God as time passes. Love does that. Let me explain this to you by using the analogy of the electronic on-off switch that is on computer equipment. Your heart is like the rocker switch having only two positions; "0" is for OFF and "1" is for ON.

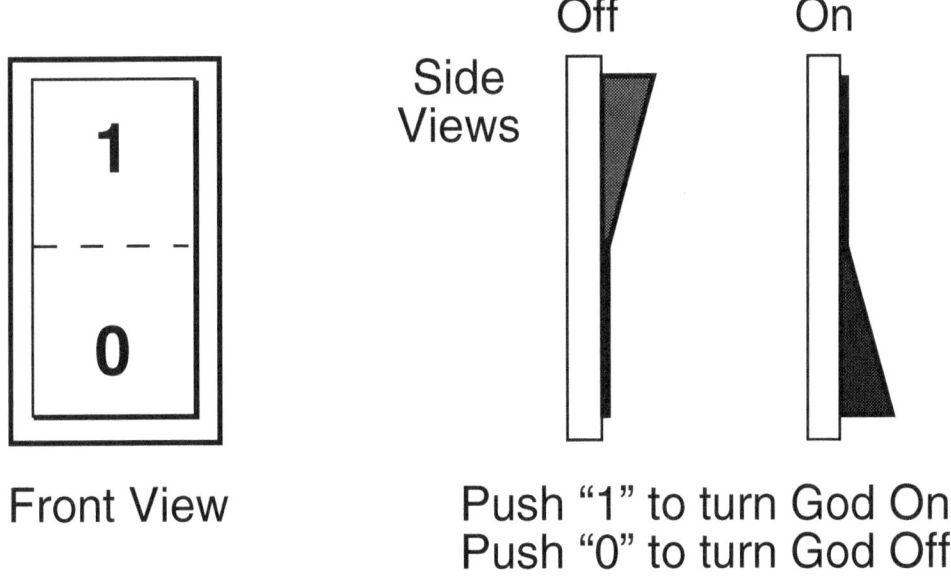

The False Salvation Doctrine

The spring-loaded power switch does not have three positions; it cannot straddle the center of the OFF (0) & ON (1) snapped positions. Your heart is the same way as far as God is concerned. If you are trying to straddle the fence [be in the middle or lukewarm towards God], it is a death sentence. That is why God has taught us in the book of Revelations the following:

"So then, because you are lukewarm, and neither cold nor hot, I will vomit you out of my mouth." Rev. 3:16

"But since you are like lukewarm water, I will spit you out of my mouth!" Rev. 3:16 NLT

Do not think you can play on both sides of the fence of righteousness with God. It doesn't work. Make a choice with your heart to follow God's ways. God's righteousness will lead you to eternal life. END MEMO.

It seems like I have suffered tremendously as I try to get beyond the fourth month anniversary of Jackie's death. One of her favorite questions was to ask me: "Do you miss me?" Of course, I would always answer that I did. Before she died and sitting only inches from me, she asked the question often and of course I answered yes. That is because true love can feel the effects of a spiritual absence even if physically within inches of each other. I think we started that dialogue early in the seven and a half years I spent in the U.S. Navy. We were separated many times by Naval travels. Recently I have found myself expressing often the thought "I miss you honey."

Today, however, I have asked God to take me beyond the self-talk of "I miss you honey" and into the self-talk of "I will remember you honey and I will honor your memory." Yes, I find I can no longer think of Jackie being physically absent from my side. The emotional pain is too horrific. I have asked God to take me beyond those mental thoughts, to transcend my mind into the joyous memories of our past together. Simply put, there can be no further earthly memories that Jackie and I can share. I must move on in life. I must <u>transcend</u> the thoughts of the past on this matter of our love.

The False Salvation Doctrine

This is no easy task for me. I am literally fighting 43 years of mental thoughts concerning my love for Jackie. To state my mind expects her to be at my side and that I might have to reprogram my thoughts and change my thinking to go forward in this earthly life is a huge understatement. I need to transcend the mental programming of my past. God will help me move on.

The same thing is true with most of Christianity concerning the issue of salvation. For over two thousand years the word of God has been abused. You think that being able to state from your mouth that Jesus is Lord will save you, don't you? This apostle is here to tell you that you can claim Jesus as savior till you are blue in the face and still find yourself in Hell. Why? It's because of a "false salvation doctrine" & "where your heart's loyalty is!"

God can help you transcend the fixed thought patterns of your mind's program. This is the stuff Christianity has fed you with through the years. Before we proceed, let me offer a prayer to God Almighty on this subject.

PRAYER. "Awesome and magnificent God Almighty, it is my prayer that YOU will open the hearts of those who belong to YOU and of those who belong to YOU through YOUR only begotten Son Jesus Christ. As I ask YOU from the depths of my soul to transform my own thinking beyond the thoughts of how much I miss my beloved Jackie, I ask YOU from the depths of my soul to transform the thinking of those who read this chapter. Show those with an open heart towards YOU the truth of YOUR salvation." Edward

MEMO. If you have opened this book and are beginning with this chapter, I would ask you to stop and go back to the beginning of the book. God has given this book to me in a specific sequence. The entire book deals with the issue of salvation. While I expect that this chapter will stand on its own, the real context of its message lies within the framework of all that God has given my hand to pen. Go back, start at the beginning. END MEMO.

I touched on the issue of judgmentalism at the end of the last chapter. It is a close cousin to rationalization. Indeed, judgmentalism is often a lens in which you and I view our life and the events or issues that confront us.

The False Salvation Doctrine

In order for you to get the most out of this chapter, you need to understand that as you read, you may be thinking to yourself thoughts of how the Apostle Edward has to be errant on salvation Scriptures. Instead, you should focus on what the Scripture citations are teaching you. God gave me an illustration on the subject of judgmentalism and how it can impact the way we think about life and even Scripture. Here is how judgmentalism recently affected my own thinking on the simple issue of house repairs.

While Jackie was dying, an exterior contractor came to the door in the spring to offer a free hail inspection for damage to our siding and roof. I was not interested and chased them away. They might have thought I was rude. I believe I said something like: "Leave me alone. My wife is dying and I have my hands full." They specialized in insurance claims and offered the prospect of a new roof paid for by the insurance on the house.

Enter my judgmentalism. Parts of my roof were 30 years old; some other parts 18-25. Part of the 30-year old section was repaired about 20 years ago. Thus the roof was of a mixed age. It looked bad and definitely needed replacement. While the main area of the house was not leaking, my office area was experiencing some problems. I had made a mental note that as soon as resources were available I would replace the roof. I have talked to my nephew Jay, himself a contractor, about the roof. He told me at the time to have the contractor look at the roof. Let him be your representative.

Of course, my judgmentalism said: "Edward, you should just replace the roof. Look at its age, etc." I figured I could have a roof party and that family and friends could help. Jay could head up the project and had all the necessary tools to get the job done fast. Many houses around me had the siding and roof replaced since I was first contacted. Jay had a heart attack.

As I dialogued with God on the subject, the message I got from HIM was: "What business of yours is the roof?" Huh? That's right, weird to me. Finally, I had to concede to God that whether or not the roof was repaired or replaced by the insurance company was not really my business. It is true that a violent storm racked the house less than a year earlier. My personal diary provided an historical record of that violent storm.

The False Salvation Doctrine

Now the two main questions were: A) Is the roof damaged; and, (B) Is the damage covered by the insurance on the house? The contractor came and made an assessment of the roof, which was not my area of expertise. He then represented the damage claim to the insurance company.

The contractor and insurance claims adjuster examined the roof in detail. They took pictures, measurements and chalked out damaged areas. When they were done, the insurance adjuster told me that the roof had been damaged by the storm and that they would replace it. Today, I have a new roof. However, I had to get out of the way. God told me that it was my own judgmentalism that was in the way of the roof getting replaced. HE also said that it wasn't my business. It was the contractor and insurance company's business. It was they who had control over what happened to the roof, not I. For my part, if a loss on the property was suspected, God informed me that I had a duty to myself, and the mortgage company, to report the suspected loss to the insurer for their examination.

The same thing exists with you and your ideas about salvation. What business is it of yours if God has something different to teach you in the Holy Bible about HIS salvation? If God tells me to show you Scriptures on salvation that are opposite to your pastor or denomination's teaching, you then have to make a choice. Do you accept God's Word on the issue of HIS salvation? Or, will you allow judgmentalism and rationalization to keep you from the truth about salvation? Live in a house for 30 years and I guarantee you will have some judgmentalism about that house. It can color the way you view things and even offer you a basis for rationalization. It can even get in your way of doing what you need to do or learning what you need to learn. Get taught Christian mythology all of your life and I guarantee that you will have judgmentalism about the subject of God's salvation.

Now the primary question for Christianity is this. Is there salvation apart from Jesus Christ? The answer is yes, there is! The very next question is whether just claiming Jesus Christ is assurance of your salvation. The answer is no, Jesus may say to you: "I never knew you." This chapter will show you why these answers are true and why God's eternal salvation transcends Jesus Christ.

Copyright 2005 Edward G. Palmer, All Rights Reserved.

The False Salvation Doctrine

Before we get any further, it is necessary for you to understand exactly what Christianity's false salvation doctrine is. To illustrate it, I will show you five examples of Christian teaching on salvation. Think carefully about each of these examples and if it reflects your current understanding of salvation. No doubt, you have heard one or more of these teachings during your life as a Christian. Yet, I do doubt if you will ever think the same way about these half-baked salvation teachings after you finish this chapter.

Example One

John Hagee [2] nationwide television statement: "There are two families; one of the evil one and one of God. If you haven't accepted Jesus Christ, you are of the family of the evil one. You cannot call God your FATHER if you are not saved [having accepted Jesus Christ]." *Paraphrased*

> Commentary: *It is a fact that in established Christian dogma and teachings, no one is saved that does not proclaim the name of Jesus Christ. There should be no dispute that the above message is common in the pulpit of the Christian Church. The message implies that Jews, Muslims and righteous people throughout the world are of the evil one and are headed to Hell. Is this true? The answer comes shortly.*

Example Two

Princeton First Love Fellowship pastor writes in the local [3] paper: "Jesus — The only way! Because Jesus said unto him, 'I am the way, the truth and the life; no man comes to the FATHER but by me.' " John 14:6

> Commentary: *John 14:6 is often cited as scriptural proof that there is no salvation outside of Jesus Christ. However, the Scriptures provided on the opening page of this chapter should give you a clue that this interpretation is not exactly correct. So, if this Scripture doesn't mean that Christ is the only way to salvation, what does it mean? The answer comes shortly.*

The False Salvation Doctrine

Example Three

Salvation prayer from Morningstar Ministry tract: [4] "If you want to accept Jesus Christ as your Lord and savior, pray this prayer: Dear heavenly FATHER, I come to you in the name of Jesus. I know that I am a sinner, and I want to turn away from my sin. I believe in my heart that Jesus Christ is the Son of God. I believe that he was raised from the dead for my justification, and I confess him now as my Lord. Thank you, Lord, for coming into my heart and saving me."

> Commentary: *Some variation of the above message is common in tracts handed out in Christianity today. The message is half-baked and anyone who makes the above prayer is just as likely to go to Hell as to Heaven. Why? The answer comes shortly.*

Example Four

Salvation prayer from Houston's Lakewood Church web site[5]**:** "Jesus, come into my heart. Save me. Be my Lord. Be my savior. I repent of my old way of living. Jesus, I want to serve you all the days of my life. I'm not everything I want to be Jesus, but I know you'll make me into what you want me to be. Jesus, I'll serve you all the days."

"That if you confess with your mouth, 'Jesus is Lord,' and believe in your heart that God raised him from the dead, you will be saved. For it is with your heart that you believe and are justified, and it is with your mouth that you confess and are saved." Romans 10:9-10

> Commentary: *The prayer and Scripture citation of Lakewood Church are good. However, both the prayer and the Scripture citation are half-baked. You could literally follow the above instructions and still find yourself in Hell. Why? The answer comes shortly.*

Copyright 2005 Edward G. Palmer, All Rights Reserved.

Book of Edward—Chapter 12

The False Salvation Doctrine

Example Five

Emotion can accompany the message of salvation. Indeed, the very subject of eternal life is packed with emotion since most of us are familiar with death in our family. My sister-in-law Candy recently emailed me the touching story shown below. I share it with you because it represents the message of Christianity in simple lay terms. The original writer is unknown to me. Listen to the words of a sincere Christian who tells the story of salvation in Jesus Christ in an honest and heart-tugging way. All of us can understand the story. However, is it the truth of salvation according to the words of the Holy Bible? The email story is titled: "A letter in the night."

A letter in the night

One day a woman named Louise fell asleep in her bed, and dreamed a very fitful dream. She dreamed that someone in Hell wrote a letter to her, and it was to be delivered to her by a messenger. The messenger passed between the lakes of burning fire and brimstone that occupies Hell, and found his way to the door that would lead him to the outside world. Louise dreamed that the messenger walked to her house, came inside, and gently but firmly woke Louise up.

He gave her the message, saying only that a friend had written it to her from Hell. Louise, in her dream, with trembling hands took the letter and read:

> My Friend,
>
> I stand in judgment now,
> And feel that you're to blame somehow.
>
> On earth, I walked with you day by day,
> And never did you point the way.
>
> You knew the Lord in truth and glory,
> But never did you tell the story.

The False Salvation Doctrine

>My knowledge then was very dim;
>You could have led me safe to him.
>
>Though we lived together on the earth,
>You never told me of the second birth,
>
>And now I stand this day condemned,
>Because you failed to mention him.
>
>You taught me many things, that's true,
>I called you "friend" and trusted you,
>
>But I learn now that it's too late,
>You could have kept me from this fate.
>
>We walked by day and talked by night,
>And yet you showed me not the light.
>
>You let me live, and love, and die;
>You knew I'd never live on high.
>
>Yes, I called you a "friend" in life,
>And trusted you through joy and strife.
>
>And yet on coming to the end,
>I cannot, now, call you "my friend."
>
>   Marsha

After reading the letter, Louise awoke. The dream was still so real in her mind that sweat dropped from her body in pools. She swore she could still smell the acrid smell of brimstone and smoke from her room. As she contemplated the meaning of her dream, she realized that as a Christian, she has failed in her duty to "go out to all the world and preach the gospel." As she thought of that, she promised herself that the next day, she would call Marsha and invite her to church with her.

The False Salvation Doctrine

The next morning she called Marsha and this was the conversation: Yes, Bill, Is Marsha there? Louise, you don't know? No, Bill, know what? Marsha was killed last night in a car accident. I thought you had known.

Is this your testimony? Are you witnessing to your friends that you are with everyday? Or will there be a friend of yours, in Hell, asking you why you did not tell them about Jesus?

As your friend, if you don't know Jesus, here's how: "If you confess with your mouth and believe in your heart that Jesus died on the cross for your sins and God raised him from the dead, you will be saved." *Note: writer claims this paragraph is Romans 10:9-10, the "proof" scripture.*

If you have not done so, just pray this prayer: "Dear God, I confess with my mouth and believe in my heart that Jesus is your Son and that he died on the cross for my sins. Jesus, forgive me of my sins and come into my heart and become my personal Lord and savior. In Jesus' name, Amen."

> Commentary: *Here is basically what I told Candy: "It's a very touching story. However, Marsha still could have gone to Hell if she were only taught the first half of Romans 10:9-10 like the writer presents. It is Romans 10:10 that gives the outcome of sincere and true belief, in that one 'believes in their heart unto righteousness.' I.E. They change their ways and subscribe to God's righteousness or HIS idea of what is right and wrong."*

Five Half-Baked Salvation Messages!

There you have five different messages on salvation from Christian teachers. Two are national televised ministries of whom I like to listen to. One is a friend's ministry. One is from a charismatic church twenty miles away. And, of course, the touching story from an anonymous Christian.

The False Salvation Doctrine

Yet, if these messages were all that people heard, they represent only part of Apostle Paul's writings. The above five messages are half-baked. They are just as likely to lead people to Hell than to Heaven. Why you ask? It gets back to the full text of Apostle Paul's teachings on salvation in Romans. Two of the above ministries actually quoted the first part of Paul's teachings. However, they both left out the most important second part. I have touched on this subject in an earlier chapter. Let us go back and study Apostle Paul's teachings to get the whole salvation recipe for Jesus Christ.

You would not find success if you only followed half of a food recipe while cooking food. For example, if you left out an important ingredient, one that allows success or failure, you would surely meet with failure. Not a lot to think about when it comes to following food recipes. Apostle Paul's teaching on salvation through Jesus Christ message is the same way. It is a spiritual recipe for salvation and you need to use the whole set of ingredients in Apostle Paul's recipe, not just half of it. That's if you claim salvation through Jesus Christ. Don't expect if you get to Heaven, that you can tell Jesus that Paul didn't give you the complete salvation recipe, he did.

The current salvation theology of most Christians, as shown above, is sheer mythology being taught. Solomon writes the following:

"There is a way which seemeth right unto a man, but the end thereof are the ways of death." Proverbs 14:12 KJV

The above salvation teachings are a pathway to Hell and similar to a homosexual's salvation logic. Call on the name of Jesus — all you want on your way towards Hell. If your salvation doctrine does not acknowledge God's righteousness from within your own heart, it is just fantasy.

Listen to this apostle. The church of Christ in the United States of America is currently and earnestly collecting souls for Satan, not God. That is because the church offers a half-baked message, which leads Christians to falsely believe that all they have to do is "call on the name of Jesus." Listen, don't you think that is exactly what those Christians were doing when they complained as Jesus told them: "I never knew you?" Think about it.

Copyright 2005 Edward G. Palmer, All Rights Reserved.

Book of Edward—Chapter 12

The False Salvation Doctrine,
— Limits Christ's Salvation —
To Primarily Calling On the Name of Jesus!

Time and again God's Holy Scripture is taken out of the context of the Bible and especially out of the context of God's eternal character. You will hear the message of salvation generally restricted to simply "calling on the name of Jesus." The Scripture lifted out of context is one of several. I.E.

"Anyone who calls on the name of the Lord will be saved."
Romans 10:13 NLT

Apostle Paul is actually providing us with a citation from the book of the Prophet Joel in reference to God Almighty, not Jesus, as follows:

"And it shall come to pass that whoever calls on the name of the LORD shall be saved." Joel 2:32

Popular translations like the NIV, NRSV, KJV interpret the word "Lord" in Romans 10:13 by using the Greek word *Kurios*. It can mean Jesus Christ. The NKJV clarifies Paul's reference to the Prophet Joel by using small caps on the word Lord. Therefore, it reads LORD, which means God or Yahweh [vs Jesus Christ]. It is my opinion that the statement should read: "Anyone who calls on Yahweh [God] and HIS righteousness, shall be saved." The reason for that conclusion should become apparent to you.

Let's assume for discussion that Romans 10:13 is actually a reference to "calling on the name of Jesus." However, if you want to count salvation on that verse, you should also be aware of these words that Jesus spoke.

"But why do you call me 'Lord, Lord,' and do not do the things which I say?" Luke 6:46

The False Salvation Doctrine

Jesus' own words summarize the difficulty of those who promote the false salvation idea of "just calling on the name of Jesus." Christ translates your calling on his name into a direct challenge of your obedience to the commandments of God. Jesus ultimately rejects those who "just call on his name" but exhibit no obedience to God's commands [Matthew 7:21-23]. Jesus says: "I never knew you — you who practice lawlessness." Jesus will filter his sheep with the simple criteria of obedience to what he has taught. Therefore, call on his name until you are blue in the face and you can still simply wind up in Hell when you are disobedient from your heart.

Jesus Said: "They Worship God In Vain!"

"And in vain they worship ME [Yahweh], teaching as doctrines the commandments of men." Matthew 15:9

The Apostle James tried to teach Christians obedience when he said: "faith without works [obedience] is dead." Now, how did we get to this point where the average Christian may be just as likely to be headed to Hell as Heaven even though we all "call on the name of Jesus?" It gets back to the false salvation doctrine of Christianity, which is first of all a half-baked presentation of Apostle Paul's teachings. Listen to what Apostle Paul taught about sin and God's eternal character [subject of prior chapter].

"Awake to righteousness, and do not sin; for some do not have the knowledge of God. I speak this to your shame."
1 Cor. 15:34

Apostle Paul gives a clear warning concerning sin. "Awake to righteousness, and do not sin!" He goes on to explain that some who claim Jesus Christ as their savior are actually ignorant of any knowledge of God Almighty. How can that be except for false doctrines and 8-minute sermons from the pulpit? Let me clarify this for you. What Paul is talking about is that some of those "who call upon the name of Jesus" are actually ignorant of God's eternal character. It is their ignorance that is leading them to Hell since they refuse to repent from within their hearts to God.

The False Salvation Doctrine

Paul touches on the idea of continued sin many times. Having studied Paul's teachings in depth, I cannot understand how so many people can use his teachings to justify their desire to continue in sin. Except for the sole answer that those people are Satan's servants headed to eternal damnation.

> **"But if, while we seek to be justified by Christ, we ourselves also are found sinners, is Christ therefore a minister of sin? Certainly not!" Galatians 2:17**

> **"I have been crucified with Christ; it is no longer I who live, but Christ lives in me; and the life which I now live in the flesh I live by faith in the Son of God, who loved me and gave himself for me." Galatians 2:20**

Do you offer a filthy vessel of sin for Christ's spirit to dwell in? Do you honestly think that the Spirit of God and the spirit of Christ would occupy a vessel that willfully continues to sin? Or, can you understand the Apostle Paul's admonishment to "awake to righteousness" and get to know the God that you claim to serve? Apostle Paul knew God and exactly how offensive willful sin is to HIM, do you?

> **"Blessed is the man to whom the LORD [Yahweh] shall not impute sin." Romans 4:8**

Talking about the second half of Paul's salvation recipe in the book of Romans takes you smack into the middle of behavioral issues, into the middle of our continued willful sins. It literally forces us to address and take into consideration what God says is right and wrong behavior in this earthly life. We are asked through Jesus Christ to return to God's righteousness, which was discussed in detail in the last chapter. Yet for two thousand years the Christian Church has only fed its people baby milk. The consequences of that baby milk are now coming to roost in a huge flock within the Christian Church headed towards Hell instead of Heaven.

Christianity Feeds The Flock Baby Milk!

The False Salvation Doctrine

Are you thriving on righteousness or are you still drinking baby milk in a carnally lived life?

> "And I, brethren, could not speak to you as to spiritual people but as to carnal, as to babes in Christ. I fed you with milk and not with solid food; for until now you were not able to receive it, and even now you are still not able; for you are still carnal. For where there are envy, strife, and divisions among you, are you not carnal and behaving like mere men?" 1 Cor. 3:1-3

Babes Unskilled In Righteousness!

> "For everyone who partakes only of milk is unskilled in the word of righteousness, for he is a babe." Hebrews 5:13

Apostle Paul's Salvation Recipe!

The full salvation recipe from Apostle Paul is in Romans 10:9-10. Consider that even though Christianity often references the proper Scripture, it then only cites verse 9 or Part I in its salvation writings.

Verse 9: Part I

> "If you confess with your mouth the Lord Jesus and believe in your heart that God has raised him from the dead, you will be saved."

Verse 10: Part II

> "For with the heart one believes unto righteousness, and with the mouth confession is made unto salvation."

True Belief Is <u>Unto</u> Righteousness!

The False Salvation Doctrine

Take a moment now and go back to the five examples of Christian salvation teachings that I showed you earlier. Notice that not even a single teaching talks about a change in your heart; a change in which you turn away from your sins and take up God's righteousness. Notice also that two of those examples even cited the above salvation recipe from Romans yet left off the idea of a changed heart, which is now a slave unto righteousness. Have you really "put on the new man?" If so, then you exhibit that fact by being a slave unto God's righteousness. It is the "sign" to all that you now belong to God and are saved through either HIS grace or by the gift of the blood of HIS Son Jesus.

> **"And having been set free from sin, you became slaves of righteousness." Romans 6:18**

> **"But now having been set free from sin, and having become slaves of God, you have your fruit to holiness, and the end, everlasting life." Romans 6:22**

Now in the practical sense, such a conversion and change of heart means that you would, if needed, see your own death hanging upside down on a cross like the Apostle Peter did — before you would forsake God's righteousness. You would, like all the apostles, understand that you must stand up for the truth of God's Word. If you cannot state this as a fact in your life, the blood of Jesus Christ does not save you. Further, the grace of Yahweh does not save you. In short, you do not belong to God unless you are willing to die for God.

The lack of the church teaching a changed and righteous heart is the primary element of the false salvation doctrine. If you take a moment and reflect on exactly how few Christians would lay down their life, it will give you a sense of why Jesus said that few will find the way home and many will stay on the path to Hell.

The nature of today's Christian Church draws in souls for Satan. If you don't believe this is a fact, just try to take a righteous stand for the truth of God's Word within your church and see what happens to you.

Copyright 2005 Edward G. Palmer, All Rights Reserved.

Book of Edward—Chapter 12

The False Salvation Doctrine

I am happy to find out that there appears to be a schism taking shape within the Episcopal Church over the recent ordination of the homosexual bishop. This is great spiritual news. It means there are some righteous Episcopal assemblies. I heard a homosexual Episcopalian on the news and he estimated that if the "conservative" wing of the church bolts, it would only be a membership loss of about 13%. He said it was nothing to worry about suggesting they would become small like the Quakers. Let me tell you something. It will be better for you if you are a part of a small group of righteous believers than a member of a large unrighteous church. You are not a righteous person unless you stand your ground for God's righteousness and His truth. That is what it means to "live by faith." Faith in God!

So, go ahead all you willful sinners [unrighteous people] and call on the name of Jesus Christ as your "Lord" for your salvation till you are blue in the face. Then see where your unrepentant and unrighteous heart has gotten you when you come face to face with Christ. Without a doubt, this apostle confirms to you from God that Jesus Christ will tell such a person: "I never knew you, depart from me you who practice lawlessness."

That a changed heart is a requirement of "living unto God in faith" is so fundamental with God that it is not debatable. What are debatable are the subtle reasons of exactly why Christianity has ignored the full salvation message of Paul. Yes, the gift of salvation is from God's grace. Yet, your receipt of God's salvation is acknowledged through your changed heart unto God's righteousness. Perhaps this would be a good time to go back and read the first seven chapters of this book. You know, the "Matters of the Heart."

Consider for the moment that you have one really good and close friend. It's the kind of person that you can share anything with. Jackie's friend Dorothy was that kind of person to Jackie and vice versa. This is the kind of friend that loves you so much that no matter what you tell them, they will not condemn you. Can you relate to this type of friendship? I hope so as everyone in this earthly life deserves such a friend. The friendship and love you share with such a person runs so deep that you wouldn't think of doing anything that you know would certainly offend them.

The False Salvation Doctrine

For instance, suppose your friend owned the local home improvement store in the last chapter that gave you an easy pass on walking out with an extra $110.00 in merchandise free because the clerk made a mistake and failed to ring up a purchase. You wouldn't even think about not correcting the clerk's error and paying the full price would you? Why? It is because you love your friend and their friendship is more important to you than anything physical on this planet. You reason correctly that your friend would interpret such an action as a theft. Therefore, as far as your friend is concerned, you believe in the commandment, "Thou shall not steal."

Suppose you stopped by your friend's house only to find out she was gone and wouldn't be home for hours. Her husband offers you some coffee, which you accept. You find your friend's husband a very attractive person. However, you reject and restrain all lustful thoughts you have towards your friend's husband, because you reason correctly that nothing on this earth is worth jeopardizing the close friendship you share with her. Therefore, as far as your friend is concerned, you believe in the commandment, "Thou shall not commit adultery."

Suppose someone known to both you and your friend meets up with you and starts to talk about your friend to you. In fact, they state some outrageous thing you know for certain is an outright lie about your friend. You do not keep silent because you know the truth. You reason correctly that if you do not tell the truth, you are then bearing a false witness against your friend by default. Therefore, as far as your friend is concerned, you believe in the commandment, "Thou shall not bear false witness."

Suppose your friend has acquired something in life that is desirous to you. Something you would like to personally own. Your friend is well off, but you are poor and cannot afford such a luxury. Because you value your friendship so much, you learned to rejoice in the good things of your friend's life. You reason that your joy in life can be an extension of your friend's joy in life so you reject all thoughts of covetousness towards anything that your friend owns. Therefore, as far as your friend is concerned, you believe in the commandment, "Thou shall not covet."

The False Salvation Doctrine

Suppose your friend has a brother that does hateful things towards her. You despise the brother because of his hateful behavior. However, you and your friend are members of a "conservative" congregation that places great value on human life at all stages of development. Plus, your friend loves her brother despite his terrible and often hateful behavior. You reason that your friend loves her brother and you reject all thoughts that this hateful brother should be murdered. Therefore, as far as your friend is concerned, you believe in the commandment, "Thou shall not murder."

Your friend has great respect, love and honor for her parents. They have come to know you quite well. Despite the fact that sometimes they may be wrong in life, you have come to honor them by showing deference to their opinion. Therefore, as far as your friend is concerned, you believe in the commandment, "Thou shall honor thy Father and Mother."

Do you get the picture? You would not think of doing anything that intentionally offends your friend would you? That is not the way we live in this earthly life. If we are fortunate to obtain such a friendship, we do all we can to respect and honor that friendship. We wouldn't for example, take our friend's belongings, sleep with her husband, curse at her parents, murder her brother, tell lies about her or otherwise offend her and expect such friendship to continue. We are all smart enough in life to understand that you do not treat close friends that way. So why do Christians treat God in a much less favorable way than they would treat a close friend? Will God understand?

What if that close friend was God or HIS Son Jesus, who both offer you salvation simply by "calling on their name?" Do you honestly think they will have salvation waiting for you if you did not care enough about them to restrain from behavior that is offensive to them? Hello, anyone home? The illustrations above are exactly what it means to live in faith. It means that you live for God's righteousness and that you understand your heart must be right towards God like your heart is right towards a close friend or loved one. This is not rocket science. It only means that you treat God and Jesus as you would any close friend you love. Do not intentionally offend them in anyway. Treat God and HIS Son Jesus Christ as your close friends and you will see eternal salvation at the point of your death.

Copyright 2005 Edward G. Palmer, All Rights Reserved.

The False Salvation Doctrine

A Heart For God Values His Friendship!

Now, what do friends do for each other when they get in trouble? They stick up for one another, don't they? So what if you really blow it big time with your friend? Do they condemn you? No, they don't. It's the same thing with God when He is your friend. You will not be perfect for any close friend. There will be times of difficulty when you will need to just trust in the love your friend has for you to help you get through life.

Remember King David's adultery with Bathsheba in the last chapter? This is an excellent illustration for you to remember that when you walk with God, He will take care of you. If you blow it big time, it doesn't mean you won't suffer some consequences of your actions. However, it also does not mean you will be condemned by your friend. By way of illustration, let's return to the two-zone graphic of righteousness and unrighteousness.

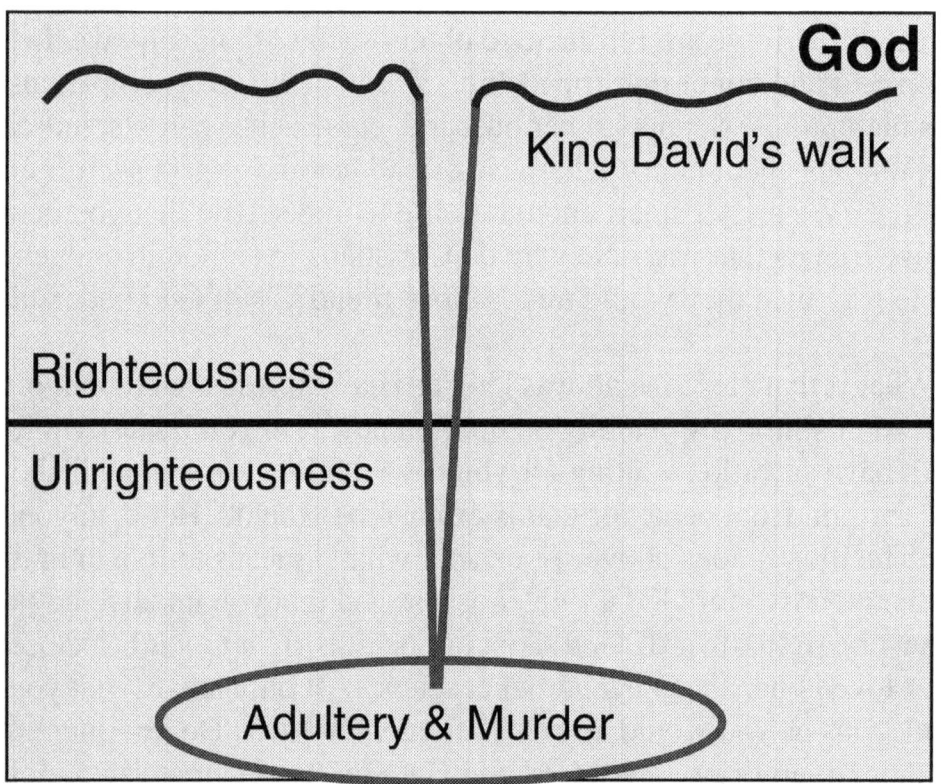

Copyright 2005 Edward G. Palmer, All Rights Reserved.

Book of Edward—Chapter 12

The False Salvation Doctrine

This time, I have drawn a line representing David's walk with God and the adulterous and murderous affair he had with Bathsheba. Think about the ramifications of King David's behavior and you will see that God has never expected our behavior to be perfect. God only expects us to respect HIM like we would respect any close friend. King David violated two of God's Ten Commandments. "Thou shall not murder" and "Thou shall not commit adultery." Go back and study the story in 2 Samuel 12. You will find out that God had mercy on King David. Why? It is because that behavior was not the normal behavior of King David. He had a heart for God and walked closely with God.

Now flip the graph upside down and picture the spike as the only one that goes into the realm of righteousness. Many Christians live in the realm of unrighteousness and on occasion do something visibly righteous. Do you think God will view that person as a friend? No. When you walk with God, HE will walk with you. It doesn't mean that there won't be consequences for unrighteous behavior. It does mean that if you are close friends with God, you can expect the love, mercy and care that a close friend will give you.

Truncating Paul's Teaching Is Apostasy!

Truncating the salvation teachings of Apostle Paul in Romans 10:9-10 is a major aspect of the false salvation doctrine being taught in the Christian Church. The failure to teach Christians that hearts must actually "change unto God's righteousness" is the failure to teach Christians that they need to treat God and Jesus at least as respectful from a behavioral point of view as they would treat any close friend. This involves not offending your friend because that is what friends do for each other. Friendships dissolve when respect for one another's beliefs dissolves. Therefore, eternal salvation is only reflected within those Christians that adhere to the commandments of God. That adherence to the commandments is reflected within our actions, statements, morals, politics, etc. It demonstrates respect for God Almighty.

God Values HIS Friends Too!

Copyright 2005 Edward G. Palmer, All Rights Reserved.

The False Salvation Doctrine

The second major aspect of the false salvation doctrine is the false teaching that you cannot be saved apart from life in Jesus Christ. The Christian Church today has the mistaken idea that the Bible is all about Jesus. The reality is that the Bible is all about a loving God called Yahweh.

Let's consider John 14:6 for a moment in the context of the next verse. Study these verses for a moment. Can they be used to state that there is no salvation outside of Jesus Christ? Then consider the graphic below.

> "Jesus said to him, 'I am the way, the truth, and the life. No one comes to the FATHER except through me.' If you had known me, you would have known my FATHER also; and from now on you know HIM and have seen HIM."
>
> John 14:6-7

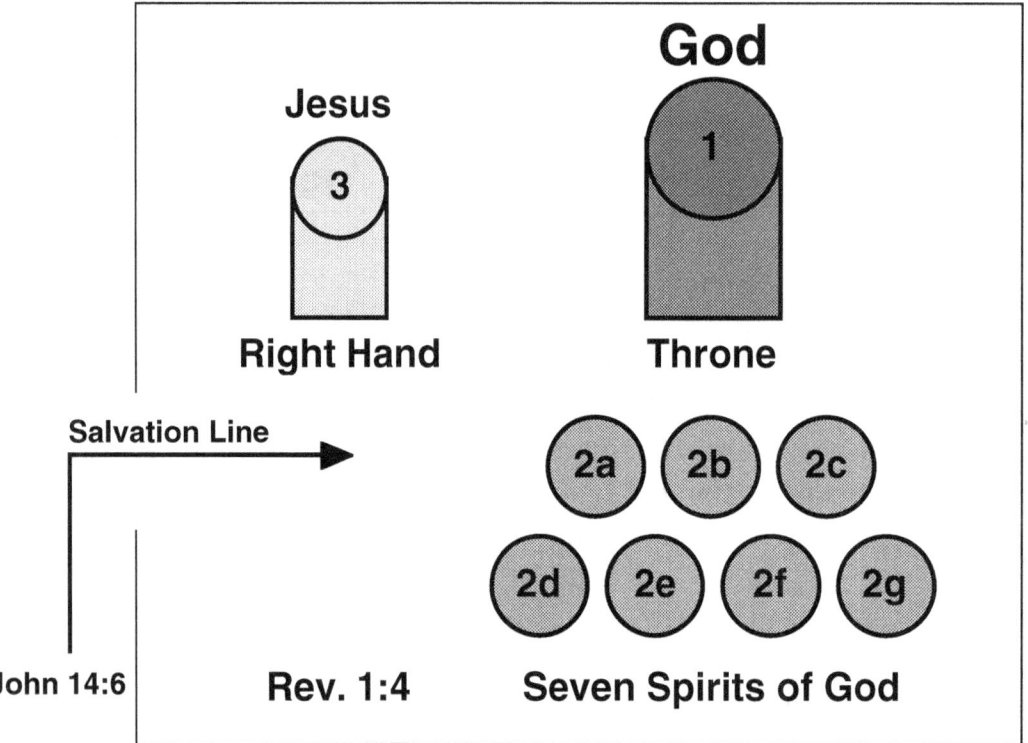

Salvation Line Forms At Jesus' Right Side

The False Salvation Doctrine

If you are trying to read this chapter on its own, you will need to go back and study the conversation on page 301 concerning God's *seven* Spirits to fully appreciate the graphic above.

Let me tell you what John 14:6-7 does not say. It does not say that Jesus Christ is the only form of salvation. What Jesus said and did was what the FATHER told him to say and do. Therefore, the way, the truth and the life are "the words of God Almighty" as given to mankind via Jesus Christ who was the messenger of God. The phrase that "no one comes to the FATHER except through me" is easy to understand when you realize that Christ sits at the right hand of God the FATHER [Yahweh]. It is also easy to understand when you realize that God has appointed Jesus as Judge. When you realize that you can call on the name of Yahweh to be saved [Joel 2:32], the verse makes sense that all will go through Jesus before they "come to the FATHER."

To put it plainly, the salvation line forms to the right of Jesus. He will decide whether or not you belong to his flock. If not, Jesus will lean over and say to YAHWEH something like this: "FATHER, I do not know this one, do YOU?" Thus there are two defined groups of souls that will be saved in the Holy Bible. One group is those souls who know Jesus and call upon his name. The other group is those souls who know God and call upon HIS name. Of course, knowing someone in this instance is akin to being friends.

Now consider John 3:16 and who the gift of sacrifice is for.

"For God so loved the world that HE gave HIS only begotten Son, that whoever believes in him should not perish but have everlasting life." John 3:16

The gift of God is for "the world" and whether or not Christians like it, this includes all who are righteous and all who know God. It means that righteous Muslims and Jews will see eternal life. But Edward, you say — doesn't the verse specifically indicate that it is Jesus who must be believed in? Actually, it doesn't if you fully understand Scripture. Since most of

The False Salvation Doctrine

Christianity does not, let me explain the full truth of John 3:16. The truth is unveiled by a careful study of Jesus' words in John 12:44.

> **"Then Jesus cried out and said, 'he who believes in me, believes not in me but in HIM who sent me.'" John 12:44**

Now put the pieces of the puzzle together and you will realize the following teachings of Jesus Christ:

1. Jesus Christ was a messenger of God.
2. He was God's only begotten Son in the flesh.
3. He was the image of God Almighty before our eyes.
4. He only spoke what God told him to say.
5. He only did what God told him to do.

Therefore, Jesus says that if you believe in him, you really believe in the FATHER who sent him. Think about this. Is it easier to believe in a God that you cannot see or is it easier to believe in someone who claims to be the Son of God who stands before you in the flesh like any other human being? How about the human Son of God who willingly goes to the cross to die for your sins? If you think it is easier to believe in Jesus, you are wrong. Yet with the miracles God performed through him, it was made easier and more real to those who were able to see and touch Jesus at the time.

True belief in Jesus Christ equates to belief in God Almighty and HIS realities, HIS commandments and HIS righteousness. Therefore, Jesus made it clear that those who "really believe" in him would obey God. What were the main points of Jesus' earthly mission? First, it was to provide one final and perfect sacrifice for all of mankind. Second, it was to point everyone back to Yahweh with the Gospel of Christ, which is "repent and be saved."

Therefore, the focus of Christianity is wrong. It focuses on Christ, yet Christ himself focused on the FATHER, his God [Yahweh]. Christianity has its priorities mixed up and has conjured up various doctrines to rationalize its salvation only in Christ doctrine. However, Joel 2:32 and many other verses stand in sharp defiance to this false Christian teaching.

Copyright 2005 Edward G. Palmer, All Rights Reserved.

The False Salvation Doctrine

> "And it shall come to pass that whoever calls on the name of the LORD [Yahweh] shall be saved." Joel 2:32

Salvation Only In Christ Is Apostasy!

Now, consider for the moment that all manner of willful sinners in Christianity like to grab onto Romans 10:13. Their idea of getting saved is simple; call upon the name of Jesus. If this is reasonable theology within the Christian Church, why is it unreasonable theology for Jews and Muslims to call on the name of Yahweh (or Allah) as God states in Joel 2:32? The Jews call God, Yahweh and the Muslims call God, Allah. Yahweh is the Hebrew name for Abraham's God and Allah is the Arabic name Abraham's God.

Is it any wonder why Christians are often viewed as hypocrites when they teach against their own Holy Bible? Most of those in Christianity have been programmed with so much apostasy that they don't know what is right and wrong from God's perspective. If you want to deprogram yourself, it will take some serious study of your Bible. The wrong focus of Christianity is shown in the graphic below. Consider all the teachings of Jesus.

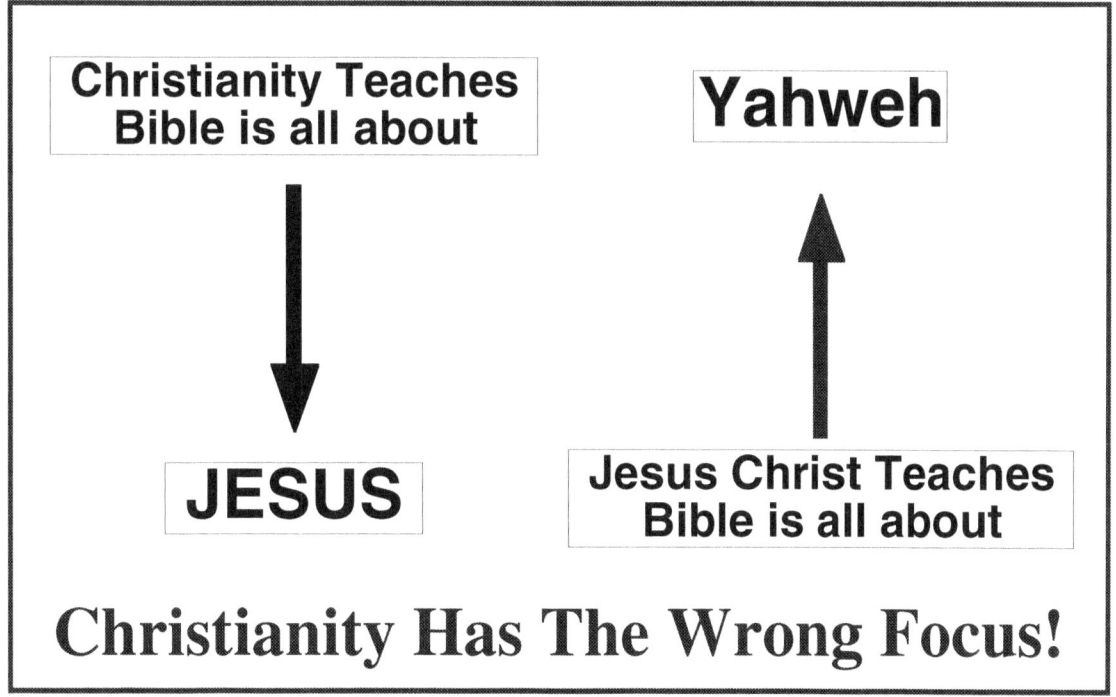

The False Salvation Doctrine

Now when you realize that Jesus made it clear that belief in him was tantamount to belief in Yahweh and that if you are a "sincere believer" your behavior will reflect obedience to God, it is easier to understand what John is really teaching us. Here then is a spiritual translation of whom we are to believe in John 3:16 based upon what Jesus taught in John 12:44.

Original Wording

"For God so loved the world that HE gave HIS only begotten Son, that whoever believes in him should not perish but have everlasting life." John 3:16

Spiritual Translation

"For Yahweh so loved the world that Yahweh gave HIS only begotten Son Jesus Christ as a final and perfect sacrifice to atone for the sins of the world. Whoever truly believes in Jesus Christ adopts God's righteousness into their heart and this results in obedience to God's ways. Since the heart changes and adheres to God's righteousness, it is not really belief in Jesus Christ, but belief in Yahweh that has been established through Jesus Christ. Such a believer will not perish but have everlasting life." John 3:16 — *Paraphrased*

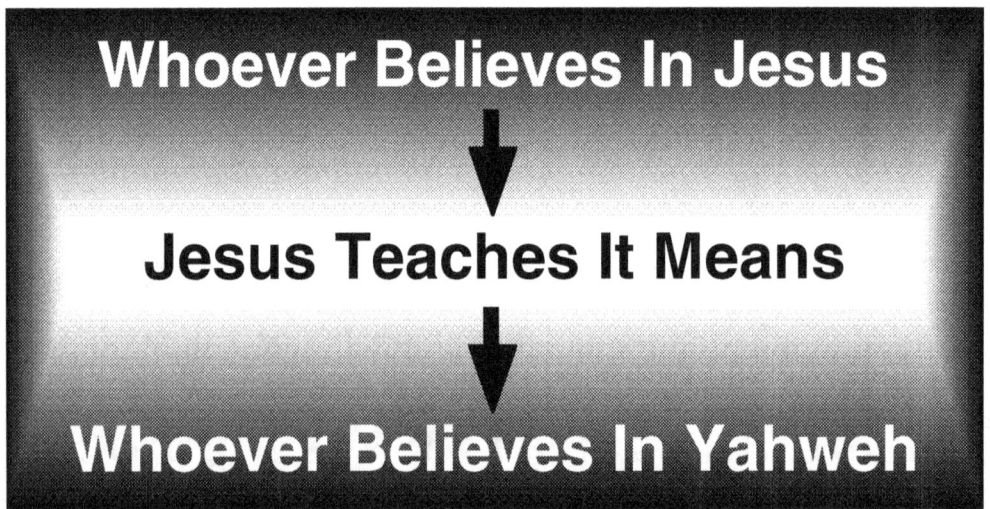

The False Salvation Doctrine

Now study carefully the verses cited on the opening page of this chapter. I could have given you many pages of Scripture references, but they would only amplify those I already gave you. I'm sorry to inform you that you have been taught Christian mythology with the teaching that salvation is only through Christ. If you do a sincere study of Romans 10:13 and the other verses like it, you will also find that it is really those who call on the name of Yahweh that are saved. That should give you pause for concern. Consider also these words of Jesus in John.

Original Wording

> "Most assuredly, I say to you, he who hears my word and believes in HIM who sent me has everlasting life, and shall not come into judgment, but has passed from death into life." John 5:24

Spiritual Translation

> "Most assuredly, I say to you, he who hears the words that I Jesus speak and sincerely believes in Yahweh as a result, has everlasting life, and shall not come into judgment, but has already passed from death into life." John 5:24

Specific teachings of Jesus include:

1. Those who really hear Jesus Christ will believe in Yahweh.
2. True belief in Yahweh is always coupled with a heart for HIM.
3. True believers in Yahweh adopt HIS righteousness standards.
4. Those who believe in Yahweh already have everlasting life.
5. Those who believe in Yahweh shall not come into judgment.
6. Those who believe in Yahweh have already passed from death into eternal life.

He Who Believes In Yahweh Has Everlasting Life!
This is the teaching of Jesus Christ!

The False Salvation Doctrine

Ezekiel 18 contains specific teachings from God Almighty that directly contradict the teachings of Christianity, which would have you believe that salvation came into being with Jesus. It didn't. In fact, all that true and sincere repentance will get you with God through Jesus Christ was and still is available aside from Jesus Christ. If that is so, why do we need Jesus you ask? The *Gift of Jesus* is two chapters away. I will explain it at that time. For now, consider these words of God Almighty on the subject of repentance and eternal life. Remember, these are the words of God, not I!

Salvation <u>Outside</u> Of Christ — Ezekiel 18:4-32

The word of the LORD came to me again …

[4] "Behold, all souls are MINE; the soul of the father as well as the soul of the son is MINE; the soul who sins shall die.

[5] But if a man is just and does what is lawful and right;

[6] If he has not eaten on the mountains, nor lifted up his eyes to the idols of the house of Israel, nor defiled his neighbor's wife, nor approached a woman during her impurity;

[7] If he has not oppressed anyone, but has restored to the debtor his pledge; has robbed no one by violence, but has given his bread to the hungry and covered the naked with clothing;

[8] If he has not exacted usury nor taken any increase, but has withdrawn his hand from iniquity and executed true judgment between man and man;

[9] If he has walked in MY statutes and kept MY judgments faithfully--he is just; he shall surely live!" Says the LORD God.

All Souls Belong To God!

The False Salvation Doctrine

[10] "If he begets a son who is a robber or a shedder of blood, who does any of these things

[11] And does none of those duties, but has eaten on the mountains or defiled his neighbor's wife;

[12] If he has oppressed the poor and needy, robbed by violence, not restored the pledge, lifted his eyes to the idols, or committed abomination;

[13] If he has exacted usury or taken increase--shall he then live? He shall not live! If he has done any of these abominations, he shall surely die; his blood shall be upon him.

[14] If, however, he begets a son who sees all the sins which his father has done, and considers but does not do likewise;

[15] Who has not eaten on the mountains, nor lifted his eyes to the idols of the house of Israel, nor defiled his neighbor's wife;

[16] Has not oppressed anyone, nor withheld a pledge, nor robbed by violence, but has given his bread to the hungry and covered the naked with clothing;

[17] Who has withdrawn his hand from the poor and not received usury or increase, but has executed MY judgments and walked in MY statutes--he shall not die for the iniquity of his father; he shall surely live!

[18] As for his father, because he cruelly oppressed, robbed his brother by violence, and did what is not good among his people, behold, he shall die for his iniquity.

[19] Yet you say, 'Why should the son not bear the guilt of the father?' Because the son has done what is lawful and right, and has kept all MY statutes and observed them, he shall surely live."

The Soul Who Sins Shall Die!

The False Salvation Doctrine

[20] "The soul who sins shall die. The son shall not bear the guilt of the father, nor the father bear the guilt of the son. The righteousness of the righteous shall be upon himself, and the wickedness of the wicked shall be upon himself.

[21] But if a wicked man turns from all his sins, which he has committed, keeps all MY statutes, and does what is lawful and right, he shall surely live; he shall not die.

[22] None of the transgressions which he has committed shall be remembered against him; because of the righteousness which he has done, he shall live.

[23] Do I have any pleasure at all that the wicked should die? Says the LORD God, and not that he should turn from his ways and live?

[24] But when a righteous man turns away from his righteousness and commits iniquity, and does according to all the abominations that the wicked man does, shall he live? All the righteousness, which he has done, shall not be remembered; because of the unfaithfulness of which he is guilty and the sin, which he has committed, because of them he shall die.

[25] Yet you say, 'The way of the LORD is not fair.' Hear now, O house of Israel, is it not MY way, which is fair, and your ways, which are not fair?

[26] When a righteous man turns away from his righteousness, commits iniquity, and dies in it, it is because of the iniquity which he has done that he dies.

[27] Again, when a wicked man turns away from the wickedness which he committed, and does what is lawful and right, he preserves himself alive."

Turn Away From Wickedness And Live!

The False Salvation Doctrine

[28] "Because he considers and turns away from all the transgressions, which he committed, he shall surely live; he shall not die.

[29] Yet the house of Israel says, 'The way of the LORD is not fair.' O house of Israel is it not MY ways, which are fair, and your ways, which are not fair?

[30] Therefore I will judge you, O house of Israel, every one according to his ways," says the LORD God. "Repent, and turn from all your transgressions, so that iniquity will not be your ruin.

[31] Cast away from you all the transgressions, which you have committed, and get yourselves a new heart and a new spirit. For why should you die, O house of Israel?

[32] For I have no pleasure in the death of one who dies, says the LORD God. Therefore turn and live!"

Spend some time and study these verses from Ezekiel 18 and you will realize that God is serious about sin resulting in death. Notice also that all the righteousness you have done vanishes when you turn to wickedness. Has anything really changed in God's eyes because of the New Testament in regards to sin, repentance and salvation? The answer is no, it hasn't and the Apostle Paul reinforces this fact with the following verse.

"For the wages of sin is death, but the gift of God is eternal life in Christ Jesus our Lord." Romans 6:23

Paul can confidently teach you that the "gift of God" is eternal life in Christ Jesus our Lord because he knows that true believers actually believe in Yahweh like Jesus taught. This belief engenders a close friendship with God and HIS Son Jesus. It's a friendship in which you give up all offensive behavior. The gift is manifest by both a changed heart and obedience.

The False Salvation Doctrine

You've learned that two major aspects of the false salvation doctrine are: a) the half-baked presentation of Paul's salvation recipe; and, b) the false idea that salvation only comes through Jesus Christ. Now consider the following table of 25 biblical teachings on the issue of salvation. For our purposes, you can consider that the terms life; eternal life and salvation are all the same. Note: The letter *S* stands for salvation in the table below.

Salvation Truth Table

Teaching from Holy Bible	Says Who	Reference
Salvation belongs to Yahweh	David	Psalm 3:8
Salvation belongs to Yahweh	John	Rev. 7:10
Salvation belongs also to the Lamb (Jesus)	John	Rev. 7:10
Salvation belongs to Yahweh	Jesus	John 5:26
Salvation belongs also to the Son (Jesus)	Jesus	John 5:26
Whoever praises Yahweh has salvation	Yahweh	Psalm 50:23
Whoever orders his conduct aright has S	Yahweh	Psalm 50:23
Whoever believes in Yahweh has S	Jesus	John 5:24
Whoever calls on name of Yahweh has S	Yahweh	Joel 2:32
Whoever believes unto righteousness has S	Paul	Romans 10:10
Whoever obeys what Jesus taught has S	Jesus	Luke 6:46
Whoever is awake to righteousness has S	Paul	1 Cor. 15:34
Whoever does not sin has S	Paul	Romans 4:8
Whoever is set free from sin has salvation	Paul	Romans 6:22
Whoever believes in Yahweh via Christ has S	John	John 3:16
Whoever is faithful to the LORD God has S	Yahweh	Ezekiel 18:9
Whoever turns away from wickedness has S	Yahweh	Ezekiel 18:21
Whoever gets a new heart and spirit has S	Yahweh	Ezekiel 18:31
Benefactors of righteous prayers may have S	Yahweh	Ezekiel 14:14
Benefactors of apostle's forgiveness have S	Jesus	John 20:20
Obeying the Ten Commandments means S	Jesus	Matt 19:17
Having a minimum righteousness means S	Jesus	Matt 5:20
Obeying two great commandments means S	Jesus	Matt 22:40
Righteous people will see salvation	Solomon	Wisdom 5:2
Righteous people will see salvation	Jesus	Matt 13:43

The False Salvation Doctrine

The preceding Scriptures make it abundantly clear a false salvation doctrine is being taught within Christianity. Not only is Apostle Paul's salvation recipe taught in a half-baked way, but also many Scriptures that teach opposing instructions from God and HIS Son are simply ignored. There are 148 salvation Scriptures in the NKJV Bible and I have studied virtually every one of them in that translation and others. If you cannot accept the Scripture citations, you owe it to yourself to conduct a detailed study on your own. Search on the word "salvation" in any Bible software to obtain a study list or use a good concordance like *The Guideposts Family Concordance*.[6]

> **"And he opened their understanding, that they might comprehend the Scriptures." Luke 24:45**

> **"And we know that the Son of God has come and has given us an understanding, that we may know HIM [Yahweh] who is true; and we are in HIM [Yahweh] who is true, in his Son Jesus Christ [when we believe unto God's righteousness with a new and changed heart]. This [Yahweh] is the true God and [HIS is the only] eternal life." 1 John 5:20**

> **Jesus said: "He who is of God hears God's words."**
> **John 8:47**

"When you understand God's salvation, you realize that it transcends just mouthing the words —'Jesus is my Lord.' You realize that salvation even transcends Jesus Christ himself and that salvation exists in God and righteousness despite the teachings of modern day Christianity. God has not changed and salvation has always belonged to HIM!" The Apostle Edward

When God's Word Speaks To You, You Know That Christianity Teaches …

The False Salvation Doctrine

Book of Edward

Chapter Thirteen
A Light On My Path

"Your word is … a light for my path." Psalm 119:105 NLT

"Search me, O God … And see if there be any wicked way in me, and lead me in the way everlasting." Psalm 139:23-24 KJV

"You will show me the path of life." Psalm 16:11

"You enlarged my path under me." 2 Samuel 22:37

"It is God who … makes my way perfect." Psalm 18:32

"Make me walk in the path of Your commandments, for I delight in it." Psalm 119:35

"For this is what the high and lofty One says—He who lives forever, whose name is holy: I live … with him who is contrite and lowly in spirit." Isaiah 57:15 NIV

"He comforts us in all our troubles so that we can comfort others. When others are troubled, we will be able to give them the same comfort God has given us." 2 Cor. 1:4 NLT

"Keep a close watch on yourself and on your teaching. Stay true to what is right, and God will save you and those who hear you." 1 Tim. 4:16 NLT

"Lord, You will grant us peace, for all we have accomplished is really from You." Isaiah 26:12 NLT

A Light On My Path

What is the proudest one thing you have ever done in your life? That was the question posed by a family relationship game card, being discussed over the radio a few days ago. It is apparently a game designed to build deeper relationships within the family between parents and children. I wasn't listening closely enough to get the name of the game, so you will have to track it down if you are interested in it. When I heard the question posed, I reflected on it and could not come up with an immediate and easy answer. It is an interesting question; it is also a very deep question. So, if you could only name one thing you have done in your life that represents the proudest thing you have done [or moment in your life], what would it be? Think about it for a while and take your time. That is exactly what I did.

At some point during the next 24 hours, the answer came to my mind and I knew it was the only answer for me. So, for my grandchildren and children who are now eagerly wanting to know, here is the answer. The single proudest thing that I have ever done in my life was to "surrender myself 100% to God." I can also tell you that the second proudest thing that I did in my life was to "give everything that I owned away." That was the day I opted out of ownership and instead chose to be only a steward for God.

The first choice set my soul and spirit free even while my body has continued to live in this earthly realm. The second choice set my soul free emotionally; it also set my body free physically even while I continue to live in an earthly vessel. Indeed, those two choices confirmed to God that I am indeed an alien on this planet. Yes, it's true; I simply do not belong to this world. All you UFO buffs should understand that this is a metaphor. I am an earthling; I am not from another planet. Yet I am from God and I belong to God, even now, and no matter what life brings. Listen to God's word.

> **"I will come near you for judgment; I will be a swift witness against sorcerers, against adulterers, against perjurers, against those who exploit wage earners and widows and orphans, and against those who turn away an alien — because they do not fear ME, Says the LORD of hosts."**
> **Malachi 3:5**

A Light On My Path

I did not state that this "proudest" one moment was when I "knew about" God. For thirty-two years I had been given information and known about God. The proudest moment I had was when I actually surrendered myself into His loving hands. There is a difference. Knowing about God involves the head and all the mental thoughts of God and who He is. The "surrender" to God involves a decision from your heart to enter into an everlasting relationship with God. A relationship that starts at the present moment right smack in the middle of your now earthly journey, even your earthly difficulties and even in the middle of your earthly trials and sufferings. Yes, even in the middle of a very difficult moment of your own life, you can find yourself in the hands of a loving God who will guide you from that point forward—if you make the right choice from your heart.

Did not Jesus say you would "do greater works than he did?"

"Most assuredly, I say to you, he who believes in me, the works that I do he will do also; and greater works than these he will do, because I go to my Father." John 14:12

How could you ever expect such a reality of "greater works" to occur if you didn't fully surrender yourself to God? How could you ever expect such a reality if you were still "tied" into a physical and materialistic world? You have entered life as part of this world's material and physical system. The choice now from God is clear; you are either a friend to this world or a friend to Him. Listen to the Word.

"Adulterers and adulteresses! Do you not know that friendship with the world is enmity with God? Whoever therefore wants to be a friend of the world makes himself [or herself] an enemy of God." James 4:4

Memo. When you fully appreciate the above three scriptures, you will realize the depth of the false doctrines that ask you to be entangled with this world's systems. Such teachings as modern tithing and Jesus as a rich man [in the material sense] are abominations unto God Almighty. He will have the last word with those who continue to teach such lies. End Memo.

A Light On My Path

This chapter is about the spiritual journey that led me to the point of surrendering my heart to God and that special moment in time when I just "knew God" throughout my whole being. That whole being is my body, soul and spirit. Paul teaches on your "whole" being and it is also expressed by the graphic shown below.

> "Now may the God of peace HIMSELF sanctify you completely; and may your whole spirit, soul, and body be preserved blameless at the coming of our Lord Jesus Christ." 1 Thessalonians 5:23

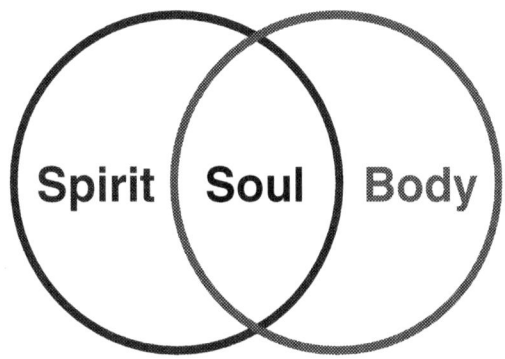

Your Whole Being Is "Spirit, Soul & Body!"

God has just given me the above illustration. I had prayed about this issue several times, asking God for clarity on this subject of our "whole being." Some Christians believe and translate the word "soul" only as your breath of life. When you stop breathing, they believe it is the temporary end of your existence. Atheists believe it is a permanent end. However, those Christians who believe it is our temporary end, believe we will exist again at the time of our bodily resurrection, a subject discussed in the last chapter.

Anyone who has ever closely witnessed death can testify that the soul departs from the body. I believe it leaves with the spirit and returns back to God. The soul is often thought of as the seat of our emotions and will. It is associated with emotions, the heart and the mind in the Holy Bible.

A Light On My Path

The soul lies between the spirit and the body, which war against each other for control [of your soul]. At the end of the day, which side expresses itself through your own soul's behavior, your spirit or your flesh [the body]? Obviously, the soul is our human expression and the totality of who we are on earth and of which side controls or reigns within us, the spirit and good or the flesh and evil. It is an interesting analogy, isn't it? Moses taught the following concerning the soul departing from Rachel when she died.

"And as her soul was departing, for she died, she called his name Ben-Oni [son of my sorrow]; but his father called him Benjamin [son of the right hand]." Genesis 35:18 AMP

I witnessed Jackie's last breath of life. I can tell you that I also bear witness that her soul departed from her body along with her spirit. I can also tell you that her soul was in between both worlds for several days and there was no fear in her of where she was headed. I kept telling her it was okay for her to go, that I would also be okay. At one point she quipped back: "Don't rush me, I am not ready yet!" Jackie knew precisely where she was going and who was waiting for her at the appointed time. Jackie's bravery and lack of concern for herself was clear evidence to me that she knew she was traveling to a place of happiness and joy. It would be a place without further pain and suffering. The facts concerning her soul's departure cannot be denied and I am not the only person who bears witness to them. Her death demonstrated to me the truth of the teaching of Moses that the "soul departs from the body at death."

Job teaches us that the "soul" can choose death over the body.

"So that my soul chooses strangling and death rather than my body." Job 7:15

Jesus teaches us that the body and the soul can be killed.

"And do not fear those who kill the body but cannot kill the soul. But rather fear HIM who is able to destroy both soul and body in Hell." Matthew 10:28

A Light On My Path

James teaches us that the body without the spirit is dead.

"For as the body without the spirit is dead, so faith without works is dead also." James 2:26

Some think they can express the spirit, soul and body [this whole] in a form of overlapping circles as you might see the trinity doctrine expressed. I am here to tell you that the soul manifests itself from within the overlapping spirit and body forces. It is the synergistic output of your total life and an expression of the battle that is waged spiritually from within and without. Therefore, you would never see a separation of the body force from the spirit-soul force except when death occurs.

Thus, visually, the death of our whole being takes on the following separation of forces. The spirit-soul force returns to God. This is the essence of who we have become. Our body then returns to the dust of the earth. Simple enough to understand until you get into various resurrection doctrines.

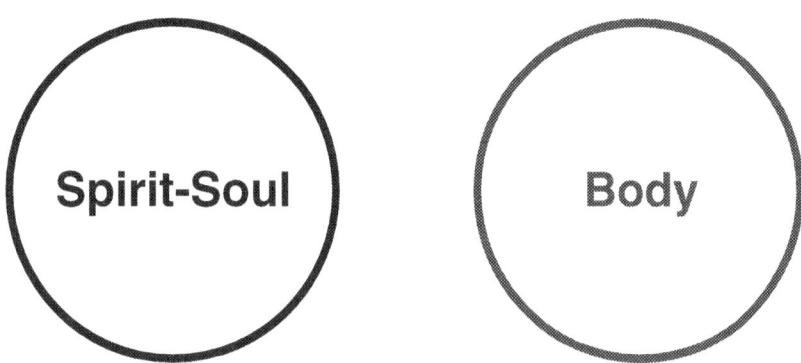

Death Occurs When Our Spirit-Soul Leaves Our Body!

It makes sense that we will be with God when we die given what Jesus and Paul taught. Consider that Jesus taught, "those who believe in God Almighty [HE who sent Jesus] already have everlasting life." They have passed into eternal life and will not come into judgment. Example: I am physically on this earth, yet I have already passed into eternal life.

A Light On My Path

> **"Most assuredly, I say to you, he who hears my word and believes in HIM who sent me has everlasting life, and shall not come into judgment, but has passed from death into life." John 5:24**

I recently discovered an interesting paradox in the teachings of Jesus. Consider that Jesus taught us in the above verse that those who believe in Yahweh [HIM who sent Jesus] already have everlasting life and has passed from death into life. Then contrast this with the teachings of Jesus that he will pick up his followers on the "last" day. I am wondering if this is a reflection on those Christians who are righteous yet worship Jesus instead of God? If I get the answer from God on the subject, I will let you know and try to explain it. For now, think about these words of Jesus. Interesting!

Then there is Apostle Paul's teaching that when we are absent from the body, we are present with the Lord.

> **"So we are always confident, knowing that while we are at home in the body we are absent from the Lord. For we walk by faith, not by sight. We are confident, yes, well pleased rather to be absent from the body and to be present with the Lord." 2 Cor. 5:6-8**

Exactly what is Paul talking about if he is not talking about our spirit-soul force and the real essence of us—being present with the Lord? I have to conclude that I will be with my God and HIS Son the moment I die. My spirit-soul force will return to them and my body will return to dust. Later, at God's appointed time, there will be a bodily resurrection. At that time, my spirit-soul force will be reunited with a new resurrection body. It will be a very exciting time. I am drifting a little, but bear with me. All this will be tied together shortly. If you want more discussion on the resurrection, you will find it in the last chapter.

Paul also taught that the spiritual battle for our souls couldn't be fought with our flesh. We will need to put on God's "spiritual" armor to make it to our heavenly home and to fight the good fight here on earth.

Copyright 2005 Edward G. Palmer, All Rights Reserved.

Book of Edward—Chapter 13

A Light On My Path

"For though we walk in the flesh, we do not war according to the flesh." 2 Cor. 10:3

Comment: The battle for our soul is a spiritual battle. It is waged between the spirit and the body [flesh]. Successful control of the soul is demonstrated by our behavior, driven either by the spirit or the flesh.

"There is therefore now no condemnation to those who are in Christ Jesus, who do not walk according to the flesh, but according to the Spirit." Romans 8:1

Comment: Those in Christ have totally surrendered to God and His Son. Their lives are no longer a spiritual contest between Satan and Christ.

"For those who live according to the flesh set their minds on the things of the flesh, but those who live according to the Spirit, the things of the Spirit." Romans 8:5

Comment: The spirit says: "Do Not Sin!" The flesh says: "Go for it!" Those with Christ have a heavenly focus. Those with Satan are focused on this world and its systems. That includes obsession with material things and riches according to the world's definition. They have not learned "to set their minds on the things of the Spirit."

"But you are not in the flesh but in the Spirit, if indeed the Spirit of God dwells in you. Now if anyone does not have the spirit of Christ, he is not his." Romans 8:9

"Clearly you are an epistle of Christ, ministered by us, written not with ink but by the Spirit of the living God, not on tablets of stone but on tablets of flesh, that is, of the heart." 2 Cor. 3:3

Paul makes it clear that those with God have His commands written on the tablets of their heart. This transcends the mere thoughts of our mind.

A Light On My Path

The heart is tantamount to the transmission of a car when the engine represents the mind. You won't get far with just your mind's thoughts unless your heart is right with God. It is the transmission that moves the car in the right direction. Likewise, your heart is the spiritual transmission that moves your soul in the right direction. When I surrendered to God's will, I engaged my spiritual transmission [heart] to move my soul in God's direction. Prior to that moment in time, God was just a bunch of mental thoughts. God was just a roar of my engine [mind]. Our minds can also engage our mouth and still get us nowhere with God. That is why God says: "Their mouth is close, but their heart is far away; they worship ME in vain."

> **"I say then: Walk in the Spirit, and you shall not fulfill the lust of the flesh. For the flesh lusts against the Spirit, and the Spirit against the flesh; and these are contrary to one another, so that you do not do the things that you wish. But if you are led by the Spirit, you are not under the law. Now the works of the flesh are evident, which are: adultery, fornication, uncleanness, lewdness." Galatians 5:16-19**

Let me see if I can tie these thoughts together with some graphics. When you start to walk in the spirit, the soul joins forces with the spirit and they jointly start to move in the right direction overwhelming the force of the flesh or body. The graphic looks like this in which the body is demoted.

Soul Starting To Obey Spirit's Direction

A Light On My Path

At some point God's Spirit and your spirit are linked up and they exert full control over your soul and body. You are headed for Heaven and your earthly walk then looks like this.

Walking In The Spirit

Notice that there is not a perfect overlap. In other words, you could still stumble and be subject to a limited control of your flesh. However, this graphic reflects what it means to walk in the spirit. It means that your soul or essence of who you are is not focused on fleshly concerns. It is the spirit that exercises primary control over your soul. Your soul then focuses on heavenly things, not on earthly things. When I gave myself to God in the full 100% surrender of my heart, the above is what it looked like spiritually.

Walking in the flesh is an exact opposite and it looks like this. In this instance, the Spirit exhibits little control over the soul. This is a life of sin.

Walking In The Flesh

Copyright 2005 Edward G. Palmer, All Rights Reserved.

Book of Edward—Chapter 13

A Light On My Path

At the time of our death, this is a graphical view of what will happen to our "whole-being." The destination of the spirit-soul is a choice we make.

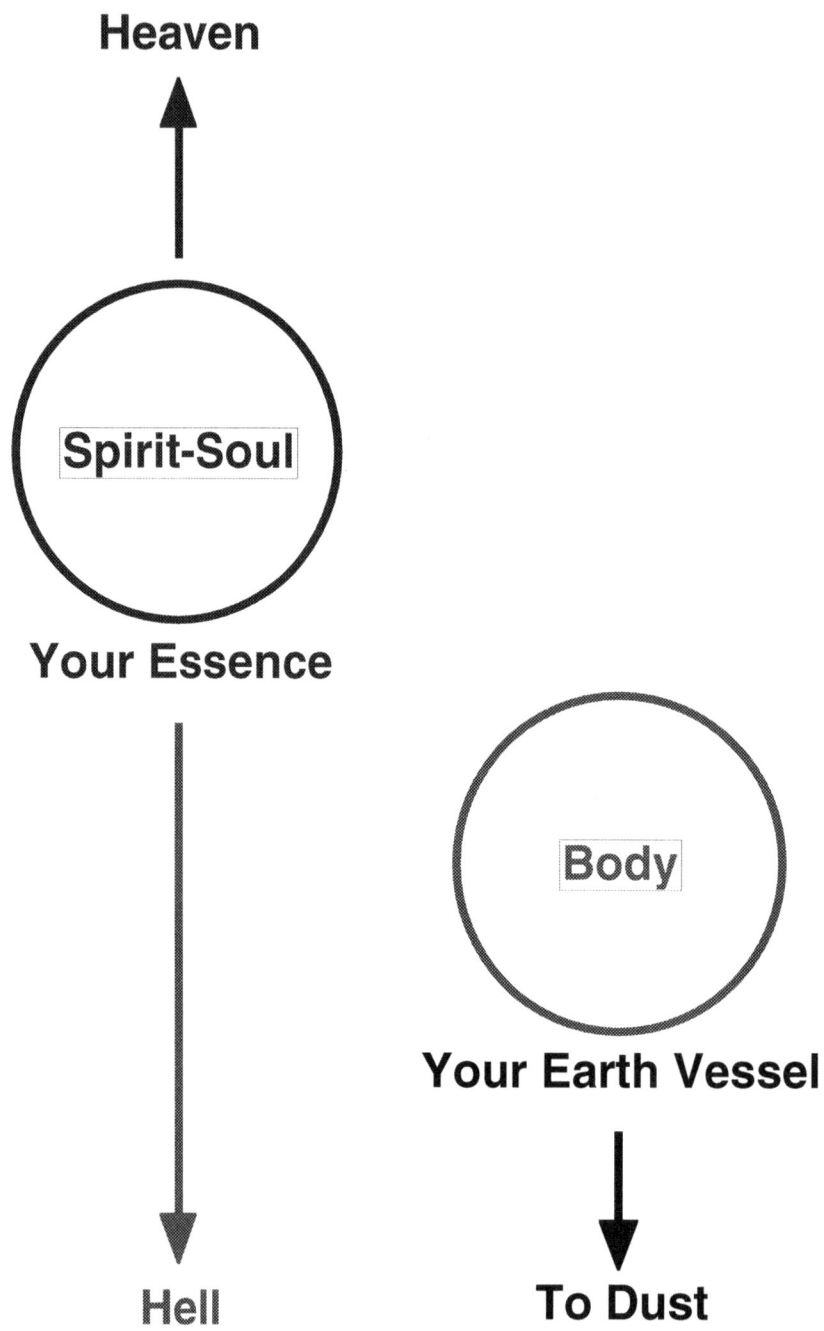

What Happens To "Whole-Being" At Death!

Copyright 2005 Edward G. Palmer, All Rights Reserved.

Book of Edward—Chapter 13

A Light On My Path

All of this is to let you know that the decision of my heart had some consequences. I was ready and willing to let God take over. I honestly had come to the conclusion I had given it my best shot in life and had come up short. Certainly, for me, there had to be a better way to live. There had to be more truth to this existence that I had not explored. There was and all it took to find it—was for me to surrender my heart 100% to God. I have heard it preached that the heart is actually the mind. This is not true and I want you to fully understand what it is that I actually surrendered to God. Therefore, let's look at another graphic that expands on the "soul" picture and considers the mind, heart and emotions. The essence of who you are is expressed by your soul. The spirit and flesh [body] are two spiritual forces exerted on the soul trying to control, who it is or will become. The soul looks something like this graphic albeit this is an incomplete illustration.

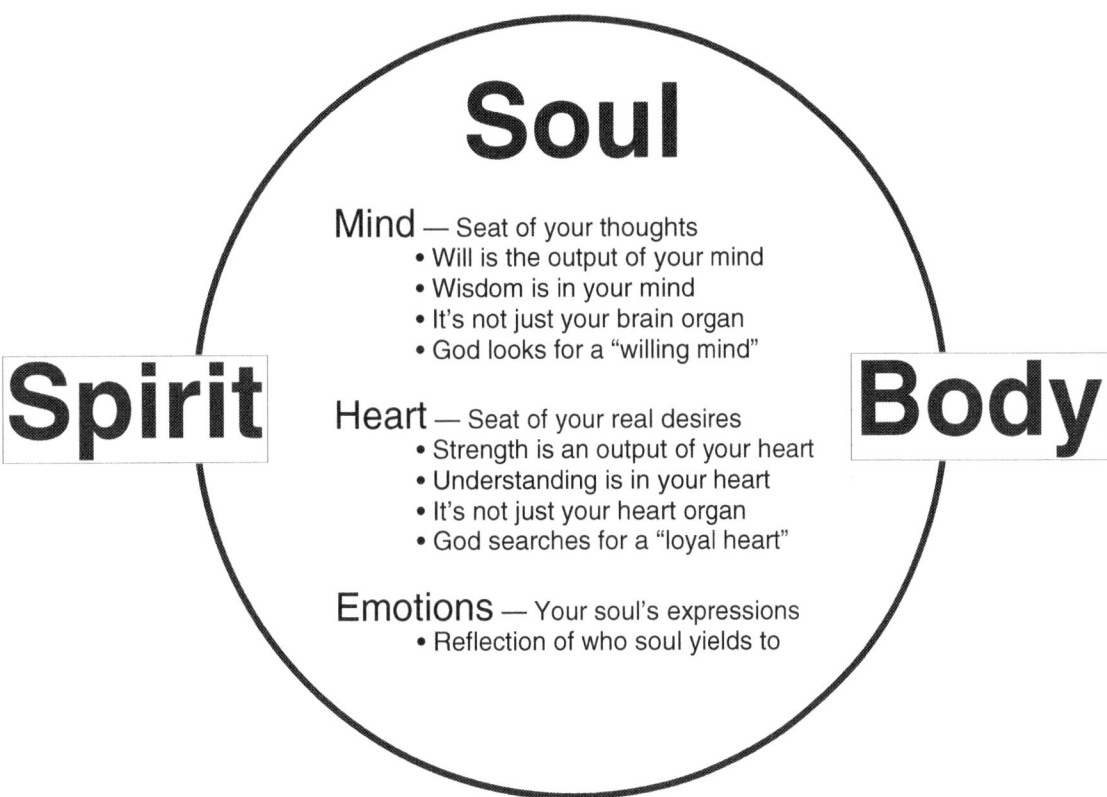

Your Essence Manifested To Humanity

A Light On My Path

It is clear in the Bible that the mind and heart are not the same thing; and, both are shown in various scriptures to be separate from one another. Therefore, the mind cannot be substituted for the heart in any doctrine. To do so is to foist apostasy onto you. Bill if you are still reading, you should listen to the word of the LORD.

> **"Who has put wisdom in the mind? Or who has given understanding to the heart?" Job 38:36**

> **"But, O LORD of hosts, YOU who judge righteously, testing the mind and the heart." Jeremiah 11:20**

> **"I, the LORD, search the heart, I test the mind …"**
> **Jeremiah 17:10**

> **"But, O LORD of hosts, YOU who test the righteous, and see the mind and heart." Jeremiah 20:12**

In retrospect, all my life I have felt God tug upon my soul in one way or another. Yet HE could not get past my mind and into the bowels of my soul until age 32. I believe I had to exhaust all that "human" capability from within me first. Yes, the LORD looks into our souls. HE sees the mind and its intent. HE sees the heart and where its loyalty lies. HE tests both our mind and our heart to see if they are true to HIM. For those who walk with God, HE places wisdom in their mind and understanding in their heart.

When you study the mind in the Bible, you will find these kind of attributes: Being renewed; being of one mind; willing; ready; comes to; recalled by; grieved; vexed; remembered by; anxious; debased; fleshly. You will also find in Romans that the mind serves the "Law of God." In contrast, the flesh or body serves the "Law of Sin." Therefore, the spirit in our whole being is the conduit for our soul's mind back to God's Spirit. Our spirit is literally God's channel of influence into our soul. It is how HE lets us know HIS mind, HIS heart and HIS voice. And we only perceive God's inputs when we quiet ourselves down from the noise of this world. That is why we are instructed by God to "be still and know HIM" in Psalm 46:10.

A Light On My Path

Study the word loyal in the Bible and you will find it associated with the heart and not the mind. You will not find the phrase "loyal mind" in the Bible. You will find several verses where it is taught to have a "loyal heart" towards God. Thus the loyalty of our soul emanates from within our heart. I can phrase this a little differently for you by saying that what is in your heart is what you really believe in. That is to say, your actions speak of what is actually within your heart. The old adage to watch what they do and not what they say is true. In another sense, the truth as our soul sees it emanates from our heart, not our mind. Real, sincere belief comes from the core of your soul. It comes from the bowels of the soul where the heart resides.

What's In The Heart—Is What Is Really Believed!

"For the eyes of the LORD run to and fro throughout the whole earth, to show HIMSELF strong on behalf of those whose heart is loyal to HIM." 2 Chronicles 16:9

In the spring of my thirty-second year of life, I gave God my whole heart without any reservation or hesitation. I said: "I get it now God; I now understand. From here on, YOU lead and I will follow." That was my real salvation prayer; it was from my heart to God's heart and I will never forget the event or the fellowship with God that occurred. It was an epiphany for me. When you have a quiet conversation with God and tell HIM the same thing, you will find that your life suddenly changes. Mine certainly did.

In essence, I finally opened up the door of my heart and let God in. That completed HIS communication channel to my heart, the center of my soul. God communicates to us through the spirit. The channel is God, HIS Spirit, and HIS Son's spirit communicating directly with our spirit. Our spirit is like the remnant God placed in married couples to give them one flesh. Do you remember? Our soul is given such a remnant of God's Spirit. It allows our soul to see where we come from, to understand that there is an eternity. From the spirit of our soul, the communications then goes to our mind. However, if this is all the farther God's communication can get, there cannot be any permanent change in our life.

A Light On My Path

God's communications must actually get to our heart, the bowels and core of our soul. Don't think of the mind and heart as simply those muscles and organs in our physical body. When the Bible speaks of these, there is much more involved from a spiritual perspective than just a physical body part. For example: Being of the same mind; having the mind of Christ, etc.

Graphically, when I gave my heart to God, I opened the doorway from my mind to my heart so HE could have control. It was a choice I have never regretted. Life has been very exciting for me since that day. Now, can you understand statements like: a) He or she doesn't have a heart for it; or, b) Let's get to the heart of the matter? All such statements acknowledge that at the core of who we are, our soul has a heart in which true beliefs are kept.

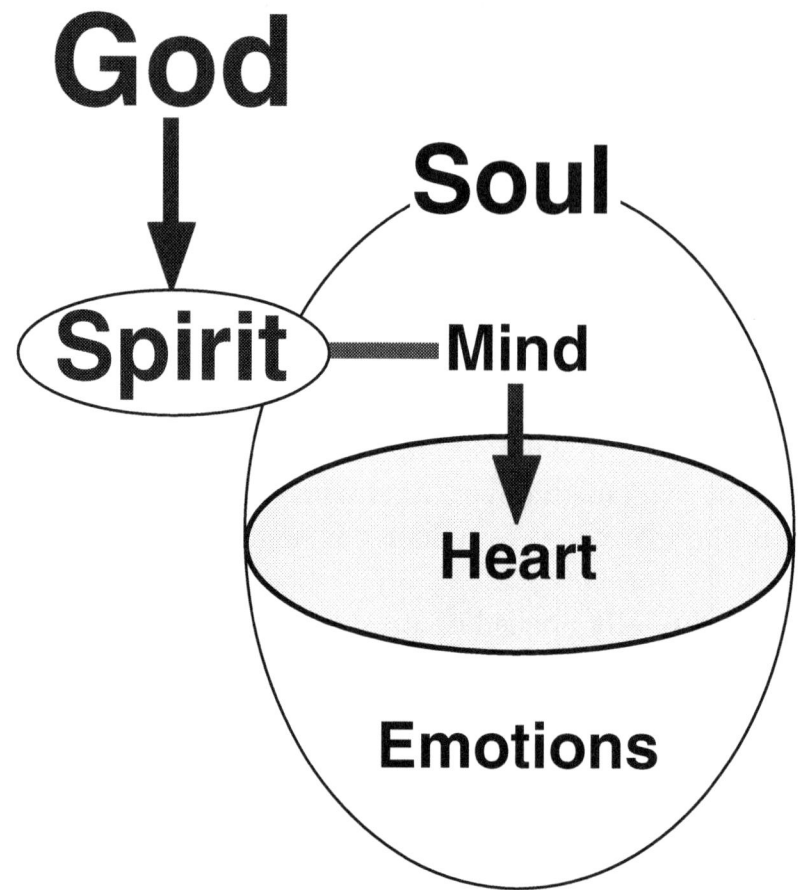

God's Communication Channel

Copyright 2005 Edward G. Palmer, All Rights Reserved.

A Light On My Path

We have been given the power of a strong mind and Paul taught us that with the "mind" we will serve the law of God and that with the "flesh" [body] we serve the law of sin. God doesn't make a play on your emotions to get anything out of you. God will come in through the front door of your mind and then tug at the door of your heart. When your mind is convinced, you yourself will willingly open up the door of your heart to God Almighty. In contrast, Satan will come through the back door of your emotions. He will use your flesh [body] to manipulate your emotions to get into your heart in a false and evil way. You should beware of any ministry that trades on the emotions of the crowd on a regular basis. God has said: "Come and let us reason together" and reason transcends our human emotions. Get it?

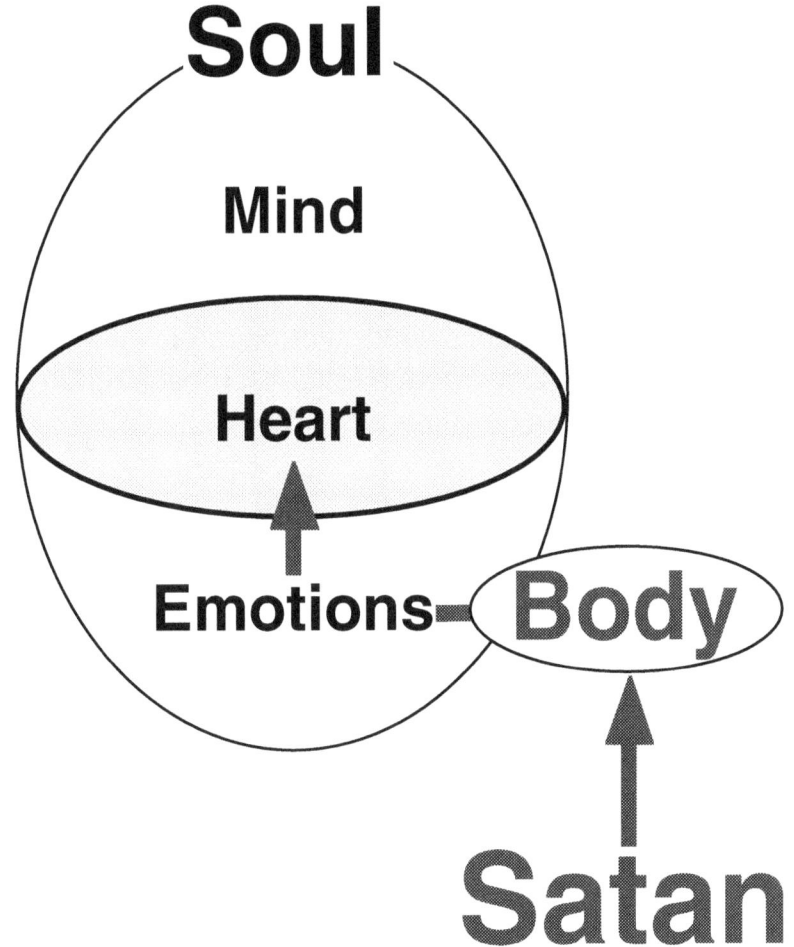

Satan's Communication Channel

A Light On My Path

I have had two people I know tell me that when their kids got old enough they could make their own choice as to whether or not they will believe in God. I wish it were so simple, it isn't. Satan's forces are deployed on the body and throughout our life to influence our heart in an evil way. If you fail to teach your children about God, Satan will use society to teach them there is no God; there is no right and wrong. Remember, this is about reason in our mind, not emotion. How could your kids make the best decision of their mind without knowledge of God? Few will listen to what is written on their mind and heart without external input. Satan will make sure he gets his input into your kids. Has not God taught us to "train up a child in the way he should go?" Yes, you can expect some vacillation between the forces of the spirit and the body on the soul; but there is no neutral position. You are either being trained by God or by Satan.

I wasn't with God for 32 years of my life even though HE constantly tugged at my heart's door. A friend of mine who led the Bible study group at one of my jobs told me that he sung in the choir loft for 35 years and knew then that he was not really saved all those years. Of course, he felt good singing in the choir on Sundays; but, that is not the same thing as having God inside your heart. One is our emotion in play and the other is the mind serving the "law of God" with a loyal heart backing up reason. Don't ever think your soul can be a neutral observer; it can't!

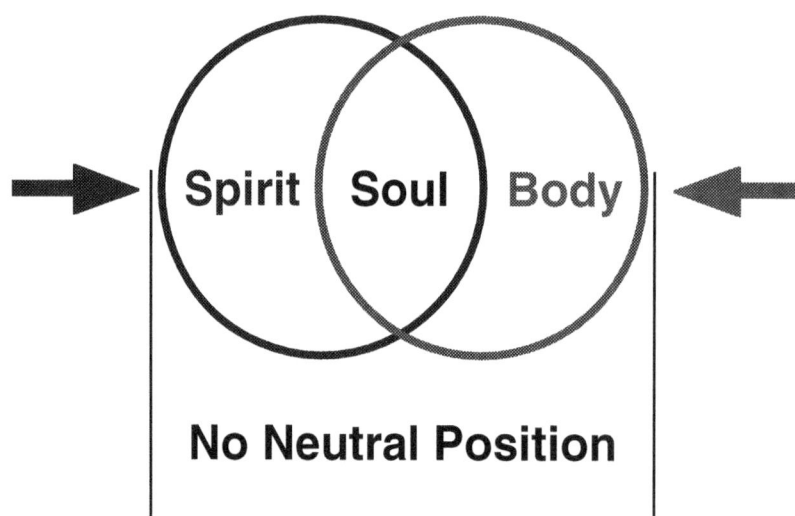

Copyright 2005 Edward G. Palmer, All Rights Reserved.

A Light On My Path

The arrows at the right and left of the graphic above represent the spiritual forces in life putting pressure on the soul to join up with the spirit and move right to be with God or to join up with the flesh [body] and move left to be with Satan. If you are not consciously walking with God you are not walking with HIM. That is why the Spirit testifies to our spirit concerning everlasting life. Those who have it actually know it.

Those Walking In The Spirit, Consciously Know It!

When I was only 14 years old I kissed Jackie for the very first time. I knew at that brief moment in my life that she was the girl for me. I swung wide open the door of my heart to her soul. Life was never the same after that kiss. Now, for only the second time that I can recall, I swung the door wide open again. This time I did it at age 32 and that significant other was God Almighty. When you can understand the facts that we all guard our hearts closely and are fearful of letting people that close to us, you can understand the significance of opening up your own heart to God. Let's face the reality of exactly where heartbreak comes from. It comes from those who reside in your heart. When you understand that if we walk with God, there can be no second place for HIM — you will appreciate why HE must reside inside your heart. That is where your true love for anyone will reside.

I guarded my heart from anyone other than Jackie because no one ever taught me how to really open it up to God or for that matter that I even had to. Then, there is the matter of the wedding band that was around my heart for Jackie. Let me explain our wedding rings and their significance.

When I gave Jackie's eulogy, I made note of the symbolism of her missing wedding ring. I had the wedding ring she had worn for thirty-nine years taken off of her hand. In its place, I had a crucifix placed within her hands. The crucifix has Jesus nailed to the cross; it is different than just a blank cross. God had showed me Jackie holding this crucifix when I chose the casket. HE literally showed me a vision of her lying inside the casket with the crucifix between her hands. It brought tears to my eyes then, even as it does now.

A Light On My Path

Many preachers in the charismatic movement like to preach an empty cross; he is risen is the message. Yet God told me that you couldn't even come close to appreciating HIS Son Jesus until you realize that Jesus was actually a 100% human being on that cross. Jackie no longer belonged to me or anyone else on this earth; she now belonged to God and HIS Son. Indeed, Jesus came back for her according to his scripture promise. That wasn't the only ring symbolism. I, myself, never wore a wedding ring after the first year of our marriage.

My wedding ring was lost in Hong Kong harbor 38 years ago when I was in the Navy. I pointed the funeral crowd to the pictures of my skinny body when I was in the Navy. I lost too much weight on my first Vietnam cruise and the ring was falling off my finger. I didn't want to lose it, so I picked up another ring at the ship's store. It was also too big for my finger, but I reckoned that I could reduce its size by cutting it and re-soldering it back together. Our ship had arrived in Hong Kong harbor and I was on duty that night. That meant I could not go ashore and had some onboard duties.

I was in the middle of reducing the new ring in size when suddenly a security drill was launched. I was one of the guards at a rocket launcher so I picked up a 45-caliber gun, its ammo and raced up to the launcher. Before I left the computer room where I worked, I placed BOTH of the rings on my wedding finger thinking that they would be safe with me during the drill.

Another shipmate arrived on the launcher deck with an M-1 rifle. I used to be part of a drill team earlier in the Navy. We traveled on weekends flipping Springfield rifles up in the air with bayonets attached doing various stunts in tight formation among each other. I had amazed even myself that I could be coordinated enough to actually do all the rifle stunts. Reflecting back on those skills, I asked my shipmate for his M-1 rifle stating that I would show him some of our drill team's aerial tricks. As I spun the rifle in circles with my right hand, I came at it with my left hand to then make the stopping movement. The rifle did stop. However, as I swung my left hand fast to catch the rifle, both of the wedding rings went sailing off my finger over the ship and into the depths of Hong Kong's dark brown harbor. At the time, they dumped sewage in the harbor and it smelled. Good-bye rings!

A Light On My Path

I never wore another wedding ring. Needless to say, at first Jackie seemed a little suspicious I might not be telling the whole story. Yet there it is, a simple and dumb event. Why didn't I ever wear another wedding ring? It is simple. My heart had a wedding band wrapped around it for the entire thirty-nine years we were married. I knew it was not what was on my hand that really mattered when it came to being faithful to the love of my life. Seven and a half years in the U.S. Navy taught me that much, just observing the behavior of sailors and my own mental considerations while traveling. I learned that it was what was in my heart that really mattered; not what was on my wedding finger.

No amount of jewelry that beckons you to loyalty will keep your heart from adultery if it is intent on sin. Now, when I was young, I can't say that I dated a ton of young women. I certainly dated quite a few. However, I can say with absolute conviction that not a single woman in my life ever entered into my heart except one, Jacqueline Lee Bowers. And, she entered my heart during that kiss when I was 14 and she was only 13. I knew it at the time too. I always knew that as long as she was the woman in my heart, she had nothing to worry about. Jackie came to appreciate that truth after a short while and nothing could replace the ring she first put on my finger except the band that was wrapped around my heart. I eventually quit wearing all forms of jewelry, including even a watch.

When you think about it, the love of our life has to be in our heart or else the statement [love of our life] isn't true. However, isn't this fact also true for all of those you love? You bet it is. In simple terms, those who you really love have a special place in the bowels of your soul [heart]. That is why we guard our hearts, isn't it? We really want to be careful who it is we actually let in that close to our soul. Well, is it any wonder why God Almighty might want the same consideration from us? True love finds a place in the soul's heart. That is what I gave to God on that spring day in the thirty-second year of my life. I gave God my whole heart. Just like I gave Jackie my whole heart for the thirty-nine years of our marriage.

God Wants Your Whole Heart — A Loyal Heart!

A Light On My Path

What happens to your behavior when you give someone your whole heart? It is simple, isn't it? You want to do everything in your power to show your love for such a person, don't you? One of the ways we show our love is to honor such a person. In fact, we are admonished by God to honor the wife of our youth. True love doesn't stop such honor because of age.

While Jackie was dying, she asked me: "Ed, will you do me a favor and paint the small bedroom?" She asked me this 2-3 times and I always answered yes. I haven't gotten around to this task yet. However, it is on the list of the things that I have to do. Not because I personally want the room painted. In my maleness, the room is acceptable as is. No, I will paint the room because I want to honor Jackie. I will paint it because she asked.

Therefore, part of our honoring of those we love is to actually do what they would like us to do. Jackie's spirit is always around me. When I reach for the wrong shirt to go with some pants, I can still hear her voice saying: "You can't wear that shirt with those pants." She also liked to keep a clean and neat house. So guess what? I keep a clean and neat house just to honor her. She liked the bed made and every day that I make it — I know that I honor her memory. In short, when we really love someone, we honor him or her with our actions. This honor in their absence is also in the form of behavior that is inline with what they would want done had they been here with us. Isn't that what we hope our kids will do when we go on vacation without them? Honor us with their good behavior? And it really doesn't matter if that special someone is physically with us on earth, does it? Honor as a character trait seems to be losing devotees lately. Obedience is also a part of honor. When we love one another, we honor and obey each other. Often, it's our obedience that demonstrates our honor. It shows our respect.

It is the same thing with God and HIS Son. Jesus says that if we really believe in him, we will honor him just like we honor God. That involves our obedience to both their instructions. Listen and consider the word of God.

> **"That all should honor the Son just as they honor the FATHER. He who does not honor the Son does not honor the FATHER who sent him." John 5:23**

A Light On My Path

The result of the surrender of my heart to God was to fully respect and honor both God and HIS only begotten human Son Jesus Christ. This was similar in nature to what I had already given Jackie. When she got my heart, she got my full respect and honor. It's the same thing with God. The question for you now is this: Has HE got your heart? Do you respect and honor both God and HIS Son? Indeed, the issues of respect and honor are the responses from the heart to anyone you deeply love. Respect and honor also means submitting to that person's desires for you. It means obedience. When that someone is not with you physically to look over your shoulder — that will be the time when your love will be tested. That is when God will take a look inside your soul to see the intent of your mind's thoughts and the loyalty of your heart. Will you pass the test? Have you really chosen?

> **"I have chosen to be faithful;**
> **I have determined to live by YOUR laws.**
> **I cling to YOUR decrees.**
> **LORD, don't let me be put to shame!**
> **If YOU will help me,**
> **I will run to follow YOUR commands." Psalm 119:30-32 NLT**

The New King James and King James Version end the preceding scripture with "For YOU shall enlarge my heart." Indeed that is exactly what happens. You won't have to worry about giving up any part of your heart for those who you love. You will find that God will enlarge your heart. HE will enlarge it so much you will "run to follow HIS commands." Just like I have done. You will find like I have that my capacity to love others has grown into the love of Christ and of the FATHER. My love is now unlimited.

For LORD, YOU Shall Enlarge My Heart!

Test your heart now with these three questions; use some blank paper.

1. I honor those whom I love on earth by _____?
2. I honor Jesus Christ whom I love by _____?
3. I honor my FATHER in Heaven whom I love by_____?

Copyright 2005 Edward G. Palmer, All Rights Reserved.

Book of Edward—Chapter 13

A Light On My Path

So, what led me up to this point of surrender in my life? How did I actually get there? What all actually took place during that epiphany? What happened afterwards? When did real change occur in my life? All these are good questions. I cannot offer a complete detailed biography here, but I can provide some background information and at least try to cover some spiritual highlights as they come to mind. Let's start at the beginning of my life and I will highlight some of the spiritual influences and issues as I recall them.

I was born on January 4, 1946 in Minneapolis, Minnesota to Hilda Clara (Winter) Palmer [age 22] and Glen Gilbert Palmer [age 42]. My father was about 20 years older than my mother. My mother was 100% German, my father to the best of my understanding was of French-Canadian descent. She was a Lutheran; he was a Methodist. My mother and father were also born in Minnesota. She was born in the rural town of Beardsley and he in Minneapolis. In the 1950's, the two religions of Lutheran and Methodist were a little like vinegar and water. They didn't blend very well and all I remember are some Lutheran teachings. I do not recall being exposed to any Methodist teachings during my youth.

I am not a stranger to death. It has been around me all my life. My father died at the age of 56 [same age as Jackie]; I was only 13 1/2 years of age. My first son Glen died when he was only 28 days old; Jackie and I were only 18 and 19 at the time. My mother died at the age of 46; I was only 24 years of age. My only sister died at the age of 53; I was 51. There were many other family deaths along the way. If you just looked at the life span of those in my immediate family, it doesn't bode well for my longevity. Yet I look only to God who has said that HE would satisfy me with a long life. I like Genesis 6:3 and also the fact that Moses made it to age 120 with good eyesight and undiminished natural vigor. It is a worthy goal for me.

> **"With long life I will satisfy him, and show him MY salvation." Psalm 91:16**
>
> **And the LORD said, "MY Spirit shall not strive with man forever, for he is indeed flesh; yet his days shall be one hundred and twenty years." Genesis 6:3**

A Light On My Path

> **"Moses was one hundred and twenty years old when he died. His eyes were not dim nor his natural vigor diminished."** Deut. 34:7

All of our married life, Jackie informed me she would die before the age of 60. I never took her seriously until it actually was happening. It is my belief that God told her early on in our life how long she would live. I'm glad I did not believe her; it would have prolonged the suffering I have had to endure in my heart from her loss. During our life, I studied longevity and in the fourteenth year of our marriage decided that I accepted Genesis 6:3.

Science is just catching up with the Bible in realizing that our bodies are designed to live to 120. The only family background that indicates it may be possible for me to live a long life is my paternal grandparents, who both lived well into their nineties. We'll see how long I last; I am certainly satisfied with my life at this point. It has been interesting and I consider life well worth the physical and emotional sufferings I have encountered. Like Jackie, I have no fear of shedding this earthly vessel. Like Jackie, my life is in the hands of the LORD. My children and grandchildren can bear witness to how long God allowed me to stay on this earth.

My mother and father did not have an easy life. I noted by age 10 that my mother suffered from polio first and then from multiple sclerosis (MS). She eventually died from MS while I was in the Navy. By the time she died, her body had degenerated severely to the point she didn't even have control of her eye movement. She was wheelchair bound the last decade of her life and she suffered greatly from a physical perspective. She once told me: "Ed, if there is a Hell — it is right here on planet earth." If so, one could muse of the justice of recycling people until they get it right. Of course, that's not the case since we read in Hebrews 9:27 that we only die once and then the judgment comes. Still, the point that we suffer should not go unnoticed by Christians given what we are taught in the Bible.

> **"For to you it has been granted on behalf of Christ, not only to believe in him, but also to suffer for his sake."**
> **Philip. 1:29**

A Light On My Path

> **"Therefore let those who suffer according to the will of God commit their souls to HIM in doing good, as to a faithful CREATOR." 1 Peter 4:19**

> **"Do not fear any of those things which you are about to suffer. — Be faithful until death, and I will give you the crown of life." Rev. 2:10**

If you are a true believer and you do not suffer in this earthly world, you should be concerned. It might be time for a heart check up. Do I worship a God that expects all of us to suffer? The answer is no. However, you cannot dismiss the teachings of Jesus and the apostles that tell us we will suffer. When you understand that you are not a friend of this world and that you are an alien like I am, you can understand why the world may target you. And the more power you exert for God in this world, the more of a target you become for Satan. The devil doesn't care about those mediocre Christians who won't even talk about God to their close friends. Get it?

Now, think about all the false preaching that teaches Christians just the opposite. If you are suffering, you must not be tithing. Heard that one? Listen, God will take care of these false teachers in HIS timing. Just study the issue of suffering in the Bible and learn the truth about it. Then focus on your endurance when it comes. I have been in various degrees of physical pain for the last 23 years following a couple of accidents. In the early 1980's I took 5,000 – 8,000 mg of Motrin to just take the edge off of back pain. I am happy to report I am better than I was in those days, but I still have a lot of persistent pain. The more I use the computer, the more pain I experience. In one accident, I damaged some tissue behind my right shoulder blade. Every time I am at the computer for any length of time, I suffer greatly. Yet, here I am anyway. I don't complain of pain, because I have to put it in the perspective of what my mother and father suffered. I have nothing compared to their physical sufferings. The best pain medicine I know of is to just get on with your life; that is what my parents did.

Real Believers <u>Will</u> Suffer On This Earth!

A Light On My Path

My father contracted scarlet fever as a child. As a result of the disease, he suffered from grand mal seizures all the days that I knew him. Those seizures manifested themselves in epilepsy like attacks and for the longest time I wondered if I would have any or for that matter have troubles with MS. In spite of the physical attacks on my mother and father's earthly bodies, my memories are only filled with the love my mother and father gave to me. I do not remember hearing any statements of how much either suffered. Reflecting back, I realize how much pain they both suffered in life. In those days, it was common knowledge to just grin and bear what you cannot change. To make the most of the life you have regardless of the pain and suffering you are confronted with. Hey, stuff like medical insurance didn't even exist in the late 1950's. Think about that. Do you rely upon medical insurance to keep you on this earth? You should rely upon God.

By year one, I was baptized as a baby in a Lutheran church. Even though the Lutheran community believes this helps to provide eternal life, I can tell you that all it does is sprinkle water on babies. It is true that support for the sprinkled baptism of an adult can be found in the Bible. However, Baptism through full body immersion after the age of accountability is the preferred method. The age of accountability is generally thought of as age 12 when a young person is able to discern the consequences of their adult decisions. Jackie and I were re-baptized by full immersion as older adults.

After my baby baptism, the next significant spiritual thing I remember was attending Ascension Catholic School in north Minneapolis during kindergarten back in 1952. I've often wondered if I made some kind of promise or deal with God at a young age and then forgot about it? I can't remember much about the experience other than walking back and forth to school. However, I do believe it was the first time I was made aware of God from someone outside of my family. Certainly, if my Catholic teachers had anything to say about it, I learned something about God at the early age of six. My birthday in January got me off to school at the age of six. Jackie's December birthday got her off to school at the age of four. It was God's timing, as HE knew we were predestined for marriage as young adults. HIS timing put us in the same high school class. I guess I'll have to stop grousing about getting a late start to school on that basis alone.

Copyright 2005 Edward G. Palmer, All Rights Reserved.

Book of Edward—Chapter 13

A Light On My Path

The kindergarten was conveniently located about four blocks away from the apartment building we lived in. I wasn't raised Catholic and other than kindergarten and later dating some Catholic girls — that was the extent of my experience in the Catholic faith. Talk about a conflict of religions, you would be considered treading on dangerous ground if you were a Lutheran boy dating a Catholic girl in the early 1960's. Of course, that is only if her parents found out. If they did, it would be time to discuss your possible conversion to Catholicism. I know from first hand experience.

I have always had a thirst for knowledge and truth. Beyond anything else in life, I have valued the truth. I have observed that not many people desire to know the truth like I do; sometimes it can really hurt. Then there's that old adage that "ignorance is bliss." Is it? I think its just ignorance.

During that kindergarten time when my family lived on Dupont avenue in Minneapolis, I remember lighting a birthday candle and putting it on a play cup saucer and placing it underneath a big double mattress. It was my first memory of seeking out some light and lucky for me my father was able to pitch the burning mattress over the rail of our second story apartment before the fire got serious. That wasn't the first time my curiosity got me in trouble. In fact, I've always had a propensity for adventure. As a young man, I also got in trouble. Especially after my father died. I remember mom telling me at about age 14: "Ed, one day you are going to get yours." I wondered at the time exactly what she was talking about as she pointed her finger angrily towards me? Now I know. I think I got paid back in spades.

> **"Do not be deceived, God is not mocked; for whatever a man sows, that he will also reap." Galatians 6:7**

What You Sow, You'll Reap — I Know!

I've lost track of the number of garbage cans of mine that were tipped over at the end of my driveway. I can say with certainty that the number of incidents greatly exceeded the times I tipped over a trash can during my teen years. Young people take heed; this is an unyielding law from God.

Copyright 2005 Edward G. Palmer, All Rights Reserved.

Book of Edward—Chapter 13

A Light On My Path

I have now lived long enough to see the truth of this law come to bear on the younger generations that I have watched grow up. Parents teach your children to live good lives in their youth so their level of misery later as adults will be minimized. That is when the payback arrives! The teaching should start with the true meaning of "honoring your mother and father;" that the activities of children can either honor or dishonor parents.

I was confronted with stealing, drinking, fornication, homosexuality, smoking and to some other problems that are common to mankind. Listen to the word of God on what we are confronted with during this earthly life.

"No temptation has overtaken you except such as is common to man; but God is faithful, who will not allow you to be tempted beyond what you are able, but with the temptation will also make the way of escape, that you may be able to bear it." 1 Cor. 10:13

My family was poor so I started to earn my own money to spend at the age of seven. I shined shoes outside of seven bars in South Minneapolis by myself. Can you imagine allowing a seven year old to do something like that in these days? Not a chance. Times have changed. Our society is not so innocent today, mainly because we can't seem to administer justice in a way that keeps from recycling criminals or deterring crime; that is my humble opinion. By the time I was ten years old, I had paper routes and was literally buying my own clothes. I didn't seem to mind because that is what my parents expected of me. If I wanted something, their message was to go out and earn the money to pay for it.

Both mom and dad had some business aspirations. When I shined shoes in south Minneapolis, it was only a few blocks from a bar that they owned. The bar business didn't pan out and a later adventure in a Chinese take out restaurant didn't make it either. Still, they imparted a sense of entrepreneurism into me that has lasted all my life. My father was a music writer and musician. At one point he had his own band. He played several instruments including the piano, banjo, clarinet, guitar, drums, saxophone and the bones. I saw him play these instruments and he was very gifted.

A Light On My Path

The grand mal seizures were a problem for dad getting jobs at most nightclubs. But even worse was his sense of wanting the freedom to work where he wanted to, when he wanted. The 1940's to 1950's were a time of increasing union activity in the musician field in Minneapolis. It eventually became him refusing mostly union jobs because he refused to join the union. The influence of my father was not just his love; it was also his sense that we should be able to make it on our own in life. Wow, that from a guy that suffered grand mal seizures. My dad and mom never let their disabilities stand in the way of the progress they sought to make. I admired that. I too have learned that to press on in life will ease our pain. I have also found out that getting into God's presence can wipe the pain away. Focus your mind on your tasks in life and on God; then your pain will not be so noticeable.

In stark contrast to my father, Jackie's father was a union man all the days of his life. As a manual laborer, I have to admit, the union probably helped him from being taken advantage of by the big company he worked for. We always had some interesting discussions in the family since we grew up with this contrast between belief in unions and disbelief in unions.

First grade was spent in Seward Elementary School close to the bar my mother and father owned. I remember being taken out of school for an hour each day as our class marched up to a local church to learn about God. I do not recall any specific teaching other than God exists. Therefore, I can tell you spending an hour a day with God in school certainly didn't hurt me. I understand that many will disagree after reading this book. Back in the mid 1950's, God was a part of our public education system. I suspect that is why a seven year old could shine shoes outside of a bar in those days. Since our public education exposed all of us to morality, we were a moral people. Now, you can wind up in jail teaching morality to children. Who has won the battle to influence your kid's mind in the public education system?

Somewhere around the age of 11, I stole a Christmas tree on the night before Christmas. My father made me take it back immediately that same night. The tree lot owner gave it to us anyway since it was the night before Christmas and he felt sorry for our poor family. I never forgot that theft mainly because of the way it hurt my father. Of course, I got caught because

A Light On My Path

he questioned me on how I got the tree and I did not lie to him. It was a good lesson for me, but it didn't stop some other attempts at theft.

I wasn't a thief at heart. However, I hot-wired a few cars for joy rides. I remember making the decision to walk away from some friends of mine and abandon stealing cars as a losing proposition in life. God was guiding my thoughts at the time. That decision saved me from getting arrested and sent up to juvenile prison. I had joined some friends on a joy ride one night. We had ditched the car in an industrial parking lot near downtown Minneapolis. We used to walk by the site on a regular basis. Three weeks later, the car was still where we left it. My friends decided to take it again. When they asked me, I said: "I don't want any part of it."

That night the police were waiting for my friends as they picked up the car. I will never forget how grateful I was at making that decision. The lesson I learned at age 15 was that bad company would corrupt character. If you want to be engaged in the good things of life, don't fellowship with those who want you to engage in the evil things of life. Is this a surprise?

Do not be misled: "Bad company corrupts good character."
1 Cor. 15:33 NIV

This is where Christianity has really gotten lost. We are now taught to go out and get sinners and bring them into our fellowship. Willful sinners do not belong in church according to God's Word! Repentant sinners who have turned to righteousness belong in church. If you want to know why so many churches are corrupt just look at the make up of members. Righteous people are mixed with sinners. It is against God's Word and is there any doubt about why the Church is no longer relevant to many people? Church going people used to be different. The statement, "they are Christians," has lost its meaning today, because so many churches are just social clubs. They mirror the mix of the local area and fail to exclude willful sinners into their membership. Visiting sinners should know that righteousness is expected in an Assembly of God. You cannot build God's house with Satan's kids.

"Sinners ... have no place among the godly." Psalm 1:5 NLT

A Light On My Path

God saved me from a life of crime by guiding me away from those who would lead me astray. Along the way, I gave up a several friends. True friends will not lead you into doing anything evil. Then there is the matter of smoking. I started at the age of 10. My dad caught me smoking at the age of 11 and made me sit down in the living room and smoke a cigar. He liked cigars and I think he thought inhaling it would make me sick. It didn't and after that I smoked cigars too, when I could get one. Smoking is a sin against our body. Its evil effects are well documented and even the major tobacco companies now admit it causes serious health problems. Yet, listen, when Jackie and I were growing up — these companies were advertising the health benefits of smoking. Yes, I am serious. We were taught that smoking was good for us. Eventually sinus and chest pain would force me to quit.

One day at the age of 20, I found myself lighting up a cigarette as I arrived on board the USS Berkeley DDG-15. I hacked nonstop for a solid ten minutes and as I coughed it felt like a knife was being twisted around in my chest. The pain was so severe that I immediately threw the cigarettes over board and quit cold turkey. I had smoked up to three packs a day at times. That is the short hand version of how I quit smoking. Suffice to say that God enabled my body's pain to speak to my heart. I got the message. Smoke, you get pain; don't smoke, you won't get pain. It had been going on for the prior six years of my life. I only regret that I was unable to get Jackie to quit with me at the time. The smoking eventually became a contributing factor in her pancreatic cancer.

Drinking had also been a problem for me in my youth. At age 15, I was well on my way to becoming an alcoholic. I was putting down several quarts of booze a week. Not good. Jackie didn't like it and informed me of that fact. She was my saving angel. At least she tempered what I thought of as fun in those teenage years. I stopped drinking completely at age 34, a couple years after starting my new walk with God. I would usually only have two drinks in a given evening, but God showed me how those two drinks affected both my mood and my mental thinking the next day. I gave up drinking because I wanted a clear mind for my fellowship with God. I will have a glass of wine on rare occasion now. I also offer real wine to those who participate in the communion services of my ministry.

A Light On My Path

I was also seriously rebellious and left home at age 15. I wandered from one friend's home to another and at times I went back home for a brief time. Life became very tough and unstable after my mother remarried and the family moved out to the suburbs. I had been attending Vocational High School in downtown Minneapolis where I studied Radio-TV electronics for three hours a day. I owned my own car and had jobs to support it, so for a while I traveled long distance to the school, which was over 12 miles from my house. After the school found out my family moved to the suburbs, I was disqualified from continuing on in the inner city trade school.

The net result of all of this was that I quit school in the middle of the eleventh grade and joined the Navy. Grades weren't an issue for me and I was always a B average student; I loved the educational experience and learning new things. However, continued schooling as it was then presented to me was no longer an option in my mind. At the time, young men were obligated to six years of service to the country either on active or inactive service. Since the Vietnam War was underway, I opted for the U.S. Navy. It was a good choice for continuing my education, but I did not realize it.

I took the GED High-School equivalency immediately and passed. I then spent over 2 1/2 years in advanced electronics courses during my 7 1/2 year Naval career. In total, I have accrued over 5,000 hours of class training in electronic engineering. You can compare that to a college BSEE degree in which about 1300 hours of class training would be encountered. I have a non-traditional education today that well exceeds a BSEE, MBA and Ph D. I am well educated albeit non-degreed. I am satisfied with the results of my education and I usually put in 400 hours annually in continuing education. I have for the last 30 years. So, while some might want to view me as a high school dropout that would not be accurate. After I got out of the Navy, it took 15 years before consumer electronic equipment reached the level of my engineering and technical expertise. I also took equivalency tests while in the Navy for the first two general years of college and passed them. Before leaving the Navy I completed all of the regular high school courses as if I would have attended North High in Minneapolis and not a trade school; I studied consumer electronics; and, I studied for my FCC First Class Radio Telephone exam. I obtained the license with the ship radar endorsement.

A Light On My Path

In the Navy, I worked on missile system computers and search radars. I rose in the ranks fast to first class petty officer and before I left the Navy, I was assigned to be an instructor at the Damneck Guided Missile base near Virginia Beach, Virginia. Needless to say, Jackie and I had two girls by then and we opted out of the Navy. I was honorably discharged in December of 1970 after returning from my third Vietnam cruise. We had bought a house in Minneapolis near Jackie's folks prior to leaving for Vietnam. She stayed at the new home with the girls; I finished my final cruise on the USS King.

When I got out of the Navy, unemployment was about 13% in the local engineering markets around the Minneapolis area. I joined a group of unemployed engineers and technicians selling Nutrilite products and was exposed to vitamins. I soon got a job at RCA installing television antennas and later repairing consumer electronic goods. I wound up with an unsold inventory of Nutrilite vitamins. Amway later acquired Nutrilite products and I believe the vitamins are still available. I didn't sell any vitamins; I even wondered at the time if people would pay $30 a month for them. I couldn't see them going to waste, so I consumed the vitamins myself at the age of 25. I couldn't believe how much better they made me feel and since then I have always taken vitamins. If I had the vitamins, minerals and herbs I would like to have on hand, it would be nothing for me to consume 50 tablets in the morning and another 20 or more at night. I have consumed vitamins for the last 32 years in various amounts. I could never get Jackie interested in them and admittedly it takes a little courage to get them down daily in that kind of volume. Occasionally, it is just not in me either.

While at RCA and then later at WCCO-TV as a broadcast engineer, I started to repair consumer electronic products in my basement during the evenings and weekends. It eventually led me into various business ventures over the course of the next eight years. After leaving WCCO-TV for one business venture that quickly failed, I accepted a job as a computer repair engineer. It quickly led into the manager's position where I directed a team of seven engineers in repairing stock brokerage, utility company and bank computer systems. I was still the field service manager for the Minneapolis Bunker Ramo office when Jackie and I decided to move in 1972. We had three children and Minneapolis announced an unacceptable busing plan.

A Light On My Path

Jackie and I moved to Elk River, Minnesota in 1973 where our kids wouldn't be bused in three separate directions all their school lives. I soon left Bunker Ramo and restarted a local electronics repair business out of my home. I already had all the equipment and it was an easy start up. For the next five years, the business was in various phases of development. It had evolved into the manufacturing of a security system I designed, but all was not well financially. The business was always under capitalized. I can tell you that business is always fraught with difficulties that will challenge any person's mental sanity. I tried every business skill I learned in business journals and books. What could go wrong did go wrong and I was rapidly headed towards bankruptcy. I had struggled for many years in business and Jackie was sick of it all. She even threatened a divorce as we entered 1978. Both my business and home life were under some serious stress.

I have always been a possibility thinker. I enjoy the intellectual tests that confront business people. However, I was overextended and had run out of options. I had used up every bit of mental, physical and emotional power I could muster. About a year and a half earlier I had been given a tape of Earl Nightingale's Strangest Secret. It sat on the shelf until one day in May 1978, the thirty-second year of my life. I picked up the tape and decided to listen to it for reasons I cannot recall. Within the tape, the author cited the words of Jesus contained in Mark 9:23.

> **"Jesus said unto him, if thou canst believe, all things are possible to him that believeth." Mark 9:23 KJV**

I recall the initial shock and disbelief that those words were actually in the Bible. I went and found a Bible and opened it to that scripture. I had been living life to the best that I was able to do with everything of my own personal being. In other words, I knew intellectually I had reached my own internal capacity and that it was simply not enough. I thought there had to be something in life that I was not factoring in, something that would make a difference. God was showing me that life could be different with HIM at that particular moment. I felt God's awesome presence and I simply knew God instantly in a moment of time throughout my whole being. I'll never forget the moment. It would change my life instantly and forever.

A Light On My Path

It was an epiphany, a moment in my life when everything spiritual came together and became crystal clear to me. I remember looking at the ceiling and telling God: "I get it LORD. I understand. From now on, YOU lead and I will simply follow." It was a deep spiritual connection that was made from my heart to God's heart. I acknowledged to God that all that I am was not enough for this earthly life. I knew then that I needed HIS guidance and I gave my life to God.

I was baptized as a baby into the Lutheran faith. I was confirmed at the age of 13 into the Lutheran faith. I remember that at my confirmation my stomach was ready to explode at the altar. I was nervous and had a sick feeling. I thought clearly at the time I wasn't supposed to be there. How could confirmation cause such a sick feeling? I was confirmed at Redeemer Lutheran Church in spite of my ill physical feelings at the altar. I managed to get through Lutheran confirmation in only eight weeks when my older sister Barbara spent two years in class. This always irritated my sister. I don't know how I managed to get through on an accelerated basis. My mother must have pulled some strings, because I have no other answers. In the Navy, I signed my pledge to Jesus Christ in the Gideon New Testament that I was given. I still have it.

However, neither my baptism, nor my confirmation nor my New Testament pledge to Jesus Christ in the Gideon Bible penetrated the bowels of my soul [heart]. Nothing reached my heart; everything about God was only in my mind prior to the point in time of my surrender. When I told Jackie that I had found God, she asked me: "What took you so long?"

Life for me changed immediately. I picked up the Bible and read it from front to back, because I wanted to really know the God I had pledged to serve with my soul. I then got an Apocryphal Bible and read those books. I have studied the Bible in depth ever since having now accrued thousands of hours of study over the course of 25 years. I have left the realm of mere study and now flow into HIS Spirit throughout the week. I have learned to rely upon HIM for all my needs. So life changed immediately at the point of that epiphany. Life has been a great adventure with God ever since that time. Jackie decided that I would be okay after all.

Copyright 2005 Edward G. Palmer, All Rights Reserved.

Book of Edward—Chapter 13

A Light On My Path

This short version of the events that led up to the decision of my heart gives you a brief view of what my life was like. How I grew into God's apostle is a subject for another time. My mind had become sophisticated through years of advanced education. Yet all that I learned was meaningless in this life. I wandered around spiritually during the first thirty-two years of my life until one day in which I had an epiphany from God. On that day, I "knew" God throughout my whole being. God showed HIMSELF to me and HE taught me. From the FATHER, I readily came to know and appreciate Jesus Christ HIS only human Son. For me, Jesus is a teacher of God's ways not his own. In other words, Jesus always points the way to the FATHER.

If you will open the door of your heart to God, it will complete HIS communications channel to your soul. Nobody ever told me the difference between God being in the mind and God being in the heart. Now you know. You can make the choice to take God deeper into your own soul as a result. You can let God into the bowels of your soul where your heart is guarded. When you embrace God with your whole heart, you will find a thirst for HIS Word; it will become more important to you than any words from a pulpit. At that time, YAHWEH'S Word will become a light unto your own path.

"YOUR Word [YAHWEH] is a lamp to my feet and a light for my path." Psalm 119:105 NIV

"God's metaphysical manifestations in my life became observable and intense after I willingly opened the doorway to my heart for HIM to enter in. At that moment, the communications channel for God's instructions became completed and HE became a bright light on my path." The Apostle Edward

When You Give God Your Whole Heart, HE Becomes A Light On Your Path, Just As HE Is …

A Light On My Path

Chapter Fourteen
The Gift of Jesus

[Jesus] replied, "You are permitted to understand the secret about the kingdom of God. But I am using these stories to conceal everything about it from outsiders." Mark 4:11 NLT

"Don't forget to pray for us, too, that God will give us many opportunities to preach about his secret plan-that Christ is also for you Gentiles." Col. 4:3 NLT

"For this lawlessness is already at work secretly, and it will remain secret until the one who is holding it back steps out of the way." 2 Thess. 2:7 NLT

"But when the seventh angel blows his trumpet, God's mysterious plan will be fulfilled. It will happen just as he announced it to his servants the prophets." Rev. 10:7 NLT

"Without question, this is the great mystery of our faith:

> Christ appeared in the flesh and
> Was shown to be righteous by the Spirit.
> He was seen by angels and
> Was announced to the nations.
> He was believed on in the world and
> Was taken up into Heaven." 1 Tim. 3:16 NLT

"Because of the cross, God sent HIS Spirit to dwell with those who believe. It's our return to Eden and direct fellowship with God. This is the greatest gift of Jesus." The Apostle Edward

The Gift of Jesus

Few Will Find Eternal Life!

"The MOST HIGH made this world for the sake of many, but the world to come for the sake of only a few. But I tell you a parable, Ezra. Just as, when you ask the earth, it will tell you that it provides a large amount of clay from which earthenware is made, but only a little dust from which gold comes, so is the course of the present world. Many have been created, but only a few shall be saved."
2 Esdras 8:1-3 NRSV

Jesus said: "For the gate is narrow and the road is hard that leads to life, and there are few who find it."
Matthew 7:14 NRSV

Its been over twenty-five years since I first encountered the words of Jesus in Matthew 7:14. "Few will find eternal life" is the message of Christ. Not only that, but the road that leads to that eternal life is hard. Yet today a lot of Christians think they've got an easy pass on life; an easy pass on their continued willful sins. The words of Jesus mirror the words taught to Ezra. These words disturb me today even as they did back then; they mean many lost souls in plain and simple language. It grieves my spirit.

It is easy for me to imagine now that you have just skipped the entire first thirteen chapters of the book and are turning to this chapter. After all, isn't this the crux of the matter for Christianity? Exactly what is the gift of Jesus? Does that gift of Jesus give us a pass on our sins? Total forgiveness of what evil has been done and what evil we may choose to do in the future?

If you have flipped the book to this chapter as a starting point, go back and read the first thirteen chapters. You will not get from God all of what you need to understand from this chapter alone. It is the conclusion of the second volume and while there will be good stuff in this chapter; it does not stand alone in this writing. It stands as the fourteenth chapter in a sequence that God has given me. Taken alone, it is taken out of context. Isn't taking scriptures out of biblical context what many Christians do every day? Yes!

The Gift of Jesus

They also respond emotionally when they should be engaging their brains in reasoned discourse to learn the truth from God's Holy Word. This means that anytime Scripture is cited, your ears should perk up to the word of God and you should not become defensive. Listen to the word of God on the subject of reason, your sins and the implications for your salvation.

> **"Come now, and let us reason together," says the LORD,**
> **"Though your sins are like scarlet,**
> **They shall be as white as snow;**
> **Though they are red like crimson,**
> **They shall be as wool." Isaiah 1:18**

Now consider these words from the Apostle James on wisdom.

> **"But the wisdom that is from above is first pure, then peaceable, gentle, willing to yield, full of mercy and good fruits, without partiality and without hypocrisy." James 3:17**

> **"But the wisdom that is from above is first of all pure (undefiled); then it is peace-loving, courteous (considerate, gentle). [It is willing to] yield to reason, full of compassion and good fruits; it is wholehearted and straightforward, impartial and unfeigned (free of doubts, wavering and insincerity)." James 3:17 AMP**

Godly Wisdom Yields To Reason!

The Apostle James also states the following on listening:

> **"Understand [this], my beloved brethren. Let every man be quick to hear [a ready listener], slow to speak, slow to take offense and to get angry. For man's anger does not promote the righteousness God [wishes and requires]."**
> **James 1:19-20 AMP**

Are you willing to yield to the reason of Scripture? If not, why?

The Gift of Jesus

What I am telling you now—you need to understand! You can either choose to listen to the word of God as contained in the Scripture citations that I am providing or you can ignore them at your own peril. It is easy to simply dismiss my writings as "being deceived" as one woman recently did. I might add that she hadn't even read as much as a single page of this book before coming to that conclusion. However, responding to scriptures in that manner only demonstrated to me that she did not possess godly wisdom. If she did, she would have been open to discourse on God's Word. Not only that, if she really loved God with all her heart, she would jump at the chance to learn "anything" from HIS Scripture—even if it was a direct challenge to her basic understanding and belief about salvation and Jesus Christ.

Does Holy Scripture rank higher throughout your whole being than the words of your priest or pastor? If not, why? Listen to what God says comes from the mouths of many who claim to serve HIM.

"[You priests & ministers] have wearied Yahweh with your talk. You ask, 'How have we wearied HIM?' When you say, 'Any evil-doer is good as far as Yahweh is concerned; indeed HE is delighted with them.'" Malachi 2:17 NJB

"For the lips of a priest should keep knowledge, and people should seek the law from his mouth; for he is the messenger of the LORD of hosts." Malachi 2:7

Want an illustration of great apostasy from those who represent God? Consider the recent consecration of a practicing homosexual in the person of V. Gene Robinson into the office of bishop of the New Hampshire Diocese in the Episcopal Church. An estimated 50 Episcopal bishops supported his consecration and that included the head of the Episcopal Church of America. They are all headed for Hell now having committed the unforgivable sin of blasphemy against the Spirit of God. They have attributed the sanctioning of the sin of homosexuality, an abomination, to God HIMSELF. HE will repay.

God Almighty HIMSELF said: "You shall not lie with a male as with a woman. It is an abomination." Leviticus 18:22

The Gift of Jesus

If God's Word does not out rank the mouth of your priest or pastor, you might as well close this book right now. You will not be able to gain anything from it. Why? It takes someone who loves the truth to listen when scriptures are presented that challenge a core Christian teaching. This book is a message to Christians that inform them why many are going to Hell. If you don't value the Word over the priest or pastor's opinion, you are already lost. You will be one of those whom Jesus says: "I never knew you."

For the moment, consider how difficult it is for a trinity believer to accept anything from God's Word in this book in the form of scriptures that speak to the contrary. I have already told you that the trinity doctrine is false. Go back and read the many scriptures cited in chapter 10 that speak to this fact if you don't believe it. I have also told you that the typical salvation doctrine that is taught is false. Go back to the chapter 12 scriptures if you don't understand it. I have told you that your own righteousness counts and that continued willful sin on your part is forbidden if you expect to claim salvation through Jesus Christ. Go back and study the earlier chapters until you understand these scriptural facts.

Will you accept such facts when shown corroborating scriptures? Or, will you dismiss out of hand such facts because they are in opposition to established Christian teachings? I suspect the latter with many, because they are headed for Hell. And despite their claims to the contrary, they are not willing to accept what Scripture teaches as fact. This can be because they are spiritually lazy people and will follow anyone. It can be because they place their faith in a priest or pastor instead of in God's Holy Word.

I had been invited to a Christian gathering for a sing-a-long a few weeks ago. There were about thirty Christians who gather on a regular basis for some good clean fun and fellowship. Sharon, a friend of the family, felt it would be good for me to get out in the wake of Jackie's death. Since the event was being held at her home, she insisted that I come over and check it out. She even told me that plenty of food would be available. That is good enough for most males albeit I already had dinner planned that Saturday night. I didn't think I would go; I even watched a movie first. Two of my adult kids encouraged me to go, just to get out of the house. Sharon had

The Gift of Jesus

indicated that at least part of this group was meeting together in a small cell discussing Bible truth. That interested me and it peaked my curiosity enough to go. I like surprises and who knows what God had planned. I also felt God's Spirit nudging me to go. I realize now that God was giving me some insight into the typical Christian mindset regarding the trinity dogma.

Everything seemed to go fine as we discussed various subjects including some health issues. Then, Sharon introduced me to another couple and encouraged me to discuss the book I was writing with them. As we talked about the book and I cited scriptures, I noticed the couple getting tense and disturbed by what I was telling them about the Bible and why I was writing the book. They did not want to talk about the scriptures I cited. That gave me a clear clue that it wasn't Scripture that interested them, it was their church tradition and doctrine.

Jesus said: "Thus you have made the commandment of God of no effect by your tradition." Matthew 15:6

I indicated that Scripture made it clear that continued willful sin was unacceptable in God's eyes for those who claimed salvation through Christ Jesus. I also told this couple that it was clear that salvation was also from God Almighty. At some point shortly afterwards, I was told: "You need to pray about that book because you are deceived." Another statement that followed shortly stunned me. The woman said: "I willfully sin each and every day; I can't help it." Wow. Let me say that anyone who actually does this will meet with the words from Jesus: "I never knew you."

God showed me that this would be a familiar response of many in Christianity today. God's truth now takes second place to church doctrine in the mass of Christendom. Perhaps in over 80% of those calling themselves a Christian. Do you remember that Jesus taught it would be difficult for a rich man to enter the kingdom of Heaven in Matthew 19:23? Here is a new teaching the Spirit of God has given me. It is similar in nature.

"Verily I say to you that it is hard for a trinity believer claiming salvation in Jesus Christ and living in continued willful sin, to enter the kingdom of Heaven." The Apostle Edward

The Gift of Jesus

Why do I say they are similar? The rich man relies upon his wealth instead of God's Word. The trinity believer relies upon Church orthodoxy instead of God's Word. As far as the LORD is concerned, they are the same.

I can also point out that the teachings of sin have perverted God's Word to the point that every single word you misspeak is considered a sin in the eyes of many. You just can't help yourself, can you? That was the impression I got when talking to the couple about the book. Christianity has perverted God's Word so that every single thing in life can be thought of as a sin. Yet, once again, it is God who defines sin. Jesus taught that if you obey the commandments of God, you would have eternal life. Listen to the words of Jesus if you claim him as savior.

Jesus replied: "Only God is good. But to answer your question, you can receive eternal life if you keep the commandments." Matthew 19:17 NLT

Now for those of you who claim that there is no other way to eternal life, you need to reconcile that dogma with this teaching from Jesus. Go ahead, open up your Bible and study the issue. Is Jesus a liar? Don't even think it. Don't think I have taken Jesus out of context either as I haven't. Study and meditate on this verse until you understand that the salvation doctrine taught today is mythology; it is far from the truth of God's Word.

Getting back to the idea that you just can't help yourself, because everything is sin nowadays. I am sure this is what the couple I talked to believe. However, as I started to ask which commandments the woman breaks every day, she had no answer. Here is the list. If you are a willful sinner, check off the commandments that you break every day—willfully.

- ❏ You have other gods
- ❏ You make graven images
- ❏ You take God's name in vain
- ❏ You don't keep Sabbath holy
- ❏ You don't honor parents
- ❏ You commit murder
- ❏ You commit adultery
- ❏ You steal
- ❏ You bear false witness
- ❏ You covet neighbor's property

The Gift of Jesus

If you found it easy to check off commandments that you willfully break, you are in trouble with God. That is the essence of Hebrews 10:26. Somehow, I do not think that the couple I talked to had the idea of breaking God's commandments in mind. They have just been pulverized into the Christian dogma that they are sinners and just can't help themselves. If fact, everyone is, aren't they? Again, listen to the word of God on this issue.

> **"There was in the days of Herod, the king of Judea, a certain priest named Zacharias, of the division of Abijah. His wife was of the daughters of Aaron, and her name was Elizabeth. And they were both righteous before God, walking in all the commandments and ordinances of the LORD blameless." Luke 1:5-6**

Once again, as a Christian, you have to confront the false teachings of the church that takes Scripture out of context to teach you that no matter what you do, you cannot be a good person on your own. It is a lie, because you have free will. That free will allows you the freedom to make a choice for good or a choice for evil. So, the next question is do you even try to be a good person given today's teachings in Christianity? Do you actually obey God's commandments? If not, why? Is it because you have no free will?

You can see that you can be righteous, because both Zacharias and Elizabeth were righteous before God. You can also see that this gave them eternal life no matter what is taught from your pulpit. Not because I said so, but because Jesus made this fact clear. Do righteous people have to repent? Not if you believe what Jesus said, that he did not come down here for the righteous. Jesus came down to earth for the sake of sinners with a message of "repent and be saved" from God Almighty. Was it just another reminder from God or is there more? Why did God need two prophets on the scene?

> **Jesus said: "For I did not come to call the righteous, but sinners, to repentance." Matthew 9:13**

> **Jesus said: "Repent, for the kingdom of Heaven is at hand." Matthew 4:17**

The Gift of Jesus

John the Baptist preached the same message as Jesus did. It was a message of repentance for sinners to get right with God again. Both John and Jesus offered the same good news that all of the preceding prophets before them did. Yet why two prophets? There had to be more to Jesus.

The Real Definition of Good News!

The real good news is that God will forgive your sins if you simply repent of your evil ways and walk according to His ways. That is the exact message in Ezekiel 18 from God Almighty HIMSELF. That is the message in Joel 2:32 from God Almighty HIMSELF. So, Christian, how do you explain away the words of Jesus and of his fellow prophets on this simple message of salvation: repent and be saved? How do you explain away the words of God Almighty who reiterates the same simple message of Christ that those who sincerely repent will be saved? If you love God's Word like I do, you will not simply ignore it or try to rationalize it away with some orthodox dogma that allows for continued willful sin. Clearly God has something else in mind with repentance; it is why Christ said: "Go and sin no more."

> **"In those days John the Baptist came preaching in the wilderness of Judea, and saying, 'Repent, for the kingdom of Heaven is at hand!'" Matthew 3:1-2**

Clearly the message of John the Baptist was virtually identical to that of Jesus Christ concerning eternal life. The Bible makes it clear that many took advantage of this opportunity for the forgiveness of their sins.

> **"Then Jerusalem, all Judea, and all the region around the Jordan went out to him [John the Baptist] and were baptized by him in the Jordan, confessing their sins."**
> **Matthew 3:5-6**

Now, the question arises: Are those who repented and were baptized by John saved? The answer is yes if the repentance was sincere and it resulted in them following God's ways. To say otherwise is apostasy.

Copyright 2005 Edward G. Palmer, All Rights Reserved.

The Gift of Jesus

Jesus has certainly not given us an excuse for continued sin. Consider the following Scripture. Jesus makes it clear that you will have no excuse for sin in the first citation. This is interesting because many Christians *use* Jesus as an excuse for their sin. Apostle Paul also makes it clear that mankind will not have any excuse for not knowing God Almighty. Atheists take heed that the second citation is a direct challenge to the falsehood that there is no God.

> **Jesus said: "They would not be guilty if I had not come and spoken to them. But now they have no excuse for their sin."**
> **John 15:22 NLT**

> **"From the time the world was created, people have seen the earth and sky and all that God made. They can clearly see His invisible qualities - His eternal power and divine nature. So they have no excuse whatsoever for not knowing God."**
> **Romans 1:20 NLT**

So if Jesus is not really God, if salvation existed before he came along, if he is not an excuse to sin and people can be righteous without Jesus, exactly what is (are) the gift(s) of Jesus? That is the big question of this chapter. I will attempt to answer it from a biblical perspective and clarify what God has accomplished with His only begotten human Son. I wish I could tell you that when I am done with this chapter, that all Jews, Muslims and Christians will have the same understanding of Jesus Christ. They won't. However, perhaps Christianity will have some clarity on the subject of what God's Word actually says about who Jesus Christ is. Lets summarize the biblical truth about Jesus that we've already discussed.

Item	The Truth About Jesus	Yes	No
1	Jesus is God Almighty		✔
2	Jesus is the only way to salvation		✔
3	No one is righteous apart from Christ		✔
4	Jesus is an excuse for Christians to sin		✔

The Gift of Jesus

I suspect some of you are now angry at the four non-characteristics of Jesus shown in the table above. If so, did you start at the beginning of this book? An angry person would come from three distinct sources. 1) How dare you. This means you really haven't read the first thirteen chapters and are ignorant of the many Bible scriptures previously cited that support the four facts above. 2) I've read the chapters, but still don't believe you. This means you don't believe God's Holy Word. 3) I've read the book from the front and studied the scriptures, but don't accept this teaching because it goes against what my church teaches. This means that the word of God is less important than the doctrine of your church. Take a deep breath and open up your heart to God's Word. Maybe you need to take a break?

Are you ready to proceed with a calm mind? Okay. Let's look at the phases of spiritual influence on man that have transpired or are in process.

The Phases Of Spiritual Influence Upon Man

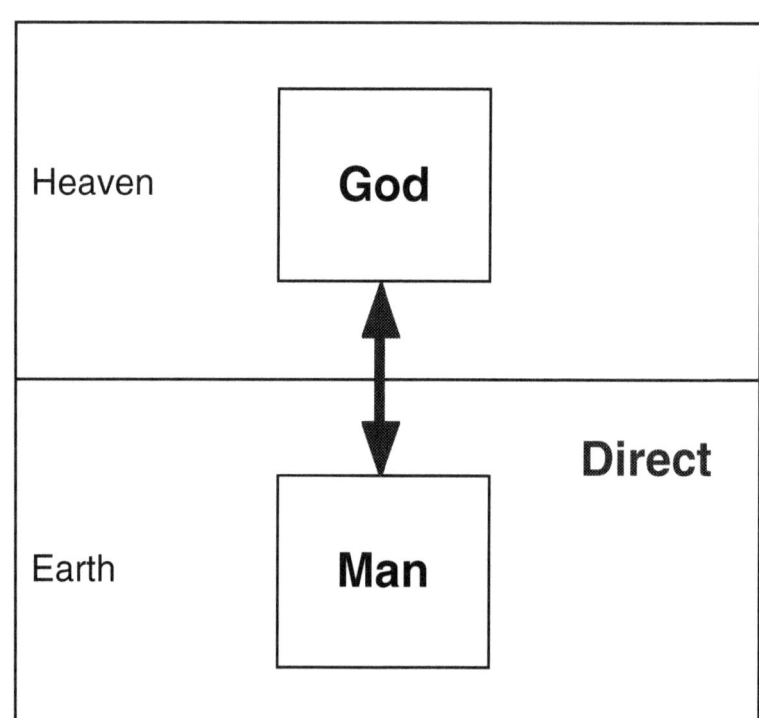

Phase 1: God Starts With A Direct Relationship

The Gift of Jesus

It is certainly easy to understand that in the beginning there was a creation and that both man and woman dealt directly with God. This is Phase 1 and it constituted a simple and direct relationship between God and man. For visual graphics and writing ease, I have used the term "man" but this should be understood to also cover woman. Can you imagine how simple and wonderful communications were between God and man? It is also clear that there were no intermediaries involved. This was God's plan and design. It was going to be Heaven on earth and everything was simple to grasp. At the time, mankind did not know that it was naked and neither did it have knowledge of the evil side of life; the things that God hates!

"And God saw every thing that he had made, and, behold, it was very good. And the evening and the morning were the sixth day." Genesis 1:31 KJV

When Eve and Adam committed sin against God, the picture for mankind took an immediate and permanent alteration for the worse. Instead of God's primary influence and direct dialogue, man was now confronted with both good and evil thoughts on a regular basis. Mankind's spiritual influence picture took on a new third level with Satan. In the process, God withdrew HIS presence in anger and the earth became a place of human toil. Where once mankind had no idea it was naked, it now felt shame over the idea of bare flesh. We literally went from a paradise into a land of toil.

"But of the tree of the knowledge of good and evil you shall not eat, for in the day that you eat of it you shall surely die."
Genesis 2:17

Did mankind "die" on the day that Adam and Eve ate from the tree of knowledge of good and evil? The answer is yes they did, despite various resurrection theories that take a different position. The death that occurred was an immediate spiritual death. God, in some large degree, stepped away from the direct fellowship that HE originally planned for man.

When Christ cried out on the cross: "My God, my God, why have you forsaken me?" — It was because Jesus Christ also had to first endure and

The Gift of Jesus

suffer through a spiritual death. Christ was made to suffer a spiritual death prior to suffering the physical death of his body. This is the same way that Adam experienced life. For Jesus Christ to understand our full humanity, he would be born into the same flesh as ours, made to live life and experience it as we do, endure it and suffer through it just like we have to. How else could he learn to be a merciful and faithful High Priest for us before God?

> "Therefore, it was necessary for Jesus to be in every respect like us, his brothers and sisters, so that he could be our merciful and faithful High Priest before God." Hebrews 2:17

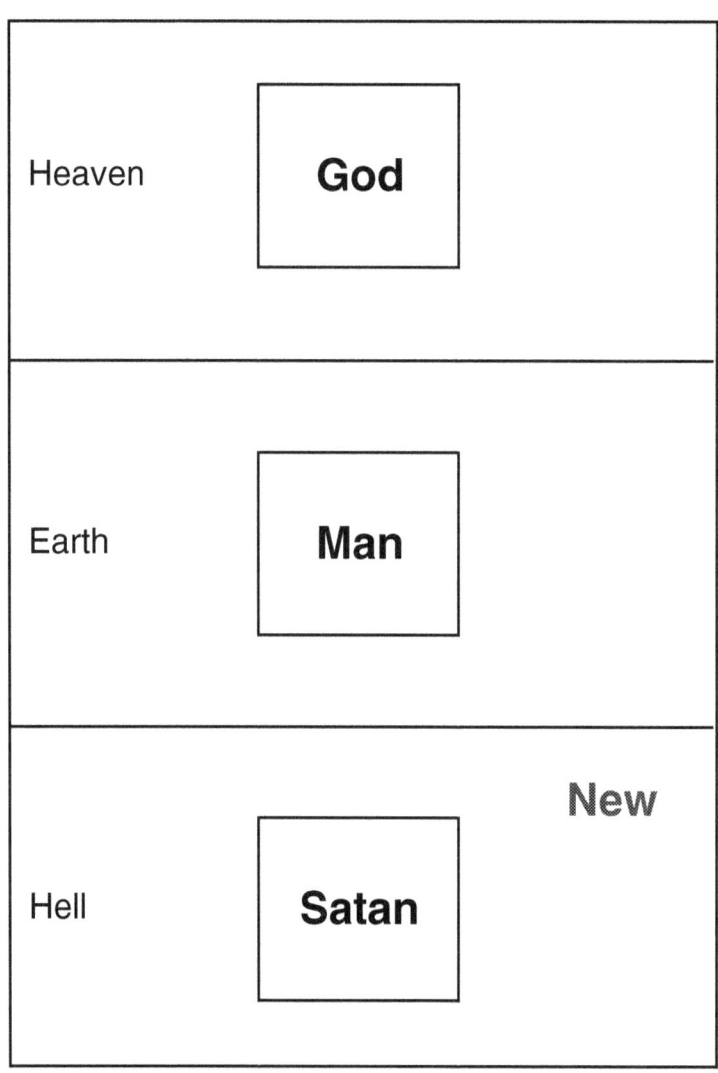

Phase 2: Sin Alters Spiritual Influence

The Gift of Jesus

The world degenerated towards almost complete evil in the days of Noah. God had enough and destroyed everything living on the earth except for Noah and those with him. Many feel today that evil is again rampant.

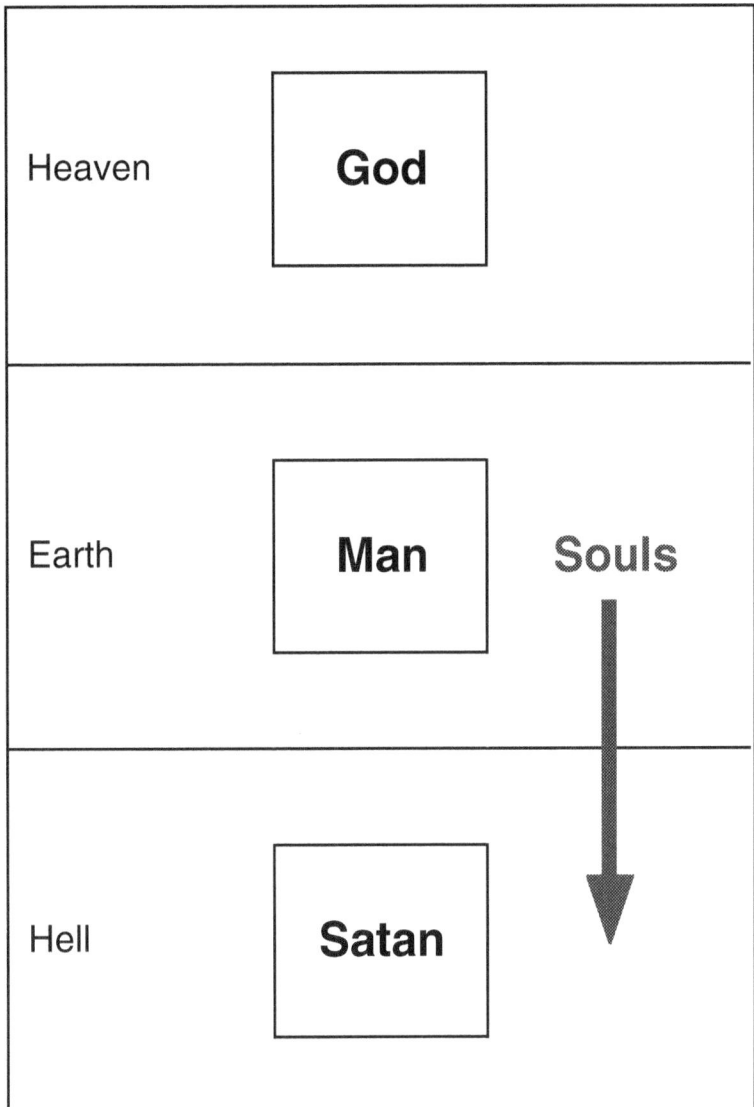

Phase 3: Satan Wins Man's Souls

Clearly Satan reigned during Phase 3. Only one righteous man named Noah and those who were with him were saved at the end of Phase 3. Don't tell me that you cannot be a righteous person. Even if the whole world is unrighteous, you can still choose to walk with God just like Noah did.

The Gift of Jesus

Think about the ramifications of the ending to Phase 3. Remember that it was a righteous person who was saved. Remember also that Jesus has stated you will need a minimum level of righteousness yourself to be saved.

> **And God said to Noah, "The end of all flesh has come before M**E**, for the earth is filled with violence through them; and behold, I will destroy them with the earth."**
> **Genesis 6:13**

> **Then the L**ORD **said to Noah, "Come into the ark, you and all your household, because I have seen that you are righteous before M**E **in this generation." Genesis 7:1**

Clearly Satan was in control of the world and was winning when Noah entered the ark. Where did all the souls that died in the flood go? They didn't go to Heaven, did they? And, they never will. I tell you this because some believe that all who are evil will eventually wind up in Heaven. That is the stuff of true Christian mythology.

Christ was the first of God's creations, according to the book of Revelation. He was sent down by God to alter the spiritual dynamics in the world. Christ took on a human form and was then called Jesus. He was a 100% human being in every respect, just like you and I. He was born of a human woman from her womb. He was born as a baby and raised as any child would be raised. He suffered from his flesh just like we suffer from ours. He waged a battle between his spirit and his body, just like we do. He willingly accepted God's plan so that we could learn to "walk in the Spirit" by following his example. Only the spirit of the Antichrist denies any aspect of the full humanity of Jesus Christ. Apostle John makes this point clear.

> **"For many deceivers have gone out into the world who do not confess Jesus Christ as coming in the flesh [or deny an aspect of his flesh]. This is a deceiver and an Antichrist." 2 John 1:7**

The Spirit Of Antichrist Denies Christ's Humanity!

Copyright 2005 Edward G. Palmer, All Rights Reserved.

Book of Edward—Chapter 14

The Gift of Jesus

Verily I say to you that the Christian Church is now filled with the spirit of the Antichrist. It is a spirit that creates doctrine condoning continued willful sin. If anyone denies the flesh of Christ in any manner, this is of the Antichrist. It is the spirit of the Antichrist that says Jesus is 100% man and 100% God. This is not from God, because HIS Word teaches us different.

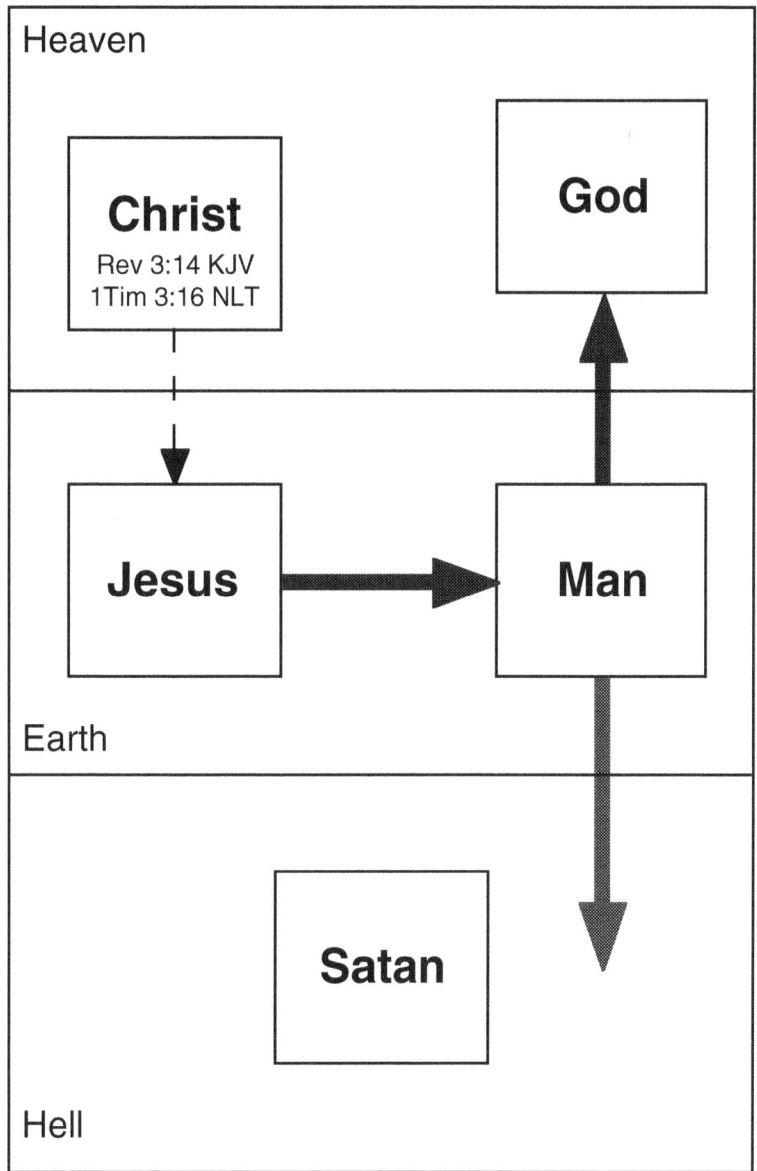

Phase 4: God Sends Sacrifice of Christ

The Gift of Jesus

> **Jesus says: "If I had not come and spoken to them, they would have no sin, but now they have no excuse for their [continued willful] sin." John 15:22**

I have lost track of the incredible dumb or stupid things I have done in life. I have also lost track of my failures in this life. Yet, listen, dumb and stupid things along with failures are not continued willful sin. They are just dumb, stupid and failures. To try and alter John 15:22 to cover any form of human error is not justifiable. Go back and study the many prior discussions on Hebrews 10:26 if you are still uncertain on this subject of willful sin.

Since continued willful sin is no longer allowed and we no longer have any excuses for such behavior, it means that Jesus Christ was the final and perfect blood sacrifice for man's sin. Without the shedding of his blood, there would be no atonement for the sins of the world. Therefore, the blood of Jesus and his perfect sacrifice are key gifts of Jesus. They demonstrate the love that he had for both the FATHER [his God] and for us.

> **"And … without [the] shedding of blood there is [can be] no remission [for our sins]." Hebrews 9:22**

Jesus walked with God and did what God told him to do. He also spoke to us exactly what God told him to say. Go back to the false trinity chapter if you don't understand these facts. When Jesus went back to God, he did not send the Holy Spirit back to us. That is because it didn't belong to Christ. Instead, Jesus asked God to send the Holy Spirit to us. Listen to the Bible and quit being confused on the simple teachings of Jesus.

> **Jesus said: "And I will pray the FATHER, and HE will give you another Helper, that HE [God] may abide with you forever." John 14:16**

> **"But the Helper, the Holy Spirit, whom the FATHER will send in my name, HE will teach you all things, and bring to your remembrance all things that I said to you." John 14:26**

The Gift of Jesus

> "But when the Helper comes, whom I shall send to you from the FATHER, the Spirit of truth who proceeds from the FATHER, HE will testify of me." John 15:26

Another gift of Jesus is his prayer to the FATHER [his God] to send us the Spirit of truth. Note: this Spirit proceeds from the FATHER [not Christ].

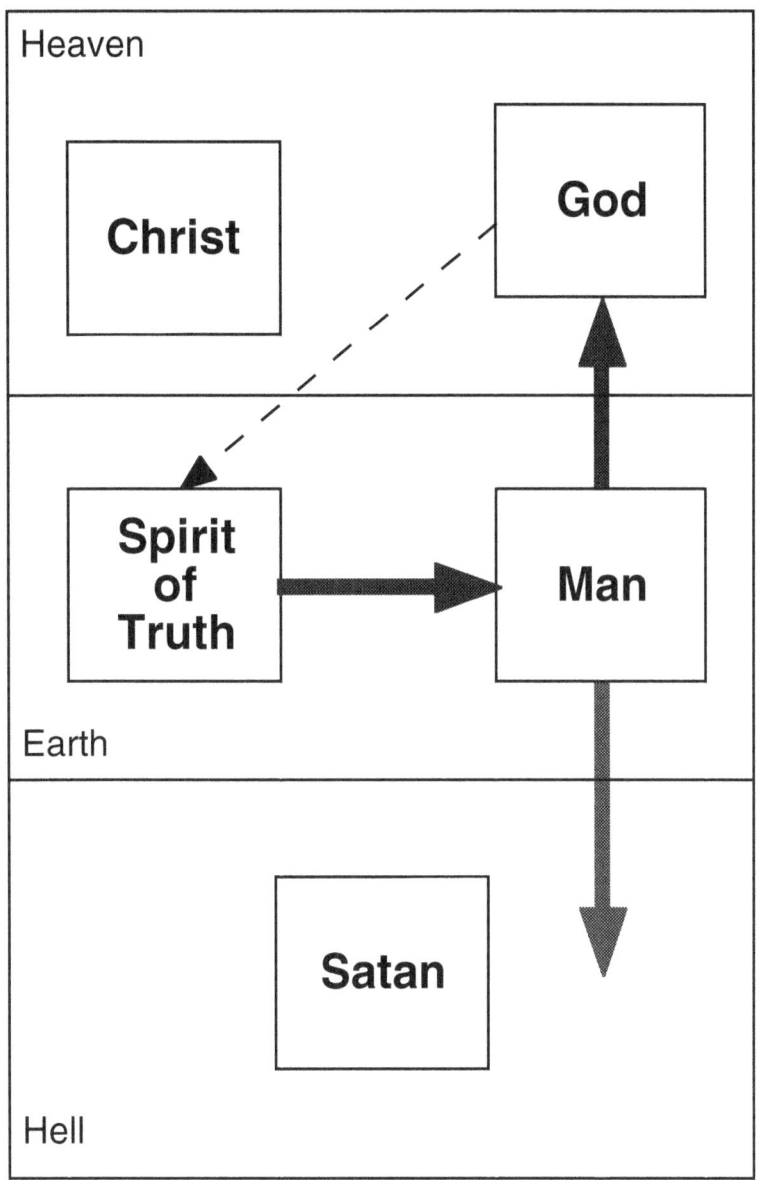

Phase 5: God Sends Spirit of Truth

The Gift of Jesus

It is a simple enough plan that Christ makes clear from God's Word. It was God who sent Christ as a perfect sacrifice for the collective sins of the world. It was the prayer of Christ that petitioned God to send man the Spirit of truth or Holy Spirit to *"Live Within Us!"* Those who have God living inside of them are obedient to HIS Word; they are slaves unto righteousness.

God changed the playing field through Christ and the Holy Spirit in regards to the spiritual influences man was faced with. However, today we live in a world filled with many evildoers living alongside few good people. The United States is culturally split down the center. The Church at large is also split and half or more of the Church now serves Satan instead of God. Is it any wonder why society in the United States is in rampant moral decay when those who should be from God have no salt [truth]? These phases constitute an influence power graph. We are now in the sixth phase; like the days of Noah, evil is rising. Satan has won the battle for the majority of human souls, but God has made a way for all who choose to serve HIM.

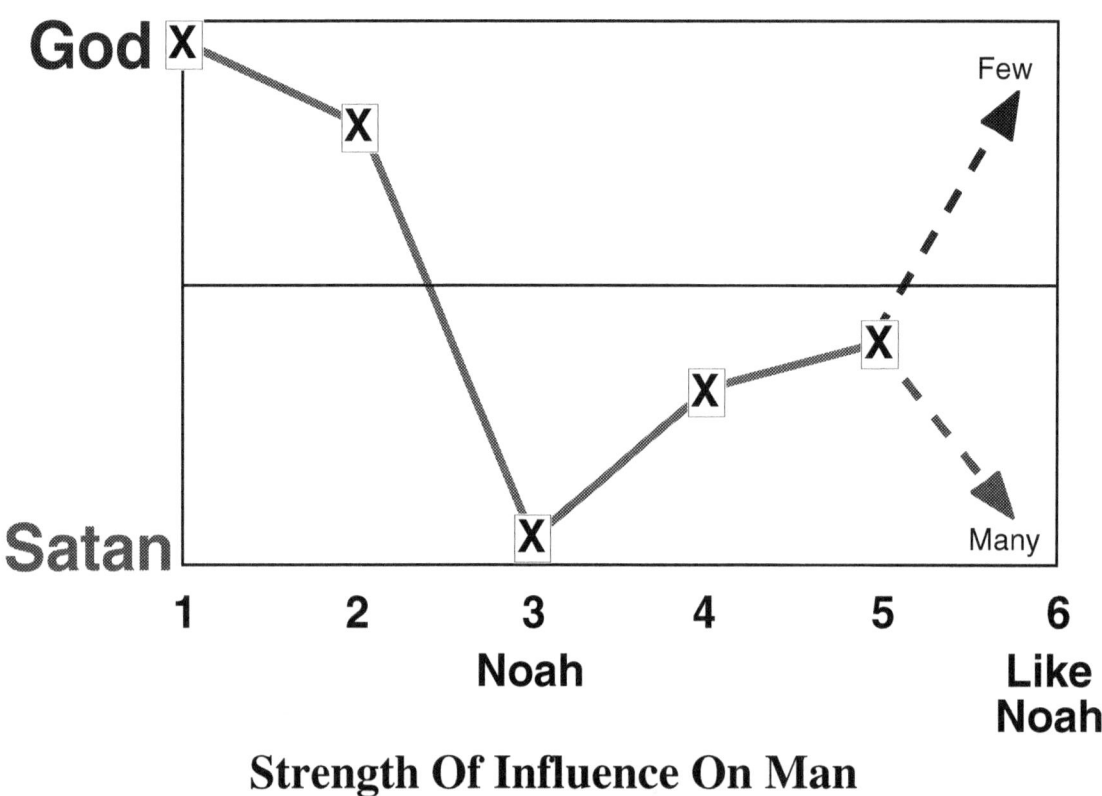

Strength Of Influence On Man

Copyright 2005 Edward G. Palmer, All Rights Reserved.

Book of Edward—Chapter 14

The Gift of Jesus

Indeed the salt of Christianity has lost its flavor due to the corrupt teachings of orthodox Christian dogma. Many Christians now walk a path towards Hell. Righteousness no longer matters in life. However, Christ has the last laugh because while the "forces of Hell shall not prevail against the Church of Christ"—few realize that the real Church are those who sincerely believe in God Almighty. It is collectively those who walk in God's light. Church buildings and those who visit them are irrelevant in eternity. God dwells in the praises of HIS people, not in man made buildings. Your heart will determine your eternal fate, not where you attend church services.

Jesus said: "You [righteous people of God] are the salt of the earth; but if the salt loses its flavor [truth], how shall it be seasoned? It is then good for nothing but to be thrown out and trampled underfoot by men." Matthew 5:13

Examining the phases of spiritual influence on man and the resulting curve will reveal God's secret plan for Christ. These characteristics are summarized in the table below. Phase 6 is only shown on the graph. When evil bottoms out in Phase 6, it will be the second coming of Christ as a Lion of Judah. Many souls will be destroyed by sin, but God saves the righteous.

Phase	Strength of Influence Characteristics
1	God communicated verbally and direct with man. It was HIS plan to have a heavenly place on earth for man called Eden. God would watch over man and take care of him; HIS voice would be the primary influence on man.
2	Eve and Adam disobey God. That is the first time sin entered the life of man. The sin they committed revealed the other side of knowledge, which is the part involving evil. A new and permanent level was established in which Satan would operate from. Man was now subject to the daily thoughts of evil from Satan as well as the good thoughts from God. God dropped the plan HE originally had for a direct verbal fellowship. Man died an immediate spiritual death in the form of separation from God. Later, God limited man's earthly life to 120. [Gen. 6:3]

The Gift of Jesus

3	The majority of mankind succumbed to the evil side and finally during the time of Noah, God destroyed all that was on the earth except those with Noah. It was Satan who won the majority of souls at the time of Noah, because man chose to follow Satan's influence. Noah and family started to rebuild life on earth. It was a fresh start. However, mankind rekindled its desire to sin and Satan was again gaining ground with man. God in response sent many deliverers including Moses, the Judges and the Prophets. Clearly man listened for a short time during their presence, but he soon resumed his evil ways.
4	God in HIS compassion and grace decided to make a way for those who would choose to follow HIM. HIS ultimate plan was to dwell once again with those who chose HIM. The first part of this plan unfolded when God sent Christ down to become Jesus. In order for God to come dwell again with man, HIS justice for our collective sin had to be satisfied. Jesus willingly went to the cross as atonement to God for the collective sin of mankind. Christ prayed and requested that God send HIS Holy Spirit to man. This was the next step in God's larger plan.
5	As a result of the cross, God did send HIS Spirit back to earth to once again dwell with those who would choose to serve HIM. The combination of Christ's earthly ministry and the coming of the Holy Spirit functioned as a permanent offset to the strong influence to sin from Satan. The direct verbal input that Adam received from God was replaced by a quieter input into our soul from God's Holy Spirit. To hear God speak now requires that we make a strong effort from our heart in a calm and quiet manner. That is why God said: "Be Still and Know ME!" God in HIS infinite wisdom knows that the majority of man's souls will once again be lost to sin as a result of Satan's influence. However, for those who choose God, HE gives the Spirit of truth to show their souls the way home to a heavenly domain. Few find the way because the forces in this world warring against the spirit are very strong. It will take 100% of your heart from within the bowels of your soul to overcome the world's forces you face if you choose to walk in God's light.

The Gift of Jesus

6	We are once again in a time similar to that of Noah where evil seems to abound without limits. The restraining force that keeps evil in check to some limited degree is slowly being removed to let man become as evil as he chooses to become in his heart. Those who choose to serve God have been given an escape path by way of HIS Holy Spirit. Yet even this will not keep them from suffering just like Jesus did in his earthly existence. Our goal is to walk with God in the narrow path that Jesus talked about. This is the path of righteousness that both Zacharias and Elizabeth walked. The Antichrist has infiltrated the established Church of Christ and now leads many on a pathway to Hell through false doctrines that justify the sins of the flesh. No longer is mankind judged as a group collectively, because the new covenant from God is with each man and woman individually. You alone will determine the ultimate destination of your soul based upon the choice of your heart. Choose "life" while you can!
7	Phase 7 will start with the second coming of Christ when evil reaches a similar level on earth as it did in Noah's day.

Reading these phases of spiritual influence almost seems like reading a mass murder plot. That is until one realizes that Scripture makes it clear that the mass of human souls will be lost due to their sin. What happened to souls in Noah's time will happen to souls in the last days; righteous souls will be saved. Christ did not come so that everyone can have a happy home in Heaven. That is the stuff of Christian mythology. Christ came in the flesh to set the record straight for God's people who were lost and in confusion over God's ways. Most of Israel is still lost. However, there are Jews who walk with God just like there are Muslims and Christians who walk with God. The gift of Jesus applies to all of mankind in whosoever will choose to walk with God. The proof of this fact is that God said HIS new covenant would deal with each of us on an individual basis. Not on a collective basis like HE used to with Israel; certainly not on a basis of any religion like that of Judaism, Islam, Christianity, Catholicism, Lutheranism, etc. It is only you and God. You'll find God with all your heart. If not, your soul is lost.

What Is The Greatest Gift Of Jesus?

Copyright 2005 Edward G. Palmer, All Rights Reserved.

The Gift of Jesus

From the phase of influence discussion, did you recognize the greatest gift of Jesus? Think about these two facts. God started with man by direct verbal communications. God walked with us on earth. As a result of the cross, God has returned to us in a deeper more meaningful way. God now dwells within us, and HIS light guides our earthly path. While we still may suffer on this earth, HIS Spirit comforts us and confirms to us where we are headed. Thus we have come full circle back to direct fellowship with God.

Like Apostle Paul, I tell you that God lives inside of me with HIS Son and HIS Spirit(s). Do Jews or Muslims recognize this indwelling of God? They should! Verily I say unto you that this return to fellowship with God is the greatest gift of Jesus. It is why the Apostle Paul can say:

> "I have been crucified with Christ; it is no longer I who live, but Christ lives in me; and the life which I now live in the flesh I live by faith in the Son of God, who loved me and gave himself for me." **Galatians 2:20**

Because Paul received the greatest gift of Jesus …

> "The Holy Spirit, whom HE [God] poured out on us abundantly through Jesus Christ our savior, that having been justified by HIS [God's] grace we should become heirs according to the hope of eternal life." **Titus 3:4-7**

Because God ordained this new covenant for each of us …

> "For you are the temple of the living God. As God has said: 'I will dwell in them and walk among them. I will be their God, and they shall be MY people.'" **2 Cor. 6:16**

And Jesus confirms this new covenant is for those who obey …

> Jesus replied, "All those who love me will do what I say. [Then] My FATHER will love them, and WE will come to them and live with them." **John 14:23 NLT**

The Gift of Jesus

Jesus was a gift of God to settle HIS need for justice. It was a final atonement for the collective sins of mankind. The result of that atonement is the pouring out upon man of God's Holy Spirit. However, this is only done for those who are obedient to the word of God. Jesus states clearly that it is those who obey what he said who would receive the gift of fellowship with God. What Jesus said was only what God had told him to say. Therefore, true obedience is the acceptance of God's Word and the adherence to it. God will only dwell within those who truly submit to HIS will.

God "draws" people to Jesus for his ministry and other purposes. Not all can come to Jesus, but only those who the FATHER draws.

> **"No one can come to me [Jesus] unless the FATHER [God] who sent me draws him; and I will raise him up at the last day." John 6:44**

In the very next verse, Jesus makes it clear that all who are taught by God Almighty will come to him. This means that all Jews and Muslims who truly know God and who submit to HIS Word will find and recognize Jesus Christ as their brother. Have you been taught by God? If so, God's Spirit will confirm the truth of Jesus Christ and his sacrifice on the cross to you.

> **"It is written in the prophets, 'and they shall all be taught by God.' Therefore everyone who has heard and learned from the FATHER comes to me." John 6:45**

When John 6:44-45 are taken together, there is the direct implication that if you do not know the FATHER, you will not see the salvation of Christ!

> **"Most assuredly, I say to you, he who hears my word and believes in HIM [God] who sent me has everlasting life, and shall not come into judgment, but has passed from death into life [even while still alive on this earth]." John 5:24**

Jesus makes it clear that those who know God already have eternal life. Verily I say to you that this is the meaning of what Jesus taught.

Copyright 2005 Edward G. Palmer, All Rights Reserved.

The Gift of Jesus

The matter of belief in the cross is a serious issue between the three major religions who believe in the God of Abraham. The majority of Jews believe Jesus was a righteous rabbi at best, at worse a rebel. They do not accept his sacrificial death on the cross as a final atonement for their sins. I read that Jews stopped animal sacrifices for sins and now rely on prayer. I am curious about the history behind the change and when it took place.

Muslims believe that Jesus was a prophet of God and as such they are expected to honor him, but the Quran at Surah 4:157 teaches it only looked like Jesus died on the cross. The Quran states that Christ did not die and suffer crucifixion because "God raised him up." The Quran implies Jesus was switched with someone else who suffered crucifixion. Thus, Muslims also deny Christ's final atonement for their sins. Verily I say to you that the atonement for mankind's sin by Jesus on the cross applies to both Jews and Muslims whether or not any of them believe in this gift of God.

In Gnostic Christianity, there is a belief that Jesus did not come in the form of a man but only appeared as one. This heretical theology is called "Docetism" and it first appeared in Gnostic theology circa 140 A.D.

To deny the humanity of Jesus comes from the spirit of the Antichrist. To deny the cross also denies God's perfect sacrifice and the blood of Jesus Christ HIS Son. Jesus made it clear that blasphemy against the FATHER and he would be forgiven. Such teachings appear to be blasphemy. Still, there is the matter of honoring Christ. In this regards, I believe it is possible to be confused on a physical or theological level and yet still honor Christ. Failure to honor Christ is failure to honor the FATHER who sent him.

> **"For the FATHER judges no one, but has committed all judgment to the Son, that all should honor the Son just as they honor the FATHER. He who does not honor the Son does not honor the FATHER who sent him." John 5:22-23**

Indeed Jesus was more than a prophet for God. He was HIS begotten human Son. This does not make Jesus into God and Scripture is clear he is not God. Yet to understand the gift of Jesus one needs to recognize that his human death on the cross was a final atonement for man's sin.

The Gift of Jesus

Understanding Jesus makes it easy to honor him as we are instructed. Since Jesus has been given authority as our judge, it makes sense that all the children of Abraham understand whom he really is and what he did for God.

To the extent that Jews and Muslims obey God's Holy Word and submit to HIS Will — they are in obedient to what Jesus taught. This shows that they do honor him even if they do not understand him. In contrast, Christians are taught mythology today and even that they do not and cannot obey God's Word. Verily I say unto you that all who fail to adhere to the words of Jesus will never see the kingdom of God. The words he taught from God require obedience "unto righteousness" from within our hearts.

You are the temple of the living God and the greatest gift of Jesus is a return to fellowship with our God. Right here on planet earth you too can be walking with God. Those who have HIS eternal light know it as a fact. Like me, you too can return to Eden on earth and even experience HIS joy in the midst of earthly sufferings. When I had the epiphany over 25 years ago, God filled me with HIS Spirit and came to dwell with me. It was ten years later that I was baptized by immersion. For me, that water baptism was a moment in which I proclaimed to the world that I belonged to God.

The Greatest Gift Of Jesus Is God's Fellowship!

In preparation for this chapter, I studied for days the so-called lost gospels of Christ. The Church had reportedly purged and burned certain books and writings in its early days circa 200 A.D. that were considered heretical. It presumably did this in the process of establishing an orthodox Christian belief system. If you claimed to be a Christian in the early days of the Church, belief in orthodox doctrine was expected. However, in 1945 an Egyptian peasant found an earthenware jar in northern Egypt that contained 13 ancient manuscripts.[1] These manuscripts contained Gnostic texts that apparently survived the purge of the original orthodox construct. Gnostic Christians believe that these manuscripts contain additional gospels and scriptures that are critical to understanding God. These manuscripts were only recently translated and are still being researched by scholars.

Copyright 2005 Edward G. Palmer, All Rights Reserved.

Book of Edward—Chapter 14

The Gift of Jesus

For example, in the "Apocryphon of James"[2] — we read the following from our Lord Jesus:

> Jesus said: "Verily, I say unto you, none will be saved unless they believe in my cross. But those who have believed in my cross, theirs is the kingdom of God."
>
> "Verily, I say unto you, none of those who fear death will be saved; for the kingdom belongs to those who put themselves to death. Become better than I; make yourselves like the son [or daughter] of the Holy Spirit!"

These teachings in the Gnostic book of James indicate the importance of our belief in the cross. It doesn't mean belief that Jesus is God or that he is the only way to salvation. It is consistent with canon Scripture. The issue of putting yourself to death is to crucify your flesh. It means to not be a friend of this world; be a friend of God. Believing in the cross means doing what Jesus said to do; that means obeying God's Word.

Another Gnostic example is in the "Gospel of Thomas"[3] — where we read the following in verse #70:

> Jesus said: "If you bring forth what is within you, what you have will save you. If you do not have that within you, what you do not have within you will kill you."

This teaching is consistent with the kingdom of God being inside of us. What all of us need to do is to acknowledge the truth of God that is in each of our souls and then submit ourselves to the will of God in this earthly life. Thomas again confirms what the canon Gospels teach about who it is that is the brother or sister of Jesus. In verse #99, it reads:

> [Jesus] said to them, "Those here who do what my FATHER wants are my brothers [sisters] and my mother. They are the ones who will enter my FATHER's kingdom."

Copyright 2005 Edward G. Palmer, All Rights Reserved.

Book of Edward—Chapter 14

The Gift of Jesus

The word *Gnostic* is derived from the Greek word *gnosis* and in a general sense just refers to spiritual knowledge. Gnostic Christians believe in the trinity concept albeit they assign the feminine name of Sophia to the Holy Spirit. Since I have read most of these documents, let me say that only a few of them have anything material to say. Most are a form of mythology to me and often they contradict the teachings of the biblical canon. So, do not waste your time on Gnostic scriptures unless you want to delve deeper into "Christian mythology."

I can contrast the Gnostic scriptures, which by and large are a mixture of various religious theologies to that of the Apocryphal books taken out of the Protestant Bible circa 1300 A.D. The biblical canon that I believe in is the Catholic Bible canon or any other Bible translation that also contains the Apocryphal books. These books are intermixed within the Catholic Bible. They are located in between the Old and New Testaments in other Bibles. I highly recommend reading and studying all of the Apocryphal books. Of the Gnostic texts, I found these documents relevant to the biblical canon.

1. The Gospel of Philip
2. The Book of Thomas
3. The Gospel of Thomas
4. The Gospel of Truth
5. The Gospel of Mary

The "Secret Book of John" aka "The Apocryphon of John" and many others like it I found to be of a highly suspect nature. They were filled with jargon of a mythical nature and seemingly geared more towards supporting Gnostic doctrine instead of reinforcing canon Scripture. I reviewed the Gnostic documents to reflect on their teachings of Jesus. To the extent they support and reinforce canon teachings, I believe they may be authentic.

It is important to make a decision exactly which text or texts you will take into your confidence. Intellectually, you cannot believe in opposing texts. I.E. In Genesis 1:31 God says "behold [creation] is good." However, in Gnostic scripture, it is called a mistake. Therefore choose carefully what you study. This book is written for believers in the Holy Bible, any version.

The Gift of Jesus

Another Gnostic example comes from the "Gospel of Philip." [4]

"If one goes down into the water and comes up again without having received anything, and says *I am a Christian*, he has borrowed the name at interest. But if he receives the Holy Spirit, he has the name as a gift. He who has received a gift does not have to give it back, but of him who has borrowed it at interest, payment is demanded. This is the way it happens to one when one experiences a mystery." Gospel of Philip

Note: Only canon Scripture is shown in boldface type indented, unless a large section of Scripture is being provided or the Scripture is shown at the start of the chapter. It is November 15, this day of my LORD.

Many people call themselves Christian today. However, many who call themselves Christian have never received anything from God. Indeed, true repentance from the heart leads to the gift of Jesus during either water or spirit baptism. That means many people are simply fake Christians who do not have the Spirit of God inside of them. These fakes are the ones who can conduct willful open sin in the name of Christ. God will have the last word. Is this a surprise to you? How else do you explain both righteousness and unrighteousness coexisting within the church of God? Do you really think they are compatible with one another? Those of the light should not walk in fellowship with those of the darkness!

"Then Jesus spoke to them again, saying, 'I am the light of the world. He who follows me shall not walk in darkness, but have the light of life [Spirit of God].' " John 8:12

The "light of life" that Jesus talks about shines down from the FATHER, our God. Those who actually follow Jesus have acquired this light from God Almighty and do not willfully sin. God's light is inside of them. If you find that you can disobey God's commandments without much mental conflict, it only means that you are not one of God's kids. You belong to Satan because you have not had a permanent change inside of your heart. This changed heart *within us* towards God is also a gift of Jesus.

The Gift of Jesus

> "Whoever has been born of God does not sin, for His seed remains in him; and he cannot sin, because he has been born of God. In this the children of God and the children of the devil are manifest: Whoever does not practice righteousness is not of God, nor is he who does not love his brother." 1 John 3:9-10

We Practice Righteousness; Christ Fills Any Gap!

Therefore, two gifts of Jesus are the indwelling light of the FATHER and Christ's ability to fill a gap in our righteousness. You don't have Jesus unless your heart is changed towards God. You don't acknowledge the FATHER as God unless you repent and are obedient to HIM. If you worship Jesus the Son instead of the Son's God [FATHER], you mock the gift of the FATHER [God] whose purpose was to provide you with HIS light. This light from Jesus' sacrifice is the gift of understanding God [the FATHER].

> "And we know that the Son of God has come and has given us an understanding, that we may know HIM [God] who is true; and we are in HIM [God] who is true, in HIS Son Jesus Christ [when we have repented and returned to righteous ways]. This is the true God and eternal life." 1 John 5:20

In the Gnostic Gospel of Philip [5], written circa 100-200 A.D., we read about those misappropriating the use of the word *Christian*. Today the word *Christian* has become corrupted and cannot be faithfully used to describe someone who walks in God's light. C.S. Lewis in his 1943 classic "Mere Christianity" [6] explains how misuse started to corrupt the meaning of the word *Christian*. In the preface, Lewis explains what he means by using the illustration of the corruption of the English word *gentleman*.

> "The word *gentleman* originally meant something recognizable; one who had a coat of arms and some landed property. When you called someone 'a gentleman' you were not paying him a complement, but merely stating a fact. If you said he was not 'a gentleman' you were not insulting him, but giving information. …

The Gift of Jesus

There was no contradiction in saying that John was a liar and a gentleman; any more than there now is saying that James is a fool and a M.A. But then there came people who said—so rightly, charitably, spiritually, sensitively, so anything but usefully—'Ah, but surely the important thing about a gentleman is not the coat of arms and the land, but the behavior? Surely he is the true gentleman, who behaves, as a gentleman should? Surely in that sense [David, Jim, etc.] is far more truly a gentleman than John?' They meant well. To be honorable and courteous and brave is of course a far better thing than to have a coat of arms. But it is not the same thing. Worse still, it is not a thing everyone will agree about. To call a man 'a gentleman' in this new, refined sense, becomes, in fact, not a way of giving information about him, but a way of praising him: to deny that he is 'a gentleman' becomes simply a way of insulting him. When a word ceases to be a term of description and becomes merely a term of praise, it no longer tells you facts about the object: it only tells you about the speaker's attitude to that object. (A 'nice' meal only means a meal the speaker likes.) A *gentleman*, once it has been spiritualized and refined out of its old coarse, objective sense, means hardly more than a man whom the speaker likes. As a result, *gentleman* is now a useless word. We had lots of terms of approval already, so it was not needed for that use; on the other hand if anyone (say, in a historical work) wants to use it in its old sense, he cannot do so without explanations. It has been spoiled for that purpose.

Now if once we allow people to start spiritualizing and refining, or as they might say 'deepening,' the sense of the word *Christian*, it too will speedily become a useless word. In the first place, Christians themselves will never be able to apply it to anyone." C.S. Lewis, 1943

The Word Christian Is Now Meaningless!

The Gift of Jesus

After a full one-half century and more since Mr. Lewis' observation on the beginning of the corruption of the word *Christian*—I tell you that the word is corrupt and now meaningless. In the common use of the word today there are three observable definitions: a) A good person, or b) Someone who believes in the orthodox trinity dogma, and c) Someone who claims Jesus as their savior yet continues to live a life of sin. How else could you explain a nation that claims to be 80-90% Christian in polls; yet with a cultural divide wherein 50% of evangelicals vote opposite of each other in most elections? Indeed, the use of the word *Christian* is meaningless today and far from its original and intended meaning. It simply does not faithfully describe people belonging to God anymore. Many grossly misappropriate the word.

> C.S. Lewis concludes: "We must therefore stick to the original, obvious meaning. The name Christians was first given at Antioch (Acts 11:26) to 'the disciples,' to those who accepted the teaching of the apostles."

Of course, these were followers of the teachings of Jesus Christ. In that sense, these were people who "submitted to the will of God," because that is what Jesus did and that is what he taught his followers to do. Yet how many Christians today can say that they submit to God's will?

Followers Of Jesus Submit To God's Will!

I am a follower of Jesus Christ and I submit daily to God's will. That means I do exactly what Jesus taught us to do. It means I obey God's Word; I don't try to alter it to cover any sins. Yet many Christians would call me a devil and a deceived person. That alone proves how useless the designation *Christian* is to me. I will settle for the term "child of God." That works for me too. What about you; your family; and, your friends? Do all of you accept the teachings of Jesus and his apostles? Or, do you believe in a more user friendly God who unconditionally sanctions all of your sins?

You can get right with God by starting to get real about Jesus and who he was and what the gift of Jesus is all about. It starts with righteousness.

The Gift of Jesus

I'm going to pull together an outline for you shortly of the attributes and characteristics of the gift of Jesus. I suspect it will not be all-inclusive. However, it will get the main points together so you can continue your study of Jesus. Indeed, Jesus is now back again in Heaven as Christ our High Priest and judge who sits at the right hand of God Almighty. The line for our returning souls forms to right of Christ and all souls will go before him on their way to our God who sits on the throne. Christ will execute God's judgment in Heaven, not his own. Therefore, take heed and get to know both Jesus the human begotten Son of God and the FATHER his God. You do not know God if you think he is Jesus [the human begotten Son] in some kind of a triune arrangement. You must recognize both the FATHER [as God] *and* Jesus [as human Son] because failure to do so is a doctrine of the Antichrist.

> **"Who is a liar but he who denies that Jesus is the Christ [the one sent from Heaven by God]? He is Antichrist who denies the FATHER *and* the Son." 1 John 2:22**

> **"Who is he who overcomes the world, but he who believes that Jesus is the [human begotten] <u>Son</u> of God?" 1 John 5:5**

The terminology *Antichrist* is a reference to those who deny that Jesus was in human flesh like us. And denies that Jesus was the Christ sent down by God. You do not read in the Bible about an "anti-Jesus." What you read about are those who do not believe that Jesus is the Christ who came from Heaven. Recognizing that Jesus is the incarnation of Christ acknowledges that Jesus is not God even though Jesus experiences oneness with God.

> **"By this you know the Spirit of God: Every spirit that confesses that Jesus Christ has come in the flesh is of God, and every spirit that does not confess that Jesus Christ has come in the flesh is not of God. And this is the spirit of the Antichrist, which you have heard was coming, and is now already in the world." 1 John 4:2-3**

The Antichrist Started 2,000 Years Ago!

The Gift of Jesus

The word *flesh* used in the above Scripture is derived from the Greek word *sarx* defined in Strong'S Concordance[7] as Greek #4561. *Sarx* means a human being or the body of a human being as opposed to the soul. The use of the word *flesh* connotes the same meaning whether it is applied to you, I or to Jesus. Therefore, to deny that Jesus Christ has come in the flesh is to deny that the humanity of Jesus Christ was the same as our humanity. Who does this except the spirit of the Antichrist? That is the teaching of Apostle John, not I. Why is it important to the Antichrist that you believe Jesus was God? Denying the struggle of the flesh of Jesus and the limitations of his human existence raises the level of his human sacrifice to that of a God. Instead of being an example for us to follow with our flesh, he becomes an excuse for our sins. It is the Antichrist's way of telling you that you cannot help yourself, and by the way, God understands. Hello … God doesn't!

Clearly the spirit of the Antichrist is influencing all believers in the trinity doctrine because the very essence of the trinity doctrine denies that Jesus is 100% human flesh like you and I. It also denies that Jesus was the Christ sent down from Heaven by God. Verily I say unto you, the Christian orthodox doctrine of the trinity is from the Antichrist. It started to unfold during the time of the apostles circa 100 A.D. As a backup strategy for Satan, the Gnostic teaching on Docetism was started circa 140 A.D. Satan has little to worry about since the trinity doctrine is entrenched in orthodox dogma and Christian orthodoxy has become a home for Satan's people.

Now let me state an important biblical fact about the cross itself. The sacrifice on the cross was not a gift from Jesus Christ. It was and remains to mankind only as a gift from God Almighty. It was God's grace and love for mankind that led to this solution for the propitiation and justification of man. "For God so loved the world that HE gave HIS only *begotten* Son." This gift of God applies to all of mankind regardless of belief, religion or theology. It was a full, final and perfect atonement for the collective sins of the world. It does not just apply to the sins of Christians or those who can mouth Jesus as their savior misappropriating the use of the word.

> **"And he is the propitiation for our sins: and not for ours only, but also for the sins of the whole world."**
> **1 John 2:2 KJV**

The Gift of Jesus

To be "in Christ" is to put on the new man and shed our old earthly concerns. It means we shift our focus to eternity and to God's ways. It means we stop all willful sins and we walk in the light of the FATHER. This light of the FATHER is present in all who obey God's Word regardless of what religion they practice. The real Church of Christ is the collection of souls that walk in obedience to God's Holy Word. Sin no more was the message of Christ from God. It was also the message of the apostles.

Christ is your advocate. Christ is not your sin excuse to God.

"My little children, these things I write to you, so that you may not sin. And if anyone sins [by mistake inadvertently, unknowingly or by accident], we have an Advocate with the FATHER, Jesus Christ the righteous." 1 John 2:1

There is no blood sacrifice of Christ to those who willfully sin.

"For if we sin willfully after we have received [Jesus] the knowledge of the truth, there no longer remains a sacrifice [of the blood of Jesus] for [our] sins." Hebrews 10:26

There is no blood sacrifice for those who do not walk in the light.

"But if we walk in the light as [Jesus] is in the light, we have fellowship with one another, and the blood of Jesus Christ — [God's Son] cleanses us from all sin." 1 John 1:7

If you think you can just mouth Jesus as your Lord and that's it, you are wrong. If you think there are no conditions to the blood of Jesus, you are wrong. The gift of salvation is free from God's grace to those who choose. That much is true in orthodox dogma. However, if you accept God's free gift of salvation, some responsibilities or strings are attached. Therefore the blood of Jesus that "cleanses you from all sin" talked about in 1 John 1:7 is conditional and applies only to those who walk in the light of our FATHER. Walk in the FATHER's light and you will know that your sins are forgiven and that you have God's eternal life. Has Christ brought you back to his God?

The Gift of Jesus

God Is Light! — 1 John 1:5

Apostle John's instructions seem clear enough, but I will repeat them here so there can be no mistake. We are taught to walk in the light like Jesus did. We are taught that this light is from God. Finally, we are taught that IF we do walk in God's light as Jesus walked, that is when "the blood of Jesus Christ cleanses us from all our sin." John amplifies what I have taught you by making clear that obedience to God's Word is a characteristic of all those who belong to the light, who belong to God.

> **"And how can we be sure that we belong to HIM? By obeying HIS commandments. If someone says, 'I belong to God,' but doesn't obey God's commandments, that person is a liar and does not live in the truth. But those who obey God's Word really do love HIM. That is the way to know whether or not we live in HIM. Those who say they live in God should live their lives as Christ did." 1 John 2:3-6 NLT**

Jesus Lived Life In Obedience To God!

A while ago, the United States launched the Hubble telescope into space. When scientists attempted to look into the depths of our universe, they were shocked to find a corrupt image of everything they looked at. What they saw was distorted by a faulty lens that they had to look through. Eventually, the lens was replaced and they could then see things clearly as they looked into the vast expanse of outer space.

Orthodox Christian doctrine contains a false lens in which Scripture is viewed. That false lens includes both the idea of Jesus as God and salvation in no other way. To rationalize countless scriptures that speak against such teachings, various doctrines such as our soul sleeping after death and Jesus speaking instead of God [Yahweh] have been developed. Christians cannot understand the gift of Jesus unless they understand that orthodox trinity and salvation doctrines are also a corrupt lens in which scriptures are viewed.

The Gift of Jesus

Characteristics of The Gift of Jesus

I. Fellowship Attributes

1. We return to direct fellowship with God.
2. God dwells within us.
3. One or more of God's seven Spirits dwell within us.
4. God pours HIS Spirit of truth on us abundantly.
5. The spirit of Christ dwells within us.
6. We have access to the Holies of Holies anytime.
7. We live and walk in God's light just as Jesus did.
8. We are obedient to God's commandments.
9. We teach the truth that righteousness matters to God.
10. We ask of God directly and no longer ask of Jesus.
11. We are faithful to God even unto our own physical death.

II. Salvation Attributes

1. Jesus brings us back to his God, our heavenly FATHER.
2. Jesus is the teacher sent by God to correct our errors.
3. Jesus gives us an understanding of God so we can obey HIM.
4. Jesus willingly did his part in God's plan to redeem souls.
5. Jesus willingly gave his own human life to redeem mankind.
6. Jesus gave his own blood as a final perfect sacrifice for man.
7. Jesus gave his own blood as a spiritual atonement for man.
8. The blood of Jesus was the propitiation for the sins of the world.
9. The blood of Jesus was God's way of justifying man's existence.
10. Jesus was the incarnation of Christ whom God sent from Heaven.
11. Jesus first died a spiritual death on the cross.
12. Jesus secondly died a physical death on the cross.
13. Jesus suffered crucifixion on the cross like any human would.
14. God resurrected Jesus into a perfect body.
15. Jesus is another chance for God's people to return to HIM.
16. Jesus is a new opportunity for all gentiles to walk with God.
17. Jesus is not an excuse for any continued willful sin.
18. Jesus fills our righteousness gap when we make mistakes.
19. Jesus petitioned God to send back to man the Spirit of truth.
20. God sent back HIS Spirit of truth to guide our earthly lives.

The Gift of Jesus

III. Heavenly Attributes

1. Jesus was known as Christ in Heaven and now has a new name.
2. Jesus was an angel of God and the first of God's creations.
3. God chose Christ as atonement for mankind's sin.
4. Christ now sits at the right hand of God Almighty.
5. Christ serves as judge of souls executing God's will in Heaven.
6. God gave Christ a higher status than angel because he was Jesus.
7. The oneness of Christ and God is the same oneness of believers.
8. Christ had unlimited love for God and submitted to HIS will.
9. Christ had unlimited love for man because of oneness with God.

III. Earthly Attributes

1. Jesus was a human in every respect just like you and I.
2. Born of Virgin Mary who was impregnated by God.
3. Born through a mother's womb like you and I.
4. Raised as a baby and child like you and I.
5. Assumed the adult ministry that God called him to.
6. Walked in a fellowship of oneness with God.
7. Jesus was God's "in your face" call for mankind's repentance.
8. God's Word was manifested to *all* men by Christ's humanity.
9. Jesus reiterated God's timeless message to "repent and be saved."
10. Jesus spoke only what God told him to say.
11. Jesus did only what God told him to do.
12. Performed God's miracles to help us understand the kingdom.
13. Brought back the Word to reawaken God's chosen people.
14. Showed us by example a sinless and righteous life all could walk.
15. An historical record of Jesus exists that cannot be denied.
16. The resurrection of Jesus provides proof of an eternal afterlife.
17. Jesus documented only a few souls will walk God's narrow way.
18. Jesus documented many souls will be lost because of their sin.

IV. In Christ Attributes

1. We are a new creation when we put on the new man.
2. We walk in the spirit's control instead of the flesh.
3. We become slaves to righteousness and all sin is anathema to us.
4. We have the spiritual strength to walk in righteousness.

The Gift of Jesus

5. Our sins are immediately forgiven.
6. We cease all willful sins knowing that it mocks God.
7. When we make mistakes and sin, we have an advocate in Christ.
8. When we make mistakes and sin — even those sins are forgiven.
9. We have perfect peace with God dwelling inside of us.
10. We have perfect joy with God dwelling inside of us.
11. We have perfect love with God dwelling inside of us.
12. We know God because we first knew Jesus HIS *begotten* Son.
13. God's light dwells within us and we walk in the light.
14. We are "hot" for God, not lukewarm or cold.
15. Our consciences are clear because we walk in the light.
16. We suffer like Christ suffered in this world yet still have joy.
17. When we die, we know that we have eternal life immediately.
18. At some point we will receive a resurrection body like Christ.
19. We are given the name of Christian if we walk in God's light.
20. We bear the name Christian because we have Christ inside of us.

Jesus Was Only A Part Of God's Plan To Save Souls!

Study your Bible and locate the scriptures for the above attributes. Orthodox Christianity would have you believe the Bible is all about Jesus, but it isn't. It is a book about a loving God called Yahweh. Jesus points the way to God and never once advocated that you substitute him as your God.

Jesus said: "And I have declared to them YOUR name [God], and will [always] declare it, that the love with which YOU loved me may be in them, and I in them." John 17:26

"I have manifested YOUR name [God] to the men whom YOU have given me ... they have kept YOUR Word."
John 17:6

God hasn't changed despite what orthodox and mainstream churches may teach you. Instead of Jesus being an end to your spiritual search, Jesus should be the beginning of your fellowship and walk with his God.

The Gift of Jesus

Only an estimated 22% who say they are born-again say they believe in moral absolutes. Therefore, the word *Christian* and term *born-again* are both useless in describing God's people. Unless you walk in the light of God as Jesus did, your soul is lost. One orthodox writer laments that no one is paying attention to orthodox teachings. I say it is just the opposite. It is orthodoxy that they *are* listening to! In 2,000 years, orthodoxy has evolved to where Christians are taught that their sins no longer matter. "Once saved, always saved!" In fact, "You can't obey the Ten Commandments if you tried!" — "That is why you need Jesus!" Given such apostasy, why should Christianity be surprised when it produces *Christians* like former U.S. President Bill Clinton whose behavior demonstrates that they don't believe in moral absolutes?

> **Jesus said: "The thief does not come except to steal, and to kill, and to destroy. I have come that they may have life, and that they may have it more abundantly." John 10:10**
>
> **"But when the kindness and the love of God our SAVIOR toward man appeared, not by works of righteousness which we have done, but according to HIS mercy HE saved us, through the washing of regeneration and renewing of the Holy Spirit, whom HE poured out on us abundantly through Jesus Christ our savior, that having been justified by HIS grace we should become heirs according to the hope of eternal life." Titus 3:4-7**

"The real mystery of Jesus Christ is that through our faith both he and Yahweh will live inside of us while on earth. We demonstrate our receipt of God's eternal life when we walk in HIS light just like Christ did while on this earth. That requires obedience to God's Word." The Apostle Edward

If You Understand The Mystery Of Our Faith, You Will Truly Understand God <u>And</u> ...

The Gift of Jesus

Copyright 2005 Edward G. Palmer, All Rights Reserved.

Book of Edward

Volume II
Notes & Bibliography

Forward section notes are located in the back of Volume I and in Volume IV Appendix H.

Chapter 8

1 — (p178) Ibid.

2 — (p180) Reid, David R. (1997) *Hermeneutics Study Guide: Hermeneutics Handout #3*. River Forest, Illinois: Growing Christian Ministries, Inc.

3 — (p191) Ibid.

4 — (p192) Ibid.

5 — (p198) Bristol, Claude M. (1948) *The Magic of Believing* (p64). New York: Pocket Books.

Chapter 9

1 — (p206) Kazantzakis, Nikos. (1975) *The Last Temptation of Christ*. New York: Simon & Schuster. Translated onto film in 1988 by director Martin Scorsese and stars actor William Dafoe as Jesus Christ. Comment: I never read the book, but the film is a piece of satanic apostasy, which has little resemblance to the Jesus Christ known in the Holy Bible.

2 — (p210) Miles, Jack (2001). *Christ, A Crisis In The Life Of God*. New York: Alfred A. Knopf. Comment: An excellent guide to a full understanding of our modern day Christian mythology. The best intellectual

Notes & Bibliography - Volume II

case for the trinity doctrine even if it is filled with apostate misunderstanding and lack of scriptural support from the Holy Bible. Few Christian leaders would openly state what Miles is intellectually forced to conclude having based his theology on the supposition that the trinity doctrine is actual truth. However, his writing reflects an honest intellectual examination of theology having the myth of the trinity doctrine to support.

3 — (p211) Ibid. See page 243-244 of Miles' book.

4 — (p212) Ibid. See page 222 of Miles' book.

5 — (p212) Ibid. See page 224-225 of Miles' book.

6 — (p216) Example. (2000) *The One-Year Chronological Bible*. Wheaton, Illinois:Tyndale House Publishers. <u>Comment</u>: This NLT Bible arranges Scripture according to the time line of actual events. This is in contrast to the canon [out of order] sequence developed by Jerome in the early church. Other translations of the Chronological Bible are available.

7 — (p216) Example. (1981) *The Guideposts Parallel Bible*. Grand Rapids, Michigan: Zondervan Bible Publishers. <u>Comment</u>: This parallel version has the KJV, NIV, LIV and RSV side by side so that all translations can be compared with one another. Other versions have been published and they too make a great study aide. *The Complete Parallel Bible* with Apocryphal/Deuterocanonical Books is also in my library. It has the NRSV, REB, NAB and NJB side by side for comparison.

8 — (p217) Ibid.

9 — (p217) Ibid. Example: See Strong'S Hebrew Dictionary.

10 — (p217) Ibid. Example: See Strong'S Greek Dictionary.

11 — (p217) Robinson, James M. (Gen. Ed.). (1988). *The Nag Hammadi Library: The Book of Thomas*. New York: HarperCollins Publishers.

12 — (p219) Ibid.

Notes & Bibliography - Volume II

13 — (p223) Ibid.

Chapter 10

1 — (p252) Trinity Episcopal Church, Parkersburg, West Virginia. Web site location on 4/20/03 at http://www.trinity-church.org.

2 — (p253) *Trinity Times Electronic Edition 01/18/99*. Web site location on 4/20/03 at http://www.trinity-church.org/archives/Times_19990118.htm.

3 — (p254) I.E. (10/02) Internet site http://www.av1611.org/nkjv.html.

4 — (p255) (1997) Hagee, John C. (General Editor). *Prophecy Study Bible, New King James Version.* Nashville, Tennessee: Thomas Nelson, Inc.

5 — (p255) John Hagee Ministries on Internet site is http://www.jhm.org.

6 — (p255) Ibid. See page 1429 of *Prophecy Study Bible*.

7 — (p277) Ibid.

8 — (p277) You can research Tertulian on the Internet. One excellent article is located at http://www.newadvent.org/cathen/14520c.htm. This article states that Tertulian "was learned, but careless in his historical statements." From his writings, it is evident that Tertulian possessed limited Scripture writings. I.E. He "did not know James and II Peter."

9 — (p278) Herbert Armstrong died in 1986. He was the founder of the Worldwide Church of God. Extensive information about him is on the Internet and his organization was often referred to as a cult. I found his radio teachings during my travels fascinating, but I could never match his teachings up with Scripture at the time.

10 — (p278) Ibid.

11 — (p280) See http://www.carm.org/doctrine/trujesus.htm on Internet.

Notes & Bibliography - Volume II

12 — (p283) (1961) *New World Translation* (NWT). Published by the Watchtower Bible and Tract Society of New York. Jehovah Witness. See Luke 23:43 in the NWT and how the comma has been shifted in translation to allow NWT Scripture to agree with Jehovah Witness resurrection and salvation doctrine. <u>Comment</u>: The NWT Bible stands in contrast to many excellent translations and runs counter to the character of Jesus as explained.

13 — (p287) (2001) Hendrickson, Bryn. *Is Jesus The Alpha and Omega?* See Issue No. 11 (Vol. I No. 11) or reference Article #107 when requesting a copy. Published by Growing in the Word Ministries. 7964 Brooklyn Blvd, #208, Brooklyn Park, Minnesota 55445. <u>Comment</u>: Bryn publishes a monthly study and Bible commentary.

14 — (p289) Ibid.

15 — (p289) Ibid. See page 224-225 of Miles' book.

16 — (p295) Ibid.

Chapter 11

1 — (p319) <u>Comment</u>: Research the ordination of V. Gene Robinson, a practicing homosexual to the position of bishop of the New Hampshire diocese by the Episcopalian Church during 2003. Meeting occurred in Minneapolis, Minnesota and volumes of commentaries exist.

2 — (p322) <u>Comment</u>: Research "Gay Pride" on the Internet if interested.

3 — (p322) <u>Comment</u>: An atheist is attempting to have the words "under God" removed from the Pledge of Allegiance in the United States. A monument of the Ten Commandments was ordered removed from a Court House in Alabama. Both issues are well documented on the Internet and are reflective of the cultural attempt to excise God from society.

4 — (p327) Charles Stanley is on the Internet at http://www.intouch.org.

Notes & Bibliography - Volume II

5 — (p339) (1993) Hill, Paul J. *Should We Defend Born And Unborn Children With Force?* <u>Comment</u>: Paul J. Hill was the first pro-life activist in the United States that was convicted of killing an abortion doctor. His article on 9/5/03 was at http://www.streetpreach.com/Abortion/pjh01.htm. Paul J. Hill advocates the killing of all doctors that willfully kill babies by legalized abortion methods. Kill one person, save thousands is his logic. His arguments and Scripture citations do not carry biblical truth.

6 — (p339) <u>Comment</u>: MSNBC online at http://www.msnbc.com carried extensive articles and commentaries on the Paul J. Hill murder conviction.

7 — (p340) (2003) Bray, Michael. *The Murder of God's Prophet in the Year of Our Lord 2003.* Article dated 2 August 2003 and found on the Internet at http://www.bowiereformation.org/Main/commentary.htm. Comment: The Reverend Bray mistakenly believes Paul J. Hill was a Prophet and that the U.S. executed a man of God doing HIS will. Bray is errant for the reasons cited in Chapter 11.

8 — (p342) Ibid.

9 — (p354) <u>Comment</u>: Extensive writings have been made concerning the U.S. Supreme Courts ruling in 1973 that legalized the killing of babies in the name of female privacy. Whatever else is said about *Roe V. Wade*, one fact is clear and undeniable after 30 years. Over 40 Million babies have been killed or executed. Our society worries about losing a few hundred soldiers who died honorably in the Iraq war. However, it should be hanging its head in shame over needless baby killings. A price will be paid for the shedding of innocent blood and there can be no doubt it is an abomination to God!

10 — (p367) Ibid. See Jewish Bible references in Forward.

11 — (p367) Ibid. See Holy Bible references in Forward.

12 — (p370) (2001) *The Qur'an.* Text, Translation and Commentary by Abdullah Yusuf Ali. U.S. Edition 2001. Elmhurst, New York: Tahrike Tarsile Qur'an, Inc. <u>Comment</u>: The Koran can be found on the Internet at http://www.koranusa.org. The Qur'an [or Koran] is freely distributed on the

Notes & Bibliography - Volume II

Internet as a set of text files. The above version was found online. A second version can be located at http://www.submission.org, which is another Islamic site. This second version is said to be free of the influence of writings outside of the original text as given to the Prophet Mohammed. The first version is said to be influenced by Islamic traditions instead of being simply an accurate translation. I cannot speak to these issues, but have observed that the second version has concluded that all righteous people will go to Heaven regardless of religion. That obviously is what I conclude from our Christian Holy Bible and the teachings of our Lord Jesus Christ.

13 — (p371) The Apostle Edward's definitions based upon his own studies of the three main religions.

Chapter 12

1 — (p383) Mac Hammond Ministries can be found at http://www.lwcc.org.

2 — (p388) Ibid.

3 — (p388) Article printed in the Elk River Star News, Elk River, MN.

4 — (p389) <u>Comment</u>: Tract is the standard type of tract passed out by most Christian Ministries in an attempt to win Christian converts.

5 — (p389) Lakewood Church is located at http://www.Lakewood.cc.

6 — (p415) (1982) *The Guideposts Family Concordance To The Bible*. Guideposts. Carmel, New York: Thomas Nelson, Inc., Publishers.

Chapter 13

None.

Chapter 14

1 — (p477) (1988) Robinson, James M. (General Editor). *The Nag Hammadi Library in English*. HarperSanFrancisco, a division of Harper Collins Publishers.

Notes & Bibliography - Volume II

2 — (p478) *The Nag Hammadi Library in English: Apocryphon of James.*

3 — (p478) *The Nag Hammadi Library in English: Gospel of Thomas.*

4 — (p480) *The Nag Hammadi Library in English: Gospel of Philip.*

5 — (p481) Ibid.

6 — (p481) (1952) Lewis, CS. *Mere Christianity.* New York, N.Y.: Macmillan Publishing Co., Inc.

7 — (p485) Ibid.

Appendix A
A Real Salvation Prayer

OPENING PRAYER: FATHER God, let everyone who utters this prayer of salvation unto YOU, with a sincere heart, immediately feel the presence of YOUR Holy Spirit and equip them with the internal strength of conviction to stand tall for YOUR righteousness at all costs and even unto their own human death. Verily I say unto YOU that this is YOUR expectation of their [my] sincere heart. The Apostle Edward

INSTRUCTIONS: Pray out loud and offer up to God Almighty outstretched arms and the following prayer, on your knees, in the privacy of your prayer closet [private room, alone], and with your sincere heart. Verily I say unto you that your soul will see eternal life in Heaven upon the death of your earthly body if your heart is sincere with God to the point that your behavior turns to righteousness. Mark down the time, date and place of this gift of your heart to God and feel free to share this moment of time when you made a commitment to walk in God's ways with HIS priorities over your life.

PRAY: Heavenly FATHER, the only ONE and True God. YOU, who are also the FATHER and the only ONE and True God of my brother Jesus Christ whom YOU sent down as a living human sacrifice for the sins of all the humans in this earthly realm and world, hear this prayer from my sincere heart. This prayer comes from within the bowels of my spirit-soul and I fully understand that this is a one-way decision of my heart.

A Real Salvation Prayer

FATHER, I believe in YOUR only human begotten Son Jesus Christ. I believe that YOU sent Christ down to this earth and that he became the human being Jesus Christ [Yashua] in the flesh just like the flesh I have. I believe he had bones like I do, flesh like I do and blood like I do. I believe that his body on the cross was no different than any other human body on the cross. I acknowledge Jesus Christ is the Son of God; he is not God.

FATHER, I believe that he only spoke what YOU told him to say and that he only did what YOU told him to do. I believe that he was the final and perfect blood sacrifice for the forgiveness of the sins of mankind. FATHER I believe that includes my sins.

LORD, I fully acknowledge that by accepting Jesus Christ as my personal savior and brother that I am inviting his perfect spirit into my life to share this earthly body with me. Along with his spirit, I understand that you will also give me YOUR Holy Spirit and that YOU also will dwell within me.

I believe that the end result of my sincere acceptance of this gift of YOUR Son is the Oneness that I will share with YOU and him. Christ has taught me that I might live in perfect Oneness, Peace and Joy with YOU and him. O LORD, this is truly the sincere desire of my heart. I no longer want to be spiritually alone.

Therefore, I accept the precious gift of YOUR Son Jesus Christ and I repent of my past sins and sincerely regret every thought, action, behavior or anything that was displeasing unto YOU. I understand that with the precious gift of YOUR Son, YOU expect me to live a righteousness life the rest of my days on this earth.

Such a life entails living up to YOUR expectations and obeying what YOU and YOUR Son taught us in Holy Scripture. LORD, I acknowledge that I cannot be perfect in and of myself. I realize that to be like Christ requires that I "practice" righteousness and that I avoid sin to the best of my ability. I acknowledge that to continue willfully to sin is a tacit rejection of the gift of Jesus.

Copyright 2005 Edward G. Palmer, All Rights Reserved.

A Real Salvation Prayer

I also acknowledge FATHER that there will be unintentional and unknown sins that will come in my life. I understand that YOU and Christ will cover those types of sin and function as a guide in my life to keep me on the narrow path to Heaven.

FATHER, I acknowledge that YOUR Son is not a free pass on sins like so many Christians believe. Therefore, when I realize I have sinned against YOU in any way, I promise to confess that sin immediately and to keep a short list of my missteps with YOU. I know YOU are faithful to forgive under such conditions, but I also realize that if any life is filled with such confessions that it will be a testimony of an insincere heart. I recognize YOUR instructions in Ezekiel 18 and that Jesus has not altered YOUR criteria for punishing sinners. Therefore, keep me under YOUR wings O God and give me a pure heart unto YOU.

Having said this FATHER, I pray that you will dwell within me and help me to be the man [or woman] that you want me to be. I ask all of this in the name of Jesus Christ whom I confess with my mouth that he came in the flesh as YOUR only begotten SON. I acknowledge with my heart that YOU expect righteousness, a new life with changed behavior; behavior that glorifies YOU.

FATHER, help me to be an instrument of YOUR will even as Christ was such an instrument. Let this day be the first day of the rest of my life and help me to put away all offensive behavior and sin, which YOU hate. In the name of YOUR only begotten and beloved human Son Jesus, I pray. AMEN

Date and Time of Prayer: _____

Place of Prayer: _____

I First Told To: _____

_____

Copyright 2005 Edward G. Palmer, All Rights Reserved.

JVED Publishing

18140 Zane Street NW #410
Elk River, Minnesota 55330

www.jvedpublishing.org

Special Acknowledgements

The Apostle Edward would like to thank Dean and Jackie Mattila along with Vernon Enstad for their spiritual and emotional support during his four plus years of writing. Without their godly personal support and input, this work for God may not have been possible. This book was a spiritual journey for all four of them. A special thanks is also due Brian Mechler for his proof reading assistance. Book updates and errata data will be posted online at http://www.edwardtheapostle.org. For people in countries where the book is not available in print form or for those who prefer, it may be read and searched free online in English via web browsers at this web site.

The Apostle Edward asks ...
Are You Ready?

When he returns for souls, will Christ find you going about God's business? Will he find your spiritual light shining? If not, why? Do you even know why Christ stated those two salvation requirements?

There is an exodus from established churches by Christians who have found out that many churches no longer teach God's truth. The trend is worldwide and was the subject of a recent newsletter I received. These Christians read the Bible and compared what their church taught. They found that the Church supported many evil things that God abhors. In the process, they have asked themselves some fundamental spiritual questions:

- Can we support abortion if God abhors the shedding of innocent blood?
- Can we support Gay rights if God says homosexuality is abominable?
- Can we support a political party that seeks to excise God from everyday life?
- Can we support world friendship when it makes us HIS enemy?

Christian mythology is rampant. The Book of Edward discusses the above and many other important issues that the Church is now confronted with. Will you personally obey God's Word and the teachings of Jesus? If not, you are not saved. This book can reawaken your spirit and save your soul. At the very least, it will educate your heart.

I can remember the first experience in which I felt betrayed and confused by a pulpit teaching that did not line up and match what the word of God actually said. The basic choice you have, as a Christian, is whether you will adhere to God's Word or to the man made doctrines of your social group, your church, its hierarchy or its denomination.

There lies the main issue of salvation. You'll have to decide on God's Word if you want eternal life for in the end analysis you will be held accountable to HIS Word. Christians are leaving the established church and finding small fellowships or home churches as described in the New Testament. God has opened their eyes to HIS truth and if you read and study the Scriptures in this book, HE will open your eyes.

If desired, you may write to me in care of JVED Publishing. May your soul find the true salvation contained in the teachings of Jesus Christ. The Apostle Edward

www.ingramcontent.com/pod-product-compliance
Lightning Source LLC
Chambersburg PA
CBHW082106230426
43671CB00015B/2623